MEDIA MANAGEMENT
A Casebook Approach

LEA'S COMMUNICATION SERIES
Jennings Bryant/Dolf Zillman, General Editors

For a complete list of titles in LEA's Communication Series, please contact Lawrence Erlbaum Associates, Publishers, at www.erlbaum.com.

MEDIA MANAGEMENT
A CASEBOOK APPROACH

Third Edition

Jan LeBlanc Wicks
University of Arkansas

George Sylvie
University of Texas at Austin

C. Ann Hollifield
University of Georgia

Stephen Lacy
Michigan State University

Ardyth Broadrick Sohn
Sam Houston State University

Contributing Author:

Dr. Angela Powers
Northern Illinois University

 LAWRENCE ERLBAUM ASSOCIATES, PUBLISHERS
2004   Mahwah, New Jersey   London

Acquisitions Editor:	Linda Bathgate
Textbook Marketing Manager:	Marisol Kozlovski
Editorial Assistant:	Karin Wittig Bates
Cover Design:	Kathryn Houghtaling Lacey
Textbook Production Manager:	Paul Smolenski
Full-Service & Composition:	UG / GGS Information Services Inc.
Text and Cover Printer:	United Graphics Incorporated

This book was typeset in 10/12 pt. Times New Roman and Italic. The heads were typeset in Zapf Humanist Bold, Zapf Humanist Italic, and Times New Roman Bold Italic.

Lawrence Erlbaum Associates, Inc., Publishers
10 Industrial Avenue
Mahwah, NewJersey 07430
www.erlbaum.com

Library of Congress Cataloging-in-Publication Data

Media management: a casebook approach/Jan LeBlanc Wicks . . . [et al.].—3rd ed.
    p. cm. — (LEA's communication series)
    Includes bibliographical references and index.
    ISBN 0-8058-4715-4
    1. Mass media—Management—Case studies. I. Wicks, Jan LeBlanc. II. Series.

P96.M34M4 2003
302.23'068—dc21

2003040808

#5155919 8

Books published by Lawrence Erlbaum Associates are printed on acid-free paper, and their bindings are chosen for strength and durability.

Printed in the United States of America
10 9 8 7 6 5 4 3 2

CONTENTS

ACKNOWLEDGMENTS

Jan LeBlanc Wicks
Thanks to Rob and Ian for their support.

George Sylvie
Thanks to Kathy, Emily, and Ryan for putting up with me during this.
Thanks also to my students who have given me valuable feedback
on the material over the years.

C. Ann Hollifield
Dr. Lee B. Becker, Director of the James M. Cox Jr. Center
for International Mass Communication Training and Research,
Grady College of Journalism & Mass Communication,
University of Georgia
George Daniels, Department of Journalism,
College of Communication and Information Sciences,
University of Alabama

Stephen Lacy
Thanks to Leslie Lacy for all of her help over the years.

Ardyth Broadrick Sohn
Professors Hugh Fullerton and Ruth Pate of Sam Houston State University
are thanked for their support and encouragement during the writing of
chapters. Journalism student Yvette Keener and administrative assistant
Sandy Baker of Sam Houston State University are thanked for their
research and transcribing assistance.

PREFACE

This volume marks an improved version of the 1999 edition. All primary authors from the second edition were involved in writing and revising the third edition. The central approaches of the book and chapters, as well as chapter order, are unchanged because a user survey suggested all were appropriate. Each author reviewed the relevant scholarly and trade literature to update the theories, research, industry practice, trends, examples, and appropriate statistics in their chapters, as well as to add information on the Internet and new media.

The author's reviewed the cases accompanying their chapters to update or change them if necessary. New extended cases were added as well. Our goal is to give students practice in solving simple and complex problems and provide professors a variety of choices for assignments. Ardyth Broadrick Sohn noted our reasons for using the case study approach in the second edition's preface:

> Case study . . . is ideal for students and management because it takes into account flexibility, individuality, and creativity as students face realistic problems and opportunities mirrored in the professional world. It provides practice in role playing, leadership, communication, and decision making with consequences. All are valuable intellectual and professional exercises. Students are encouraged to distinguish among acts, activities, actors, meanings, relationships, and settings of importance. By recognizing the components individually and collectively students can see the options and choices more clearly. Discussion and debate are hard to avoid when examining cases, and as students recognize themselves and their peers as part of the issues surrounding media study, they will become more adept at finding their own place within the media workforce.

Here is how each author revised or wrote each chapter to help you and your students use the case method more effectively. Stephen Lacy revised chapter 1 (Managerial Decision Making) and chapter 10 (Budgeting and Decision Making), updating research and examples to reflect the current state of the industry. Ardyth Broadrick Sohn revised chapter 2 (Leadership and the Workforce) and chapter 7 (Planning), updating material on convergence, new media, and international aspects as well as their influences on leadership and planning. George Sylvie revised chapter 3 (Motivation) and chapter 5 (Technology and the Future), updating research and information about new media, the Internet, and their future implications for media managers. Angela Powers revised chapter 4 (The Global Structure of Media Organizations), incorporating new material on the structure of Internet, new media, converged, and international media organizations.

Jan LeBlanc Wicks revised chapter 6 (Media Regulation and Self-Regulation) and chapter 9 (Marketing and Research). Updated Internet, new technology sections, and online resource sections were added to chapter 6, and updated information and examples on data used by advertisers and media organizations were added to chapter 9. Wicks wrote Extended Case 1 (The Case of Change at a Newspaper) to allow students to conduct Internet and database research, analyze it, and apply it when examining several major problems from a broad perspective, incorporating all chapters in the book. (See the Introduction to the Extended Cases.) C. Ann Hollifield revised chapter 8 (Market Analysis) and wrote Extended Case 2 (The Case of the Newsroom Restructuring). Chapter 8 incorporates new media, international material, and the implications of new technologies and international markets in market analysis. Extended Case 2 involves planning and decision making regarding cutbacks, layoffs, and restructuring a media organization while maintaining product quality.

In summary, this new third edition retains its core content and approach while incorporating new material and cases to reflect contemporary research and professional practice. Our method of using case studies enables students to learn the importance and application of theory and research in real-life media settings. A student who understands not only what occurred in a media management situation, but why and how it happened, and what the consequences of various solutions could be, is better prepared to face the complex, rapidly changing field of media management.

—Jan LeBlanc Wicks

CHAPTER

1

MANAGERIAL DECISION MAKING

Managers carry out a wide range of organizational activities. They budget, evaluate employees, plan product changes, give raises, and more. All of these activities require decisions, and managers need to know how to make good decisions if their organizations are to achieve their goals. Simon (1960), the most noted scholar in the area of decision making, equated the decision process with managing.

Decision making is so central to managing that most managers select among options without thinking about the process by which they decide. Making decisions without reflecting on the process can work reasonably well on a day-to-day basis. However, decision making is a skill. To improve that skill, managers must think about the process they use to solve problems. The purpose of this chapter is to help students understand how decisions are made so they can better benefit from using the cases in this book. The cases following each chapter provide decision-making practice in a number of managerial areas. This practice is more effective if a person understands the decision-making process.

DEFINING DECISION MAKING

There are many definitions of *decision making*. For example, Simon (1960) wrote, "Decision-making comprises three principle phases: finding occasions for making decisions; finding possible courses of action; and choosing among the courses of action" (p. 1). Harrison (1987) defined a *decision* as

'. . . a moment, in an ongoing process of evaluating alternatives for meeting an objective, at which expectations about a particular course of action impel the decision maker to select the course of action most likely to result in obtaining the objective.' (p. 2)

Many of the traditional definitions of *decision making* concentrate on the process as a rational one that involves a person or group with common goals. However, Taylor (1984) emphasized the role of organizations' sociopolitical contexts and environments. This approach suggests that decisions are not as

1

deliberate as often assumed, but occur from interaction among people and groups with sometimes conflicting goals.

The range of definitions for decision making suggests that defining this process is somewhat arbitrary. However, some concepts are common to most definitions. Decisions almost always involve resources, they usually address goals or objectives, they always involve people, and the environment in which these people work always affects decisions.

With these common concepts in mind, we define *decision making* as the allocation of scare resources by individuals or groups to achieve goals under conditions of uncertainty and risk. This definition has six important terms. First, *allocation* means that things have been distributed among alternatives. Just as a family allocates its income for food, clothing, housing, transportation, and entertainment, media managers must decide how to distribute their resources.

Scare resources reflect that a manager never has all of the resources she would like. Available resources are people's time and money. To a degree, these two resources are interchangeable. If you have money, but need time, you can hire others. If you have time, but need money, you can sell that time. Certainly, other forms of resources are available, but all are related to time and money. For example, technology is a way of increasing the effectiveness and efficiency of time and is acquired with money. Other forms of resources are derivative of time and money, or they are ways of improving the allocation of time and money.

The word *scarce* is equally important. If resources were not scarce, decision making would not be central to management. With a limitless supply of money and time, people simply could try every alternative until they found the one that worked best. Scarce resources limit the time and money spent on a decision.

The third term includes *individuals and groups*. Decisions can be made by one person or by two or more people functioning as a unit. All other things being equal, it takes less time for one person to decide than it does a group. However, ease of decision is not the same as effectiveness of decision. Groups make some decisions better than do individuals.

Goal is the fourth term. *Goal* means a decision has a purpose. The nature of business goals is complex and has been the subject of much debate and research. The cases in this book may or may not state specific goals, but no decision can be made adequately without considering the goals of that decision and the overall goals of the organization.

In pursuing goals, managers can assume they act in a strictly rational way or they act with bounded rationality. Managers act in a strictly rational way when their goal is to maximize some aspect of business. Simon (1957) defined a *rational decision* as occurring when a decision maker confronted with alternatives selects the one that has the highest return. This definition of rationality is the basis of classical economic theory and has resulted in the idea that business should maximize some goal, whether it is profits, revenues, or sales.

Acceptance of the assumption of rationality began to crumble after World War II, as scholars began to recognize the limits of the "rational man" approach. Cyert and March (1963) said the profit maximization assumption for businesses was not realistic because people within organizations do not have single-minded purposes. People pursue a variety of goals. Cyert and March also added that firms do not have the perfect knowledge necessary to maximize profits. Maximizing profits occurs when the cost of an additional unit of a product equals the price a consumer pays. This maximizing point is a theoretical idea because such detailed price and cost data are impossible to collect.

In place of this rational assumption for decision making, Simon (1957) suggested the principle of *bounded rationality*. This principle recognizes that humans cannot be rational in the strict, traditional sense, but Simon was not willing to say people act randomly. Rather, he proposed that humans pursue goals in a purposeful manner, but this pursuit is limited by the nature of people and the social environment in which they live. As a result, people seek goals and make decisions that work to satisfy instead of maximize their benefits from the decisions. This *satisficing* approach means people adopt goals and decision outcomes that are acceptable within the constraints faced by the organizations.

Uncertainty is the fifth term of the definition that needs discussion. *Uncertainty* means all decisions are probabilistic. No decision outcome is 100% certain. Reducing uncertainty starts with a subjective estimate of the probability that an outcome will occur. A graduating public relations major, for instance, might estimate that she has a 50% chance of finding a job within a month. Part of the estimate is figuring out the factors that affect outcomes. Once a person has made such an estimate, the reasons behind the estimate can be used to reduce uncertainty.

These estimates of probability may be as crude as a statement that an outcome is more likely than not, or they may be as sophisticated as a derived mathematical statement of probability. For instance, a person might bet another person that Michigan State University will beat the University of Illinois in a football game. This is a statement with subjective probability, as is the statement that there is a 60% chance of rain tomorrow.

However, all such subjective estimates share two characteristics: (a) They are based on analysis of information, and (b) they are based on assumptions about measurement and time that limit their objective nature. The accuracy of the information and quality of analysis determine how well the subjective statement of probability predicts rain or the football game winner.

Uncertainty then rests on a continuum from 0% to 100% uncertainty about a decision outcome. This is shown in Fig. 1.1. Because perfect knowledge is impossible, 0% uncertain decisions do not exist, and a 100% uncertain decision would be a random solution. As Bass (1983) pointed out, in the absence of other information, people fill in with their experience or that of their acquaintances. As uncertainty increases, the difficulty of making an effective decision increases.

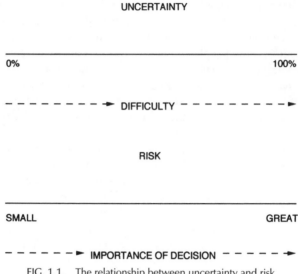

FIG. 1.1.   The relationship between uncertainty and risk.

The word *risk*, the final term in the definition, is used differently here than in traditional decision-making literature. *Risk* refers to the amount of resources committed to accomplishing a goal and, therefore, the amount of resources that might be lost. Risk also exists on a continuum shown in Fig. 1.1. The risk runs from small to great. Small means few resources are allocated, whereas great means a large amount of resources is involved. As with uncertainty, organizations rarely operate at the ends of the risk continuum.

Few organizations allocate a large percentage of their resources to a given project, much less a single decision. Risk is a relative term. Allocating $1 million would be a huge proportion of resources at most weekly newspapers, but a relatively small proportion of resources at a large media corporation such as CBS or Microsoft. The greater the risk, the more important the decision is for a company.

Figure 1.1 can be used to illustrate the importance and difficulty of decisions to a media organization. A decision that concerns a relatively great risk and a high level of uncertainty is important and difficult. In fact such a venture might not be undertaken. A decision that has little risk and uncertainty would be relatively unimportant and easy to make.

TYPES OF DECISIONS

Decisions fall into two types: programmed and nonprogrammed (Simon, 1960). A *programmed* decision sets up a rule that states an action will take place once a certain condition has been reached. A *nonprogrammed* decision is one that cannot be made by referring to a rule. Programmed decisions tend to be highly structured with established goals and channels of information. Nonprogrammed decisions have poor structure, vague goals, and ambiguous information. Determining an employee's pay every month is an example of a programmed decision. Publishers at a newspaper do not have to decide how much money to pay their employees at the end of each month. The amount and form have been set up in advance, usually on an annual basis, and most organizations have computers that issue the checks.

Nonprogrammed decisions occur at irregular intervals and require information and analysis that is specific to a particular set of options. A newspaper's decision to provide free Web-classified advertising would be a nonprogrammed decision if it were not a regularly occurring promotion. Because nonprogrammed decisions—such as hiring a new news anchor on TV or starting a magazine—happen irregularly, an effective programmed policy is difficult or impossible to develop. Each time new information and analyses must be conducted for an effective decision to be made.

The distinction between programmed and nonprogrammed decisions is an important one. If a decision can be programmed effectively, it is wise to do so. The greater the number of programmed decisions, the more time a manager will have to spend on more difficult nonprogrammed decisions. Whether a decision can be programmed depends on the uncertainty and risk involved. The lower the uncertainty and risk, the more likely a programmed decision will work.

The two types often occur in the same process. News selection, for instance, involves both programmed and nonprogrammed decisions. News values are a form of programmed decisions. If an automobile accident kills several people in a city, it will be on the evening TV news in that city. It has the news values of proximity (it is local) and impact (extreme consequences). There is little debate because applying the news values to such events has become programmed. The difficulty comes in deciding whether an event truly represents certain news values.

Proactive and Reactive Decisions

Another way to categorize decisions has to do with the impact of external events and trends on an organization. Managers tend to react to changes in the business environment with either proactive or reactive decisions (Ivancevich, Lorenzi, Skinner, & Crosby, 1994). *Proactive decisions* are made in anticipation of external changes, whereas *reactive decisions* are made as a result of external changes.

Examples of these two types of decisions can be found in the reaction of a newspaper company to Web sites that provide information about the newspaper's community. If the newspaper went online in 1995 with a Web site about its community, it is likely that managers made a proactive decision to establish a source of information before other companies did. If the newspaper managers waited until competitors had already established a community Web site, say 1998, then they made a reactive decision.

Proactive decisions can work well when they promote solutions to problems before they become particularly burdensome. Reactive decisions often occur after a company's competitor has gained a foothold in the market, which can put the reacting company at a disadvantage. However, a company can be proactive to an imagined problem and end up wasting money solving a problem that does not exist. Successful proactive decisions require accurate predictions of future external trends and events. Successful reactive decisions require that an organization not wait too long in responding to changes in the business environment. Timing is crucial.

THE DECISION PROCESS

Despite variation in the names given to the steps in the decision process, most decision-making models are similar. For example, Drucker (1983) gave six steps: (a) classify the problem, (b) define the problem, (c) specify what the decision must do, (d) seek the right decision, (e) build in the action to carry out the decision, and (f) use feedback to test the decision's effectiveness. Griffin and Moorhead (1986) offered a model that incorporates the difference between programmed and nonprogrammed decisions and acknowledges the role of information at each step.

The model shown in Fig. 1.2 is called a *decision wheel* because it represents the cyclical nature of the decision process. It differs from the Griffin and

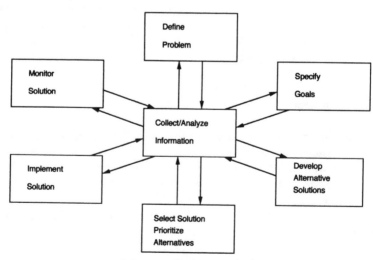

FIG. 1.2.   The decision wheel.

Moorhead (1986) model in two ways. First, it does not include the idea of programmed versus nonprogrammed decisions. Programmed decisions, although important, are not the basis of the case study approach. Although creating a policy may be the solution to a case, this solution results from a nonprogrammed decision process.

A second difference between the decision wheel and other models is the central placement of the collection and analysis of information. Just as decision making is the heart of management, the collection and appropriate analysis of information are the hubs of decision making. All steps of the decision-making process must involve the collection of information and its appropriate evaluation. Analysis, which breaks down the information and then examines and classifies it so it can be used, is a key to effective decisions. Correct analysis with little information often is more useful than poor analysis with abundant information.

Defining the Problem

The first step is defining the problem to be solved. It involves the collection of information about some form of behavior, either inside or outside the organization, that is a problem for the media firm. This information must be analyzed in a way that allows the managers to frame the problem appropriately. For example, a TV news department that is losing audience has a problem. To define the problem behind this decline in ratings, management must develop a list of possible causes and collect information about them. Then the information about the potential causes must be analyzed to decide what the cause may be. Perhaps the audience does not like the hard-news focus of the news shows or they may not like the anchors. Each problem holds several possible causes; in most cases, problems may have more than one cause. The ability to reverse the sliding ratings, however, depends on management's ability to define the problem in a way that the causes can be identified correctly.

Specifying Goals

After the problem is defined, the next step is to specify the goals of the decision. The goals need to be concrete. Vague statements about reversing a trend does not allow for effective decision making. The goals should be as specific as the problem and available data allow. Usually the decision process addresses multiple goals. All goals should have a time frame for accomplishing them.

In the free Web-classified ads decision mentioned earlier, the newspaper publisher decided the newspaper needed to draw more visitors to its Web site, specifically to its classified ads page. The goal could be to generate an additional 200 visitors a day within a month, generate 400 new visits a day within 3 months, and to retain at least 200 of those visitors when the promotion ends after 3 months. These specific goals allow better monitoring and force managers to use detailed data analysis. Managers can set up several goals at various times. For example, the publisher could have a goal of 200 new visitors at 1 month, 300 at 2 months and 400 at 3 months, and a permanent increase of 200 visitors at 6 months, which would be 3 months after the promotion ended. The crucial element of goal setting is degree of specificity and a time for meeting the goal.

Developing Solutions

The third step in the decision wheel is developing alternative solutions. This step should yield as many viable alternatives as possible. Inadequate solutions can always be rejected, but a solution that has not been considered can never be selected. A weeding out process follows the listing of the solutions. Here the obviously unsuitable solution can be dropped, leaving those that have some possibilities for accomplishing the goals.

As with all steps, the narrowing process requires the acquisition of information and its analysis. Two questions for developing this short list are: (a) Will the solutions actually accomplish the goals? (b) Will the costs of the solution outweigh the gains to the organization? If the answer to the first question is no, the solution should be dropped. If the answer to the second question is yes, the solution should be dropped.

If a newspaper decided it needed to increase visitors to its Web site, the managers might list the following options:

1. Partner with a local TV station and stream news video.
2. Hire a reporter to write just for the Web site.
3. Set up live Web cams around town to stream live video from popular community locations such as malls and parks.
4. Partner with local news/talk radio stations and stream news audio.
5. Give away free Web-classified advertisements for 3 months.
6. Acquire additional news services to load online.

These are just some of the possible solutions. Only a few of these will get serious consideration, but examining all possible alternatives will help managers identify plausible ones.

The two-question test can be applied to eliminate some of the listed alternatives. For example, acquiring additional news services such as *The New York Times* service probably will not attract more visitors because many sites already provide these news services. In addition, Solutions 1 and 3 might require an investment in live video-streaming technology and employees to use the technology. The investment might exceed the increased revenue from additional Web site visitors.

Selecting a Solution

With a short list of solutions, a manager moves to Step 4, which involves selecting one solution to the problem. The solution may be a combination of more than one alternative solution, but the next step requires a decision to pursue a specific solution.

The collection and analysis of information are crucial at this point. When one solution is selected, the alternate solutions should not be forgotten, however. Often the original solution does not work as well as management would like. As a result, managers have to return to the problem and either generate new solutions or choose one of the solutions dropped in Step 4. It is a good idea to prioritize the solutions not used based on the information and analysis in Step 4. This may save time if the chosen solution fails.

Selecting solutions is always a matter of costs and benefits. Often more than one solution will work so the correct option involves one that balances costs with the benefits. One solution may generate more visits than another, but the costs would be so high as to consume the entire increase in revenues from getting more visits. At the same time, a solution may be inexpensive, but the results will not reach the specified goals.

Returning to the problem of increasing visits to the newspaper Web site, we find the managers considering three options not eliminated by a quick two-question test. They reject Option 4 because the newspaper exists in a medium-sized market that does not have a commercial news/talk station.

The two remaining solutions involve either investing in new employees, which will increase expenses, or allowing free classified ads, which will reduce revenue because some of the people using the free ads would have paid for ads. Both of the solutions would result in a reduction of profits in the short run to increase profits in the long run. Over time the goal of increasing visits will allow the newspaper to charge higher prices for online advertising, particularly for online classified ads.

Comparing the two options, the managers realize that hiring an online reporter may be a good idea, but it will require a permanent increase in the number of employees and a continuing increase in the budget. Giving away free ads for 3 months will reduce revenues only temporarily. The managers also realize giving free online classifieds will bring people who are looking at classified, and it will possibly bring the advertisers results that will encourage them to buy classified ads in the future. This is a double benefit that might not derive from the exclusive online reporter.

Implementing the Solution

Once the solution has been selected, it must be implemented. This is the fifth step in the decision wheel. The solution means nothing unless it is applied correctly. This requires a detailed plan of action with a timetable for specific actions, a budget, and a breakdown of who has responsibility for carrying out the changes. The details should be as specific as possible.

Therefore, the decision to provide free online classified ads is just the beginning of a string of decisions. To accomplish the goals, the free ads must be promoted, the process by which ads will be taken must be planned, and the managers must decide how to measure the impact on visits. Promotion can occur through the print edition of the newspaper, on the Web site, and even through other media such as radio ad spots. The promotion will most likely involve a variety of activities, but the cost will have to reflect what the managers think the return will be. It is likely that the existing classified ads staff will place the free ads, but the newspaper might have to hire temporary help. Finally, the managers must decide how to measure the impact, which would involve measuring a baseline of visits over several weeks before the free ads are offered so that any change in number of visits can be compared with this baseline.

Monitoring the Solution

The final step is monitoring the implementation in light of the goals. This monitoring should provide feedback on a regular basis to judge progress toward the goals and be part of the implementation plan. For example, the newspaper Web manager would examine the data from Web site visits weekly, with special attention to visits on the classified ad pages. Every 2 weeks or so, the managers would discuss the results to see if they need to change the promotion that draws people to the free ads. Of course they might have to deal with problems from having a larger number of free ads than were anticipated. A rush for free ads could increase the expenses more than anticipated, which would generate new problems.

Crucial to the monitoring system is a timetable. A solution that is not working should be given an adequate test period, but a media organization should not remain committed to a solution once it becomes obvious that it will not work. Times should be established during the implementation process at which the managers must decide to continue or end the plan.

This monitoring process makes the entire decision process cyclical. If the solution is not working, this becomes a problem that starts a new cycle of decision making. The same steps are taken in a new cycle, but some may take less time and effort because the previous decision process already provides relevant information. However, managers must always be careful not to assume that they have all the information they need. An effective manager continues to acquire information until the cost of additional information outweighs the probable benefit from having that information.

CONSTRAINTS ON THE DECISION PROCESS

The decision wheel is an ideal. It is a blueprint that is seldom followed exactly because of practical constraints that fall into two types: (a) who makes the decision, and (b) time available for the decision.

Decision Makers

Both individuals and groups make decisions. Whether a group or individual makes the decision influences the efficiency and effectiveness of the decision. In some cases, individuals may decide best. In other cases, group decisions work better. Huber (1980) listed three advantages and four disadvantages of group decisions, whereas Harrison (1987) gave nine strengths and four weaknesses. Griffin and Moorhead (1986) presented six advantages of group decision making and three advantages of individual decision making. Table 1.1 summarizes the advantages and disadvantages of group decision making and categorizes them under the headings of *timing, uncertainty*, and *goals*.

TABLE 1.1
Advantages and Disadvantages of Group Decision Making

Advantages	*Disadvantages*
Timing	
Slower decision process	Slower decision process
Division of labor for complex task	Disagreement over goals may result in no decisions
Uncertainty	
Larger amounts of information and knowledge generated	Political behavior of group members reduces acceptance of information from others
Fewer errors in analyzing information	Groupthink—The tendency of group members to think the group is infallible
More alternatives generated	
Goals	
Groups can clarify goal understanding	Groups sometimes act in ways inconsistent with goals
Participation increases acceptance of group goals	Groupthink

Interestingly, weaknesses of group decision making can also be strengths. For example, one of the advantages and disadvantages of group decision making is its slow process. Group decision making usually increases the time needed for a decision because of problems in organizing meetings and in the long process of forming consensus among people with conflicting positions. An individual decision maker does not have these timing problems. Whether the time element is an advantage or a disadvantage depends on the decision. If timing is crucial, individuals make quicker decisions. If timing is not crucial and risk and uncertainty are high, a slower process has advantages.

Deadlines exemplify the timing importance in news departments. News stories do not get used if they are not ready by the printing or broadcast deadlines. So individuals make most decisions about what stories will run. However, important stories are exceptions to this rule. An example of a group decision involving a news story is the case of the Pentagon Papers. The Pentagon Papers were a secret report about the history of the Vietnam War. They were prepared in the late 1960s for Secretary of Defense Robert S. McNamara, who served for President Lyndon Johnson. *The New York Times* got the report from Daniel Ellsberg, who helped prepare it. After four installments of the Papers ran in *The New York Times* in June 1971, a federal court issued a restraining order. Meanwhile *The Washington Post* had obtained a copy of the report. A group of 10 managers at the *Post* met for 12 hours to discuss whether they should publish parts of the report. They published (Witcover, 1971).

The inherent lack of speed in group decisions is not the only advantage or disadvantage of groups. When complex tasks are involved, groups have the advantage of division of labor. Dividing tasks among group members actually can speed up the process because no one person must learn the wide range of complex information required for complex decisions. Buying a new computer system for a newspaper is an example. Because such systems often serve multiple departments, it would make sense to include someone from each of these departments in the decision-making process. It is easier to have people from each department who know the departments' computer needs than it is to have one or two people learn about the computer needs of all the departments.

Advantages and disadvantages of group decisions also fall under the heading of uncertainty. Group decision making can reduce uncertainty in three ways. First, having more than one person increases the amount of information and knowledge brought to the process. Second, it can decrease the number of errors. The cliché "two heads are better than one" applies here. Having more people also can reduce information errors because people can evaluate each other's information and analysis. Third, groups generate more alternative solutions. The ability to compare alternatives with each other can result in better solutions.

Although uncertainty will decline with some groups, it can increase with others. The probabilities that develop from the satisficing approach are subjective. The attitudes and perceptions of other group members influence this subjectivity.

Political behavior among group members can create doubt as to appropriate goals and desirability of solutions. For instance, when a city editor and sports editor try to persuade other group members that each department is key to improving quality, the process of persuasion can cast doubt on either department being effective at attracting readers. The result is uncertainty of actions.

Just as dangerous as political behavior, which can divide, is the phenomenon of groupthink. *Groupthink* occurs when group members are so set on sustaining unanimity that they fail to properly appraise the alternative solutions (Janis, 1982). Although the group feels it has reduced uncertainty because it agreed on the best alternative, it actually decreased the probability that any one solution will work. The solution does not get an adequate evaluation.

The final heading in Table 1.1 is goals. Because of the number of people involved, groups often develop a better understanding of the organization's and decision group's goals. Reading a statement of goals adopted by an organization does not mean automatically that the employees understand those goals. Hearing others discuss the goals can help clarify them.

Another advantage is that participation in group decision making will increase acceptance of the goals and solutions that are adopted. Increased acceptance can translate into increased effort in accomplishing the goals. People tend to accept more readily those decisions in which they participated.

A disadvantage of group decisions with respect to goals is the tendency of some groups to develop their own goals that may be inconsistent with the organization's goals. For example, a group set up within a media organization to develop ways to cut costs may decide that cost cutting is not a proper goal. The result is a conflict of goals between management and the decision group. Resulting decisions are less likely to accomplish the aims of management.

The many advantages and disadvantages of group decisions create problems for deciding when groups or individuals should make decisions. Vroom and Yetton (1973) said that individual managers are likely to make decisions when the problem is well structured, information is plentiful, a previously successful solution to a similar problem is available, and time constrains require a quick decision.

Individual Decision-Making Styles

As with all human skills, managers vary in the style of decision making they use. A decision-making style has to do with common patterns of reaching decisions. Most managers exhibit more than one style, but often a particular style emerges under pressure.

Driver, Brousseau, and Hunsaker (1993) identified decision style by the way managers use information and how they focus on solutions. *Use of information* involved either satisficing or maximizing. As mentioned earlier, satisficing requires collecting information to reach a satisfactory conclusion that may not result in as good a result as possible. Maximizing involves collecting information until a decision maker has enough to reach what he feels is the best decision. The difference is related to how long the decision makers will collect information before acting.

Solution focus concerns the use of data to identify possible solutions. *Unifocus* people collect information and identify one solution they think is best, whereas *multifocus* people collect information and provide a variety of solutions to a problem.

These two dimensions were combined to produce the following five decision styles:

Decisive Style. This style involves people who are satisficers and are unifocus with respect to solutions. These people collect a limited amount of information and act quickly. Once they identify their solution, they are unwavering in their support of that solution.

Flexible Style. Flexible decision makers are satisficers who have multifocus on solutions. They also act on limited information, but they show more flexibility in using solutions. If one solution fails to work, they turn to another.

Hierarchical Style. This style involves maximizing and unifocus. These decision makers act slowly because they collect large amounts of information to select the one best solution, which is pursued using a detailed plan.

Integrative Style. People using this style are maximizers with multifocus solutions. They tend to take their time in collecting and evaluating information, but unlike the hierarchical style, these people consider more than one solution to the problem.

Systemic Style. This style incorporates both the integrative and hierarchical styles in a two-step process. The first step involves using the integrative style of evaluating large amounts of information and dealing with multiple solutions. The second step is more hierarchical in that the solutions are prioritized with one or more criteria being considered the best. This style is more contemplative than the hierarchical style, but involves more organized and active solutions than the integrative style.

These types of decision-maker classifications can be useful in understanding decision making, but care must be taken. Often managers exhibit a combination of these styles with individual decisions and in decisions across time. The usefulness of the classification is its emphasis on types of goals (satisficing and maximizing) and nature of focus (unifocus or multifocus).

Types for Group Decisions

Just as individual decision makers exhibit different styles, so do groups. McEwan (1997) listed 10 ways that groups can reach decisions; they vary by the degree the entire group participates and the quality (how effectively the decisions result in reaching goals) of the resulting decisions. The group decision styles are:

Decision by Authority Without Group Discussion. This is not really a group decision, although it may be presented as such, because one person makes the decision for the group. It yields a fast decision, but the group does not become involved.

Decision by Default. A group failing to make a decision can be a form of decision. Group inactivity results in either someone else making the decision or the problem going away.

Self-Authorized Decisions. One or more members assume they have the authority to make a decision when they do not. Such decisions have little support from members left out of the process.

Decision by Clique. A few individuals form a subgroup to make decisions and then impose that decision. This breaks the decision-making group into competing factions, which reduces quality of decisions.

Decision by Expert. A person within a group makes the decision, but how the expert is selected can create internal disagreements.

Decision by Averaging Individuals' Opinions. Members' opinions are asked separately, and the results are averaged. Group members have no actual part of the decision because group interaction is missing.

Decision by Authority After Group Discussions. Group members advise the person who has authority to make the decision. This can result in competition for authority's attention or telling authority what the group members believe will please her.

Decision by Minority. A subgroup is given the authority to make decisions. This makes other members wonder why they were put in the group.

Decision by Majority Vote. The group does as the majority wants. The effectiveness depends on everyone's commitment to this method, whether they are in the majority or minority.

Decision by Consensus. The group reaches a decision that everyone can support, but it can be time-consuming. This may be the best method if time allows because it results in high-quality conclusions.

All of these types of divisions have advantages and disadvantages depending on the decision's goal. It is helpful for groups to understand how they are making decisions because it allows them to analyze the weaknesses of these decisions. Suppose a magazine company appoints a committee to plan a long-term strategy for incorporating the World Wide Web in its product strategy. Members should represent the various departments in the company, as well as a variety of Web experience and technological knowledge. The group might be tempted to let the person with the most technological knowledge (decision by expert) make the decisions, but that person might not know how advertisers and viewers want to interact with the Web. The company's chief operating officer (CEO) might make the decision after hearing all sides (decision by authority after group discussion), but the techies and nontechies might form subgroups and compete for the CEO's support.

The best type of group decision making depends on a variety of factors about the problem and the people involved. One of the most important factors is timing of decisions.

Time and Decision Making

In addition to classifying decisions by type of decision-making style, decisions can be broken down on the basis of time available. Three general timing patterns seem appropriate. Nonprogrammed decisions can be classified as immediate, short term, or long term. Immediate decisions must be made quickly. The time that is available between Steps 1 and 5 in the decision wheel is measured in hours or even minutes. Story decisions on deadline are the prime examples in media.

As a result of deadlines, it is common to find individuals making content decisions at newspapers, magazines, and TV news departments. However, the deadline pressure hides the danger that individuals will begin making *all* decisions quickly and alone out of habit. No decision should be made before time requires it. If a decision need not be made immediately, participation of others should be sought.

Short-term decisions are ones that need not be made immediately, but they must be made within a reasonable period of time. At a newspaper, the plans for a breakdown of news and advertising space for the coming week would be short term.

Small groups usually make these decisions even if one person has responsibility. For example, the publisher, who has final authority for space in a newspaper, may meet with the advertising manager and editor to determine news holes for a week. Often the publisher has determined a breakdown for the year between news and advertising space. The meetings are monitoring sessions by which the three managers discuss news-editorial needs in light of the year's goal, previous use of space, and the newsroom's space needs for the week.

Long-term decisions are those that affect the organization over a period of years and, therefore, warrant a longer decision-making process. This type of decision includes selecting network news anchors and format changes at a magazine or newspaper. Because of their complexity, these decisions require participation by a large number of people in groups and as individuals. In effect, a long-term decision, such as what next year's budget should be, requires hundreds or thousands of smaller decisions.

Overall, time acts as a constraint on the process shown in the decision wheel by limiting the time available for each of the six steps. These limits determine how much information can be collected, how much analysis can be conducted, and how many people can participate in the decision. Immediate decisions allow little time for each step and for information collection and analysis. Long-term decisions should include adequate time for each step.

The timing of various types of decisions places a premium on different types of managers. When an immediate decision is needed, a satisfactory solution is more important than an optimal solution. So the person who has command of a great deal of information in an area and who can analyze quickly will perform best. This person need not be as good at working with people as a manager who deals with short- and long-term problems. Decisive and flexible decision styles work well here.

A manager faced with short-term decisions needs both people skills and the ability to reach decisions within a reasonable time. In contrast, managers who must make long-term decisions are better served by skills that allow them to work with people and examine a problem from several angles. This person should be good at analysis, but it is analysis with a different time frame. This manager must be good at developing many alternatives and evaluating them against each other. The variation of needed skills explains why some people make better upper level managers, such as editor, than lower level managers, such as assistant city editor. Long-term decisions that involve high risk and uncertainty work best with integrative or systemic styles for decision makers.

The key to effective decision making is to put people in positions where their abilities serve them best and then train them in the areas where they are weakest. The ability to understand and handle time constraints is essential if a person is to be promoted within the media organization.

TOOLS OF MANAGEMENT

Just as time constrains decision making, so does the quality of information and analysis, which relate directly to the skills of the decision maker. As with all skills, collecting and analyzing information can be improved through learning. This section briefly addresses the sources of information and some of the tools of analysis.

Sources of Information

Because information plays so important a role in all six steps, it is useful to examine where one gets information. Basically, information comes either from one's own efforts or the efforts of others. The efforts can take various forms, however, and those forms can affect the quality of information. The two main types of efforts are experience and research. Experience involves participating in events or processes, and research is the application of generally accepted systematic methods of examining events or processes. Someone who works at a news magazine has experience in magazine journalism. Someone who conducts a survey of news magazine reporters is conducting research about magazine journalism. Experience differs from research in that it does not have accepted standards for analyzing data. Experience is inseparable from the person having the experience. Yet a researcher, if conducting research properly, should have a limited impact on the events or processes being studied.

Research should be more objective and systematic than experience. *Should be* are important words because quality of research depends on the researcher's skills, just as quality of experience depends on the wisdom of the person experiencing the event. A manager can analyze experience systematically and somewhat objectively, just as a researcher inadvertently can alter the result of his research through poor use of methods.

Managers have roughly four sources of information: their own experiences, the experiences of others, their research, and the research of others. The tendency among media managers is to depend on their experiences and the experiences of trusted colleagues. Experience has the characteristic of being specific to a particular situation. This can be an advantage when a decision must be made about a situation similar to previous events. However, using one's experience becomes a liability when that experience is applied to a problem that differs from the original experience. The result in such situations is often a poor decision.

Managers should know the value of all forms of information and seek many diverse sources of information, especially in the monitoring step. A successful manager analyzes past decisions so the next decision can be made more effective. The results of every decision should become information for future decisions, but the usefulness of this information depends on the ability to use tools of analysis.

Cost–Benefit Analysis

A manager with few analytical skills or little knowledge and experience will end up depending on others to judge the reliability and validity of information. This can be a problem. Managers who understand analysis are in a better position to select information appropriate for decisions. Analysis involves ways of processing information. Several different types of analysis, which vary in complexity, are available.

Perhaps the most recognized analytical tool is cost–benefit analysis, which is an attempt to estimate the costs and benefits that would result from alternative actions. McKean (1975) listed five steps: (a) identifying benefits to be achieved, (b) identifying alternatives that will reach the goal, (c) identifying costs for the alternative methods, (d) developing a model or set of relationships that explain the impact of alternatives on the costs and benefits, and (e) a criterion involving both costs and benefits for selecting the preferred alternative. These steps sound familiar because they correspond to steps of the decision wheel.

The traditional approach to cost–benefit analysis is to place a monetary value on all costs and benefits and compare the resulting differences (Huber, 1980). Because this is difficult to do with many types of costs, cost–benefit analysis may include the "dollar-equivalency technique" (Huber, 1980, p. 80), which is the development of money equivalents for costs that are difficult to measure in dollars. Obviously this becomes problematic when costs and benefits involve human behavior.

Two concepts are useful in dealing with the nonmonetary aspects of cost–benefit analysis: opportunity costs and intangibles. *Opportunity costs* are the expenses that accrue from giving up alternative actions. It is equivalent to the old saying: "There is no free lunch." For every alternative selected, a person loses what she would have gained from another alternative. For example, a manager is hiring a reporter and must pick from two candidates. The first is stronger at writing and the second at reporting. If the first is hired, an opportunity cost is the reporting ability that will be lost from not hiring the second. If the second is hired, an opportunity cost is the writing skill that will be lost from not hiring the first.

Intangibles are the things that cannot be measured well. This may be leadership in a manager or the ability of some people to raise morale in an organization. Whatever the attribute, a dollar amount cannot be assigned adequately. These intangibles are often ignored in formal tools of analysis because they cannot be measured well.

Opportunity costs and intangibles are the Achilles heel of cost–benefit analysis and most other types of formal analysis. These two concepts relate to all decisions, although sometimes they are more important than at other times. Despite these two problems, cost–benefit analysis can be useful even if it simply allows a manager to think more clearly. The following example demonstrates the potential use of cost–benefit analysis in a situation where quantification is difficult.

The *Times-Leader* recently conducted a readership survey in which 48% of the readers said they would like to have more in-depth local coverage. Managing Editor, Jane Smith, has been assigned to come up with a plan for doing this. Her first observation is that it can be done either by hiring a new reporter or using existing staff. She comes up with the benefits and advantages presented in Table 1.2.

The monetary benefits for either alternative are equal in Table 1.2 and amount to $54,000 per year. These benefits are based on retaining 250 readers a year and attracting 250 more readers annually as a result of increased in-depth coverage. Two main areas of monetary benefits are saving $4,000 from not having to replace the 250 readers and making $50,000 in advertising revenue that would be lost if the 500 readers were not taking the newspaper.

Both approaches also have intangible benefits in the form of staff morale and the promotional advantage of having in-depth coverage that will generate recognition of the newspaper's journalistic efforts. The use of existing staff has an

TABLE 1.2
Cost–Benefit Analysis of Increasing In-Depth Reporting at the *Times-Leader*

| Costs | Alternatives | |
	Hiring a Reporter	*Using Existing Staff*
Monetary	$30,000 a year salary	$10,000 a year additional overtime
	$5,000 a year expense for travel & research	$5,000 a year expenses for travel & research
	$13,000 for 26 additional pages at cost of $500 per page	$13,000 for 26 additional pages at cost of $500 per page
Opportunity	Dissatisfaction among existing staff because they will not be allowed to do in-depth work	Use of staff for in-depth reporting will reduce time for day-to-day reporting
	Editing time lost on day-to-day coverage due to increased editing needs of day-to-day coverage	Editing time lost on day-to-day coverage due to increased editing needs of day-to-day coverage
Intangible	Possible negative impact of new reporter in the newsroom	Added effort needed to balance in-depth reporting
	Benefits[a]	
Monetary	Save $4,000 needed to gain 250 lost readers	Save $4,000 needed to gain 250 lost readers
	Save $50,000 in advertising revenue that could be lost with decline of 500 readers	Save $50,000 in advertising revenue that could be lost with decline of 500 readers
Intangible	Increased morale among staff from increased quality of the newspaper	Increased morale among staff from increased quality of the newspaper
	Promotional value of expected recognition from in-depth coverage	Promotional value of expected recognition from in-depth coverage
		Increased staff morale for those who do in-depth reporting

Note: The goal is to increase the amount of in-depth coverage by one page every 2 weeks.

[a]Benefits are based on an estimated retention of 250 readers and attracting 250 new readers as a result of increased in-depth coverage.

added advantage in that it will increase morale of the staff because they will be allowed to spend time on more lengthy projects.

Monetary costs of hiring an additional reporter are about $20,000 more a year because the new reporter would earn $30,000 a year, whereas overtime needed to use existing staff would only amount to $10,000. Both alternatives have opportunity costs. Each alternative would require about the same amount of additional editing, which would have to come from the time spent on editing of day-to-day stories.

Two opportunity costs and two intangible costs stand out as important factors. First, hiring a new reporter could create dissatisfaction among the existing staff members who would like to pursue in-depth reporting. Reporters usually look on in-depth work as a kind of reward because it is more satisfying and interesting than most day-to-day coverage. However, taking time from day-to-day coverage has the opportunity cost of reducing the amount of space and effort spent on everyday reporting. This could negatively affect circulation.

The intangible costs also involve the staff's reaction to a new plan. If a new reporter is hired, he or she may alter the chemistry among people in the newsroom. This impact, combined with the possible resentment, may have negative consequences. Yet a new reporter might add to the newsroom chemistry. Whether this becomes a cost would depend on who is hired as the new reporter. The use of existing staff means an added cost for the editors because they must ensure that the in-depth assignments are distributed fairly. Otherwise staff resentment could develop.

By examining Table 1.2, a manager could see that the question of which approach to take comes down to whether the additional $20,000 cost of a new reporter and the potential newsroom disruption exceeds the impact of reducing the day-to-day coverage in the newspaper. This, in turn, is related to the adequacy of the current staff. If the newsroom already is understaffed, expanding the work required could be disastrous. More readers might drop the paper because of poor day-to-day coverage than would take the paper because of increased in-depth reporting. To make an appropriate selection, a manager needs to have an understanding of the nature of the reporters currently working and an awareness of the informal organizational setting in the newsroom.

An important point of this illustration is that many of the costs and benefits are not quantifiable, but this should not lead to these costs and benefits being ignored. A second point is that the analysis is only as good as the information that goes into it. The monetary costs and benefits should be accurate, but the knowledge of the people in the newsroom needs to be just as reliable and valid.

Evaluating Information

As the decision wheel illustrates, information and its analysis lie at the center of effective decision making. The invention and development of computers, and personal computers in particular, have generated a flood of information that can help or hurt managers in making decisions. Computers have created this information flood for two reasons. First, they allow for the faster collection and manipulation of data about all types of human behavior. From sales information to surfing on the Internet, computers collect data in minutes what would have taken days or months before computers. As computers have grown faster and smaller, more data can be processed more quickly. Second, computers allow the instantaneous distribution of large amounts of information anywhere in the world. Multiple employees of an organization can share the same information at the same time, so group decisions can be made in a more timely fashion. This allows decision makers to live in different parts of the world and still make group decisions.

Of course computers also have reshaped the way media organizations distribute information to consumers, but this impact defines the type of decisions for media companies more than the decision process. Media companies experience the same impact of computers on the decision process as all organizations. Information is more accessible now than it has ever been, but accessibility is not the same as accuracy. Accessibility concerns how easily a given piece of information is to obtain. The Internet and other information distribution systems have made information much more accessible. However, this availability may be a Trojan horse—allowing information into the decision process that could lower the effectiveness of decisions.

Accuracy of information concerns whether the depiction of human behavior in numbers or words is a valid representation for that behavior. For example, if a readership survey supposedly represents what readers think about a magazine, the issue of accuracy addresses whether it truly does. Computers certainly make information more accessible, but whether information becomes more accurate depends on by whom and how the information was generated. Although an excellent researcher can use computers to generate even more accurate information, an incompetent one will only provide more inaccurate information.

Before using information for decisions, managers need to be able to determine whether the accuracy of that information is sufficient enough to make effective decisions. The accuracy level of information involves probability. Little information used for making decisions is 100% accurate if for no other reason than decisions involve future actions and the future is always uncertain. However, some information is more accurate than other information, and managers need to determine whether any given information meets that test. Because the only true test of information's accuracy is how well it can predict future behavior and events, accuracy can only be estimated. The following steps can be useful in evaluating information's accuracy.

1. Decide whether the material under consideration is information or opinion. Information is a description of behavior or phenomena, whereas opinion is a person's belief about the behavior or phenomena. An example of information would be the evaluation of accounting data that show publicly owned newspapers are more likely to have a smaller percentage of revenues devoted to the newsroom budget than do privately owned newspapers. An opinion would be a statement from a critic that publicly owned newspapers do not spend enough money on their newsroom budgets. The

information is a statement about budgeting behavior, and the opinion is a statement about whether the budgeting behavior is good or bad.

Opinion often can masquerade as information. A person not trained in data analysis might interpret the accounting data incorrectly. Without proper training on how to analyze data, the conclusions from the data will be no better than opinions and can even lead to ineffective decisions because the manager mistook the opinion for information.

2. Know accepted procedure for creating information. The process of creating accurate information has certain procedures that are accepted as appropriate by scientists and scholars who create knowledge and information. Scholars use the scientific method or critical method to generate information. Whether the information is considered valid depends on the procedure used by the scholars. Journalists also have generally accepted rules for reporting and writing stories. However, the two processes differ because scholars must report their method as part of their scholarship, whereas journalists are not expected to do so.

Managers, who use information to make decisions, should understand research procedures considered appropriate by the community of scholars and scientists. Knowing the methods for creating information allows decision makers the ability to evaluate its accuracy. Media managers should understand how surveys and content analysis are conducted so they can evaluate the research methods and ask researchers intelligent questions if they doubt the accuracy of information they are supplied.

3. Know who created the information you use. Even if managers understand research methods, and especially if they do not, it is a good idea that the sources of information be identified and evaluated. As mentioned, not all researchers and journalists are equal in their ability to generate accurate information. When acquiring information for decisions, a manager should know the source of the information. This is why companies often have their own research division; if they do not, they tend to use a research company proved to produce information that has resulted in effective decisions. One of the great problems of the Internet is that sources and method of information are often absent.

SUMMARY

Decision making is the heart of managing. Decisions are either *programmed*, which means the solutions take effect under prescribed conditions, or *nonprogrammed*, which requires attention to the individual problems that must be solved. Nonprogrammed decisions are more difficult to make. All programmed decisions originally were set up by nonprogrammed decisions.

Decisions can also be classified as *proactive* and *reactive*. Proactive decisions anticipate changes in the environment that will affect the organization, and reactive decisions are made as a result of environmental changes.

Reaching decisions has an abstract form presented here as a decision wheel. The steps in this wheel occur to some degree in all effective decisions, although the time and effort devoted to the individual steps varies with the conditions surrounding the individual problem.

Just as decision making is at the heart of management, so analysis and information collection are the hubs of decisions. Both lack of information and poor analysis of information account for a high percentage of decisions that fail to achieve their goals. Several tools are available to improve analysis and information collecting, including social science theories and cost–benefit analysis.

As with the majority of human endeavors, management can be made better with thought and practice. The remainder of this book is designed to facilitate thought and provide practice through cases. Each chapter also presents background to help explore the cases. The principles, theories, and research presented in the early part of the chapter should be used to analyze the information that is either provided with the case or needs to be collected from outside sources. In all cases, the decision process applies.

Case 1.1
Looking at Past Decisions

People often make important decisions without properly preparing or fully examining the decision process. The purpose of this assignment is to have you think about your decision-making process by concentrating on a specific decision. Select an important decision (choosing a college or college major, moving in with someone, etc.) that you made during the past few years that has disappointed you. Think about how you made that decision and why you were disappointed. Using the decision wheel from chapter 1, try to remember the actions you took that would have fit into the various steps in the wheel.

ASSIGNMENT

Write a brief summary of the decision and then answer the following questions:

1. Did you take all of the steps in the decision wheel? If not, which ones were not taken and why?
2. Did you complete each step as thoroughly as you should have? If not, which ones were not completed thoroughly and why?

3. If you could make that decision over again, what would you do differently to improve your decision?

Case 1.2
Using Individual and Group Decision Styles

Dan Smith, publisher of the *Lincoln Daily Chronicle*, sat at his desk thinking about the e-mails he had just received from one of his reporters, Susan Kelley, and from the director of advertising, Jane Seymore. Both messages concerned the Web site for WZZY, the local CBS-affiliated TV station. The Web site was not new. Yet unlike the other local TV station sites, WZZY had just added a section of classified advertising.

Kelley had e-mailed Smith because she found the site while buying a set of used golf clubs. Seymore had seen an advertisement that WZZY wanted to run in the *Daily Chronicle*. Smith has to make two decisions. First, he has to decide whether the newspaper will run the advertisements for the classified advertising on WZZY's Web site. After all, WZZY is now a competitor with the *Daily Chronicle* for classified advertising. Second, he has to decide what to do in response to this new competition for classified advertising. Currently, about 35% of the *Daily Chronicle*'s total revenues came from classified advertising. Before the Web, the cost of delivering classified ads to consumers had kept down competition for this lucrative market.

ASSIGNMENT

Using the material in this chapter, answer the following questions:

1. What type of individual decision-making style would work best for deciding whether to run WZZY's advertisement for its classified Web page? Why would it be best?
2. Should Smith use group decision making to decide how to react to the threat to the newspaper's classified advertising revenue? Why?
3. Assuming a group will be used to make the decision, which of the 10 group decision types would work best? Why?

Case 1.3
Improving the Web Site

Your newspaper, *The Daily Bugle*, currently places its staff-produced content on its Web site. In addition, it has recently added a reporter to produce daily copy just for the site. However, the publisher is still not convinced that these efforts will build the visits that are necessary to sell more online advertising. She knows that local businesses are skeptical that enough people visit the *Bugle's* Web site to make advertising effective. Currently, the site is pretty much an electronic version of the print newspaper.

ASSIGNMENT

Generate ideas for how to draw more users to the Web site and make them visit regularly. Develop additional methods of generating content for the site, prioritize them as to how likely they are to generate repeat users of the site, and provide information to support the priorities you assign.

Use the Web to identify particular elements of Web sites that might be attractive to people in a community and find research that explains how people currently use such elements. The research may be available online, in databases such as Lexis/Nexis or in newspapers and magazines found in the library.

2

LEADERSHIP
AND THE WORKFORCE

Managers oversee and assess the work of others, design plans for their unit, are responsible for specific timely actions, adhere to a budget, and guide their subordinates to contribute to the overall success of the organization. Recently media managers have faced harsh economic climates requiring worker layoffs and reevaluation of staffing needs. Converging technology has altered product and service expectations, and unstable global diplomacy has affected workplace conditions. The best managers handle the routine as well as the unexpected, but also are outstanding leaders. This chapter focuses on the importance of leadership in media management.

Leaders are nimble reactors as well as alert predictors. They know how to adjust to challenges and respond enthusiastically to opportunities. Yet even more important, they have a vision of where their organization should be headed and are clear about their accountability in the process. Leaders, not just managers, are needed in the next decade, which promises to be challenging for media companies. This chapter identifies the characteristics, behaviors, and theoretical assumptions for positive leadership by media managers.

THE ROLE OF LEADERSHIP IN MANAGEMENT

One of America's best-known leaders, Mayor Rudy Giuliani, became a symbol of pragmatic action after the September 11, 2001, attack on New York City. Giuliani, in a keynote address to the University of Colorado at Denver Business School in May 2002, said there are at least two characteristics shared by all great leaders: having a vision and being accountable. "There is no such thing as a leader without a philosophy . . . it is the power of their (leaders') ideas that captivates the people," Giuliani (2002) said.

In a recent Columbia Journalism Review survey, media employees said they expect managers to take responsibility and share their visions with employees, punctuating Giuliani's emphasis on accountability and vision. "Managers should make the mission clear, and make it a mission we can succeed with," said one respondent, whereas another said, "Definitive, creative, and attentive LEADER-SHIP (read management) that demands the best, yet is accountable and idea/ideal driven—that's what we need badly" (Hickey, 2001, p. 38). Media companies are interested in exploring several models of leadership.

For instance, when Julia Wallace was named the new managing editor at the *Atlanta Journal-Constitution*, she began her editorship by talking with her new staff about how the newspaper could make the leap from good to better. These conversations led to a new company vision that was backed up by action. ". . . Layers of editors were thinned, beats re-thought, and 20 percent of the staff applied for 108 new or newly configured newsroom positions" (Cunningham, 2001, p. 36).

Wallace's bottom–up strategy for designing a company's vision, which relies on consultation with staff members, does not follow traditional bureaucratic models, but it is consistent with management models described by Jim Collins who wrote *Good to Great* (2001b). Collins found that leaders who did not begin by setting a new vision and strategy ran great companies. "We found instead that they first got the right people on the bus, the wrong people off the bus, and the right people in the right seats—and then they figured out where to drive it" (Collins, 2001a, p. 13). Collins' research empirically demonstrates that ambitious leaders—but ones who are more ambitious for the company's success than their own—manage great companies. Leaders of great companies focus on finding the right people for the right positions and then trust those people to create the vision. "They deflected attention away from themselves, shunned the limelight and quietly focused on the tasks at hand. One described himself as, 'more plow horse than show horse,' an apt description of all the good-to-great leaders we studied," Collins (2001) said (p. 1).

Although Collins did not include a media company in his final list of 11 great companies, he did single out one media leader, Katherine Graham, for recognition.

> When Graham became president of the Washington Post, she did not position herself as the great leader or savior. In her own words, she was "terrified." . . . If you were to interpret Katherine Graham's genuine personal humility as a sign of weakness, you would be terribly mistaken . . . she pinned the newspaper's success principally on other people, the enduring core values of the Post, and good luck. (Collins, 2001a, p. 1)

Leadership Roots

Guiliani, Wallace, Graham, and Collins are examples of leaders who demonstrate firm commitments to vision-directed management as well as personal accountability. Such models have been part of the empirical leadership literature for at least four decades. However, there is frank admission that media managers are often uninformed and poorly trained.

> Management training for newsroom editors has been mostly an afterthought. Editors, who typically rise from the reporting ranks, learn to manage by being managed . . . . In the early 1990s, newsrooms began to open up a bit. The first wave of Generation X journalists—the 23 to 38-year-olds who currently make up 80 percent of all new hires in any industry—joined the field, with their less patient, more transient view of the job. (Cunningham, 2001, p. 36)

Whether a new generation of workers or competitive forces triggered the change, it is clear that today's managers are interested and attentive to leadership theory and method. Although it is not possible to thoroughly cover leadership theory here, among the most significant research of the past four decades was the Michigan Leadership Studies (Likert, 1961), which involved interviews with managers and subordinates to determine effective leadership behaviors. The studies isolated and identified at least two major supervisor orientations. They were: (a) job-centered or task-oriented behavior, and (b) employee-centered or relations-based managerial behavior. Researchers assumed the two types of managerial orientations were exclusive and represented two ends of a continuum, with managers being either one or the other, but not both. However, later studies have refined the model that shows that outstanding managers alternate styles as circumstances change.

Media Leadership Challenges

Communication theorists and historians agree there are significant professional differences between media workers and suggest such differences can be traced to the early origins of each medium. For instance, advertising theory and practice grew out of understanding and adherence to principles tied to profit margins, the radio and TV industry developed from entertainment interests, and newspapers began as partisan tools during the Colonial period. Today's media manager balances not only historical expectations, but also internal tensions between and among departments, which may have different functions or missions (i.e., advertising vs. news content).

Looking at just one set of workers (journalists), Powers and Lacy (1992) outlined a model to illustrate how: (a) factors within journalists (i.e., individual variables), (b) leadership characteristics, (c) organizational settings, and (d) market factors affect a local TV newsroom. All four factors affect the perception of goal accomplishment or effectiveness, which in turn affects job satisfaction.

Powers and Lacy found that employees are more satisfied with democratic-oriented leadership than with leadership that is autocratic in nature. They said, "this does not mean news directors cannot make their own decisions, but rather that many, if not most, decisions should also include participation by the journalists"

(p. 18). This is how Wallace approached her quest for a better newspaper. The important lesson in the Powers and Lacy study is that employees from different media have different expectations, and the wise manager understands that when a corporation owns several properties (e.g., radio, TV, newspapers, ad agencies, book publishers, public relations firms, Internet sites, film companies, etc.), not all employees will respond equally well to the same stimuli.

Communication and Leadership

Communication is key to the efficient and effective management of a work force. Managers who are adept at communicating can unite, commit, and motivate employees to cooperate successfully for a common goal. Managers who are poor communicators can alienate, distract, and destroy employee momentum and energy. Managers communicate informally and formally with staff and intend for messages to be heard and understood. However, they should be aware that misunderstandings are to be expected, and feedback with quick correction should be built into any corporate communication system.

Traditional theory was built on the assumption that leaders are rule givers who tell employees what to do and when to do it, act as disciplinarians, and punish those who do not obey company procedures (Barge, 1994). Although media managers do share some of these responsibilities, they most often supervise employees who are comfortable with autonomy and limited supervision. In addition, the media are change oriented and technology driven so that work systems have to be constantly reconfigured to meet customer needs for new and better products, markets, and better delivery systems.

Leaders, according to Schein (1985), have the ability to communicate organizational messages in at least five different ways: (a) by focusing on and measuring and controlling variables; (b) by how they react to crises or other important events; (c) by coaching and teaching; (d) by reward and status conferring; and (e) by promotion, recruitment, and excommunication. If leaders are consistent in actions supporting these five criteria and if they embellish these actions with stories, myths, and formal statements, the culture can be managed and maintained quite effectively.

Basically, leaders remind staff "who we are" and "what we do." Confusion, and even anarchy, can occur when management has unclear or dysfunctional communication. Therefore, it is important that leaders explore all the options they have to communicate.

Assessment Reviews

Discussions should occur on a regularly scheduled formal basis with all employees about the quality and quantity of work. This can occur on a monthly, semi-annual, or annual basis. These reviews provide managers with the opportunity to discuss problems, recognize outstanding performance, and motivate workers who may need support or encouragement. However, informal encounters are also important and should be scheduled so that managers can observe and notice behaviors and complaints that need minimal and immediate attention before they build into major problems.

A reporter who now works on a large metropolitan daily in the southwest provides one example of effective communication. The best leader she ever knew was her editor/publisher on a small family-owned publication in Washington.

> He actually treated everyone on the staff differently. I mean, he knew exactly what button to push on everyone. He told me—everyday—that he couldn't believe how productive I was, which just made me work that much harder . . . but he told another reporter, "I understand you're just so stressed out," and he would be so gentle and understanding with her, which would have driven me up the wall. . . . But, you know, she needed it . . . and he was just perfect at doing that. (Personal interview, October 2001)

In formal scheduled settings, employees have the opportunity to self-report about their work-related successes and complaints; in the informal settings, managers have the opportunity to observe how employees are working. The manager should record both formal and informal conversations. Although the best communication is face-to-face communication and all formal performance review sessions are conducted in this way, much can be accomplished by casual conversation or even phone and e-mail.

Group Discussion

Meetings are the communication mechanism of choice for many managers. In a study of meetings from 1981 to 1995, it was found that the average number of meetings jumped from 7 to about 10 a week for all business professionals (Armour, 1997). Unfortunately, many meetings are simply a time drain rather than a productive event.

A study by 3M Meeting Network, an online resource, says that managers spend between 25% and 60% of their time in meetings, but as much as 50% of that time is unproductive (Armour, 1997). Studies even show that meetings can trigger stress in employees unless they foster creativity, reach collective agreement, or gain consensus. All meetings should have an agenda, time limit (20 to 40 minutes is ideal), and provide follow-up information about decisions made during or following the meeting.

In the United States, business meetings tend to have action as the focus. In Japan meetings may be called to gather information or analyze data, whereas in Italy meetings may provide a way for managers to assert authority. Such examples serve to remind us that even strategies for communication in a meeting must be considered within the context of worker values and expectations that may be tied to national, professional, or personal orientations.

CULTURAL CHALLENGES

As media companies adjust their organizational structures to accommodate competitive challenges, converging and emerging technology, a demographically diverse workforce, and expanded global arenas, managers are required to respond to various dimensions of cultural analysis. That is, symbols, language, task definitions, and acceptable behaviors vary among workers, countries, and even different media. Hence, a manager balances personal style or preference with complex situational variables in making decisions about the best way to lead.

Culture is a construct that underlies behavior and beliefs within a company and the society in which it operates. It guides, explains, and predicts processes and products of a media company. Organizational culture can be observed through categorizing and noting patterns of behavior, styles of dress, backgrounds of those hired and promoted, and so forth. Likewise leaders often signal changes in management philosophy by altering all or some of these indicators. However, when an organization moves from a hierarchical to a participative model, there is nothing subtle about the cultural changes or required staff adjustments. An example of this is the trend toward shared management that requires the restructuring of departments into teams.

Team Leadership

The purpose of a team is to work efficiently and effectively to identify opportunities and problems, which may seem short term, but in reality may have long-term implications. For instance, the decision to *try out* a new media product (e.g., a newspaper zone edition, "smart" TV, or a Web site) requires a team effort to research, develop, produce, distribute, and assess its viability. This kind of team would be task oriented, with a specific product as its goal. In contrast, decision teams might define goals, prepare budgets, or study changing political and economic climates to determine long-term company strategies.

For teams to succeed, the commitment must first be strongly supported by management—particularly top levels. This means that mission statements mention it, and at least one top corporate officer is assigned to develop and provide resources for teams. Second, criteria for measuring and rewarding team efforts must be clear. Pay or salary need not be the reward for progress, but something of significant value (to team members) must be offered.

Third, resources (usually time and money) are allocated. Finally, the purpose of the teamwork is clear, with specific questions and problems identified. Most media companies converting to team management also hire a consultant to guide managers in the early stages of conversion.

If the team is working well, the goals are strong and clear to everyone (i.e., everyone in the group can independently state objectives that match what others say and think). Everyone on the team understands their role and knows how that role contributes to the goals. The work climate is positive and supportive, and trust is high among team members. People willingly communicate in open and direct ways sharing data, information, and opinions. When differences occur, they are recognized and resolved through negotiation and consensus. Everyone participates in decisions without regard to title or power. Everyone agrees to follow decisions made by the team (Dyer, 1995).

A manager must know how to select and coach a team of employees as well as train them to work as a self-directed entity. Team members may have different backgrounds, levels of education, expertise, experience, and company titles. Team members also might have different professional needs for achievement, power, or affiliation. Making a diverse group of employees into a productive team is not an easy task.

Teams spend considerable time agreeing on a common set of goals or a shared vision of what they want to accomplish. Next, they identify the resources of the team, which are the skills, backgrounds, cultures, expertise, and experiences of team members.

Team leaders can be appointed or one person can organize, train, and facilitate the team but not directly influence its work. The team can also select its own leader, rotate leadership, or even operate without a leader (committee of the whole). The team also has flexibility in terms of how often and how long it meets. For some teams, sharing information by e-mail or phone is satisfactory, but other types of teams might require a higher level of interaction.

A team working on a new magazine might meet once to agree on content, time frame, and style rules. E-mail or phone conversations handle questions or changes ordered by the publisher, but most of the teamwork would be accomplished independently. However, a news team putting out a special edition on a hurricane would work closely, conferring every few minutes about new information, pictures or film that were available, interviews that had been completed, and overall presentation choices.

A team requires commitment from all its members; when some members are passive or conform simply to avoid controversy or debate, the whole team is hurt. Artificial agreement or passive compliance occurs sometimes when team members are dependent or immature or when team members have learned over time that conformity is the least stressful option when dealing with particular team members.

Some team members also may resist participation if they have little or no trust in the leader and feel they must protect themselves. However, most problems can be reduced to differences in expectations. Therefore, one of the most important tasks of any team is to identify not only general expectations for the team, but expectations each individual holds about her role and the role of others on the team.

When *The Oregonian* changed from a traditional city desk structure to a team-based newsroom in 1994, the changes affected career paths for several newsroom workers, and it was noticed. "When you flatten the hierarchy, some people feel, well, flattened," says Therese Bottomly, who has spent all 18 of her newsroom years at the newspaper (Cunningham, 2001, p. 36). Not only the organizational culture but Bottomly's leadership style changed dramatically when she found herself supervising a team of 6 instead of the 22 employees who were formerly in her department. When she was overseeing a larger number of employees, she had tried to solve all the problems herself. However, in the new organizational culture, she learned to listen and empower employees to solve their own problems. She said, "They need to leave my office feeling smarter, stronger, and more able" (Cunningham, 2001, p. 36).

Managers must be aware of what motivates employees as well as how backgrounds affect workplace harmony. Much misunderstanding occurs because of different cultural orientations.

International Cultural Challenges

Culture can be defined in terms of shared values or assumptions workers hold about the world and human nature. Such common belief systems result in predictable behaviors and confirming rituals.

Hofstede (1980) noted that North American and West European countries stress individualism rather than collectivism. This impacts how workers and managers regard their own relationships as well as those between the company and individual. If organizational culture is seen as opposed to individualization or as something that impedes or diverts the individual, then supervisor–subordinate conflict is sure to occur in companies where Western values are prevalent. Such conflict affects morale and in turn employee production.

Other studies have found similar differences between cultures—and between types of businesses. For instance, Heller and Wilpert (1981) found that managers in Sweden and France were consistently more participative in their management decision making than were managers in Britain, the United States, West Germany, and Israel. Participative management styles were more characteristic of the oil and electronics industries than the banking and public transportation fields.

PROFILE OF LABOR AND MANAGEMENT IN THE NEXT DECADE

As we move into the next decade, managers will deal with international and generational differences between workers. Media managers must understand demographics because they will compete for and manage different employees in the next decade. Both the population and labor force will continue to grow. By 2010 there will be some 158 million people working or looking for work ("Labor Force," 2001–2002). In addition, by 2010 there will be 58 million job openings in the United States, with some 22 million new jobs created and 36 million more openings resulting from retirements and those leaving the workforce. There will be a need for at least 12 million new professionals and more than 5 million managers experts predict (Barlow, 2001). It is clear that media companies will have heavy competition from other businesses for the best employees and managers.

Salaries in the Media

The highest salaries ($30,004) for 2000 bachelor degree holders who joined media companies were earned by those who took jobs online or with Internet publishing firms. Public relations workers earned a median salary of $28,964, consumer magazine beginners earned $28,236, and newsletter and trade industry employees earned a median salary of $27,976 (Becker, Huh, & Vlad, 2001). The median annual earnings for salaried writers and authors was $42,270 in 2000, with the median annual earnings for salaried technical writers $47,790 in 2000. Median annual earnings for salaried editors were $39,370 in 2000 (Writers and Editors, 2001–2002).

Overall in 2000, newspaper general managers saw a 7.6% increase in average base salary, whereas publishers' salaries were up by 10.5% when benefits were added in. Only circulation managers showed a decrease in average base salary, down 0.2% after a 6.1% increase the previous year (Brown, 1999).

The Bureau of Labor predicts that the employment of writers and editors will increase faster than the average for all occupations through 2010. Employment of salaried writers and editors for newspapers, periodicals, book publishers, and nonprofit organizations is expected to increase as demand grows for their publications. Also online publications and services are growing in number and sophistication, creating even more demand for writers and editors (U.S. Bureau of Labor Statistics, 2001–2002). A college degree in the liberal arts, communications, English, or technical writing is needed to compete in these fields. Less competition is expected for lower paying, entry-level jobs at small daily and weekly newspapers, trade publications, and radio and TV stations in small markets (Writers and Editors, 2001–2002).

Technology-Savvy Employees Needed

The top seven fastest-growing occupations are connected to computer skills with number six being desktop publishers. All top seven offer high earnings (Occupational Employment, 2001–2002). The past two decades have seen computers invading virtually every corner of the typical publishing operations, making workers with these skills highly desirable.

Even small media organizations seek workers with technical expertise because the Internet has evened the odds for small media to compete with larger ones. Online coupon users can be draws for newspaper Web sites, and with nearly one third of U.S. citizens going online daily (Yovovich, 2000), media companies cannot ignore the potential online sales income from the Internet.

Surveys show that among Internet users who have used any kind of coupons in the last month, e-coupons represented 10% of their total coupon use in March 2000, which was up from 5% in October 1999. Some surveys estimate that the commercial e-mail market may soar to an estimated $7.3 billion in 2005 and "cannibalize direct mail revenues by 13 percent" (Yovovich, 2000). E-mail marketing is definitely part of the strategic marketing future because it is fast, cost-effective, and provides immediate feedback.

"Links are growing between magazine ads and advertisers' web sites, with 70 percent of advertisements in America's top 50 magazines using URL's or e-mail addresses to steer consumers to the web in the first quarter of 2000 . . ." (Yovovich, 2000). Although computer magazines have the most ads featuring URL or e-mail addresses, business and finance magazines as well as National Geographic and parents magazines see advertising links as lucrative and necessary (Yovovich, 2000). Print, Internet, and broadcast advertisements should be consistent across and between media for consumers who will be using converged and merged media outlets to shop.

Hiring/Retaining Employees A Major Management Concern

Managers will recruit employees who are adept at technology that melds multiple media. Recruitment likely will take place over the Internet, which is a key job search tool for technology-savvy employees. Among the world's largest companies, 79% now recruit on their corporate Web sites, up from 29% in 1998 (Yovovich, 2000). "More than 90 percent of MBAs and nearly 80 percent of undergraduates use web sites to find jobs" (Yovovich, 2000, p.10). Although salary is still an important recruitment criterion, undergraduate, business, and graduate school students from the top universities say mentoring programs and training opportunities are as important as stock options, office amenities, time off, and casual dressing options.

Recent surveys of Information Technology (IT) professionals showed that 77% of companies doing recruiting were having difficulty finding and then retaining staff. An even bigger problem for media managers is that there are particular problems staffing development, database administration, management, and Web site workers. These are the employees media organizations need most (Wolferman, 2001).

To deal with the staffing difficulties, experts recommend managers do the following: (a) keep the system and network simple so that when programmers or other staff members leave, those left behind can figure out how to keep the system running until replacement employees can be hired; (b) document everything, including all processes/procedures, because if instructions are not written down and checked frequently for updates it is nearly impossible for temporary workers to keep networks stable; (c) insist on an open system based on mainstream platforms and programming standards so if a supplier disappears operations continue; and (d) train several people in system operation and be certain that no one person is crucial or irreplaceable in the operation (Wolferman, 2001).

Competitive Recruiting Strategies

Media employees of the future want challenging assignments and good colleagues. Successful companies will emphasize those attributes in recruiting them (Yovovich, 2000). Employees with an associate degree will be most in demand. Occupations requiring a bachelor's degree will experience increases faster than average experts say (Occupational Employment, 2001–2002).

Technology will affect the delivery and production of services and products to consumers as well as communication options between and among staff members. Managers will have several tools for hiring, training, and assessing employees. Managerial excellence will be tied to effective and efficient use of the available technology. Human resources software can screen applicants and even archive resumes for upcoming openings.

Graying Workforce

Both the population and labor force will age. By 2010, the baby-boom generation will be 46 to 63 years old. They will be joined by a large group of even older seniors. "The number of labor force participants ages 65 and older is expected to increase more than twice as fast as the total labor force. The 55-to-64-year-old group will grow even faster as the baby boomers age, and the 35 to 44-year-old group will decline" (Labor Force, 2001–2002, p. 38).

Just how this older population will fit into management and employee ranks is unclear. However, it is certain many will still be active within the workplace because already a substantial number of seniors are declaring their intentions to *rewire* rather than *retire*. On the positive side, this workforce will offer a great deal of job experience and stability. These workers understand professional work standards, have faced crises, and know how to improvise. They will, however, present some management challenges.

For instance, many will require training (particularly with emerging technology). In addition, salary may not be the key issue for them, but rather benefits (like health insurance) may be most important in recruiting and retaining this group. Traditionally, businesses have considered middle-age employees less adaptable, flexible, dynamic, and responsive to new ideas and technological changes than younger workers. However, because there will be fewer young workers, there will be intense competition for the best older workers, and media companies will need to move beyond stereotypes.

In addition, seniors will be a major part of the consumer base for media companies that compete for their attention for services and products. This large older population is attentive to traditional media and addicted to the Internet. Recent surveys show that 54% of consumers ages 45 and older are Internet users and make purchases online. Older adults are the fastest growing segment of the Web market, spending more time online individually than any other age group (Yovovich, 2000). Alert media managers will pay close attention to this demographic group for an attractive workforce and a substantial market base.

Youths in the Workforce

The newest workforce generation is also of interest to managers. Younger employees realize that companies can no longer guarantee lifetime secure employment. They are described as the generation on a compressed fast-forward professional cycle. Apprenticeship was part of the traditional way new employees learned the job. However, today's work environment includes Generation X workers who may be with a company only a couple of years (or in some instances a few months). The compelling criterion for hiring this generation is not *who* you know, but *what* you know. Some managers complain that this group's expertise with computer skills, combined with inflated expectations, put the product and customer last. Regardless of whether these complaints are justified, training is always a priority for inexperienced workers. Managers should plan for and build it into the hiring process.

Most media jobs will require a bachelor's degree or at least some college. Young workers with this background should continue to find a strong market for their skills. Becker, Huh, and Vlad (2001) said the 2000 graduates of journalism and mass communication programs entered a dynamic job market with more pay than those who were hired before them. More than 8 of 10 bachelor's degree recipients had at least one job offer when they completed their studies—the highest rate of offers since the measure was first included in the graduate survey in 1988.

Becker, Huh, and Vlad (2001) reported that 16.3% of bachelor's degree students who took communication jobs worked for radio, TV, or cable, 13.2% worked for newspapers, 9.6% worked in public relations, 9.6% worked in advertising, 2.8% worked in consumer magazines, 2.4% worked on newsletter or trade publications, and 1.6% worked in online or Internet publishing. The average salary earned by 2000 journalism and mass communication graduates was $27,000, below that earned by liberal arts graduates and economics/finance majors. It is also below English majors at $30,690, political science majors at $33,690, and psychology majors at $29,931.

Female Workforce

Women will comprise an estimated 47% of the overall workforce by 2006. Many will hold college degrees in journalism. Since 1968, almost 60% of journalism and mass communication college students have been female (Becker & Kosicki, 1997). Yet the professional outlook for women managers has not been good. A General Accounting Office study of women in management positions shows that, "women continue to lag behind their male counterparts in both advancement and pay. In seven of 10 industries, including communications, the pay gap actually widened between 1995–2000" ("Another Glass," 2002, p. 6). In 1995, a full-time female manager in the communications industry earned 86 cents for every $1 earned by a full-time male manager. Five years later, a full-time female manager in the same industry earned 73 cents for each dollar earned by her male counterpart ("Another Glass," 2002, p. 6).

Newspapers have a particularly poor record of providing management opportunities to women. Women hold about 44% of the management positions in the U.S. workforce, but only 35% of newspaper management positions. Persons of color hold some 9% of newspaper management jobs, with only one third held by women ("Progress Stalled," 2002).

Women are underrepresented in editorial, circulation, information systems, and production management jobs. In the last 10 years, the biggest gains for women in newspaper management were in advertising and general management. These figures are especially significant considering "the pipeline starts out full" ("Progress Stalled," 2002, p. 3). The majority of journalism/communication college students were women who entered newspapers in growing numbers during the past three decades. Yet they tend to be clustered in low- and middle-management positions ("Progress Stalled," 2002, p. 3).

The women who work in U.S. newspapers describe newspaper management in grim terms. "Despite the recent strides, I still don't see the numbers of women making it to the top that their presence in the ranks would predict. I've grown tired of hearing that it's a generational thing—that talented women will flow upward over time . . ." (Morgan, 2001, pp. 31–32).

Another woman said there have been plenty of obstacles to overcome in her career.

> There was the copy editor who told me he liked broads in blue jeans after I wore Levis to the office in a snowstorm; the news editor who told me to get out of my Celtic' warm-up suit (a green pants suit) and look like a woman; a high-ranking editor who told me he understood the biologic necessity of my motherhood and therefore was changing my assignment. That was the easy stuff. Much harder was the overwhelmingly male culture that has trouble seeing women as leaders. (Morgan, 2001, p. 31)

In a final comment, the woman added that along the way some wonderful editors had supported and encouraged her, but they were all men, which makes the point that although women are grateful for help, there are few women mentors in a position to offer it.

Women Leaving the Field

Although women are not leaving the workforce in drastic numbers, a pattern is emerging. It could have major implications for newspaper managers facing future labor shortages as baby boomers exit the workforce. The American Society of Newspaper Editors (ASNE) reported in 2002 that newspapers experienced the greatest loss of journalists in a quarter century. Almost 2,000 editorial employees, nearly half of them women, left newspapers. Even a larger number of minority women left newsrooms than minority men.

The situation for women outside the United States is not any better. Although women represent more than a third of working journalists around the world, only 6% of editors, heads of departments, or media owners are women ("IFJ Survey," 2001). In most countries, the highest number of women journalists work in newspapers. In the United States, more women work in magazines (37%) than in any other media, with only 10% working in newspapers ("IFJ Survey," 2001, p. 2). Bettin Peters, director of the IFJ's Project Division, said, "Women are still a long way from the commanding heights of equality with men, who dominate the executive and managerial class of modern media." ("IFJ Survey," 2001, p. 1).

Long working hours (nearly two thirds of managers and professionals say they work late 3 to 5 days a week), lack of management opportunity, low salaries, or early retirements may be triggering the drain of women. Other factors may also contribute to a significant drain of women from the communications field. For example, 86% of Generation X women say having a loving family is extremely important. Only about 18% of the women in that age group say earning a great deal of money is what matters (Armour, "More Moms," 2002). "In 2000, 55 percent of mothers with children under one-year-old were working or looking for work . . . that's down from 1998, when the labor force participation rate was almost 60 percent and (it is) the first decrease since at least 1976" (Armour, "More Moms," 2002). In addition, the number of working married women with children under age 3 has also stalled (going from an annual average of 4 million in 1999 to 3.9 million in 2000). We are seeing the first leveling off since 1961 of women who work during their first pregnancy.

Media companies will have a shrinking management talent pool if well-qualified women with college degrees continue to leave traditional media management career paths. These companies may face competitors with a substantial number of well-trained and experienced women media professionals ready to challenge them for media products and services.

Media companies cannot explore and develop different (and perhaps better) work climates if the field continues to be dominated by male managers. Sheppard (1989) suggested women and men experience organizational life differently. Some theorists claim women may have a more circular, consensual, and relationship-based style of leading, whereas men tend to use linear models. Women spend more time with subordinates, listen more carefully, and develop more participative management environments where negotiation and relationships become important tools of decision making. Although male managers also develop diverse work environments, it would be more likely to happen if management were not so dominated by one gender.

Ethnic/Racial Diversity

Asian, Hispanic, and other workers will increase faster in the general work force than any other groups. Asian workers should increase by 44% and account for 5% of the total workforce. Hispanic workers should increase by 36% and account for 12% of all jobs. White non-Hispanics accounted for 73% of the labor force in 2000, but will decrease to 69% of the labor force by 2010 ("BLS Releases, 2001).

Media companies do not have a positive record with minorities either.

> While the employment market for most journalism and mass communication graduates remained solid in 2000, minority employment rates continued their decline, and the gap between the full-time employment rate of minorities and the full-time employment rate of non-minorities grew again in 2000. If those who returned to school are eliminated, minority full-time employment in 2000 was 6.9 percent lower than it was for non-minority graduates. . . . The gap between minority and

non-minority full-time employment increases to 8.3 percent if those returning to school are used in the computation. (Becker, Huh, & Vlad, 2001, p. 6)

There are recruitment and retention problems for minority media employees. There is a small pool of non-White students from which to draw. Becker, Hugh, and Vlad (2001) warned that, although the 2000 graduates (as a whole) had positive experiences, there are significant negative findings for minority students. The media employment world continues to be exclusionary in terms of race and ethnicity.

The research concerning non-White managers is largely underdeveloped and anecdotal. However, the observations of the few media executives who have crossed the color barrier are instructive. The White supervisors of one Hispanic media manager had difficulty with his style of management, which was comfortable for him and his Chicano staff members. He said it was natural and effective to develop a working climate built on affiliation rather than authority. He used a model that was closer to a family than a hierarchy. The leadership style he used worked well for his staff and took into consideration the ethnic culture from which they emerged. Yet his White male supervisors were uncomfortable and questioned his sense of closeness with the staff because he did not distance himself from his staff. Even at a corporate training session on leadership, there was no understanding of the wisdom of adapting corporate climates to employee needs. Instead the management training session was set up to indoctrinate executives into a preconceived management model. There was little room or time for discussion or acceptance of leadership styles that deviated from the White male traditions.

Leadership Reminders for the Future

Leadership is a dynamic activity. The next decade will hold challenges for the traditional corporate model as diversity within the ranks increases. More women, people of color, and older workers will join with technology-savvy young people in the media workplace of the next decade, creating a need for more complex and encompassing leadership models. All managers must recognize and capitalize on the characteristics of a diverse workforce.

Cultural and demographic differences will provide challenging training, motivation, production, and turnover issues for managers. In the next decade, experts predict managers will deal with tension, resentment, and conflict between and among workers who do not share common backgrounds or cultural orientations. Diversity goals (unlike affirmative action) are not meant to correct past inequities; they ignite dynamic thinking tuned to market demands and service opportunities for media. The development of global markets underscores that a multicultural workforce is not just politically correct, but a smart and necessary business move.

Most workforce experts predict that educational backgrounds may be the most challenging demographic variable to manage in the future. Although some staff members will lack basic educational background and/or require technical training, others will be highly educated professionals who are specialists in their fields. In fact, the Department of Labor predicts that jobs for people requiring at least a bachelor's degree will grow by 25%.

TRAINING/DEVELOPMENT NEEDS

It is clear that media managers face several challenges in the next decade, such as fusing a diverse workforce with various levels of skills, cultural expectations, and job experiences. Creating an effective and efficient workforce may be expensive. Corporate spending on e-learning alone could more than quadruple by 2005 to $18 billion (Glairon, 2002).

Training Versus Development

Experts distinguish between training (which provides employees with specific skills or corrects deficiencies) and development (which provides employees with abilities the organization will need in the future). Training is focused on the current job, whereas development is focused on both current and future jobs. Training is directed at individual employees, whereas development concerns work groups or the organization as a whole. Training should have an immediate impact, whereas development has a long-term time impact. Training seeks to fix current skill deficits, whereas development is about the future work demands of the organization (Gomez-Mejia, Balkin, & Cardy, 2001).

Effective training and development can improve performance, affect morale, and move an organization toward its goals. Some employees (especially young ones) see training and development programs as desirable job benefits. Both are generally offered in a classroom setting (either on the job site or at another location where uninterrupted focused study is possible).

Options for Learning

Media organizations with satellite connections can arrange for sessions to be offered at several locations at one time. Computer-based training can be effective with self-paced instruction delivered via a CD-Rom or the Internet. Role-playing, simulated exercises, and lectures delivered by senior managers or consultants are all possibilities for learning modules.

Most on-the-job instruction connects learning to job rotation or apprenticeship assignments and generally is aimed at employees who need one-on-one instruction. Topics can be as diverse as equipment maintenance/safety instruction to homophobia seminars that help straight employees feel comfortable working with gay employees and eliminate offensive jokes and insults from the work climate (Stewart, 1991).

Some of the newest training devices are designed as games. The creators claim games are cheaper than traditional classroom style training because they cost a flat fee and can be used by several employees. They assert games are particularly effective compared with static sessions, where one presenter talks and everyone else listens. Games also are fun and appeal to the younger workforce. "By the time young people enter the workforce they have spent more than 10,000 hours on video games, which is more than three times the time the most voracious readers have spent on reading books" (Glairon, 2002, p. 8). Wendy's restaurant uses a special board game to improve communication between managers and their teenage through senior employers. McData Corporation uses a game to help baby boomers (born 1940–1960) and Generation X coworkers (born 1960–1980) understand each other (Glairon, 2002).

Key Assessment Requirements

Without assessment managers will not know if training or development is needed. If training or development is required, managers will not know how to design or measure its effectiveness without assessment. The first step in a needs assessment process is to study the broad organizational setting, including its culture, mission, goals, and structure. Resources and climate for learning are key components because they determine how successful training will be.

A needs assessment identifies the jobs, tasks, or skills that require updating. Next employees who should be included in the educational effort are targeted. Employees who are not meeting organizational expectations or coworkers' performance levels may be identified. It is critical that careful analysis of poor performance be done. For example, if classified sales figures are not meeting organizational expectations, it may be due to market conditions or too high prices rather than employee performance. In this case, initiating training in sales techniques will be a waste of time and money.

If training is justified, a set of objectives for the training program is developed with specific and measurable behavioral goals. For example, say classified advertising sales appear to be low because a salesperson makes haphazard calls on potential customers. The goal of training is to teach the salesperson how to increase her calls by 15% per week within 2 months. If the assessment was correct and the low classified advertising revenue is due to the salesperson not contacting potential customers, sales should increase after training. If, however, the salesperson is inexperienced and needs training in selling the virtues of classified advertising, simply teaching her how to target potential markets and organize her time to visit more potential customers will not result in increased sales.

SUMMARY

Changing demographics and technology will impact both media managers and the media workforce in the next decade. Training will equalize the experience and educational differences of staff. Managers will need to provide new leadership and direction for diverse work staffs.

Flexibility in management styles will be important as top–down and authoritarian leaders are melded with team and participative management strategies. Leaders who can plan effectively will be just as important as leaders who can act decisively. The cultural context for leadership including language and communication styles will be important as workers design goals that are significant for their companies, their profession, and their personal satisfaction.

ACKNOWLEDGMENTS

The author wishes to thank the Sam Houston State University Journalism Program and Yvette Keener, student assistant, for their support and assistance during the writing of this chapter.

Case 2.1
Building a Team and a News Product

Debi, 26, has been director of new media for *The Daily Tattler* for 1 month. Debi's assignment is to create an excellent news product for the paper's Web site within the next 5 months. Maggie, the 50-year-old publisher who has little or no experience with start-up Internet products, told Debi she wants something fresh—something more than just a repeat of the daily newspaper. She wants a news product that provides services to the community, is interesting to Internet readers, and has integrity.

Debi started at the newspaper as a reporter 4 years ago after graduating from journalism school. All reporters were invited to work with the Web newspaper, but she was the only one who was interested. The managing editor does not encourage reporters to work with the Web newspaper because he does not believe it is serious journalism. The other reporters told Maggie they do not have time to do anything else beside just writing and filing their stories the traditional way.

John, 25, manages the Web newspaper, which just repeats the day's news. He has no news training, but is a good technician and software expert. He supervises two news producers (Bret, 20, and Grant, 23) who have the same skills and background as he. About 8 months ago, Debi approached John with an idea.

Debi told John she was about to publish a series on childhood diabetes and wanted to use the Web site to expand her audience reach. John was enthusiastic because she was the first reporter who had ever sought his help and his sister has the same disease. Debi's story on the Web site included sound bites, video, and several links. Debi and John even set up a Web discussion group that still meets and shares information. Debi's award-winning series caught the attention of top managers at the *Statewide Gazette*, a large metro newspaper. She was recruited and offered a higher salary to join their new media staff. Debi was tempted to take the offer because of the salary increase and opportunity to work on a Web-based news product. Maggie countered with a matching salary offer *and* promotion to director of new media, so Debi decided to stay at the *Tattler*.

Maggie agreed to add two news reporters to Debi's staff. After advertising and trying to recruit in the newsroom, she hired Ryan, a 22-year-old new reporter, who covers sports and is comfortable with technology. Although Debi wanted to hire a second reporter from the newsroom, no one else was interested. On Friday she hired Megan, a 30-year-old writer for a local weekly business magazine, who wanted to work for a daily newspaper. This completes Debi's staff. Debi and her staff are moving from temporary quarters on the third floor to the second-floor newsroom in 3 weeks.

Debi calls an organizational meeting Monday to introduce Megan to the rest of the staff. Maggie also attends the meeting with Bill McBride, corporate vice president of news. Maggie tells Debi and her staff they have her full support and that she has just sent an e-mail to all employees telling them how excited she is with their plans for a first-rate Web news product. Maggie says Bill will be an ex-officio member of Debi's team and provide any resources they need. Debi thanks Maggie for the support and tells the team Maggie has promised 5% bonus raises to all members of the team on successful launching and assessment of the new Web product. In addition, for the next 5 months, they will have no other assignments but to develop, test, and prepare the Web product. "I know you will design a product that fits into our newspaper's mission, which is to provide timely, accurate and local information that is educational, entertaining and useful to our community," Maggie says before she and Bill depart.

Debi tells her staff it will take a team effort to meet the challenges ahead. She says this team has several important tasks: (a) becoming a functional work group, (b) planning a collegial integration with the newsroom in 3 weeks, and (c) designing a fresh Web news product that provides services to the community, is interesting to Internet readers, has integrity, and is online in 5 months.

She says everyone on the team will participate in decisions because she wants 100% commitment from *everyone*. Debi says decisions will be reached through consensus, and she explains how that differs from unanimous decisions. "After discussion and debate, everyone on the team must be willing to say they support the decision and are willing to implement it even if it was not what they personally wanted. Everyone must be able to say given the time frame, the resources we have, and the company mission statement it is a good working decision. We will keep talking and exploring alternatives until we reach a solution that has consensus." Ryan asks, "Does that mean *you* don't make the final decision?" Debi assures him that is exactly what she means.

Debi also says, because there are several tasks and the team is composed of members with different backgrounds and skills, leadership will vary depending on expertise rather than title. Debi says the first step is to identify skills and asks each member of the team to write down his or her own expertise in design, news content, leadership, communication, technology, software, and so on. Next, she asks each member to write down what their expectations are for their own role and the role of others on the team. Finally, Debi tells them to think of a time when they have been particularly successful and write down what was a positive motivator for them at that time.

When Debi and the others are finished writing down their answers, she asks who would like to lead a discussion about their answers. She quietly waits until Megan volunteers, saying, "I don't know the rest of you very well, but I would like to get acquainted today, so I am very interested in hearing what you have to say." They slowly begin to talk, task forces are set up, everyone volunteers for a leadership role, and Debi agrees to provide the motivators, which range from candy bars and hand holding to "uninterrupted periods of work time with no phone calls or other interruptions."

The discussion reveals the following self-reported information:

Debi: organizes well, creative, listens well, excellent writer and reporter, has studied and knows examples of excellent news Web pages. Expects to be organizer, peacemaker, and motivator for group. Also knows she will have to do a lot of preparation to make sure the newsroom people (whom she knows have disdain for the Web project and those working on it) and the team get along well. Is motivated by challenges and standard rewards like salary and promotion.

John: familiar with most of the software for Web newspapers, worked in TV production for a short time and believes some of the same tools used in TV could work for the Web page, is a quick worker, adaptable and able to fix most problems without trouble. Expects to have more visibility with top management because of this project. Is hoping to be mentored by Debi because he would like to be a manager someday.

Grant: expert with video and audio on the Web, was an English major in college and has good editing skills, is almost as good with software as John. Expects to be putting together several pieces of software in new configurations for Web page. Is self-motivated when project is not boring.

Bret: expert at computer games, has secret desire to be a sports writer, and thinks the sports pages of newspapers should cover community sports leagues. Good self-taught programmer, likes to take risks, and hopes this new Web page is built to appeal to his age group. Expects to bring new, younger ideas to the Web page. Is motivated by training opportunities because he has not completed college. Is hoping to be mentored by Ryan and learn more about sports writing.

Ryan: good writer, studied graphic design before switching to journalism in college, likes working alone and completes work quickly, likes deadlines. Expects to contribute solid news knowledge to the project in addition to sports background. Is motivated by challenges and salary.

Megan: likes working with others, works slowly but methodically, does not know much about technology, but anxious to learn. Expects to contribute experience and a calm approach to emergencies, which she knows will be frequent with a Web page. Is a good analyzer and problem solver too. Is motivated by salary and other people's enthusiasm.

ASSIGNMENT

Select an assignment from the following:

1. Form a team of six people who play the roles of Debi, Megan, Grant, Bret, John, and Ryan. While in character, pretend you are in a meeting where you draw up a plan for the new Web product that meets all the criteria outlined by Maggie. After working together for 15 minutes, stop and write down the problems that occurred from "your" character's point of view. Write down possible solutions for dealing with each problem.
2. Referring to the section on teams in the chapter as well as your own experiences with teamwork, critique Debi's performance in this case. What did she do well? Not so well?
3. Was forming a team the best way to develop a new Web product? What were the advantages and disadvantages of this management method? What did Maggie provide or fail to provide to support the team?
4. In studying the team members, who holds the *critical* skills needed to successfully create the new Web product? If you could add a team member, what skills would that person have? If you eliminated one person, who would it be and why?

Case 2.2
Shutting Down and Moving On

Nancy is the African-American public relations vice president for a corporation moving to a new headquarters in another state. Her department is small and being downsized. Only four employees, including her, are moving. She must figure out how to complete the department's work with even fewer employees. She cannot tell her staff of the move because the president asked all vice presidents to keep the news to themselves until he makes an official announcement in 2 months. Her task is to cut her staff and reduce department salary lines.

Nancy's first consideration is expertise and level of production. She needs to retain people who work quickly and efficiently and fire people who perform marginally. She wants to retain employees who work well together because increased patience and cooperation will be required in the months ahead. Finally, she appreciates staff members who are creative and take risks because her department often develops campaigns and projects that are unusual, clever, and memorable. The president told her to cut at least $100,000 in salaries from the budget.

Although Nancy is in charge of the department, she has not worked closely with the staff because she serves as the personal advisor to the president. Nancy delegates direct supervision of the department to 52-year-old Marge, who is White and earns $75,000 per year. Marge is a design expert and has purchased the software and hardware necessary to create most PR packages internally, saving thousands of dollars over the years. Nancy hired Marge and considers her a loyal and valuable employee.

Ed, 32, is the White chief technician and photographer whose work on the recent annual reports won national awards for the corporation. His work is creative, professional, and always produced on deadline. He has taken many personal leave and sick days, which Marge suspects are spent with his family and church, because he is very religious. He earns $60,000.

Charlie is White, 28 years old, and has a background in news. He is a graceful writer who develops copy for all the corporate publications, including the annual report, brochures, and promotional packages. He also is a good photographer and designer. He is ambitious and has made friends with several corporate officers who sometimes invite him to play golf with them. He tends to gossip, which Marge has pointed out to him as a flaw. He frequently gets on Marge's nerves. Although she appreciates his talent and performance, she is cautious with him because she believes he is more concerned with his career than with the corporation. He earns $50,000.

Kisha is African-American, 32 years old, and started with the corporation as a college intern when she was 22. She is a graphic designer and works with Ed. She produces a lot of work in a small amount of time and wrote decent copy when asked in emergencies. She is creative and has made several suggestions that were followed by the department. She is quiet and has not made friends easily. Marge is not certain she is happy although her performance has been excellent. She earns $40,000.

Juan is Latino, 35, and has many of the same skills and background Marge has. He is well respected by the people in the department and is very witty. He often helps Marge with personnel issues because he recognizes problems and is able to diffuse them by drawing a laugh and soothing egos with a kind or witty word. Although he is respectful of Marge, he wonders if she is best suited to manage the unit. Her communication skills are sometimes too harsh. He genuinely loves his work, but wants a raise. Although his performance reviews have been excellent, he has been reluctant to ask for a raise because he heard rumors the corporation may be moving and could fire some employees. He earns $50,000 and needs his job because his wife has just had a baby and quit her job.

ASSIGNMENT

1. Given Nancy's three goals for retaining people (see second paragraph), make a case for three employees being retained (remember, the choices need to reflect at least a $100,000 savings in salary).
2. Write at least five questions Nancy should ask each member of the department about their work relationships and performance in private interviews to help her decide who will be retained and who will be asked to resign (or be fired if necessary).

3

MOTIVATION

Mae Tyler is a 38-year-old, 16-year veteran of journalism. She is an anchor at the local network affiliate station, for which she covered everything from the courthouse to city hall to local schools before taking 5 p.m. and 6 p.m. anchoring slots 18 months ago. She says she is happy, but Charles Gaines, the news director and her immediate boss, thinks Mae is dissatisfied. She never smiles in the newsroom, has lately been frequently ill, misses a deadline occasionally, and consistently protests when local correspondents submit a late or subpar story. Her complaints include a salary lower than that of 6 p.m. co-anchor, Mark Vigar. Lately her 5 p.m. ratings are beginning to slide—she was down 15% from last ratings period, and the show is barely holding onto second place in the rankings.

Mark wants to understand. Mae has been a station mainstay ever since she graduated from college. She was the first female to win major reporting awards at the station, and when she finally got promoted to anchor, station General Manager Anthony Llorens touted it as "a long time in coming" and said she was a "role model" for the other females at the station and across the city. Yet Mae's attitude, like a yawn, is contagious; her younger colleagues in the newsroom often take their cue from her on various matters, particularly on coverage issues such as story angles and source selection. Charles is beginning to worry that if he does not do something, he might have more Maes than he can handle. He would like to find a way to motivate her to improve; Mae thinks Charles is sexist. She has seen how he treats Mark (they joke around a lot) and how differently he criticizes the anchors: He is very direct and blunt with her and almost apologetic with Mark.

Motivation, the way Charles sees it, is being able to manipulate an employee into doing what the manager—in this case, Charles—wants. Yet Charles fails to realize that motivation involves more than action on his part. In fact, motivation may be something that he cannot control at all. Mae's problem may not stem from anything Charles is doing or not doing. Media managers supervise creative employees in settings that require enlightened thinking. Motivation is complicated, and managers must understand it in context (Fink, 1993) if they are to successfully deal with employees. The media workplace with its rapid, cyclical nature of production often presents unusual, demanding, and sometimes chaotic circumstances for managing. The media manager needs an objective-based framework for viewing motivation and motivational opportunities.

This chapter emphasizes a context for motivation that takes into account the special circumstances of media workplaces. The chapter concludes with a look at some common problems as well as some current trends in the media workplace. Charles' dilemma with Mae requires him to understand why Mae behaves the way she does. The best way to do so is to examine what factors contribute to that behavior.

MOTIVATING INDIVIDUALS

Common Needs and Influences

Each mass medium requires many tasks of its employees. For example, a TV newsroom requires anchors to write and report to be sure; but also to think critically; be skeptical (even cynical), aggressive, and curious; know how to manage time, coordinate and collaborate, and develop a sense of community and civic duty, to name a few. Whatever the medium, employees—particularly those in creative jobs—must perform an array of tasks. In doing so, they experience emotions, that may range from humor or compassion to outright apathy. Therefore, Mae has *goals* imposed on her by the mere fact of being hired.

Often managers can simply look at motivation as a basic process of *needs* (in this example, job requirements) producing *drives or motives* that then lead to goals being achieved. Abraham Maslow (1954) classified needs into a five-tier hierarchy: (a) physiological (food and thirst, sleep, health), (b) safety (shelter, security), (c) social (acceptance, belonging, group membership, love), (d) esteem (recognition and prestige, success), and (e) self-actualization (self-fulfillment of potential). Depending on the individual, job mandates may affect one or all of these needs. However, Maslow theorized only one level of need motivates a person at any given time. Needs are satisfied in order, from lowest (physiological) to highest (self-actualization), as illustrated in Fig. 3.1.

Clayton Alderfer (1972) said an employee's needs may be partially but not completely met or anyone may be motivated by two or more needs simultaneously (Alderfer, 1972). For example, Mae may be concerned about her salary (safety) and her need to grow as an anchor (esteem). If higher order needs are met—such as Mae's need for journalistic prestige—then she may become frustrated and regress to being motivated by a lower level need.

Charles would do well to analyze Mae's complaints about her salary. Yet because Mae's goal is not reached, it logically follows that there was no drive or motive—a stimulus to action. The drive in this case could be manifested in

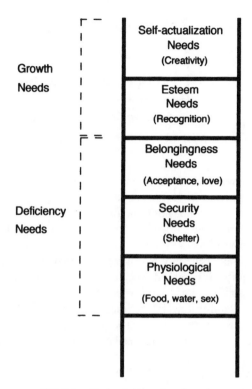

FIG. 3.1.   Maslow's hierarchy of needs.

a decision to do more health-related stories on the 5 p.m. newscast. Charles must determine Mae's needs and goals. In addition to job mandates, other factors must be considered.

Some management experts (e.g., Straub, 1984) believe that effective employee selection is a prerequisite for successful motivation. In this case, Charles would need to know whether Mae is psychologically capable, capable of carrying out the tasks required of reporters, and if her values and skills match the position. Like most media managers, Charles lacks the time and tools to do so. He must seek to become an effective motivator instead.

Motivating people requires a strategy. Besides the previously mentioned need to achieve, most people want to influence others (power) and be liked (affiliation). Psychologist David McClelland (1961) developed this typology and suggested that one of these needs usually dominates. To effectively motivate, then, managers must recognize all such needs and try to determine which is dominant for each employee. Charles sees Mae's need for power in her attempts to guide younger reporters. Her need for affiliation is less clear, although her complaints could be evidence of lack of concern for being liked. Charles probably also has

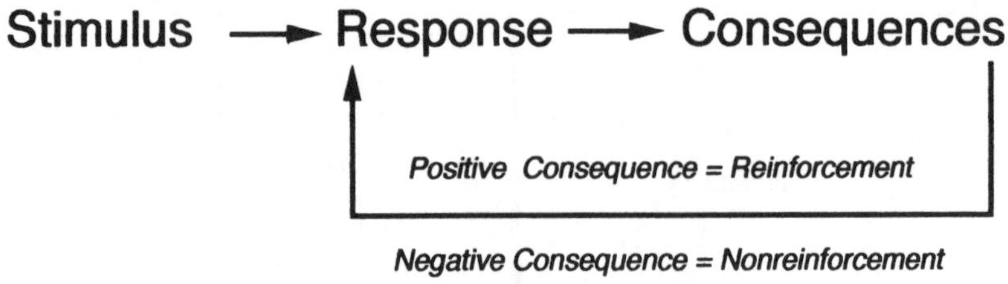

Stimulus $\longrightarrow$ Response $\longrightarrow$ Consequences

Positive Consequence = Reinforcement

Negative Consequence = Nonreinforcement

FIG. 3.2.   Operant conditioning.

a high need for power and achievement, which influences the assumptions he makes about Mae's performance (or, as Charles might say, "lack of achievement"). Yet knowing which need dominates or holds the key to Mae's motivation/job performance is only part of the battle. Charles must then know what to do with that knowledge and what results to expect.

For example, people generally repeat behavior that is rewarded or reinforced and avoid behavior that is punished. Such conditioning falls into two general categories: classical and operant. Classical conditioning tries to generate involuntary, reflexive, or semi-instinctual actions through unconditioned stimuli, as when a reporter writing a story notices she has 10 minutes before deadline. She experiences an adrenalin rush, a quickened pulse, and other symptoms indicating heightened anxiety.

Operant conditioning (Skinner, 1971) suggests—as illustrated in Fig. 3.2— reinforced behavior is repeated voluntarily and behavior not reinforced is less likely to be repeated. Reinforcement can be positive (as when Charles rewards Mae for the desired behavior of producing high ratings by giving her a raise), negative (as when Charles rewards Mae's avoidance of the undesired complaints by increasing her pay), punishing (as when Charles rewards Mae's undesired complaining with the negative consequence of firing her), or extinctive (as when Charles eliminates the unwanted complaining by not rewarding it). Regardless of how Charles attempts to condition Mae, he should be aware of options and their consequences.

Job Performance Issues

Aside from job requirements and the needs they generate, managers also need to note the interaction between job and employee. Doing so will broaden the manager's perspective on employee behavior and thus provide another decision-making tool. First, managers should know the motivation process. Three theories—equity theory, expectancy theory, and goal-setting theory—address this idea. In equity theory (Adams, 1963), the key assumption is that inequity is a motivator. When employees feel they have been unfairly treated, they will attempt to achieve a sense of equity. If Mae's unhappiness stems from inequity (she sees comparable

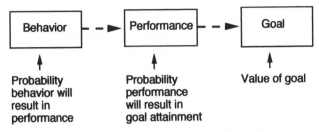

FIG. 3.3.   Expectancy theory.

anchors earning more), she could become happier by changing how much she works, attempting to increase her pay (or asking for a raise), reassessing how she compares herself, distorting the comparisons to make herself compare more favorably, or quitting.

Expectancy theory (Vroom, 1964) asserts that people will do what they can do when they want. Figure 3.3 depicts how motivation is the product of the interaction among expectancy (a person's belief that working hard will enable various work goals to be achieved), instrumentality (a person's belief that various work-related outcomes will occur as a result of doing the job), and valence (the value the person assigns to those work-related outcomes). The motivational appeal of a reward (e.g., higher salary) is drastically reduced whenever expectancy, instrumentality, or valence—together or alone—nears zero. In Mae's case, her motivation to earn a pay raise will be low if she feels she cannot do the necessary work, is unsure that the extra work will result in the raise, or places little or no value on getting a raise.

Finally, goal-setting theory says that employees behave the way they do because it helps them reach their goals (Locke, 1968). The difficulty and specific nature of the goals are particularly important. For example, planning to win an Emmy Award is a sufficient motivator for most TV writers to achieve excellence in writing. However, if a new writer sets such a goal in her first year of work, the goal can be too difficult and lead to frustration. If the writer modifies and specifies the goal (e.g., winning an Emmy in 5 years or attempting to have a certain number of ideas or scripts produced in 1 year), then she enhances the chance for honest evaluation of the goal and assessment of her writing. It is important for her manager to know what goals she has set and how that affects her behavior.

In Mae's case, Charles should familiarize himself with Mae's goals, determine their difficulty, and identify their realistic qualities and Mae's position on achieving them. This will help him discover whether he can help her meet her goals and develop strategies to do so. If Charles thinks the goals are unreachable, he can counsel Mae to help her adjust her expectations.

Managers also may look at job–employee interaction through the lens of job satisfaction. For example, it is widely assumed that a satisfied employee is

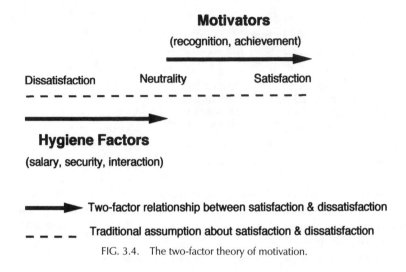

FIG. 3.4.   The two-factor theory of motivation.

a productive one. Yet sometimes satisfaction does not cause performance—it may be the reverse. An employee who performs her job is a satisfied employee (Greene, 1972). So when it comes to motivating employees, managers need to know how satisfaction works for their employees.

Alderfer's (1972) theory defines the role of frustration in terms of unmet needs. Recognizing the frustration factor implies that a manager can positively react to the frustrating item and help satisfy the employee. Frederick Herzberg and his colleagues (Herzberg, Mausner, & Snyderman, 1968) developed the dual-factor theory, illustrated in Fig. 3.4, which suggests that satisfaction and dissatisfaction are not related, but rather affected by different needs and motives.

Herzberg contended that hygiene or preventive factors do not produce motivation, but can prevent motivation from occurring. Preventive factors, such as money, status, security, working conditions, work policies, supervision, and interpersonal relations are sometimes viewed as environmental influences. If a manager attends to these items, she helps keep employees from being highly dissatisfied. However, job-related motivators such as achievement, challenging work, increased responsibility, recognition, advancement, and personal growth provide true motivation when combined with hygiene factors. Herzberg's theory has not always been supported (Griffin & Moorhead, 1986), so media managers should note the important nuances within the satisfaction concept.

For example, Chang and Sylvie (1999) found that satisfaction and dissatisfaction affected newspaper reporters differently. Wilhoit and Weaver (1994) found in a major study that journalists differ by medium as to what they consider the most important factor for job satisfaction. Daily newspaper, wire service, and radio journalists cited job security, whereas TV journalists said the importance of helping people is a primary factor. Although pay was likely to be at the bottom of most journalists' lists (regardless of their employer), wire service and broadcast journalists were more likely to cite pay as an issue in job satisfaction.

Additional studies show how elusive managing for satisfaction can be. How often a journalist received comments from managers in the early 1980s was a strong predictor of satisfaction for all journalists except those working at medium-size newspapers. The strongest predictor of job satisfaction at small newspapers was how good a job of informing the public the journalists thought their paper was doing (Bergen & Weaver, 1988). A decade later, the size influence had disappeared. Perceptions about effectiveness in informing the public and frequency of managerial comments about work were significant predictors for journalists working at newspapers of all sizes. In addition, older journalists in small- and medium-size papers were most satisfied in the 1980s, but by the 1990s the older journalists in small and large papers were most satisfied (Kodrich & Beam, 1997).

Scholars also have linked satisfaction to autonomy. Since the 1970s, journalists viewed autonomy as important in job satisfaction. Size and type of ownership also determined feelings of autonomy. Journalists who work for smaller, independently owned media are more likely to report personal discretion at work. Still Weaver and Wilhoit (1996) concluded that autonomy was not fully explained by these factors and noted that journalists' sense of autonomy had eroded since the 1980s. Recognizing such feelings of powerlessness helps Charles understand Mae's behavior and suggests managers should examine employees' resources and how they deal with job satisfaction in general.

Of course all this insight does not always help the manager. Individuals differ, national studies may obscure those differences, and sometimes other issues come into play. Typically, *different* has meant *difficult* or hard to handle. Media managers have traditionally grappled with how to treat *star* employees such as Mae. Their work performance sets them apart, often resulting from a unique, talented job approach born out of their personalities. As a result, such employees tend not to respond to typical motivational methods. So their supervisors are forced to seek alternatives (Moore, 2002) for myriad problems that arise, such as fairness (less talented employees are watching), appropriate rewards (stars do not always respond to money or promotions), evaluation (what is an appropriate work standard?), as well as recruiting and retaining stars (see this chapter's discussion of common problems).

At the turn of the century, *different* has increasingly translated to *diverse*. A growing body of research is beginning to illuminate the numerous factors that increasingly diverse workplaces introduce to the satisfaction equation. One school of thought (Pease, 1992) suggests that newspaper journalists of color are less likely than most journalists to accept promises of career advancement. They are more likely to seek alternative career paths. Particularly at risk of newspaper switching are minority females. Bramlett-Solomon (1992, 1993) found African-American and Latino journalists are twice as likely than their White counterparts to be dissatisfied and to stress job advancement opportunities (over the generally cited "chance to help people") when judging job attractiveness.

Finally, technology also affects individual motivation. When management introduces a technology to employees, the consequences usually vary along three dimensions viewed as good or bad: (a) direct (changes that occur in immediate response) or indirect (changes resulting from immediate responses), (b) desirable (helps the employee or system function more effectively) or undesirable (dysfunctional), and (c) anticipated (changes recognized and intended by management) or unanticipated (changes neither recognized nor intended). Yet from a motivation standpoint, the manager needs to ensure a good technology–employee match. Managers work to help employees see the technology is: (a) better than its predecessor, (b) compatible and consistent with existing values, (c) compatible and consistent with past experiences and employee needs, (d) relatively easy to understand and use, (e) experimentally friendly, and (f) capable of an observable job impact (Rogers, 1983). In Mae's case, Charles might introduce improved time management techniques. The key would be whether he could show Mae that the techniques would be successful without a major disruption in her work routines and personal life.

Sometimes technology is a motivator. The Internet's capacity to enhance the information-gathering abilities of journalists led many to adopt the technology with relish or, in some cases, leave their jobs for other, *hot* technology areas (D. Brown, 2002). Sometimes the choice is not so obvious. The organizational reward systems must support technology adoption. For example, the broadcast industry usually pays its salespeople on a straight commission basis. This system usually encourages staff members to sell only proved goods that are easy to sell and constitute a steady income. The commission-only system also fosters competition and conflict in sales departments (usually over who gets the best account list). The sales department head often needs to develop a system of combining commissions with salary and incentives to more effectively motivate and still meet the individual salespersons' needs (Warner, 1997).

The move toward technological convergence, whereby media expect employees to use various formats (e.g., broadcast, online, and print), has accelerated the need for alternative motivational strategies. Convergence often means more work for the employee, requiring managers to learn to motivate employees to converge. For example, the local TV meteorologist must be persuaded to broadcast the weather report, write a daily column for the newspaper, intermittently appear throughout the day on a sister radio station, and habitually update the TV Web site. As employees experience new technologies, they learn new skills, develop new ways of thinking about their jobs, and thus require new methods of motivation (e.g., Covington, 1997) and management (Killebrew, 2001). For a detailed discussion of how a manager should approach this and other technologies, see chapter 5.

In summary, managers must recognize what each employee brings to the job. Perceptions are just that—something brought to the job by an individual. Mae and Charles see her situation through different lenses. She would say her illness and complaints stem from a lack of autonomy on program budget, relatively lower pay, and lack of time to produce quality ratings. In contrast, Charles might say the problems are because of laziness, lack of ambition, and lack of time management. A good manager knows that each perception is selective or each person highlights for attention those aspects of a situation that reinforce or appear consistent with that person's beliefs, attitudes, and values. The situation evolves further in groups.

GROUPS

Media organizations are composed of groups such as committees, task forces, cliques, and entities that help the firm accomplish its objectives. To effectively motivate, media managers must become familiar with groups and group influences on the organization's well-being and development. One particular group that media managers must acknowledge is the occupational group. The occupational group is a collection of people who share a set of values, standards, and views that apply to the workplace and beyond. These groups confer, vie, and compromise with each other, thus functioning as significant participants in organizational decisions. Although hiring individuals is a key decision, when a manager places the new employee in a group, it carries an implicit obligation to learn the forces that drive the group. Thus, Charles must not only see Mae as an individual affected by personal, task, performance, and technological issues, he also must view her within the context of her group memberships.

Group Influences

Group members often get their identities or self-images from their occupational group roles, take other members as their primary reference group, and often socialize with group peers (Van Maanen & Barley, 1984). Groups develop along two basic forms: formal and informal.

Managers create formal groups when authorizing two or more people to devote time and resources to a task. Such groups include committees, task forces, project teams, or departments. Organizations cannot function without these groups, which often may gain considerable clout and power. Managers directly control groups through selection of members (and, in some cases, leadership), definition of purpose, and performance oversight. Often the group's purpose and status determine its level of motivation. For example, selection to prestigious or powerful groups fulfills certain needs for some, whereas omission or removal from a nondesirable group is a positive motivator for others, much like it would be if Charles gave Mae a promotion. Formal groups provide a way to get work done and a structural motivation tool.

Informal groups pose a more complex issue. Formal groups are part of organizational structure, whereas informal groups develop indirectly from socialization encouraged by formal structure. Creative influences on informal groups range from physical proximity of employee workspaces to the common values their jobs (and backgrounds) instill in them. These groups also serve a function, albeit not necessarily one the manager intended or devised.

As mentioned earlier, groups provide an identity of sorts for their members. Television news anchors closely identify with each other based on shared experiences and visions of what it is to be a news anchor: a witty, acerbic at times, conversationalist with an eye for news and a sense of how to entertain and accommodate TV viewers on their way to dinner or bed. Anchors may become friends with other anchors at the station or in the community. They may wear similar clothes, speak the same job-related jargon, cut their hair similarly, and carry themselves the same way in public. Employees in all departments of media organizations are subject to such conforming behaviors. Chances are their jobs bring them (or many of them) together socially so they may begin to closely identify with their jobs.

This is particularly true of journalists: Many see themselves as journalists first, human beings second. Journalism encourages a distinct pattern of beliefs, values, norms, and interpretations. Not only do journalists learn the values of news, they learn to be skeptical, cynical, critical, detached, and analytical. This requires—particularly for younger journalists—the adoption of a particular lifestyle. It is not uncommon for journalists to feel they are always *on*; they can never completely discard the journalistic lens on their environment. Journalists often speak with pride of dangerous, ordeal-like career experiences called *war stories*. Their passion for news also takes a toll on their leisure time and lifestyle, leaving little time for nonjournalistic pursuits and fostering close relationships with other journalists. Even journalists in the same organization differ, especially if their jobs differ markedly. For example, online journalists within a print organization behave differently because they have different ideas on news cycles, deadlines, and values than their newspaper counterparts (Amari, 2000).

Managers can guide the development of occupational groups by how they plan and structure work. Organizing work on a functional basis typically ensures that those performing the functions will form informal groups. Such is the case in most media organizations, although some companies organize or suborganize around certain products (e.g., an organization with a Web site needs to develop a staff to maintain it) or markets (such as when Charles' station created a regional bureau). The key for the manager is to recognize the by-products of informal groups.

One such consequence involves the pressure groups place on their members (Kiesler & Kiesler, 1969). Group members acquire shared norms and values, become cohesive as group, attracting other members, and form allegiances. The greater the attraction and loyalty to the group, the more likely the members will conform to group norms and values.

The group attempts to dissuade members from violating group norms. The pressure to conform can be enormous depending on the stray member's will and attachment to the group. The group exerts such pressure to survive and further the group's self-interests. This pressure can be subtle, as when advertising sales staffers attempting to stifle superperformers in their group jokingly deride their extraordinary peers as *brownnosers*, or when journalists call their investigative brethren *hot shots*. In each case, the message is, "you're different," and the group has indicated limits for its members. The alert media manager has three decisions to make: What is best for the group? What is best for the threatened employee? What is best for the company?

Sometimes the same action has positive ramifications for all concerned, albeit not immediately. For example, a sports reporter discovered his newspaper's star sports editor/columnist (and his immediate boss) plagiarized quotes from a news service. The reporter told the paper's editor, who then *fired the reporter*. At first, it seems the columnist, not the reporter, should have been fired for plagiarism. However, the reporter never confronted the sports editor with the allegation. The paper's editor, who realized proper channels were not followed (the sports reporter also had told several other reporters and staffers), considered the reporter's behavior a bigger threat to internal morale and organizational authority. The sports editor subsequently was disciplined and eventually demoted (but his career was saved) while the rest of the staff was outraged—at first. However, they learned what the editor considered was a valuable lesson: Follow the chain of command (and keep a tight rein on serious personnel allegations). The sports columnist continued to be one of the paper's stars—albeit with closer editing.

Another informal group phenomenon that is particularly important in media settings is the innovation that groups foster. Media constantly generate new ideas; the journalistic media do so daily. Media managers facilitate creativity without thinking about it using incentives such as bylines (in print), video stand-ups and standard out cues (in broadcasting), and merit pay. Creative media employees also naturally share the determination, eccentricity, curiosity, and experience required of ingenuity (Straub, 1984). Much innovation depends on the organizational or group culture in place and the degree to which employees feel involved with the organization. For example, one group of journalists took up a collection to help reunite a family because staffers felt it was in line with the company's tradition of doing the right thing (Petersen, 1992).

Yet informal groups also need consistently shared meanings, adaptability to the external environment, and a shared vision (Denison, 1990). These shared items are not easily found when two informal groups suddenly merge, as often occurs in the ongoing age of technological and corporate convergence. For example, prior to the newsroom staff merger of the two competing Pittsburgh newspapers, one had a corporate management staff, whereas the other was described as *freewheeling, loose*, and *breezy*. To facilitate the transition, the staff created several committees of reporters and editors from both organizations. Yet the lack of involvement with the new organization, the lack of a shared culture (inconsistency), and the initial absence of a clear mission (other than to produce a newspaper) led to conflicts in the new, combined newsroom (Jurczak, 1996). Convergent environments require constant contact between and among groups to avoid conflicting viewpoints (Killebrew, 2001).

Still groups inevitably generate conflict with other groups. As groups become more cohesive and members identify so closely with each other, the potential for self-direction (and the desire for autonomy) grows as well (Sherif, 1962). Groups come to see their goals as different from those of other groups in the same organization (Deutsch, 1949).

Various studies have shown that media are no different. For example, subdepartments in a TV production facility each brought its own agenda to the product (Elliott & Chaney, 1969); departmental membership affects how a broadcast station's employees resolve conflicts and perceived goals (Allen, Seibert, Haas, & Zimmermann, 1988). One state's newspaper managers' departmental affiliations affected how much cooperation they believed was needed in their individual newspapers (Sylvie, 1996). Part of the problem lies in the increasing complexity of modern organizations. As a company becomes more complex, it adds more tiers to its hierarchy and lengthens its chain of command. The chances for communication distortion (and thus conflict) increase. This increasing complexity convinces groups of their controlling expertise in the company, and thus discretion to lead it (Van Maanen & Barley, 1984).

As a result, productive media managers need to understand groups. Knowledge of ingroup communication networks goes far in hastening that understanding (B. Collins & Guetzkow, 1964). By doing so, managers gain a grasp on the flow of information and the group's decision-making dynamics, ultimately allowing the manager to better understand the group's motivational needs.

COMMON PROBLEMS

Labor-intensive organizations, such as media firms, inevitably run into motivation-related struggles. The following section deals with a few of the more common complications, followed by a discussion of some of the strategies a manager can use.

Retention

The ultimate motivational problem is turnover or when an employee voluntarily leaves the company. Reasons vary, but the common theme generally revolves around dissatisfaction with some aspect of the job. Turnover rates vary by company, but in media can range as high as 50%, so in a year's time half of a company's employees will leave the company. Such resignations cost because managers must then recruit, select, and train replacements. In addition, some remaining employees inevitably become concerned as to their own status.

Turnover is an inconsistent foe of media managers. In newspapers, minorities and women make up a disproportionate share of departures. In some years, certain departments have higher turnover rates than others. For example, circulation departments lost slightly more than a third of their workforce despite having only a fifth of all newspaper employees in the early 1990s. Yet even within departments, minority employees are more likely than nonminorities to leave. This should not surprise the media manager, who only has to look at studies showing that African-American and Latino journalists are twice as likely than White journalists to be dissatisfied (Bramlett-Solomon, 1993) or that women sportswriters—despite 75% of them being satisfied with their jobs—say they receive more sexist language from their newspaper colleagues than did women in news departments (P. Miller & Miller, 1995).

Add to that mix the fact that journalists at the beginning of their careers are more likely to defect than veteran journalists (Weaver & Wilhoit, 1996). Much of the problem may center on the race, gender, and age differences between managers and those they supervise. Also managers may have little time to interact with employees on an informal basis, may fear the general 1990s backlash against diversity, or see diversity as weakening operations. Finally, some experts concede they lack proper methods to evaluate minority employees (C. Phillips, 1991).

Retaining quality employees in newsrooms and other media work environments remains probably the greatest challenge for media managers. Much of the solution resides in discovering the unmet needs of the employee considering leaving. In regards to diversity, countless surveys have determined that minority groups differ in what would keep them on the job (e.g., McGill, 2000). Managers must not be quick to overgeneralize. African-American journalists working on U.S. newspapers note that editors either fail to see these journalists as persons with concerns unique to their upbringing and experiences (Newkirk, 2000b) or see them as lacking required skills (Newkirk, 2000a):

> To hear the . . . workshop participants tell it, achieving true diversity of coverage requires working through a challenging series of racial puzzles. How, many of the white managers at the workshop wondered aloud, do you confront black or Latino reporters about disagreements over stories on race. . . . Some of the managers admitted they were intimidated by the apparent anger of some of their minority reporters. Rather than challenge them, many admitted to simply retreating in silence, which ensures that conflicts go unresolved.

Stress

Media life is stressful. Many ex-journalists say they left the field because of frustration, low pay, poor management, and bad hours (Fedler, Buhr, & Taylor, 1988).

Newspaper copy editors report a higher level of emotional exhaustion and deper-sonalization than reporters (Cook, Banks, & Turner, 1993). Nearly two fifths of editors also say they have a job-related health problem (Giles, 1983). Public rela-tions practitioners say that stress is a constant factor (Butler, Broussard, & Adams, 1987). Managers must realize that stress is an inherent perception and reality for their employees.

Various scholars studied stress in various journalistic contexts and offer con-clusions about stress and its role in journalism's future. First, stress is a matter of perspective. Noting that earlier research (Giles, 1983) reported editors find dis-agreements with subordinates challenging and stimulating, Endres (1988) also reported that reporters think such incidents are stressful. Second, expectations play a role. McQuarrie (1999) discovered that professional mystique or "the expectations built up through training and through the early stages of on-the-job socialization" (p. 21) affects how journalists see their supervisor. Professional mystique creates an expectation of how supervisors behave and essentially makes journalists dissatisfied. Finally, journalism students are no more or less stress prone than professional journalists nor is their stress manifested differ-ently. Common symptoms include depression, daydreaming, less concern about work quality, and considering a change in major/career (Endres, 1992).

Stress effects vary depending on employee reaction to job demands. The media manager must be vigilant in sensing stress signals, but stress can take so many forms as to render it relatively invisible. Generally, these signals tend to stand out by their frequency, intensity, or abnormality. If an employee misses too many deadlines or reacts emotionally or out of character, the manager should make a mental note of the incident. For example, stress can be expected when major changes such as layoffs, new rules, technology, or increased expectations occur, as often happens in change-intensive media workplaces.

Some jobs or environments inherently create stress by design (Aldag & Brief, 1978). In media, such design flaws usually include deadline pressures, the need for creative content and packaging, and the need for continuous production. A recent addition to the list is the emerging pattern of misalignment between the goals of journalists and those of the media owners and managers. Many of the latter, infrequently educated in journalism, scorn in-depth, intricate stories in favor of more marketable content, which upsets or discourages journalists (Gard-ner et al., 2001). These major stressors may not be totally within the media man-ager's control, but awareness helps the manager understand and prepare for employee reaction.

Missing Inspiration, Creativity, or Challenge

Media employees crave their ability to create, react constructively, or see the meaning of their work. Since members of the Baby Boom generation began entering the workforce—whether it be news or entertainment, advertising, distribution, or production—nothing has related more to an employee's role and corporate or occupational identity than the ability to innovate or create something or overcome an obstacle in producing a quality product. A happy journalist or one contemplating leaving the profession can both be interested in a new challenge (Weaver & Wilhoit, 1996). As a media organization's lifeblood, when creativity is strangled, reduced, or obstructed, the media manager has a difficult task helping the employee relocate his or her inspiration.

Much of the problem stems from insufficient resources, staffing, and space. Other factors include long hours, inadequate supervision, an improperly designed job, and burnout. Perhaps the primary cause is the increasing need for self-determination on the job (Braus, 1992), particularly in younger employees. Two of the strongest predictors for job satisfaction in younger journalists are autonomy and "interest or challenge."

The case for managerial scrutiny of employee autonomy cannot be emphasized enough. Autonomy is cited throughout this chapter as a crucial factor in motivation. A study of Texas daily newspaper reporters' job satisfaction showed the predictors included a sense of achievement, personal growth, newsroom policy, impact on community, and autonomy (Chang & Sylvie, 1999). Older, more experienced workers often have a different view than younger employees of the day-to-day problems that seem to threaten autonomy. Like the great professional championship sports teams that dominated certain eras (e.g., Pittsburgh Steelers, Boston Celtics, or New York Yankees), veteran employees take a longer view of job pressure, changes, and stress. The opponent, the tedium and seeming-oppression that at times can characterize media work, is simply outlasted by the smarter, more patient, wiser, long-range-viewing, older employee. So media managers must be creative and innovative in battling any or all three of these typical motivational maladies, but especially when it comes to autonomy.

A study of newspaper change suggests that variables such as fear and structural politics deter change (Sylvie & Witherspoon, 2002). Reexamine, for instance, the Pittsburgh newspapers' merger. One paper bought the other, whose reporters so feared the new management that they created tension and conflict in the transition (Jurczak, 1996). Reporters also have cited concerns for traditional autonomy in rebuffing civic or public journalism as a ploy of increasingly powerful corporate interests to erode autonomy. They believe it takes the newsmaking process out of the reporters' hands and places it in the hands of local communities by letting communities define news through public forums on issues of concern. This endangers the journalistic autonomy that supposedly allows reporters protection against outside influence and bias (Gade et al., 1997; Sylvie & Witherspoon, 2002). Notions of autonomy develop early in student journalists' campus newspaper careers, seemingly implanting a feeling of autonomy that lessens the acceptance of civic journalism (McDevitt et al., 2002). Obviously, autonomy deserves singular managerial scrutiny.

The wisest course involves planning for these contingencies. Wiser still is organizing and structuring policies, procedures, and programs that prevent morale problems from arising and foster a healthy corporate culture. For example, turnover problems might be approached at various points in the employment process.

Let us return to Charles and Mae. If Charles wanted to prevent Mae's situation from ever arising, he could establish a plan for routinely addressing the issues she confronts. Because turnover results in more recruiting, Charles might want to take a closer look at the station's recruiting efforts. Typically, he might find no recruiting plan. Many established companies hire simply because there is a vacancy, without considering whether a current employee can take over the duties of the vacant position or the position has a design flaw that encourages turnover. A recruiting plan might consider the company's strategic staffing needs for an extended period of 2 or 5 years. If Charles has no power over recruiting, he can review the interviewing process.

Even if a manager examines the peculiarities of the job and the idiosyncracies of the employee in respect to motivation, the combination of the job and the person brings with it a completely new set of issues for the manager to consider. Charles should carefully reconsider the interviewing process when new employees are hired. Interviews are not just negotiations for salary, benefits, and production expectations. They should reveal how the job fits the person seeking employment.

In the case of creativity and autonomy, media managers often complain that managing creative employees is difficult because these employees want more autonomy than other perhaps lesser talented peers. It becomes an issue of whether the manager or employee has control. This is not uncommon in media organizations where employees become stars of some kind. Managers must balance pleasing employees and his or her adoring public, behaving fairly (to stars and nonstars), maintaining the indirect revenue stream the star may help generate, maintaining credibility, and perhaps maintaining self-respect.

Managers must be patient and realize their job requires pursuing and choosing the best options. One such option is to establish strong loyalty within stars because loyalty can stem turnover, which is caused by lack of challenge or autonomy. Many creative employees lack an initial strong commitment to an organization because their creativity and confidence in that creativity allows them mobility, making job security less of a need. So the media manager needs to establish trust in star performers (after all, as stars they could argue they merit stronger consideration than most employees).

Recall the newspaper editor who fired the sports reporter who informed the editor about the plagiarizing columnist. The editor engendered strong loyalty in his staff; he made them feel as if he and they were partners in the paper's news coverage ("Remember: We're David and the competition's Goliath," he often said). He even informed them of better paying positions or more prestigious openings elsewhere. Many reporters declined such opportunities because of the loyalty they felt toward him. More and more media managers are following his lead, particularly on partnering. Participative management—as a style and technique—has gained momentum in industry in general.

Teams, team building, and formal work groups have become a large part of the participatory technique. Some claim teams are developing into the basic unit of design for organizing work (Kolodny & Stjernberg, 1993). However, media adoption of teams is sporadic because of the media's long dependence on individual innovation and creativity. To suggest teamwork in some media settings is viewed as another managerial attempt at stifling creativity and autonomy. Some particularly resistant employees view it as co-opting employees. Management appears to share power, but the team actually is a ruse to squelch complaints and get employees to buy into management's agenda.

Despite such concerns, teams are beginning to blossom in media. Now it is not uncommon for newspaper reporters to work together on stories (Russial, 1997). Media managers facing change or distinct technological challenges instill a sense of *we-ness* in their staffs depending on the technology's relative advantage and compatibility with existing methods of operation (Sylvie & Danielson, 1989). More proactive managers see teams as a collective way to manage the uncertainties of change that beset media; still teams garner mixed reactions (Endres et al., 1999; Sylvie & Witherspoon, 2002) and require innovative approaches.

One media organization instituted "OrgAnalysis," a program that allowed it to focus on work flow issues. In one instance, the program looked at communication throughout the company to identify types and patterns to restructure, allowing more effective company-wide communication. Managers discovered that the personnel department generally provided senior executives with reports concerning everything from performance appraisal to applicant tracking. Further inspection revealed that senior executives were not distributing the reports, although nothing prevented them from doing so. This "Know-Flow" project was unique, however, in that it required all departments to participate. It ensured participation by tying participation in the goals and objectives (as well as performance appraisals) of pertinent managers.

Managers must create teams, including several department heads to develop mission and objective statements that meet publisher approval. The process fosters interdepartmental communication and enhances the newspaper's ability to serve its customers. Other OrgAnalysis projects dealt with specific departmental problems (S.A. Lewis, personal communication, October 1997).

Despite the approach, a media manager's leadership style is crucial to how a staff is motivated depending on the workplace and situation (McQuarrie, 1992). In TV, a gradual switch in managerial style (from authoritarian to participative) increased job satisfaction and productivity (Adams & Fish, 1987), whereas for some newspaper journalists, a manager's style did not affect their relationships with their editors (Gaziano & Coulson, 1988).

SUMMARY

As the workforce continues to change and the economy becomes more global, motivation is even more crucial to successful media management. Media organizations are too complex and unique for any manager to hope to get by without some understanding of human needs and desires.

An effective first step is to gain first-hand knowledge of the work context, such as what employees bring to the job, what the job requires, and how the two interact. That implies not just familiarity with motivation theories and concepts, but also sensitivity for how those theories factor in the workplace. In other words, for the Maes of the world, the Charleses need to know that for each action Mae takes there is a reason; second-guessing is unacceptable.

This approach requires a deep appreciation for diversity—not just demographically speaking, but also for the idiosyncracies and unique traits of each potential employee. Women and people of color bring experiences that White male media managers do not understand and perhaps fear. Yet proper motivation must be a fearless duty. Social wallflowers should not become managers because dealing with people constitutes the bulk of managing.

Finally, the media are filled with potential psychiatric bombshells in the guise of their workforce. Most people do their jobs and need no external motivation; they are self-driven. However, the efficiency orientation of the increasingly corporate and converging workplace mandates that managers know how to solve problems; thus, this chapter's focus.

The media manager should view this information not just as motivation to become a better manager, but as an incentive to help plan and structure systems that properly and adequately recognize and reward media employees. Motivation can be understood, managed, and planned. So the manager has to decide how to structure such a plan according to the needs of the workplace and the people who potentially work there. Without that perspective, motivation is seen as a problem to be solved rather than an opportunity to manage effectively. Media managing is difficult to say the least.

Case 3.1
Charles and Mae

Mae Tyler, the 38-year-old, 16-year veteran of the newsroom, and her boss, Charles Gaines, were introduced earlier. After covering everything from the courthouse to city hall to local schools, Mae took the 5 p.m. (solo anchor) and 6 p.m. (co-anchor) slots 18 months ago. She says she is happy, but Charles, the news director and her immediate boss, thinks Mae is dissatisfied. He never sees her smile in the newsroom. He has noted that she has been frequently ill lately, causing her to miss deadlines. She complains her salary (about $75,000) trails that of 6 p.m. co-anchor Mark Vigar, who is younger and has less experience. Her 5 p.m. ratings were down 15% from last ratings period, and the show is ranked second—only a half share ahead of the third-place competitor.

Charles wants to understand. Mae has been a station mainstay ever since she graduated from college. She was the first female to win major reporting awards at the station; when she finally got promoted to anchor, station General Manager Anthony Llorens touted it as "a long time in coming" and said she was a role model for the other females at the station and across the city. Mae prides herself on being a good wife and mother as well as a professional, although she has always struggled to find balance among them. Lately Mae's attitude, like a yawn, is contagious; her younger colleagues in the newsroom often take their cue from her on various matters, particularly on coverage issues such as story angles and source selection as it pertains to gender and race. Mae thinks Charles is sexist and, perhaps, unintentionally racist. She has seen how he treats Mark (they joke around a lot) and how differently he criticizes the anchors: He is direct and blunt with her and almost apologetic with Mark.

Mae is the only African American on the city staff. There have been other African Americans on the staff over the years, but none in Charles' 10-year tenure as news director. Mae feels as if she also is being singled out because of her race. Her evaluations for the last 6 months have noted her inconsistency in meeting deadlines and "an apparent lack of team spirit." Yet Mae feels these complaints are race-based and sexist primarily because, when she started to change her hairstyle, Charles told her he did not like it. He is also critical of her wardrobe choices (he tells her, "you looked good today" about once every couple of weeks) as well as her package selections ("too many talking heads," he tells her) for 5 p.m. Charles, who said there were more pressing deadline pieces, ignored her ideas for news features about schools and health and more hard news on how city policy impacts on the African-American community.

Mae asked Charles for a meeting. She wants to challenge her evaluation and find out whether Charles has a problem with women and African Americans and stories about them. She thinks the problem extends to a salary inequity too. In preparation for the following questions, review the chapter guidelines.

ASSIGNMENT

1. If you were Charles, how would you prepare for the meeting with Mae?
2. Which factor—job mandates or employee potential—seems to be most influential in this case? Is autonomy a factor at all?
3. Assign one student to play Charles' role, another to play Mae's. Have the two conduct their meeting. Afterward, (a) analyze the discussion to determine

which psychological theory—equity, expectancy, or goal setting—plays a major role in each person's approach to the conversation; and (b) determine Charles' next most logical course of action.

4. In relation to No. 3, how big a factor do the race and gender of each participant play in the meeting? Should Charles consider Mae's race or gender in how he approaches the meeting? In how he devises a solution?

Case 3.2
Memo to a Motivator

To: Deona Laurent, head, circulation & marketing department, *Today's News*
From: Jim Burns, district supervisor
Date: Dec. 31

Ms. Laurent, I've been working with the company 3 years. As you know, I am the go-between between you and our 25 newspaper carrier coordinators, who each supervise about 50 carriers. Something has come up.

Because of the recent terrorist attack (and the subsequent recession), carriers haven't had raises in quite a while. No bonuses have been given and yet the workload is still heavy; it's even increased for some who've taken up the slack for those who quit after the attack. Still, we manage and we've held our own on circulation.

But I'm afraid I've lost a little something. Of course, everybody would like a raise (it's been two years), but I know that me not having a college degree hurts my chances. Some of the coordinators are griping, too, and I can tell they don't like their jobs by the way they act at the Tuesday meetings.

I don't want to quit, mind you. I don't have time to job hunt. Sure, I could fire a few bad eggs and make *my* life easier, but these are hard-working, God-fearing people and they do their best. I just don't feel as if the company's doing right by them. In addition, I'm hoping we can do something before we have a lot of turnover.

Things are getting out of hand, though. Jean DuBreuil, one of our better carriers, came in all red-faced. This old lady (who lives on the south side) complained to Jean that she wasn't getting her money's worth from the paper, that many days it wasn't there (though we know Jean delivers it and the lady won't listen to any talk about kids stealing her paper). Jean and the lady had a falling-out (Jean thinks she hates Latinos), and I'm just warning you before the lady calls you.

What gets me is we work our tails off dealing with folks like this every day and what thanks do we get? It makes me sometimes wish I hadn't quit working on cars. *I* don't know what to tell Jean. I'm just trying to do my job.

I can't believe I've ever written something this long! I know times are tough, but could you and the folks in the office see what you can do for us?

ASSIGNMENT

1. Should Jim send the memo?
2. Using what you learned in this chapter about motivation, what alternative incentives can be developed without raises or bonuses? Is there any way Deona can spark initiative in Jim?
3. What group influences might be at work in this motivational scenario? What can Deona do to guide the carriers toward stronger loyalty to the newspaper?
4. Can Deona or Jim alleviate the stress inherent in a recession (and in the wake of terrorist attacks)? Can creativity or autonomy be factors in the problem presented by Jim? What class issues are at play and how do they figure in Deona's ability to motivate?
5. If you're Deona and you receive this memo, what do you do about Jim, if anything? Would your action concerning Jim affect his subordinates? Should you report the memo to your supervisors?

Case 3.3
Spinning Motivation

Sammy is a good kid, but unimpressive as a writer. He was assigned the higher education beat at the newspaper and really lacked initiative. When he was given assignments—they were practically spoon-fed, with explicit instructions of what to do, who to call, what to ask—he did not produce anything worth printing. Several times stories were returned to him twice for major rewrites. For example, on one assignment, the U.S. Justice Department had just put out campus crime statistics. Sammy's editor checked the Justice Web site and all three small, local colleges were listed. The editor told Sammy to do a story and that the stats would not include off-campus crime, so he would have to call the local cops and talk to them about this flaw. He produced a story that went four or five paragraphs into crimes at big colleges and universities—some not even in the state—with a light brush stroke on the local schools, and no comments from any administrators at those places. It was returned to him at least twice for revisions, and it never appeared in the paper by the time he was let go. He had been given several warnings about his lack of productivity; editors really wanted to keep him and tried to work with him, particularly for newsroom diversity reasons.

Now Sammy works in an online editing job for a public relations firm, The Spin Doctors (TSD), in a medium-size city about 2 hours west of here. Sammy feels it is a good place to work, but one person has a different opinion: chief online editor, Bob, who knows about Sammy's woes at the newspaper and is weighing Sammy's future.

The online department consists of two full-time writers, three editors, and a technical person, not including Bob, who spends most days supervising the staff and working with the TSD management to help clients tailor their messages to the online medium. The online department is considered part of the overall news operation of the firm, but rarely works with other departments. "We're a brand-new extension," Bob tells a visitor. He and his staff would like to do more, but getting convergence going within the firm is a slowly evolving project.

Bob and his staff have personalized the office as much as possible, but Sammy presents a problem. One day Sammy dropped the ball on an important, timely news release, and it did not make the Web site until the event was over; still Sammy thought he and Bob were buddies. "Whassssssuuuuuup," Sammy would always greet Bob, who would inwardly shudder because he knew the rest of the staff could see that Sammy was, in Bob's words, "a slacker without a clue." Yet Judy, a site reporter, recently told Bob she thought Sammy "could really blossom, if we push the right buttons." Judy and Sammy—unknown to Bob—were currently dating each other.

Each online editor is given a chance each day to advocate certain designs or content. This means Sammy gets to describe stories or graphics he would like to get in the next day's edition. However, often Sammy pushes an idea and cannot back it up; "I thought it would look cool" is usually his only defense. At a recent meeting, Sammy did come up with a brilliant idea to promote one client's event, but never followed up on it and, when reminded, gave only a so-so effort. Still Sammy reminds Bob of himself at Sammy's age.

ASSIGNMENT

1. If you were Bob, what would you do to make things better between you and Sammy? Between your department and the other departments?
2. You and another student should play the roles of Bob and Sammy. Bob calls Sammy in for a meeting.
3. Which is more important from a managerial standpoint: the online group's occupational loyalty, getting rid of Sammy, or helping Sammy?
4. What are Sammy's needs? Bob's? Judy's?

Case 3.4
Producing Morale

Audiences see Mae and Mark (from Case 3.1) at 6 p.m. and believe two veterans are delivering the news, but audiences do not know that most of the packages

Mae and Mark broadcast are selected and written by producer Woody Williams, who graduated from your university 2 years ago. Producers run the newscast, wielding substantial power. They select the stories, choose the order they appear, and decide the time they merit. Woody has the choice to revise anchors' and reporters' stories.

"It's tough to trust Woody because he's so damn young," Mark tells News Director Charles Gaines, who, for his part, has heard it all before. He is frustrated, too, because—although Woody's writing is often inaccurate or error filled—Charles has had a tough time keeping producers, the least glamorous spot in the newsroom. Woody's weak knowledge of current events and the market, his overconcern with production techniques, and his meager experience has caused Mae to complain, "A baby! Sixteen years in the business and I'm working for a baby!"

Veteran producers are rare. In previous years, that was not the case. With the advent of cable, the Internet (with its high-paying jobs), and increasing competition for viewers, local news programmers expanded their offerings, meaning more producer jobs are available. Even Woody says he feels intimidated by the experience gap between he and the anchors. He has told Charles that Mark regularly criticizes Woody's writing to the point that Woody is afraid sometimes to write.

Charles has tried to find more seasoned producers, but the station GM, Anthony Llorens, told him that officials at corporate headquarters are closely watching budgets. "The bean-counters are killing us all," Llorens often says, referring to his superiors' lack of TV news experience. "You can't justify higher salaries to bean-counters who don't know the workings of a newsroom," Llorens is fond of saying.

Often Woody—as the lowest paid and least experienced producer—works a weekend shift when neither Charles nor any other news managers are in the newsroom. "The station's butt is on the line and in the hands of a pimply faced kid every weekend," Charles privately complains to his wife. Woody's saving grace is that he knows computers and technology better than anyone at the station; the tradeoff comes in the quality of content.

ASSIGNMENT

1. What would you do if you were Woody?
2. What options does Charles have?
3. What options does Llorens have?
4. What should Charles say to Mae and Mark?

CHAPTER

4

THE GLOBAL STRUCTURE
OF MEDIA ORGANIZATIONS

Angela Powers

When major media conglomerates became larger in the early 2000s, as was the case when Tribune Inc. merged with Times Mirror, the structure of the merging companies changed dramatically. They assumed ownership of TV stations in many U.S. markets where they also owned newspapers. Questions immediately arose about whether such companies should be forced to divest of their newspapers or TV stations because of legalities limiting ownership. Media executives refuted rules prohibiting ownership of newspapers and broadcast stations in the same market. They argued information sources are no longer scarce, and to compete successfully in the global arena, media companies must be free to grow. Others disagreed, stating that ownership limitation rules must be upheld to preserve a multitude of separately owned voices (Hickey, 2001). Whatever the outcome, small, family-owed media organizations are disappearing, as are the rules and regulations that long limited their structure.

Debate over media structure will continue as technology melds the distinctions among print, broadcast, and online media. Some suggest the downside of ownership concentration is that journalism, among other things, will become a small part of large empires and be subject to increased commercial exploitation. In attempts to seek larger audiences across media, news could increasingly focus on celebrity coverage and lifestyle stories instead of serious news, politics, and investigative reporting. Others insist the media industry must grow larger and acquire quality resources to compete in a global media marketplace and provide quality news.

Regardless of a media organization's size, people are always at the heart of a company, and these individuals make decisions concerning news and content. A firm's overall success is achieved through the success of its unrelated parts, including top managers, news departments, programming departments, as well as regional, national, and international offices. This chapter looks at how to integrate both a formal and an informal approach to structuring global media organizations. The formal structure of media organizations defines the tasks, communication, and authority relationships within the organization, with organizational charts illustrating how the parts of a firm fit together. The informal structure analyzes ways in which managers and subordinates interact within an organization by looking at employee interactions, teambuilding, and contingency approaches. This chapter also examines how structure changes in the global environment where boundaries and cultures disappear. Taken together, formal, informal, and global structures exist to order and coordinate the actions of employees to achieve key organizational goals.

FORMAL APPROACH

A basic challenge when structuring media organizations is to decide how much authority to distribute to the top of the organizational hierarchy and how much to distribute to middle and lower levels. Should decisions be made at the local or corporate level when dealing with multinational organizations where cultural differences exist? Decisions on the structure of media organizations affect many areas. A formal approach to studying organizational structure indicates that decisions are based on a carefully developed chain of command and efficient division of labor.

Researchers have been interested in how chain-of-command, formal media organizations function in terms of content and quality. Large newspaper organizations with top–down management styles often emphasize profits at the expense of quality when compared with smaller, independently owned newspapers (Coulson 1994; Croteau & Hoynes, 2001). Yet the focus on the negative impact of size and structure on First Amendment values is often skewed (Picard, 1998). Large companies may have the resources to produce a better product (Akhavan-Majid & Boudreau, 1995; Demers, 1996).

For example, chain-owned newspapers such as Gannett papers adhere to strict format mandates, including high story count, graphics, and use of color. Because they are part of large and powerful chains, they are likely to advocate activist positions in their editorials and be more critical of mainstream institutions. Demers (1998) also found that corporate newspapers place less emphasis on profits and more emphasis on product quality because they have the latest technology. Corporate papers give their reporters more autonomy, enabling them to innovate, beat the competition, and win awards. This scientific approach to studying media organizations dates back to general management studies from the early 20th century.

In the late 1800s, a German sociologist, Max Weber (1921/1947), created a hierarchy to effectively allocate decision-making authority and control of resources. Weber developed the widely known bureaucratic model of organizational design. He viewed a bureaucracy as a logical, rational, and efficient form of organization. "A bureaucracy is a form of organizational structure in which people can be held accountable for their actions because they are required to act in accordance with well-specified and agreed-upon rules and standard operating procedures" (Jones, 2001). Organizations were to strive for one best way of administration. Weber's principles included the following:

1. Fixed division of labor among participants—The duties of each office are clearly specified.
2. Hierarchy of offices—Each office is subject to discipline from a superordinate office, but only in regard to the office's duties. The private life of the official is free from organizational authority.
3. Set of general rules that govern performance—Impersonality, as contrasted to personal relationships, regulates activity.
4. Separation of personal from official property and rights—There are no ways whereby to gain personal rights to the office.
5. Selection of personnel on the basis of technical qualifications—Hiring and promotion are governed by competence, as measured by certificated training or performance in office.
6. Employment viewed as a career by participants—Membership in the bureaucracy constitutes a career with distinct ladders of career progression (Weber, 1921/1947).

Almost every organization has a bureaucratic structure. The advantage is that efficiency of interactions among organizational members is increased. Each person's role in the organization is clearly defined. In addition, the bureaucracy separates the position from the person (Jones, 2001).

The bureaucratic model has disadvantages as well. It tends to be inflexible, and the human-relations aspects of the organization are neglected. Some of Weber's (1921/1947) assumptions about loyalty and impersonal relations are unrealistic. Nevertheless, the bureaucratic model of organization design was an important development of management theory and continues to shape administrative systems. Principles that evolved and are widely utilized today include: (a) centralization/decentralization, (b) unity of command, (c) span of control, (d) division of labor, and (e) departmentation.

Centralization/Decentralization

An organization is centralized to the extent that its decision-making power rests with one or a few individuals. In highly centralized organizations, decisions are made by one person and implemented through formal chains of command. Centralization improves coordination of organizational activities. However, it can lead to problems because often one person lacks the needed information to make good decisions or the ability to transmit decisions to lower levels. An increase in centralization and bureaucratization fosters job dissatisfaction due to diminished autonomy (Joseph, 1983; Polansky & Hughes, 1986). Furthermore, centralization can hinder innovation, increase costs, and lower performance (Stroh, Northcraft, & Neale, 2002). Reinhard Mohn, an executive of the publishing giant Bertelsmann, said, "Centralist leadership structures are no longer capable of meeting requirements in today's competitive environment. We must have the courage to decentralize responsibility. Creative people need freedom" (Fulmer, 2000, p. 179).

Therefore, the trend in many companies is to decentralize and redirect decision making and responsibility to lower levels in the organization. This benefits most media organizations because communication increases. Johnstone (1976) found that when newspaper companies become too large, face-to-face communication diminishes. Work dissatisfaction exists when management makes most decisions because of diminished autonomy (Joseph, 1983; Polansky & Hughes, 1986). Yet central management structures have their place when balance is reached between unifying divisions and providing autonomy.

Unity of Command

Despite changes in centralization, the unity of command principle states that a subordinate should be directly responsible to only one superior. To have more than one superior creates the possibility that subordinates would face conflicting priorities. However, in most newsroom situations, reporters are responsible to several supervisors.

For example, TV news directors judge overall job performance. Assignment editors evaluate coverage of a news story. Producers are concerned with story visualization and timing. When unity of command is violated, as is the case in many newsrooms, there should be a clear separation of activities and a supervisor responsible for each. In today's media organizations, strict adherence to the unity of command principle would create inflexibility and hinder performance; however, employees should know to whom they are responsible for different tasks. Those to whom subordinates report should watch for instances calling for positive feedback specific to their areas of expertise. One reporter commented in Argyris' study of a major newspaper's organizational structure, "Reporters are an irrational bunch. And the ego is high. You need to hear you're doing well" (Argyris, 1974, p. 49). Immediate supervisors are most able to identify and acknowledge work done well.

Span of Control

Media organizations that respond slowly to market needs risk becoming extinct. One way to speed up decision making is to eliminate hierarchies or change the span of control. Span of control addresses the number of subordinates a manager can efficiently and effectively direct. It determines the size of an organization's workgroups and is related to the closeness of supervision. The span of control also determines how many levels an organization has and the number of managers needed.

Managers who have fewer subordinates or a narrow span of control can supervise them more closely (Stroh, Northcraft, & Neale, 2002). Early researchers agreed that the number of people who directly report to a manager should become smaller at succeedingly higher organizational levels (Davis, 1957). For example, the span for top executives should range somewhere between three and nine. A narrow span is important when close interpersonal control of subordinates is necessary. Managers can give subordinates more attention when they have narrower spans of control.

Ideally, the wider or larger the span, the more efficient are the organizations. The span for middle managers is often between 10 and 30. A wider span of control works when tasks are well learned or easily monitored (Stroh, Northcraft, & Neale, 2002). An organizational chart with few levels of a wider span of control appears flat, whereas one with more managers appears taller. The more subordinates a supervisor manages, the flatter the organizational structure (Fig. 4.1). "Flattening the firm's structure will speed up the decision-making process, shorten lines of communication and achieve savings" (Klein, 2001, p. 47).

According to Klein (2001), several factors determine the width of the span of control:

1. Job complexity—complicated jobs require more managerial input and narrower spans of control.
2. Job similarity—employees performing similar jobs require wider spans of control
3. Geographic proximity of supervised employees—employees in close proximity can have wider spans of control.
4. Amount of coordination required to complete task—narrower spans are needed when managers spend much time coordinating tasks.
5. Abilities of employees—The greater the abilities of employees, the less need there is for supervision; thus, the wider span of control is possible.
6. Ability of management—more capable managers are able to manage more employees and less the need for a narrow span of control.

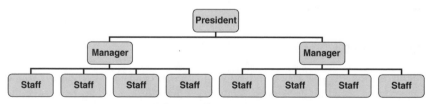

FIG. 4.1.   Flat organization.

Division of Labor

Division of labor is the extent to which jobs are broken down into a number of steps, with the responsibility for each step being assigned to specific individuals. Instead of being responsible for an entire activity, employees specialize in doing part of an activity. For example, in unionized TV stations, videotape editors are solely responsible for editing videotape. They perform this same standardized task over repeatedly.

Division of labor is an efficient way of utilizing employees' specific skills. In media organizations, some tasks require highly developed skills. Untrained individuals perform other tasks. However, if all employees were to participate in each step of producing a newscast, all would have to have the skills necessary to perform both the most and least demanding jobs. This is an inefficient method of utilizing workers skills.

Other efficiencies are achieved through division of labor. Performance skills increase through repetition of a task. As employees become more expert, efficiency is exhibited in reducing time spent in completing tasks. Training workers to perform specific and repetitive tasks is also less costly.

Finally, division of labor increases efficiency and productivity by encouraging specialized creativity. Examples of division of labor of management positions within a TV news organization include the assignment manager, who is in charge of what news is covered each day. The assignment manager creates a storyboard outlining which reporters and photographers cover which newsstory. The newsroom producers stack the newscast. They are responsible for putting the newscast together, deciding the order of stories, timing the show, and making sure the show flows. They also write stories and edit videotape for the newscast.

Similar positions exist according to division of labor within newspaper organizations. The city editor is in charge of all reporters and coordinates all hard-news coverage. The news editor supervises the copy desk and is the chief person in charge of story selection and placement, copyediting, and page design. The sports editor is in charge of producing the daily sports section. The TV news-room also has a similar sports director.

The belief that organizations should have a high degree of division of labor is a widely accepted principle. Yet it has disadvantages and can be carried too far. Too much division of labor causes boredom, fatigue, and stress that may lead to inefficiency. With the computerization of media organizations, employees are expected to handle many more production aspects. For example, newspapers eliminated many copyediting positions so reporters and editors are now responsible for proofing their own copy. Likewise, at many smaller and medium-size TV stations, new employees must be a *one-man band* with shooting, editing, and reporting capabilities. Although division of labor can be a valuable goal in planning performance in organizations, its strict adherence is rare in most situations.

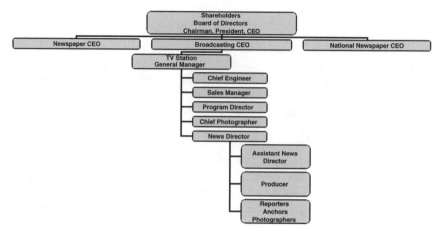

FIG. 4.2.   Gannett.

Departmentation

Division of labor creates a need for coordination of specialists. Departmentation describes how specialists are placed together in departments under the direction of a manager. The creation of departments is usually based on work functions being performed, target audience, or geographic territory.

Function

Functional departmentation occurs when organization units are defined by the nature of the work. For example, newspapers are organized into departments of news-editorial, advertising, circulation, production, and business activities. These departments, as well as departments of other media organizations, engage in distinct functions of: (a) preparing information, (b) reproducing information, (c) distributing information, (d) promoting the product to readers and advertisers, and (e) financing operations of the firm.

The Gannett media conglomerates are depicted in Fig. 4.2 based on key positions listed in its annual report (*www.gannett.com*). Gannett owns newspapers and TV stations and is structured according to function and geography. The following job descriptions explain the functions of typical management positions in different departments at broadcast and print media organizations. Each of these managers is responsible for hiring and firing personnel within a department.

Broadcast Organizations

1. The Chief Executive Officer (CEO): The CEO is responsible for overall performance of the corporation. Primary responsibilities are for the

media's relations with their perspective communities and audiences. The CEO also coordinates the efforts of all units and oversees the allocation of resources to each.

2. General Manager (GM): The GM is responsible for the overall management and operation of an individual station. The GM is concerned with matters such as income, expense, budgeting, forecasting, and long- and short-term planning. GMs hire the managers of all departments within the station and oversee the activities of each department.

3. Chief Engineer: The chief engineer is responsible for keeping the station signal on the air. This includes performing special tests required by FCC regulation. This person is responsible for maintaining technical equipment and ordering new equipment.

4. Sales Manager: The sales manager is responsible for the station's sales activities. They assign account executives to particular areas or accounts and supervise their activities. They set the rate for the sale of advertising time. They must be knowledgeable of market data, retail statistics, audience research, and all other marketing and advertising concerns.

5. Program Director: The program director is responsible for all local, network, and syndicated programming that the station broadcasts. The program director selects and schedules all programming. The program director must be knowledgeable of FCC regulations to ensure that programming complies. This is a position concerned with coordination and preparing information.

6. News Director: The news director dictates the style of the newscast and is responsible for all news operations. The news director supervises everyone in the newsroom including anchors, reporters, sports and weather announcers, producers, and assignment editors. The news director has administrative duties such as budgeting and conducting staff meetings.

7. Interactive Administrator (both broadcast and print): This person manages the Web sites for one or more media divisions. They interact with staff members, advertising clients, and third-party vendors to create Internet-based marketing solutions. They are involved with the design of banner ads, promotional concepts, and marketing solutions.

Print Organizations

1. Publisher: The publisher is the onsite chief executive officer. This person is in charge of overall newspaper operations, as well as appointing or hiring key department managers.

2. Managing Editor: This person is in charge of compiling the editorial functions of the newspaper into a quality product. This person schedules daily editorial meetings where story ideas are discussed and work assignments are made.

3. Advertising Director: The advertising manager is in charge of selling and creating classified, display, and insert advertising. This person is also responsible for setting advertising rates.
4. Business Manager: The business manager is responsible for handling administrative and general business operations. These may include payroll and personnel matters, accounting procedures, and billing.
5. Circulation Manager: The circulation manager is responsible for selling and delivering newspapers to readers. This includes marketing and promoting the product, distributing the paper in a timely manner, and collecting subscription fees.
6. Production Manager: The production manager is responsible for procedures that occur once the newspaper content leaves the editorial and advertising departments. These duties include printing, plate making, and the addition of color and words to newsprint. Production is an important component of dot.com media industries, as depicted in the organizational chart of *MSNBC.com* (see Fig. 4.3), derived from job positions listed in annual reports (*www.microsoft.com/msft/*).

The primary advantage of organizing departments by function is that it allows for specialization. It also provides for efficient use of equipment and resources. One disadvantage is that members of a functional group may develop more loyalty for the group's goals than the organization's goals. Furthermore, in today's computerized media organizations, many functions have been combined. Employees need to be adaptable and able to assume various functions. All departments must understand the organization's mission and support and strive for mutually accepted goals. Conflicts arise when different departments strive for different goals.

Target Audience.   With audience departmentation, the type of customers served divides departments. One example is a newspaper that has one department to handle home deliveries and another to handle industrial customers. This type of departmentation has the same advantages and disadvantages as product departmentation. If the home deliveries group becomes too competitive with the

FIG. 4.3.   Corporate hierarchy of *MSNBC.com.*

industrial customers group, cooperation between the two departments diminishes and the organization's overall performance could decrease.

Geographic Territory.   Geographic departmentation occurs in organizations that maintain physically scattered and independent operations or offices. Departmentation by territories permits the use of local workers and/or sales people. Media conglomerates such as Gannett own TV stations and newspapers across the country. Their large-market newspapers have branch offices to serve suburban editions of their newspapers. Such departmentation creates customer goodwill, fosters awareness of local issues, and provides a high level of service.

Different geographic territories become easier to track as media utilize more online services. New versions of media content are created daily as newspapers, magazines, radio, and TV stations go online with their products. Most job openings in these fields require computer-minded people who can provide quality content different from the print or broadcast version. Internet users want a quick product that is updated as often as possible.

Because the new technology cuts across all media, corporations depend on employees who adapt well to continual changes. Print journalists have to be broadcast journalists who also have to be online journalists. This scenario has existed for a number of years at the Tribune-owned Chicagoland TV, where print reporters are housed with news staffers of the 24-hour cable channel. Both groups provide each other with content. Each promotes the other within their news product. *The Chicago Tribune* newspaper and the cable product are available online under the supervision of one interactive administrator.

The popularity of online news media will continue to grow. MSNBC tends to be the leader and primary source for news on the Internet. This type of creativity and openness to new technology is necessary for all corporations to compete in the future.

INFORMAL APPROACH

Although the formal structure of media organizations is important, decision making and coordination often occur outside formal chains of command as people interact informally on the job. The informal approach to structuring media companies is based on the assumption that work is accomplished through cooperation, participation, satisfaction, and interpersonal skills. Managers must consider the interactions between the formal and informal hierarchies when motivating and coordinating employees (Jones, 2001). A company may have an intact formal structure, but without a willing, satisfied, and competent workforce, goals are not achieved. Employee interactions, the importance of communication and team building, and contingency approaches are addressed when studying informally structured media organizations.

Employee Interactions

Mayo (1945) was one of the first to document the importance of human interaction and morale for productivity. He studied individual characteristics such as fatigue to determine the optimum length and spacing of rest periods for maximum productivity levels. The Chicago Hawthorne plant of the Western Electric Company was the site of the research.

Management at the Hawthorne plant was aware that severe dissatisfaction existed among workers. Mayo and his colleagues experimented by changing physical conditions to determine which condition would increase productivity. They worked with variables such as lighting, noise, incentive pay, and heating. They found little support for the expected relationship between improved working conditions and improved productivity. Mayo (1945) summarized these surprising results:

> The conditions of scientific experiment had apparently been fulfilled—experimental room, control room; changes introduced one at a time; all other conditions held steady. And the results were perplexing. . . . Lighting improved in the experimental room, production went up; but it rose also in the control room. The opposite of this: lighting diminished from 10 to 3 foot-candles in the experimental room and the production again went up; simultaneously in the control room, with illumination constant, production also rose. (p. 69)

Mayo observed that work output increased no matter how the physical variables were changed. He realized it was the attention the researchers were paying to the workers that resulted in increased productivity. The workers were so pleased to be singled out for special attention that they did the best they could for the researchers and the company. This effect became known as the *Hawthorne effect*. As a result, productivity could no longer be viewed as solely dependent on formal organizational structure.

Barnard's (1938) ideas also contributed to human relations approaches. Barnard was not a researcher, but an executive of a telephone company. He stressed that organizations are basically cooperative systems that integrate the contributions of their individual participants. Barnard defined an organization as an entity where cooperation is conscious, deliberate, and purposeful. Barnard believed that goals were imposed from the top down, whereas their attainment depended on the willingness to comply from the bottom up. Barnard did not believe that authority always came down from above, noting situations where leaders claim authority but fail to win compliance. Rather he believed that authority depended on subordinates' approval.

Barnard (1938) was one of the first theorists to signify the importance of human motivation as crucial to productivity. Material rewards or economic motives were sometimes viewed as weak incentives to be supported by other types of social-psychological motivations. The most critical ingredient to successful organizations was the formation of a collective purpose. Overall, Barnard (1938) believed that when formal organizations came into operation, they created and required informal organizations. Informal structures facilitated communication and maintained cohesiveness.

McGregor (1960) developed two attitude profiles about people's basic nature. These attitudes were termed *Theory X* and *Theory Y*. A Theory X manager believes the average person dislikes work and avoids responsible labor whenever possible. These managers respond to this attitude with controls such as punishments if employees fail to produce. They assume employees prefer to be directed to avoid responsibility. Theory X managers were based on the formal, scientific approach to management theory.

Theory Y managers believe employees find work as enjoyable as play. They are self-motivated and self-directed. Employees do not need the threat of punishment to be productive because they are committed to organizational goals. Theory Y workers seek responsibility and creatively solve organizational problems. Although the beliefs of Theory X and Theory Y managers are quite opposite, McGregor assumes these to be a range of behaviors. Managers can draw on both sets of ideas depending on the situation.

Theory Z (Ouchi, 1981) makes assumptions about the culture of organizations, whereas Theories X and Y made assumptions about individuals. Theory Z contrasts American organizations with traditional Japanese organizations. Short-term employment, specialized career paths, rapid promotion, formal control, and individual responsibility characterize American organizations. They value individuality over group membership. Institutions such as churches, neighborhoods, and schools, rather than the formal work group, provide social needs. Lifetime employment, slow advancement, informal control, consensus decision making, and generalized career paths, in contrast, have often characterized Japanese organizations. Loyalty to groups is of primary concern and more important than individual achievement. Theory Z is important because it sets the stage for team building, which is the basis of many decision-making structures in media organizations today.

Teambuilding

In today's media organizations, group productivity is often more important than individual task accomplishment. Managers promote teamwork for problem solving and work improvement. Job satisfaction in newsrooms increases when subordinates are included in decision making. Adams and Fish (1987) surveyed TV news directors, general managers, and sales managers and found that participative or democratic leadership behavior related to higher levels of job satisfaction. Blanchard, Carew, and Parisi-Carew (1990) said managers who build high-performing teams within the structure of their media organizations must understand stages of group development. Powers (1991) found that when employees are more involved in the decision-making process, their levels of effort and performance increase.

When task groups initially meet, they are in Stage 1, The Orientation Stage. During this stage, team members usually have high expectations and feel eager about working. However, they are more dependent on authority and need to establish their place in the group. As team members become more familiar with each other and begin working on the tasks at hand, they move into Stage 2, The Dissatisfaction Stage. In this stage, members experience a discrepancy between early hopes and later realities. Some members react negatively toward authority and become frustrated with tasks and plans.

During Stage 3, The Resolution Stage, the team experiences more satisfaction in working together. Members start to share responsibility and control. They develop trust and respect. The final stage that most teams experience is Stage 4, The Production Stage. Here team members show high confidence in accomplishing tasks and feel positive about task successes. Performance is highest at this level.

Managers who work with teams realize they must adapt their leadership behaviors according to the stages of group development. In the Orientation Stage, a more authoritative or directing leader is needed. During the Dissatisfaction Stage, a coaching leader concerned with both relationships and tasks is needed to help the group work through conflict. As the team moves toward the Resolution Stage, the leader exhibits less directive behavior and become more supporting or relationship-oriented. Finally, in the Production Stage, the leader functions best as a delegator or just a team member.

Sometimes groups bypass the four stages of development because of a fixed time frame for completing a task. In the punctuated equilibrium model, a team sets parameters for completing a task during its first meeting and decides how it will interact, what approach it will take to the project, what its goals will be, and so on (Stroh, Northcraft, & Neale, 2002). Gersick found that, for the sake of time, task-oriented teams break out of inertia and generate new sets of arrangements, enabling the group to complete a project under pressure. Thus, the difference between the four-stages and punctuated-equilibrium models is the role of time. Teams without deadlines progress according to the internal needs of the group (Gersick, 1994). Deadline pressures, which are prevalent in newsroom situations, prompt a group to bypass its own needs in favor of the deadline imposed on the team to complete the project.

Many types of teams are formed within organizations. Barker (1999) identified four:

1. Work teams—led by supervisor or self-managed. Perform work functions such as scheduling or ordering equipment. Often the supervisor previously performed these tasks.
2. Parallel teams—perform problem-solving and improvement-oriented tasks that the regular organization is not structured to undertake. Includes people across work units. Have limited authority and usually make recommendations to managers.
3. Project teams—exist for short periods to produce a one-time product or service.

4. Management teams—provide direction to interdependent subunits for which they are responsible. Manage overall performance and provide strategic direction. The strength is a willingness to share in the responsibility for the success of the organization as a whole.

Each approach to teambuilding and informal structure is only as useful as the situation in which it is employed. Only when managers consider all situational variables that affect corporate efficiency and productivity can any single structure be successfully used. As a result, contingency theories were developed that incorporate both scientific and humanistic approaches to management study.

THE CONTINGENCY APPROACH

Contingency theories of organizational structure have developed because researchers recognize that organizations are open systems that interact with their environment (Thomas, 2002). Different combinations of situational elements require different organizational structures and management behaviors. Contingency approaches are built on differences in situational variables such as leadership styles, subordinate behaviors, work environments, and the inclusion of women and minorities. One theory that addresses situational variables is Path-Goal Theory.

Leaders and Subordinates

According to Path-Goal Theory, three important interdependent factors that organizations must consider are: (a) forces involving the manager, (b) subordinates, and (c) forces involving external and internal situations (Tannenbaum & Schmidt, 1973). Forces acting on the manager include personal value systems and leadership styles such as task- or relationship-oriented styles. Relationship-oriented behavior is the extent to which the manager's behavior promotes friendship, mutual trust, respect, and good human relations between the manager and group. With task-oriented behavior, the manager tends to organize and define the relationships between her or himself and the group in defining interactions among group members, establishing ways of getting the job done, scheduling, criticizing, and so forth (Fleishman, 1956).

Forces acting on the subordinates include ability, experience, and need for independence. People who perceive they are lacking in ability may prefer directive managers to help them understand path-goal relationships (House & Dessler, 1974). However, employees may resent directive managers if they perceive their own abilities as high. Personal characteristics include education, experience, and age. Hersey and Blanchard (1972) argued that effective management behavior varies in conjunction with the personal characteristics of subordinates. As employees' maturity level, age, and experience increase, management behavior is characterized by a decreasing emphasis on task behaviors and an increasing emphasis on relationship behaviors.

Forces acting on the situation include type of organization, time pressure, demands from upper levels of management, and demands from government, unions, or society. These environmental characteristics usually are outside the subordinate's control. For example, Powers (1991) found that broadcast news directors must be task-oriented during a crisis situation; however, once the crisis is over, they may become more relationship-oriented. Furthermore, if tasks are straightforward, the leader's attempts to direct are seen by subordinates as redundant and unnecessary. The higher the degree of formality, the less subordinates accept directive management behavior. Relationship-oriented management behavior is less critical when the work group provides the individual with social support and satisfaction. However, research indicates that relationship-oriented management behavior is the strongest positive impact on satisfaction and productivity for subordinates who work on stressful or frustrating tasks (Schriesheim & Schriesheim, 1980).

Powers and Lacy (1992) presented a model of TV newsroom management in Fig. 4.4 that modifies the situational path-goal framework. The model divides factors affecting job satisfaction into four groups: individual factors, market factors, organizational factors, and leadership. These four types of factors influence journalists' perceptions of how successful their organizations are at attaining goals such as profit, good human relations, and quality news. If journalists

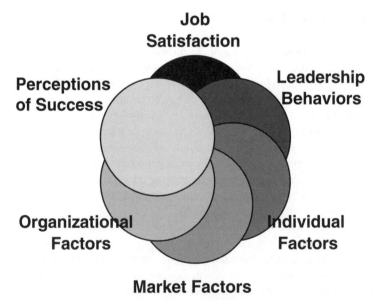

FIG. 4.4.   Model of job satisfaction for local TV news departments.

believe their organizations are successful at attaining these goals, their level of job satisfaction increases.

A negative relationship between market size and perceptions of good human relations suggests that local TV journalists in large newsrooms perceive news managers to be more task-oriented than those in newsrooms located in smaller markets. A negative relationship was also found between the organizational factor of group ownership and profit success. Local TV journalists at group-owned stations perceive no more success at profit making than did those at independently owned stations.

The most important study result for predicting job satisfaction among local TV journalists was the relationship behavior of the news directors. Employees were more satisfied with relationship-oriented managers than with task-oriented managers. Job satisfaction related to participation, suggesting that news directors should include journalists in the decision-making process if they want to retain satisfied employees.

The tone of communication is often set at the top. Phillips (1976) found that the management behavior of higher level executives sets the tone for communication at lower organizational levels. A news director who initially had a hands-on approach or participative management style felt obliged to exhibit the more authoritarian behavior emanating from corporate headquarters. Consultants are sometimes needed to change the overall management environment if a company wants to foster more participation within the entire organization. Fowler and Shipman (1982) found that newspaper managers evaluated employees on a regular basis, and interpersonal communication was the preferred and most often used means of communication. The perceived atmosphere of the newsroom was related to the amount of participation reporters had on matters of importance.

Women

Contingency approaches must address the inclusion of women and minorities in the workplace. The traditional view of organizational structures and processes persists, making it difficult to accept the idea of gendered organizations (Soundhaus & Gallagher, 2001). Rosener (1990) found men more likely than women to describe themselves as task-oriented. Men view job performance as exchanging rewards for services rendered or punishment for inadequate performance. Men were more likely to use the formal authority and power that come from their organizations. Therefore, "organizational structure and processes based on masculine values are viewed as operating on qualities such as objectivity, competition, rationality, ambition, decisiveness, unemotionality, and commitment to rules, order and hierarchy" (Soundhaus & Gallagher, 2001, p. 132).

Women describe themselves as being relationship-oriented. Women convinced subordinates to transform their own self-interest into the interest of the group through concern for a broader goal. Women credited their power to personal characteristics such as charisma, interpersonal skills, hard work, or personal contacts rather than organizational stature. Women made their interactions with subordinates positive for everyone involved. Women also encouraged participation, shared power and information, enhanced other people's self-worth, and excited people about their work.

Not all men or women operate in a particular manner, and communication styles are not mutually exclusive. Women manage organizations by adhering to the traditional, task-oriented model; some men are relationship-oriented. The larger issue is the need for organizations to question whether traditional command-and-control management is the only way to ensure results. As the workforce demands more participation and the economic environment requires rapid change, relationship-oriented behavior could emerge as the management style of choice for many organizations.

Minorities

Including minorities in media organizations continues to challenge most media organizations. As the U.S. minority population is rapidly increasing, the need for skilled minority employees to represent the population has greatly increased as well. Forward-looking media managers must cast a wider net for skilled minority applicants and, more important, produce a more hospitably diverse workplace to compete for the most talented workers.

One way to do this is by valuing workplace diversity. Managers diminish prejudice by acknowledging the problem, addressing negative behavior, and obtaining feedback. Karen Brown (1990) of the Poynter Institute for Media Studies said successful companies have open and frequent internal communications because minorities translate silence as lack of concern. Many staffers are uncomfortable pointing out offensive behavior because they fear being perceived as the minority person who has no other interests or expertise. Minorities, women, and people from varying cultures need to be comfortable discussing concerns about the work environment. Valuing diversity in the workplace means recognizing the worth and dignity of others and treating people with respect.

GLOBAL MEDIA STRUCTURES

Tomorrow's media organizations will operate in a multimedia, multiskilled environment where lower level managers and subordinates handle 70% to 80% of the tasks. The formal and informal structures of these media organizations will undergo drastic change. Shih (2002) said as long as subordinates operate within rules, they are free to appropriately proceed. If the rules do not benefit many, subordinates will make recommendations to upper levels of management.

Innovation takes place on a base of rules and knowledge. For example, a media firm with business in multiple countries must conform to local laws and have adequate information about the local culture. Local lower level managers address change and make suggestions to corporate headquarters. They need authority to control decisions in their own regions. Discussions take place across a network of divisions and countries. In a global environment, newsrooms must work in real time across multiple media simultaneously (*http://www.newsplex.org*).

With a networked approach, more stress is laid on effective resource management. In the past, resources in traditional media organizations meant time, videotape, equipment, and other physical resources. Two types of resources are becoming more difficult to deplete in the new media environment: increasing computing power and human expertise. The switch will be made from physical labor to human expertise, from the visible to the intangible, from hardware to software, and from a focus on efficiency to a focus on leadership (Shih, 2002). As computing power and talent become more accessible, organizational structures evolve into a flattened structure with greater reliance on delegation to avoid problems of the hierarchical organization. The media industry changed considerably, making many old ways of thinking about organizations somewhat obsolete.

The organizational structures of networked companies, including global media organizations such as *MSNBC.com*, will look different from traditional hierarchical companies. In a traditional company, when a division wants to undertake some change, approval is required from headquarters. In a flatter, networked company, each company in the group is independent. Decision-making procedures are independent of parent company approval. Each unit is independent and specializes in its particular area of business. Networked organizations are more effective due to speed in decision making, effective composition of working teams, and ability to adapt to change.

As media organizations think globally, survival strategies such as achieving further economies of scale increase. Globalization helps companies address local preferences not satisfied by a universal product. Expanding into new territory can be exciting, aggressive, and demonstrative of the capacity to win. Rupert Murdoch's quest to reach audiences worldwide was a personal and competitive goal. Askenas et al. (2002) listed nine reasons for going global:

1. Competitive Survival—If media companies have subsidiaries in other countries, labor costs may be cheaper and they can achieve economies of scale. Globalization gives companies leverage to reduce costs and increase profits.
2. Cost Spreading—The desire to spread or share costs for capital investments, high technology, and equipment drives many media companies to join up with other firms around the world. Neither the largest nor the smallest firms can afford to go it alone.

3. Trailblazing—Although this is founded on the drive of a single executive such as Murdoch, it benefits the entire organization. For example, Lycos, the Boston-based start-up Internet site, merged with Terra, a Spanish Internet and telecommunications firm, to form terraLycos. The assumption was that a globally based company would have a better chance of succeeding in the Internet industry.

4. Rule of Three—Often in media organizations and other industries, there are three major players. ABC, CBS, NBC dominated. In long-distance telephone, the major players were AT&T, MCI, and Sprint. The goal is to dominate in local or regional markets, as well as in worldwide top-tier positions.

5. Domino Effect—Once a media company crosses one global boundary, it becomes easier to cross another. The domino effect is when cultures and customs are similar.

6. Evolutionary Forces—Increasing homogenization contributes to media growth. People used to be more separated by their differences. Today's cultures are more similar. A *Wall Street Journal* Europe survey showed more than half of Europe's 20 best-selling brands, ranging from detergents to pet foods, are available in all European countries. This gives media companies motive to take advantage of universal advertising packages.

7. Technological Revolution—Even smaller companies can compete on a worldwide basis relatively inexpensively through Internet, e-mail, phone, fax, and so on. Time differences are minimized. Borders become meaningless in separating people from other people or information. Media companies can take advantage of the wealth of information available electronically.

8. Search for Innovation—Going global enriches a company's innovativeness by tapping into different worldwide trends that may lead to new products. AOL Time Warner used both domestic and international alliances to supplement creative efforts and obtain new technology. Their alliances reach beyond the United States into Asia, Europe, and Latin America. They have Internet companies, traditional media, and computer and satellite technology.

9. Benchmarking against other Companies—When companies see how other companies break through global boundaries, they gain confidence about their own global potential.

Operating in a global environment, managers realize that people think differently and live in different ways. Yet actions are guided, not dictated, by cultural values. Cultures exist at various levels from a group to an organizational to a national level. At the organizational level, AT&T is known for its strong hierarchy and chain of command, whereas Microsoft is known for its informal style, with people coming to work in casual attire and keeping flexible hours in a high-pressure, creative environment. At the national level, countries such as the United States are self-focused, whereas countries such as Malaysia are group-focused. People who are self-focused look to themselves to judge actions and personal goals, whereas people who are group-focused look to others to judge (Early & Erez, 1997). In the workplace, these differences are used to analyze how employees relate to each other. Americans have less equality on the job than Swedes or Israelis. In South America, top management controls authority. In Japanese corporations, respect for seniority and hierarchical order exists. American corporations struggle with the bureaucratic top–down approach to structuring. Rather American and other Western cultures often take advantage of new technology, such as mobile phones and e-mail, which facilitates corporate communication (Ashkenas et al., 2002).

To accommodate cultural differences within one company and rapid changes in technologies, media organizations experimented with creating more permeable boundaries. When worlds become unstable, organizations need the flexibility to act quickly. The focus of past organizations was on size, specialization, and control, whereas the focus of future global organizations must be on speed, flexibility, integration, and innovation.

SUMMARY

In today's media organization, structures must take advantage of traditional and innovative models. Formal approaches address how the parts of an organization fit together in terms of unity of command, span of control, division of labor, and departmentation. Informal approaches are concerned with human relations and the assumption that work is accomplished through people. Boundaryless structures address how members of global companies interact. Media managers must consider all aspects as they build their future organizations.

The ability to combine approaches rests on managers' ability and willingness to adapt to changing environments. Executives in large media conglomerates must realize that people who come from different companies, with different approaches, have no experience working together and thinking about projects to help other parts of the firm. When managers take a synergistic approach, using ideas from employees in different areas of the firm, cross-media activities take on a whole new light (Turow, 1992). Concentration of ownership changed the structure of most organizations and requires managers to use its holdings synergistically. Utilizing the contingency approach, managers analyze the relevant variables and then select the appropriate structure. Because these variables change constantly, managers must continually analyze and evaluate the efficiency and effectiveness of the structure of their organization.

Case 4.1
Structural Analysis

Effective managers make time for strategic planning to find out whether departments or media organizations as a whole are doing well. Strategic planning covers a relatively long period of time, affects many parts of the organization, and includes formulating objectives and selecting the means to attain those objectives. Tactical planning involves short-range planning such as production schedules and day-to-day procedures. Porter (1980) suggested managers should periodically analyze organizational structure by conducting a structural analysis. His analytical framework enables a company to understand its own position in the environment. Porter also suggested conducting a competitor analysis to profile the nature and success of the likely strategy each competitor might take and the environmental shifts that might occur.

There are four diagnostic components to be used for both structural and competitor analyses. These include evaluating: (a) assumptions of the firm (or the background of the firm and industry), (b) current strategies (how the business is currently competing), (c) capabilities of the firm (both strengths and weaknesses), (d) future goals, and (e) recommendations. Managers use this process to obtain as much information as possible on the organization's formal and informal structure to identify potential problems, the effect of new technology, the cutback or addition of staff, the opening or closing of divisions, or whatever else is relevant.

ASSIGNMENT

As a media specialist, you must analyze the management and organization of a media organization such as the Tribune, Edelman, Fox News, and so on. It helps if you have had an internship at the media organization, but it is not necessary.

Project Analysis.   Divide your analysis into five sections. Write out your analysis of each section.

1. Historical Overview: Provide a brief historical look at the company. For the purpose of this assignment, keep the historical overview simple and to the point.
2. Organizational Structure: Include major divisions and/or reporting lines. Use an organizational chart if the company is highly complex. Identify senior executives if prominent. Look for descriptions of their management styles and effectiveness. Include information about the company's mission statement, business philosophy, and operating approach.

3. Media Products or Services: This section consists of a content analysis of the media organization's product. For example, you could analyze the types of news sources used in reports or look at the type of advertising campaigns used. Another example is to examine the gender of subjects used in news or ad campaigns. Public relations techniques could also be analyzed. Choose a random sample and conduct a specific content analysis.

4. Financial Performance: Provide information on the company's financial performance during the past few years. Try to spot trends and patterns in terms of how the company is performing. Depending on the size and scope of the operation, review other financial indicators such as:
   a. Revenues and net income during the past 3 to 5 years.
   b. Revenues by business segments (or divisions).
   c. Revenues by regional, national, or international geographic locations.
   d. Stock prices.

   This information is standard and contained in the company's annual report and securities exchange 10K filings. Consider using the consolidated income statement and graphic displays where appropriate.

5. Discussion of Strategic Planning Issues: What are the major goals and objectives for the company during the next 3 to 5 years? What are the major challenges facing the company? Do a SWOT analysis, listing the company's strengths, weaknesses, opportunities, and threats. The following external factors can affect your company's strategic plan:
   a. Competitors
   b. Political/regulatory factors
   c. The economy
   d. Technology
   e. Cultural factors

6. Discussion: What is your overall assessment of the company's long-term growth and its ability to implement strategic plans? What recommendations can you offer to assist your company to better implement its goals and objectives, taking into consideration the external factors that may have an impact?

Case 4.2
The Debt-Laden Company

You are the head of a debt-laden foreign media conglomerate that is the second largest media conglomerate in the world. You are under pressure due to accounting practices that have been called into question. Your stock tumbled 22% on your country's exchange. In the short term, the company has to solve its liquidity situation by raising more money or selling assets. The company is saddled with about $18 billion in debt after a 2-year acquisition fest. In a recent statement to the press, you said, "I have every confidence that the company has the strengths to address its liquidity issues and find the appropriate solutions in the immediate term." In the long term, the company must chart a strategic course—something critics say is missing under your leadership. It is rumored that your board is split between two possible approaches. One is to divide the assets to create a media-centric company in the United States, leaving the rest of the company's assets in your country. Another possibility that is consistent with your practice is to keep the company in one piece and sell off noncore assets.

Your company has several attractive properties, and potential buyers are likely to size them up. Your units include:

1. TV and Film: Major movie producer and studio and theme parks, film and production assets of two major cable networks, pay-TV and Digital, and an audiovisual library that includes more than 9,000 feature films and 40,000 hours of TV programming. (Your film company is doing well and churning out blockbuster hits. There are sure to be prospective buyers. The theme parks would most likely stay linked with the movie business.) Your networks might appeal to big cable content players such as Walt Disney or Viacom, one of the financially healthiest players on the media landscape whose units include MTV Networks and CBS.

2. Publishing: You are No. 3 in publishing and No. 2 in educational publishing. You are also the No. 2 seller of PC games. (Your book publishing may be of interest to other large book publishers.)

3. Music: You supplied one in four of all albums sold worldwide last year. Artists include Mary J. Blige, Bon Jovi, Boyzone, Eminem, Elton John, Limp Bizkit, Shaggy, U2, and Luciano Pavarotti. (Music is probably the best asset in the world in terms of market share.)

4. Telecom: You own 44% of the fixed-line and mobile telecom services in your country, which has some 16 million fixed-line and mobile subscribers. Your international unit has some 10 million subscribers in countries such as Morocco, Monaco, Hungary, Egypt, and Kenya. (Your most valuable segment here is your equity of the No. 2 wireless operator in France. A lot of companies might be interested.)

5. Internet: You are the world's No. 1 Internet music service provider. You also run an Internet portal for wireless phones, cable TV, and computers. (Good for future visibility, poor for current earnings.)

6. Utility Group: You own a huge utility company like G.E. and a water and wastewater treatment firm. (A key component to your financial stability prior to your buying frenzy of media organizations. You cannot sell the stake in the water and wastewater firm for 18 months, but may be able to find a way to monetize the asset.)

ASSIGNMENT

Answer the following questions in detail using the information from the chapter and case:

1. What short-term strategy will you take to raise funds?
2. Discuss the pros and cons of the two solutions suggested by your board.
3. What is your long-term strategy?
4. How will you handle the issue of possible faulty accounting practices?

Case 4.3
Digitizing the Newsroom

CRTV is a 24-hour regional cable network owned by a large media conglomerate. It is located in one of the top five U.S. markets. The conglomerate also owns a broadcast station, newspaper, and baseball team in this same market. Management made a large investment and was among the first to create a regional cable station similar to CNN. No profit was expected the first 6 years. The station has been operating for 10 years now and is able to sustain itself with marginal success. One way to keep costs down is to hire young talent, keep salaries low, and avoid unionization, so turnover has always been high. Nevertheless, the station is in a large market, and plenty of people would love to work there.

The main evening news anchor is a female, Mandy Whithers, who has worked at the station since it started. She is 45. She has face recognition—something that few others on air have. However, she is becoming increasing unhappy because of what she sees as low standards and inexperienced employees. The new news director, Tim Fabor, recently took over and began digitizing the newsroom. He is 32 and was considered a dedicated news producer—someone who really cares about the quality of the product—before becoming news director.

The problem is to keep the news running while switching to a digital format. This has proved to be a larger headache than Tim could have imagined. Some people who would normally jump at the chance to anchor a news show have refused to do so until the system is worked out. His main anchor, Mandy Whithers, is doing the job, but has increasingly alienated many on staff. News is no longer produced live for 1 hour, but pieced together digitally in segments, requiring the anchor to remain on the desk for about 5 hours.

Mandy's view is that she's being blamed for holding up production because she finds errors in the scripts as they come in. No one is checking for factual errors or pronunciation guides. Her face is on the line, and she wants things right before going on air. She has made numerous complaints about the lack of standards for the past 6 months, but nothing has been done.

Tim's point of view is that Mandy is alienating everybody and making him look like an ineffective news director. Everything was fine before he implemented the new digital technology. Somebody has to take the fall for what is turning into a negative situation. So he is putting Mandy on 60 days notice to improve her performance or she is gone. Besides he already had to write her up once for swearing at the director.

ASSIGNMENT

Answer the following questions in detail using the information from the chapter and case:

1. What should the news director do about the anchor?
2. What should the anchor do about the accusations?
3. What could the news director and/or anchor have done to avoid the situation?
4. How should the implementation of new technology by handled?
5. What would you have done differently?

CHAPTER

5

TECHNOLOGY AND THE FUTURE

Ask most people to define *technology* and you will hear descriptions of machines, computers, and equipment of various kinds. Yet technology can be invisible—as simple as a way of doing things or a structural component of a task. That is because technology generally is a tool—a means to an end. It is the job of managers to determine how well that tool serves its purpose and what effect it has on the people who use it.

This is especially true in a media company. Knowing the technology's limitations eases the burden of operating a communications firm. By understanding the limitations of the photo equipment, a newspaper photo editor can determine what situations call for which cameras and which photographers. Similarly, technology determines internal structure. A TV station manager knows that producing the 6 o'clock news means the work must be divided into journalistic and videographic components, each with its own department and internal working composition. Consequently, technology also determines employee behavior and production efficiency. For instance, as the Internet becomes increasingly pervasive, computerized research may replace librarians in newspaper newsrooms, freeing librarians to assume other responsibilities.

As the pace of technological advances quickens, it is especially important for media managers to understand technology's strategic ramifications. Many media firms that produce time-sensitive material must adequately grasp the market significance of rapidly developing and converging technologies (such as the Internet and its World Wide Web) and learn how to adapt. The decision could mean the difference between new, growing revenue streams and a stagnant, noncompetitive future, particularly as media firms fattened by mergers and acquisitions become more organizationally complex and thus more conservative and slower in their decision making. For example, broadcasters once regarded the videocassette recorder as a fad with little potential for widespread adoption (Napoli, 1997). Technologically driven change is becoming the norm so media managers must overcome organizational culture and routinized work patterns and biases to adequately deal with that change.

A media manager's job is to turn the technology to the company's advantage. To do so, the manager must analyze the organizational role and impact of

99

technology. This chapter examines how a company uses or adopts technology and how technology impacts media organizations internally and externally. First a manager must assess the approach to the technology because that ultimately influences employees and thus the technology's impact.

APPROACH

How a manager views technology affects the company's performance. A newspaper editor, for example, sets the tone for how well copy editors use editing terminals. If the editor constantly complains about the terminal's shortcomings, staff trust in technology is undermined. However, if the editor consistently praises the machine and helps staffers master its capabilities and intricacies, the editor enhances the staff's ability to edit and design pages effectively, thus enhancing productivity.

Of course the terminal may dictate what approach the editor takes. If the machine is simple to operate and consistently performs its intended task, then the editor views it as one of several tools to aid editing. Yet if the cranky machine performs inconsistently at best, is hard to master and operate, or is so prohibitively expensive that there are not enough to go around, the editor's attitude is antagonistic or, at the least, wary and cautious. Then there is the question of management's expectations regarding the technology. If the editor expects the computer to do little more than simple editing, and if that is indeed what the computer is designed to do, then the editor's reaction most likely is positive. If the editor expects much more complex and sophisticated design effects that are not within the computer's capabilities, a different, more negative reaction occurs (Sylvie, 1995).

Consequently, there are three ways a company might approach a technology prior to adopting it: structural, technological-task, and sociotechnical. Each relates to how management can control technology and thus determines how much uncertainty and risk must be encountered.

Structural Approach

The structural approach focuses on the impact of formal devices such as rules and organizational hierarchy. This approach uses technology as a planned, controlled instrument of management, which makes conscious, intentional decisions concerning the implications of the technology. In this case, structure means considering technology as a tool for managing people (Leavitt, 1965).

A structuralist manager believes that employee behavior does not change by teaching employees new skills, rather by changing the organization's structure.

Behavioral and attitudinal change are best brought about by devices such as rules, role prescriptions, and reward structures, of which technology is a part. For example, a newspaper photo editor who adopts the latest in digital cameras does so because he believes the new technology leaves unchanged the basic structure of the work needing to be done (e.g., image development). Senior management often uses new technology to attain strategic and operating objectives, indicating factors in addition to technology help determine choices of work organization (Buchanan, 1985).

Yet in reality management does not always have such choices. Although computers facilitated various aspects of organizational life, many supervisors and lower level managers have not fully coped. Often managers' preparation lags behind technology installation or is nonexistent (Burack & Sorensen, 1976). This is particularly true in media organizations where most work centers on daily deadlines, leaving little time for any technology planning. Many managers delegate daily technological operations once they discover technology's fast pace of change.

As a result, it is difficult for media managers to be quite so calculating and control oriented in regard to structure. Management often relies heavily on employees' skills, talents, and judgment at all phases of production. For example, the reporter no longer has to physically bring a story back to the newsroom for editing; now computers can record notes and images, making editing portable and within the subordinate's control. It may be impractical to view the technology without including the employee/user in the picture—another reason many media managers try the next approach.

Technological-Task Approach

The technological-task approach complements the structural approach, albeit via emphasis on the technology's obvious, direct impact on the employee and organization. The technological-task manager sees technology as being controlled and having a measurable response in the organization. The manager chooses a technology, hoping that it increases productivity by enhancing the processes and routine tasks of work.

Such a substitution strategy (or the substitution of one technology for another) is again demonstrated by the case of a photo editor deciding to adopt the latest development software. Here the editor wishes to give photographers latitude on certain matters and thus the flexibility to shoot effective news pictures, rather than abiding by quality limits that may rule out some pictures. Similarly, using digitized graphic systems helps TV newscasters upgrade how they package their product and deliver it more quickly, all within the framework of the editing process.

Yet substituting technologies carries potential problems or trade-offs. In adopting news editing software, the newspaper's editor sought to substitute the journalists' (i.e., copy editors') expertise in design and editing for that of the nonjournalists (i.e., blue-collar composing room personnel). The editor got his wish, but he also stirred resentment in copy editors, who felt they were no longer doing journalistic work, but composing room work as well (Sylvie, 1995). These unanticipated consequences often lead managers to consider the final approach.

Sociotechnical Approach

The sociotechnical approach lies somewhere between the structural and technological-task approaches. Here the manager stresses the needs and actions of the technology's users as well as examining the technology's attributes and characteristics. Sociotechnical managers see person and machine interacting to the organization's benefit (or detriment). They view technology's purpose as dynamic and changing and to be used according to its perceived utility (Argyris, 1962).

At first glance, the sociotechnical manager seems to be today's norm. Many managers are sensitive to employee needs and growth, often recognizing that formal organizational values may infringe on an employee's personal values or skills. These managers realize that psychological and social planning play an important part in new technology introduction. They evaluate technology not just according to objectives, but also according to the process of change the technology introduces and its impact on employees' motivations, skills, and organizational competence (Blackler & Brown, 1985). For example, as the cable TV industry enhances its capabilities as an Internet service provider, it will require revisiting home subscribers to install new equipment. That means retraining employees in the new hardware and maintaining or increasing current levels of service to subscribers.

These three approaches illustrate that management has to have a basic orientation in dealing with technology. They emphasize the element of control, although some research shows managers also view technology in terms of cost and market (Noon, 1994). Regardless, managers need a basic objective when adopting technology because adoption does not occur in a vacuum. Having an objective in large part determines how well the adoption (or rejection) process occurs (Sylvie & Danielson, 1989). Managers must learn to more readily predict the impact of technology on management as well as employee and market behavior. To do so, the adoption process must be examined and placed in context.

INTERNAL IMPACTS

Technology can have several types of effects: desirable/undesirable, direct/indirect, and anticipated/unanticipated (Rogers, 1986; see Fig. 5.1). These

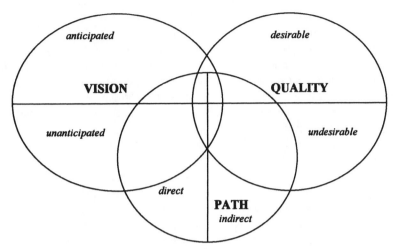

FIG. 5.1.   Types of internal impact.

consequences are placed, from a management standpoint, into internal and external categories.

Adoption Process

Internally, managers focus on the adoption process and its effects. When an organization decides to adopt a technology, several steps (Rogers, 1983) precede and follow the decision.

Agenda Setting.   This occurs when management identifies a need for a technology. The manager surveys the industry, related publications, and technological experts for potential solutions. In the media, technologies often seem to set their own agenda. For example, interest in the Internet burgeoned to the point where many media companies created Web sites to keep pace with the market for Web-based information. Yet just as often media managers respond to particular needs identified by employees in the work process.

A media organization's management chooses to introduce or adopt a technology for various reasons. Perhaps the new technology is used to obtain some strategic, operating, or control objective and management determines many choices of work and work organization. A worldwide news organization, such as CNN, uses various means of satellite newsgathering to give it a long-range toehold in the international TV news market. CNN then organizes its staff and work procedures, plans its budgets, and markets its programs to take advantage of the technology. Often this decision is an economics-based one, but that is just the beginning.

Matching. In this stage, the manager matches the problem or objective with a technology and then plans and designs a solution. Assume Channel 23, a local TV network affiliate station, has marketing problems, particularly attracting younger viewers (the station heavily depends on older adults for its viewership). The station hired a variety of consultants over a period of several months to increase viewership of its newscast. Attempts to promote the newscast proved futile, and viewership remains small compared with competitors (the station is third among the four network affiliates in town).

The general manager (GM) knows her newscast needs tremendous support at the newsstand. Younger viewers tend to watch newscasts that report much national and international news, but small stations such as hers increasingly are hard-pressed to produce a distinctive program. This is a major problem that can cause cash flow problems and threaten potential advertising sales. The general manager decides to call a GM in another city with which she attended several seminars. The friend advises her, "Try virtual sets; they give you that big-market feel." Our GM considers the idea and soon realizes this is a good match for the problem—but that is a mental match. Now she must implement the decision, which brings us to the next step.

Redefining/Restructuring. In this phase, our GM modifies or reinvents her friend's idea to fit her newscast's particular situation. She asks herself whether the organization of her news team's work process is suitable for a virtual set. Then the technology is introduced to organization members, who interact with it in various ways. There are three types of consequences from this interaction: (a) direct (changes that occur in immediate response) or indirect (changes resulting from immediate responses), (b) desirable (helps the user or system function more effectively) or undesirable (dysfunctional), and (c) anticipated (changes recognized and intended by management) or unanticipated (changes neither recognized nor intended).

Continuing the example, the virtual set idea sounds good for Channel 23. The GM evaluates these sets that make viewers believe the anchors and correspondents they see are in a large studio, bordered by banks of video monitors and a cavernous newsroom. In reality the anchors and correspondents stand or sit at a news desk in a small studio with only green walls used for superimposing the set's image. Two more months pass and she discovers that Channel 23 is beginning to garner more viewers. Yet the virtual set initially costs double the price to enlarge, rebuild, and remodel the studio. Until the set is paid for, cash reserves may be used or smaller commissions paid to ad sales account executives. Although the virtual set makes it appear Channel 23 has a large news budget, it requires the on-air talent to make adjustments such as finding marks on the floor or desk. Otherwise it appears the talent is walking through a virtual monitor or their hands are coming out of the middle of a virtual desk.

Similar employee–hardware interactions occurred when newspaper copy editors were introduced to new editing terminals. Editors were told the computerized process would give them control of the page layout process. No longer would they worry about accommodating the production staff ignoring good journalistic format, lay out pages by hand, or use rulers and pencils. However, the new machines sometimes meant shorter deadlines, computer delays/glitches, and reorganizing the workday because not enough computers existed for everyone.

These employee–hardware interactions can be mental or physical, pleasant or unpleasant, work or play, positive or negative. Media firms often experience interactions fairly quickly due to the changing nature of the product, sequential nature of the work, and routinized nature of the work. Although journalists publish or broadcast new information daily, that information is gathered in a highly structured, predictable way. Any manager implementing a technology that interrupts the routine obtains immediate feedback. This interaction is typically fed back to management in terms of costs and benefits.

Meanwhile our GM asks receptionists, secretaries, ad sales staffers, engineers, and newsroom people to develop a list of visual ideas to give Channel 23's newscast more credibility. She negotiates a loan to finance the virtual set and provide staff training. She also contracts with the local university's communication department to conduct focus groups among her newscast's target age groups. She gains access to their e-mail addresses and periodically conducts informal surveys after key, strategic newscasts unveiling new sets. Thus, the GM reinvents the typical virtual set technology to some degree, spending more than 10% of her budget on tweaking the technology's impact. Yet the process is still unfinished.

Clarifying.   Another 3 months pass, and Channel 23's viewership is up 50%—good but not great considering the loan amount. The GM confirms that the staff followed her plan correctly. The problem is that revenue has not kept pace with the audience increase. She talks individually with each ad sales account executive, stressing the value of making follow-up calls, emphasizing the telephone's role in the process, and urging staffers to talk up the new viewers to potential advertisers. The virtual set innovation has lost its newness and is embedded (via company work routines) in the station's on-air established routines. The GM must ensure all departments, including those not directly affected, take into account the technology's function in their work routines.

How adopters perceive technology is an important consideration. Such perceptions are categorized in terms of: (a) relative advantage (the degree to which employees perceive a technology as better than the idea it replaces), (b) *compatibility* (the degree to which employees perceive a technology as consistent with existing values, past experiences, and needs of potential adopters), (c) *complexibility* (the degree to which employees perceive a technology as relatively difficult to understand and use), (d) *trialability* (the degree to which employees perceive a technology may be experimented with before adoption is confirmed), and (e) *observability* (the degree to which nonadopters can see a technology's impact). Each perception or attribute can lead to good or bad consequences depending on the organization (Rogers, 1983).

Routinizing.   In this final step, the technology is firmly in place and is part of work. At Channel 23, newly hired camera and engineering staffers automatically receive a viewership-building manual and rewards for ideas such as placing promotional programs before the pertinent target markets. In this example, our GM selected a technology that controls work routines and dictates somewhat predictable outcomes.

The resulting interaction between employees and technology influences management's perceptions of the usefulness and adaptability of the technology. Employees gain experience that leads them to new and updated uses of the new technology. This in turn leads the organization to modify the desired level of use of the technology. Such a learning mechanism is self-adjusted by employees at a fairly slow pace. Organizational capabilities, development risks, and other factors shape management's perceptions, which appear as corporate cost–benefit ratios or project profitability (Stoneman, 1983; Strassmann, 1976).

Suppose Channel 23's GM wants to use the virtual set technology to produce new local sports and health shows as well as programs focusing on specific communities. The goal is to increase newscast viewership and audiences across its viewing area to eventually develop a reputation as a regional broadcaster. Reaching this goal requires market-savvy staffers who can think, create, and program with multiple markets in mind. The GM discovers such employees are in high demand and may culturally clash with old-style station staffers. She decides to train selected members of the current staff, who in turn train their colleagues.

The manager's perceptions lead her to redefine objectives and adjust technology's organizational role using various methods that reinforce or readjust the technological priorities. Relationships between technology and job content or between technology and organization structure are influenced by management assumptions, deductions, and objectives. Such influence is drastic or gradual depending on the circumstances (Child, 1972). Channel 23 may gradually use its marketing savvy, place a limit on programs to be created, or develop standards defining broadcast-worthy, quality programming.

Such routinization may lead to clarification of the technology's organizational meaning to employees or users. Clarification means that as the technology is integrated into the organization's day-to-day operation, its meaning gradually becomes clear to employees. The technology loses its newness and becomes embedded in company operations. Channel 23's virtual sets thus become part of the furniture, instead of some new toy, and an accepted or preferred way of doing business, rather than a change in the work routine.

Rules, new job descriptions, or rewards of some kind help bring about these changes. For example, one newspaper newsroom switched its structure to topic-team reporting because analyses showed that topics such as science, health, and medicine received inadequate coverage. Teams helped solve the problem, increasing such coverage; but the policy changes in coverage and news display led to adoption of a new set of news values (Russial, 1997).

Such adjustments are typical and fairly constant because managing is by nature adjustment. Typical managerial functions include planning, staffing, organizing, controlling, and motivating. Introducing technology requires the use of one or all of these functions at some time in the adoption process. The key is when to perform which function and knowing when—in the adoption process—to adjust. Nowhere is timing more important than when the adopted technology is the organizational product.

Adopting Technology as Product

Technology also is adopted as an end in itself or as the resultant product. Technology becomes more routine for managers who work in a constantly and rapidly evolving swirl of computer-driven innovations. Fierce competition in the media industry (Compaine & Gomery, 2000) leaves managers no alternative but to adopt technological products out of necessity. This necessity for constant technological change and its consequences creates uncertainty, making many media managers cautious and conservative in approach. For example, the Internet changes so quickly that authoritative-sounding advice should be taken with caution. Reckless managers risk losing face and profits quickly because the changing technology enables competitors to bring new products to market much faster than before. Savvy managers know there is a difference between the mechanically possible and the profitable.

Consequently managers must beware of market and internal organizational influences (such as the adoption process mentioned in the previous section) that accompany technology. Many managers are unaccustomed to thinking like marketers; they have previously concentrated their thoughts and management approach on internal operations and concerns. For example, in-depth interviews with 14 newspaper online executives showed they had difficulty defining their market, not to mention their primary competitor (Chyi & Sylvie, 2000).

A manager needs to adopt a broad approach, relying on as much information as possible, when considering a new product. Open system theory (Katz & Kahn, 1978) is a good tool for considering new products because it recognizes and charts the recurring organizational sequences of input/effort, change, output/production, and renewed input/effort. In other words, organizations bring in energy or materials from the environment, transform that energy/matter into some product, export that product into the environment, and then reenergize the organization from environmental sources. This allows the manager to see an organization (and thus its resulting product) as a collection of interrelated parts working in unison toward a common goal. The manager realizes that the system (organization) constantly interacts with its environment. That interaction yields a vast reservoir of relevant information with which to successfully manage. There are several implications for media managers adopting new, technologically driven products.

Strategy.   Staying competitive is always a challenge, but staying competitive in a constantly changing market is even more challenging. For media managers, this necessitates planning. Gershon (2001) said that such strategy included environmental scanning and strategy formulation.

Environment scanning means searching for significant marketplace events such as a corporate merger, an improvement in the technology (e.g., new software or enhanced capabilities), swings in consumer behavior, or some noteworthy social change (e.g., war). The manager also routinely surveys the external environment—competition, political landscape, regulatory structure, economy, technological development, and whatever affects customer behavior. Managers must continually monitor internal environmental factors ranging from operational procedures, work culture, relationships with other units within the company, to decision-making ability and everything in between.

Once the manager gathers this information, he begins to build, implement, and refine strategy. For telecommunications leaders, this is an ongoing process to make their products competitive (e.g., AOL-Time Warner must keep pace with MSN to maintain its Internet service market dominance). In practice, this means providing Internet customers with the latest in ever-more convenient services plus maintaining the capacity to forecast, plan, and develop such services while anticipating what the competition may do. Such companies continually manipulate the technology product into a positive position.

For example, *The New York Times'* online edition managers created a strategy to expand readership by leveraging the online medium to enhance and add value (Newman, 2002). Such leveraging included creating a continuous news desk to update stories from reporters and the wire. The newspaper tapped its rich archives to develop new, appealing offerings (such as Brooklyn Dodgers history and *The Times'* famed crossword puzzle) to extend established niches. Users were required to complete an electronic registration form. The information was used to offer personalized e-mail newsletters, build reader loyalty, and extend audience research capabilities. Even surround sessions were created, allowing advertisers to own a reader's online session by placing ads in major positions on every page viewed. Thus, the paper used sales and marketing innovation to generate revenue (Newman, 2002).

Strategy and planning, although useful tools, can be overdone. Because of rapidly evolving technologies, shifting customer wants, and nimble competitors, planning is often useless. Sometimes success is a matter of timing, and some plans may not be timely. For example, everyone knows about the Internet, but few remember its early 1980s forerunner, videotext, which essentially was the Internet without the Web. Then few people had computers (too expensive, with limited capabilities) and fewer had modems (too bulky and unreliable). Even fewer media companies tried to put their products online (too expensive and time-consuming because of the lack of standardized, cheap software). The few newspapers having videotext operations were seen as curiosities planning for a future they could not define rather than pioneers (Sylvie & Danielson, 1989). That is why media managers of technologically driven products must do more than simply strategize.

Resourcefulness.   Anyone can develop a strategy, but it takes a readily able manager to effectively implement it. A planned program of implementation (adequate staffing, budgeting, goals, and work environment) is needed. Plus, the media manager must create procedures and policies to support implementation (Gershon, 2001). This managerial skill is especially vital in the current convergent atmosphere transforming the media industry. Structural and technological boundaries that historically separated markets and industries were erased (Albarran, 1998), requiring managers to develop new options.

For example, where once local broadcast stations and newspapers fiercely competed for certain news, now there is cooperation and mutual promotion. Newspaper reporters appear on TV, TV news gets promoted in the newspaper, or both are promoted via a joint online venture. Editors and producers must be flexible in managing the times of their staffs; train reporters unfamiliar with print, broadcast, or online styles; and coax journalists leery of the convergence effort. Much energy is needed to maintain and nurture the partnership (e.g., Strupp, 2000).

This resourcefulness also extends to the willingness to examine honestly and openly core values and beliefs. TV station news selection is often based on ratings appeal and time allotments. Newspaper journalists operate under a sense of timeliness and urgency in selecting news. If TV station management views the relationship as a form of *scoop insurance* while dismissing in-depth, time-consuming investigative newspaper stories, this endangers the relationship. Editors and producers must recognize and deal with these different, conflicting values if convergence efforts are to succeed (Weaver, 2000).

Convergence also occurs within a medium. For example, TV stations traditionally broadcast a single signal to their viewing areas, and newspapers print their products for a local, geographically concentrated readership. Now multiple distribution is replacing single distribution due to the development of computers, digital and wireless technology, fiber optics, and the Internet (Albarran, 1998). To succeed, media managers must be resourceful and open to new ideas about process, people, and the product.

Sylvie and Witherspoon (2002) investigated how newspapers adapt to such change. When introduced, *USA TODAY* emphasized reader wants, color graphics and maps, shorter than normal stories, and detailed sports coverage. This represented a departure from central, traditional journalistic values and assumptions such as: Journalists know news/content better than readers, news is largely conveyed via text and an occasional photo, the best news is detailed, and other types of content (entertainment and sports) are lesser versions of news. Putting together this new type of newspaper was an adventure because it required a large group of journalists to change their thinking, work habits, and the end result. In essence, it required an uncommon type of journalist—one willing to risk change and view innovation as an opportunity, not a threat. Such vision, with the aid of other factors, helps change agents/managers complete their task. Sylvie and Witherspoon (2002) suggested journalists and other newspaper employees must evaluate resistance to create a longer term, more meaningful or strategic change (see Fig. 5.2) and to avoid change that is reactive, control-oriented, or based on inappropriate models. The issue then becomes, Sylvie and Witherspoon argued, how to create, properly communicate, and strategically implement the vision that enables successful change.

Vision.   Technologically driven products cannot be managed without forethought. Media visionaries continually maintain and update their understanding

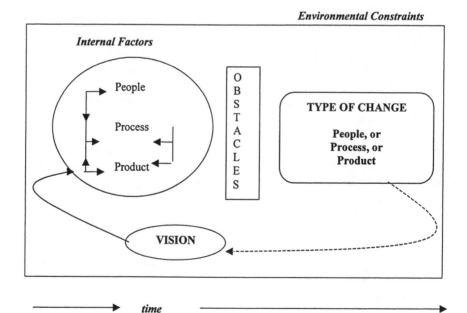

FIG. 5.2.   How newspaper change occurs.

of business/product objectives and "define their business' identity within whatever future comes" (Brown & Eisenhardt, 1998, p. 148). This is not the same as strategy or the visionary's tool or plan for executing the vision. Nor is it the same as seeing the future; even the media operations that used videotext in the 1980s were probably unaware they were working on the forerunner of the Internet.

Managers create visions not out of thin air, but through methodically thinking about the future and evaluating the wants and needs of the organization's client groups (Nanus, 1992). Managers must acquire or develop structures and processes to initiate and foster vision (Sylvie & Witherspoon, 2002). Recall the illustration of *The New York Times* online operation. Requiring users to electronically register allowed the organization to create a continuous flow of information about user habits, interests, and wants, creating an instant research and development (R&D) tool (Newman, 2002). This tool enabled *Times* managers to generate data and served as a dynamic source of constant feedback, which most open systems have in common (Katz & Kahn, 1978). *The Times* online management team used the feedback to brainstorm product possibilities and continually explore the online medium's potential to serve reader and advertiser interests. Vision became a natural, integral part of managing, enabling managers to "win tomorrow today" (Brown & Eisenhardt, 1998, pp. 127–129). The ability to constantly assess and evaluate the product permitted the online managers to take strategic, corrective action.

Brand Awareness. Enhanced, technologically driven products require media managers to understand they have a niche and an identity to maintain and expand. This works several ways. For example, local broadcasters have limited resources with which to cover and generate news. Whereas a typical small-city newspaper has one journalist per every 1,000 circulation, a corresponding local TV station might have one fifth that number. As a result, TV news directors constantly search for ways to supplement local reporting. One source is the station's affiliated network, which daily provides several hundred stories to local affiliates via satellite technology. A local station can expand its newscast, appearing to have its own regional, national, and international correspondents (Barkin, 2001), thus extending its brand.

The Internet allowed all traditional mass media to implement this brand extension. Most Web sites of local newspapers, radio, and TV stations emphasize certain distinctive types of content (Lin & Jeffres, 2001). Radio focuses on station/branding promotion; TV sites emphasize the same, plus feature e-mail, feedback, and search devices, making themselves into multisource repositories. Newspaper sites highlight community service, advertising, and news services.

Future media managers (or at least those driven by technology-sensitive products) must learn and gain advantage from the previous experience and current branding of the traditional product. For example, when video rental stores started replacing VHS-format videotaped films with films on digital video discs (DVDs), the stores were not simply trying to catch up to increasing sales of DVD players. They were learning from their experience with video customers as to what constitutes a comfortable viewing experience (Emling, 2002). That sort of thinking helped E.W. Scripps Co., traditionally viewed as a newspaper company, to branch into cable TV and start Home & Garden Television Networks (HGTV). HGTV's success led to the development of the Food Network and the Do It Yourself network (Moses, 2000). In summary, a brand-conscious media manager makes the future happen through a new technologically driven product, thus energizes the existing business (Brown & Eisenhardt, 1998).

Superior Supervising.   Finally, technology as product forces changes in the way managers handle employees, especially in the coming era of convergence (and experimentation). Cooperation is required when media converge to produce a collaborative, cross-promotional product. A national study of photo editors and Web directors of newspapers that publish online and paper editions found virtually no communication or coordinated coverage plan (Zavoina & Reichert, 2000). Managers like to talk about synergy, but *Chicago Tribune* editor Howard Tyner (Dedinsky, 2000, p. 45) noted it is easier said than done:

> You have to be hard-nosed about it. You'll run into a situation where the print people come up with an idea for a cable show, and they'll get their noses out of joint when the cable guys come back and say, "That's a really dumb idea and will never work." But the print guys will say, "How can they tell me?" Print people are not TV people and vice versa, and each looks at it in a different way.

Convergence often translates into more work for the convergee. How does a news director persuade her reporters to switch from the normal news cycle to a day of habitual online updating, several cable news appearances, sharing story information with print reporters, and producing their own stories for the last broadcast? Each 2-minute segment on the local TV news takes a newspaper reporter away from his regular work 2 to 5 hours a week (Rabasca, 2001).

Covington (1997) studied four TV stations operating in a technologically challenging market. Successful managers noted their subordinates' experiences with the product and found that what subordinates learned transformed them and helped the product. For example, experienced reporters and anchors were given increased responsibility so they did not feel caught in a dead-end job. Supervising and rewarding them required managers to use innovative approaches to motivation and evaluation. Kanter (2001) said the Internet transformed companies' internal, human aspects. Successful Web firms adopted the notion of community as an internal, organizing framework. Deep bonds developed among employees, who generally exhibited a willingness to do more because they were inspired by the company's ideals and collectively felt responsible to serve "in the cause of a greater good" (Kanter, 2001, p. 98).

Other Managerial Impacts

Open system theory teaches that managers must evaluate within the context of the operating environment. Context often indirectly shapes the technology via management perceptions about competition, market share, and legal regulations, as well as the organization's internal environment. These impacts result in change, which varies with the situation.

Level of Control. Technology changes the nature of the manager's work. Ironically, many companies adopt technologies to gain greater control over a variety of factors, including operations, the budget, the market, employee behavior, or product distribution. Although managers often see the technology as steering the process, it does not always work that way because technology has desirable or undesirable consequences.

For example, just as computerization gives a manager more time and control over deadlines and copy standards, it may make him overreliant on computers. He loses some control over his ability to work when the computers crash or electricity fails. A company that cherishes such control will experience resistance from employees who dread the inevitable new-and-improved version of the technology.

When a small public relations agency adds teleconferencing capability, the employees gain routine access to regular training without traveling. They acquire advanced skills—learning skills the agency manager alone once knew. This represents a loss to the manager, who relinquishes sole control of those skill areas. She now must place increasing trust in her staff—a fact that may prompt some control-minded executives to pause.

Functional Adjustment. Other managerial functions such as staffing, organizing, and motivating also experience the same types of changes discussed earlier. Nowhere is this more evident than in the case of the Web, where the onslaught of online publications taught managers to rethink their managerial actions to make their Web sites viable.

In general, a manager staffs by determining human resource needs: recruiting, selecting, and training employees. The Web compels the manager to recruit, select, and train employees to use the Web, the ease of which depends on the technology and company's personnel. Newspaper managers found that Web staffing varies widely depending on the site's mission and the newspaper's current Web expertise.

Consider one editor whose small-town daily started a Web page when print edition staff levels were down. There were no competent local Web writers, so the editor recruited staffers online to interview subjects by phone and communicate with the newspaper managers by Internet. Online stories were handled about the same way as print stories, with most being feature-oriented, trend-type pieces. The reporters explained their relationship with the newspaper to their sources. An editor assigning a story notified local sources that an online reporter may call.

Problems ensued from a lack of coordination of online assignments; no one knew which online writer was working on which story. The newspaper created an online editor position to confer with the reporters, make assignments, and promote their copy in daily news budget meetings. There also was low online reporter morale regarding source access. "People do not call me back, because it is long distance," one online reporter said. "They can't understand how somebody thousands of miles away could be writing a story for the (local) paper."

Adjustments followed because of management's initial view of the technology. Many managers see the Web and other technologies from the perspective of "What can it do *for* us?" rather than "What can it do *to* us?" The company's goals, objectives, and plans often predate equipment purchases and usually follow economic rather than managerial considerations. An effective media manager adjusts in a timely fashion.

EXTERNAL IMPACT

Technology's Impact on Markets

Now technology's effects on external environments are discussed. First the effects of one such external factor—markets—are discussed. Recall that technology is usually viewed as a tool or means toward some end. Media managers basically see technology as a way to change or create a market, but that change can vary.

Competition. Technology often allows entry into a market that most would have thought closed. For example, in the late 1990s, the smaller, less competitive wireless cable TV industry began to use digital compression to better compete with wired counterparts. Digital compression allows cable operators to jam more channels into less space for the same price as conventional wired cable TV. This opportunity was enhanced because many cable operators were slow to digitally equip their markets, already prone to signal outages. Add the existing interest by regional telephone companies and the cable market seemed poised for drastic change.

Similarly, the Internet changed market conceptions for electronic newspapers. No longer does a newspaper in San Jose have the safe, relative monopoly of its print edition when it starts an online version. The electronic edition allows Taiwanese newspapers to compete with the San Jose paper in the advertising and information markets for the large Chinese and Chinese-American audience (Chyi & Sylvie, 1998).

Yet technology can be so expensive that the price drives some companies out of business. To see how technology can diminish competition, compare two competing local TV stations in a market. Assume the leading station enhances its product (and market share) by investing several million dollars in capital improvements, such as a new and renovated studio, new cameras, new sound equipment, and a satellite newsgathering mobile van. The result is a clearer, crisper picture with better video footage, more colorful background graphics, and better facilities for producing high-quality local commercials. That leads to more viewers, which in turn reaps more advertisers, higher advertising rates, and more prestige. Unless the competing station has a large reserve fund or a good line of credit with local banks, it may never recover.

A similar event happened in the late 1980s due to a new newspaper's subscription-collection methods. *The St. Louis Sun*—an upstart, tabloid competitor to the incumbent *St. Louis Post-Dispatch*—attempted to generate subscribers using a pay-in-advance billing method. It relied on newsstand or single-copy sales techniques. Up to then, St. Louis residents paid for the newspaper after delivery, but *The Sun's* single-copy sales fell short of expectations and the paper failed after 7 months (Mueller, 1997).

Market Boundaries.   The Internet defies definition due to its ability to carry text, audio, and video. Advertisers want to know who is receiving their messages and how. They ask: When you view the Cable News Network (CNN) Web site and read a story, are you watching TV or surfing the web? If you find your favorite radio station's Web site, are you listening to radio, surfing the web, or both?

As media technologies converge, companies enter markets with greater ease and their products provide adequate substitutes for each other. This encourages market blurring, just as the development of radio and film increased competition for entertainment and the rise of cable and low-power TV stations delivered the same product as broadcast stations (Powers, 1990). Only by differentiating their products can these media create more distinct markets.

Revenue Alternatives.   Companies trying to weather economic downturns often attempt to diversify; new technologies make the decision somewhat easier and more attractive (e.g., Kanter, 2001). This chapter discussed the Internet at length because it has so many possibilities and the potential for so much impact. For example, newspapers form alliances and use advertising sponsors and/or subscriptions to generate revenue from their Web sites (Puritz, 1996). Although many media created a Web presence, there is doubt about the potential to raise revenue, especially as an electronic newspaper (Cameron et al., 1997). Managers know history is littered with financial technological failures, such as beta video recorders and many videotext experiments.

Yet potentially lucrative ventures exist. The future development of digital TV, which features pictures of higher resolution and clarity, allows the simultaneous transmission of news, sports, and financial statistics and software. The sale of high-definition TVs (HDTVs) will flourish as stations, networks, and program studios switch to the new digital standard. Stations can air several additional broadcasts using the higher production standard, which translates into more profits.

In short, the limit on revenue potential of new technologies is primarily dependent on the innovation and branding awareness of the manager. In the mid-1990s, Black Entertainment Television enhanced its branding mission of becoming "the preeminent provider of black entertainment" by taking profits from its cable TV beginnings and parlaying them into four cable channels, an online service, a magazine, a monthly newspaper insert, and a chain of theme restaurants. Also witness the craftiness of the person who bought video footage from British firms who run surveillance cameras (e.g., fire insurance companies, security firms, and various government agencies). Excerpts were edited and compiled into authentic, graphic scenes of unknowing couples, creating one of the most popular videotapes in Britain. The message: Technology enhances profit.

Consumer Behavior. New technology changes media consumption habits and behaviors. Consumers changed from reading news to watching it when TV was introduced (Fullerton, 1988). The Web allowed consumers to interact with the site host or the information by retrieving and sending messages. Before, the consumer was simply a passive listener/viewer/reader of information. Now consumers do not have to wait until the evening newscast for the current weather or short-term forecast. They need only find the local weather map on the Web or tune in to cable TV's Weather Channel. Cable and satellite technology provide more viewing choices so viewers became more selective in what they watch. The result is evident in the types of channels available: HBO, Cinemax, and Showtime (feature films); ESPN (sports); VH-1, TNN, and MTV (music); Lifetime (women's issues); Disney and Nickelodeon (children's programming); and Pay-TV (special events), to name a few.

Media firms particularly like technologically encouraged feedback. A Chicago TV station placed an unmanned camera in a kiosk at a nearby shopping mall, allowing consumers to comment about anything the station produces. Viewers can see themselves during newscasts or on the station's Web site. Virtually all newspaper Web sites provide either reporters' or editors' e-mail addresses; some provide online chat forums, where readers discuss news and issues (Gubman & Greer, 1997). Such devices are working: A survey found Internet use increased over time among the same group of respondents (Lindstrom, 1997).

Advertising and Promotion Strategies, Method, and Content. Remember the VCR? Viewers could fast forward past commercials in recorded programs, in effect losing the ad's audience. This led some advertisers to switch to shorter, more creative commercials to attract viewers' attention before they decide to fast forward. DVDs have enhanced this feature.

New technologies force advertisers' hands, but also allow them to be more selective about their audiences. Advertisers constantly search for new ways to target specific audiences using specific messages. Many technologies make this easier. For instance, push technology sends Web content to users' computers, rather than users' typing in Web addresses themselves, giving users what they want, when they want it. Similarly, the super VCR threatens to destroy the current advertising model in the broadcast industry. The device allows viewers to record programming as well as search and find the kind of broadcast programs they like. This may diminish the networks' capability to ensure a new program's success by placing it in a prime-time period. Such scheduling created artifices like *sweeps months*, when particularly attractive programs are broadcast to attract large audiences, increasing viewership and allowing networks to set advertising rates. The super VCR threatens that entire traditional approach (Lewis, 2000).

Advertising on the Web proved problematic for many media. Some question whether Web ads are as recognizable and memorable as print advertising (Sundar et al., 1997). Web audience measurement lacks standardization, making audience measurement and thus attracting advertisers more difficult.

On the positive side, because of the Internet's inherent targeting efficiencies, producers of some specialized sites tried to create classified advertising niches (e.g., in car buying and selling, real estate listings or employment services, or to use existing brands and spin them off into sites of their own; Newman, 2002). Others such as the regional Bell operating companies also have or plan similar vehicles to siphon off part of the local advertising market. A key driving force is national advertisers intent on reaching geographically targeted audiences using technology filters that compensate for the lack of focused content to buy (Chyi & Sylvie, 1998).

SUMMARY

To summarize, technology has internal and external impacts. Managers have to understand that technology demands adjustment. They must be sensitive as to how and when to manage. A media manager's job is to turn the technology to the company's advantage. This chapter examined managerial approaches to technology, the process of how a company uses or adopts technology, and how technology may affect media organizations and their markets.

The structural, technological-task, and sociotechnical approaches are each rooted in a slightly different managerial orientation. Each has its advantages and disadvantages. Most modern-day managers use some form of the sociotechnical approach. A media company adopts a technology for its own particular reasons. Then it introduces the technology to employees, who interact in various ways with the technology depending on the employee and nature of the task involved. Then management perceptions and employee reactions prompt a period of adjustment, ultimately leading to adoption or rejection of the technology.

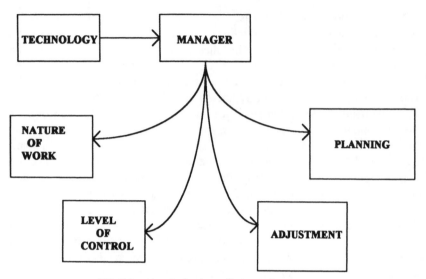

FIG. 5.3.   How technology affects media managers.

As a result, the technology affects managerial functions, including planning, organizing, staffing, motivating, and controlling operations (see Fig. 5.3). Overall technology causes a media manager to manage in an atmosphere of constant change and adjustment. How and when a manager acts has great impact on the company's future.

Case 5.1
Convergence Blues

As executive editor, Joe Chevalier runs the newsroom of *The Daily Grind*, the lone newspaper (circulation 75,000) in Matlock, a town of about 200,000. *The Grind* has just joined a venture with local TV station WOOO to cross-promote each other's news product. It is the first day that Joe will go live on WOOO's 5 p.m. newscast with a report on the city's light rail referendum. Earlier, Joe wrote a light rail story for the next morning's *Grind* and Grind Online, the paper's Web site, but WOOO producers asked Joe to provide insights in a short, on-air chat with anchorman Pete Looney. After the discussion, Looney reminds the audience to look for Joe's story "in tomorrow's *Daily Grind* and e-mail Joe and let him know what you think." Joe forgets to tell Looney that tomorrow Joe starts his vacation.

A week later, Joe came back to work with a feeling of foreboding. He knew he would have tons of e-mail messages to deal with—some harshly, some diplomatically, others quickly. After a quick, shocked look at the messages, Joe left his computer to see how the new venture had progressed.

Circulation and ratings reports suggest a small bounce in attention for the venture. WOOO's ratings are up about 0.9% compared with a year ago, while its 10 p.m. newscast continues to run second. *The Grind's* daily circulation rose about 0.5% over the week (to 75,456), and Sunday circulation dropped from 150,074 to 149,687. At Grind Online, meanwhile, page views were up 10% compared with last month.

Joe was more concerned about what he heard. Dorothy Dodson, the copy chief, said copy editors working on the floor right over the TV newsroom "have had to go out and buy some damn earplugs!" Raymond Trahan, a 10-year veteran at WOOO before he started at *The Grind* 3 years ago, is responsible for locating topics that work on TV, online, and in the paper. He also has to persuade everyone to work together. "It's like herding cats," Trahan told Joe. "I feel like the manager of the Cubs trying to coax all my right-handed batters to switch-hit. They just want to play their game and get paid."

Looney also had complained to Trahan that *Grind* reporters "looked like hell. Blue jeans and ties with ketchup stains don't look all that good" on camera. To boot, Trahan had had to remind several reporters to expect and plan for on-air shifts, as well as have two serious conversations with McCoy Metoyer, Looney's boss and WOOO news director, to "give more attention to the project." Finally, Grind Online was lobbying Trahan for more copy as well, especially video. Yet online content editor Amelia LaCour privately confided to Trahan that, "This pace is killing us; my staff's asking how much extra they're going to get paid and I keep stalling them."

Meanwhile Joe's e-mail tally had reached 257, much of it from strangers. That total is about six times what he normally receives in a day. Joe wanted to hear from everybody in his newsroom and WOOO's, as well as from the community about the new venture. He is glad the public has a hunger for greater contact to journalists, but he is not happy about the way things are working out with WOOO. His publisher, Lacadia Severin, wants a progress report in 2 days.

ASSIGNMENT

1. In what stage of the convergence adoption process is *The Grind*? E-mail adoption? Based on your interpretation of Joe's feelings, at which stage for each does Joe want to return? Which approach to adoption does Joe seem to embody on each technology?
2. What management changes is Joe experiencing or likely to experience? What functional adjustments will Joe have to make?
3. Research convergence and develop a list of alternatives for Joe to consider. What new revenue streams might be created in the process?
4. What can Joe do to improve the journalistic quality of *The Grind* and simultaneously make the news more marketable for Grind Online and WOOO?
5. What should Joe do about his e-mail dilemma?

Case 5.2
The Case of the Technology of Choice

You are the news director of KPUN, a small-market (75,000 households), network-affiliated TV station. Your three rivals—KONE, KFUN, and KTUN—have 25%, 22%, and 29% of the overall viewership, respectively, leaving you with 24%.

For years, KPUN was known as the hard-hitting, news-oriented station, with occasional top-notch investigative pieces, popular anchors, and a good sports staff. Your viewers tend to be slightly more educated than average. KONE, your nearest competitor, airs more tabloid-like pieces, emotional tearjerker stories, and sensational "gotcha" journalism. Meanwhile, KFUN and KTUN take middle-of-the-road approaches in news, but feature outstanding weather coverage. KTUN's edge is its highly popular anchors, who do a lot of community promotional work while emphasizing national and international news on the air. KFUN opts for a balance in local, national, and international news, but makes up for it by heavily promoting its total package. Each station has a Web presence, mainly as promotional vehicles for on-air content or as mechanisms to give viewers additional, nonstation-generated information. The sites typically contain the weather reports and radar (updated hourly) as well as each story (in text form) from that day's newscasts. The only other visuals are maps, charts, and still photos.

Your station GM just informed you that your budget would increase 8% over this year. You expect it to increase again the following year. About two thirds of any increase you receive will be used to upgrade equipment and/or facilities, but a mandate comes with the extra money. The GM wants an increase to second or even first place in the ratings given the closeness of the competition. You reply that an 8% budget increase is not much to go on, but she says it is comparable to what competing local newsrooms are getting. While revenues have grown, costs have kept pace, so there is no hope of hiring additional journalists. You must use current employees more efficiently to produce something distinctive that will put you at or near the top.

You decide to shop for a new newsroom system. After reading industry publications and giving the situation much thought, you narrow your choices to the following:

1. A wire service production system:
   - *A drag-and-drop interface that most likely will be adopted by major U.S. TV organizations by mid-year*. It uses a briefing button to retrieve information. The reporter types in or highlights a word and instantly accesses a catalogue of related material, including wire stories, pictures, sound clips, and maps. It also can retrieve thumbnail video images and feature links to playback and machine control for robotic cameras, still stores, prompters, character generators, and captioning systems. Training on installations has been surprisingly simple, vendors say. The system can be

integrated with the wire service's total NewsFocus product. The yearly fee of NewsFocus is based on market size, which is about $9,000 for KPUN.

2. A multitask, stand-alone system:
   - *A product that touts itself as a "lens to transmitter" technology, although still not highly adopted by other stations.* The system is designed to handle text composition, audio and video browsing, and Web publishing. As news feeds come in, the system stores them in low resolution on a server and in full resolution on tape. The user can then browse the low-resolution video and compose an edit decision list that he can then use in a tape-to-tape suite. With workstation, server software, and browse server, price can vary from $25,000 to $100,000 depending on what the customer wants to accomplish.

3. A powerful upgrade of a system KPUN already has:
   - *This system uses a database to track scripts, e-mail, wires, and archival data; allows direct access to Internet file exchange; and is the next generation of a popular system used nationwide.* It will not edit video, but allows the user to view video stored on the video server and adjust the start and endpoints for playback, which comes in handy for quick cuts. This system can be interfaced with almost any other system. The core software costs about $150 per workstation seat for the servers and $400 per seat for the database software; the software costs about $4,000. The seat prices are expected to fall after the first 10 or 15 clients.

4. An upgrade of a journalist workstation product:
   - *This product has an additional Web publisher application and a backup server; it is made by a company with a good reputation and that offers an integrated system, of which this product is a part.* The server allows reporters to perform cuts-only editing and features an undermonitor display that shows the story slug and the piece's running time. The vendor sells the system as a package with its local area network browser, which converts finished video clips to low-resolution files and makes them available to any nonediting station (including producers and news directors) on the network. A four-channel model costs about $100,000, and the workstations run $20,000 apiece.

ASSIGNMENT

1. Choose one of the four options and make a convincing case for it to the GM. Why would the option you choose be a better alternative than the other options?

2. Which technology would most help KPUN vault into the local ratings lead? Which would be least likely to help? Why?

3. Develop a projected budget of the prior options and the possible spin-off costs they may prompt. Do a costs–benefits analysis chart and present the findings to the class, which will act as your GM.

4. Should a small TV station bother to upgrade its Web presence? Is it cost-effective given computer adoption rates in small markets? Should competition drive or direct that entry? What are the adoption ramifications of creating an interactive Web page for a TV station? Would it be an improvement over the four options already under consideration? How would it change a news director's job? What kinds of Web site services and/or content would enable KPUN to set itself apart from competitors?

Case 5.3
Problems in PR

The Mark V. Looney Center for Education (LCE) faces a problem found across the country: how to integrate constantly advancing technology and electronic communication into its news and information service responsibilities. The LCE first went online a few years ago, but its site was rudimentary at best because its two-headed mission—to help improve reading and language arts performance in the state's public schools—made communication difficult. Gig Byte, the LCE's communications computer systems administrator, was talented, Web savvy, and highly energetic. However, he was constantly at his wits end in trying to get the center's internal departments to coordinate their sites.

The LCE started 15 years ago thanks to a huge grant from the Looney family. The LCE used the grant (and others from private and public funders) to achieve its mission. However, organizationally, the LCE was a bit chaotic. It was staffed by four divisions: (a) a research group that focused on theoretical and practical issues in reading and language arts; (b) a language arts group that conducted consulting and seminars across the state for schools and school districts; (c) a product division that developed reading and language arts-related materials (posters, instructional kits, handbooks, etc.) for teachers; and (d) a communications division that maintained each division's Web sites, as well as producing LCE publications such as an organizational newsletter and handling LCE public relations. All divisions were overseen by the LCE director's office, headed by Magney Tism, a well-known scholar and entrepreneurial thinker in reading and language arts who left the day-to-day operations to her associate, Chaim Able.

The center is an affiliated think tank of a local university. LCE's funding history and vision are such that each division, with the exception of communications, operated somewhat autonomously, coming together only at the behest of Tism, who seems to embody the center's mission and is, for all effects, its soul. Byte is the newest staffer; he works for communications head Chayne Jagent, who has the unenviable task of trying to keep track of what each division does while having no authority over the divisions. Chayne is often frustrated that Chaim will not tackle the LCE's disorganization woes headfirst, choosing instead to concentrate on policy matters and relationships with current and possible funders. Chayne is especially upset because the lack of organization makes his job more difficult.

Gig is feeling Chayne's pain. Gig often looks at the center's Web site and sees disarray. Each division has its own Web staffer who produces content. Gig has tried to work with these staffers, but has been unsuccessful in getting them to adopt a common vision and approach. Each division site uses different graphics, organizational styles, and writing styles, making each site unique; their only common thread is that they all link to the main LCE site, maintained in modern, efficient fashion by Gig. Still Gig only has second-hand information about what goes on in those divisions, often finding things out through the newsletter, which is produced by fellow communications staffer Hack Rider.

Failure to unify all sites hurts LCE's reputation and impedes its ability to disseminate a consistent image. Several computer problems have arisen, including server backup and problems where the network had to be taken down. Usually Gig found a quick but temporary solution. In the last 2 years, the office spent about $20,000 for new computers, printers, software, and wiring. However, only $2,000 is budgeted for technical support this year, and a systems analyst line item was permanently deleted from the center's budget.

Last week, Magney established an ad hoc Web team comprised of budget head Doll Ars, Chaim, Gig, Chayne, and the head of the other divisions. Magney is miffed that the LCE's image is relatively unknown outside of the university, teachers, and principals. "We don't get our due," Magney said. "The Web site needs an overhaul. I want to see us and the stuff we do on the news." No one in the LCE has formal public relations training.

The center's original homepage did not include a revised mission statement for the office, although one has been in the development stage since the center changed its name 3 years ago. The site contains no information about the LCE's mission or goals, nor any explanation as to how its divisions work. There is no link for the general public, much less for the news media. The center sends all its releases through the university's overworked and understaffed public relations office, which rarely, if at all, touts the center on the university's main Web site.

You—a faculty member of the university's management department—have been asked to serve as a consultant to help solve the problem.

ASSIGNMENT

1. What kind of strategic planning should the center do in regard to this problem?
2. What should be done about the agency's online presence? Should it continue or be terminated? Why or why not?

3. Should the ad hoc team be restructured? Should the team be responsible for the site's construction and content? Who should be responsible for updating and maintaining the site?

4. How can the agency make the best use of its current resources in solving this problem? What should be redone to rebuild staff confidence in the site and in its online capabilities? How important is the agency's mission to the Web site development?

6

REGULATION
AND SELF-REGULATION

Laws affecting the media change constantly. This chapter discusses how laws affecting media firms have changed and instances when legal advice should be sought. The best, most basic way to manage legal issues is to understand the laws. Laws more pertinent to media management are introduced. The goal of this chapter is to outline a few examples of practices and principles that all media managers must apply to avoid legal problems. Some online resources are identified.

This chapter is not intended to be a comprehensive discussion of all areas of law that might affect media firms. However, it highlights a few areas of contemporary interest and focuses on the prevention and response to legal actions. Readers interested in a specific legal area (e.g., libel, privacy, etc.) should review the appropriate legal resources (such as the *2002 AP Stylebook and Briefing on Media Law* [Goldstein, 2002], *Mass Communication Law in a Nutshell* [Carter, Dee, & Zuckman, 2000], *First Amendment Law in a Nutshell* [Barron & Dienes, 2000], *Internet Law for the Business Lawyer* [Reiter, Blumenfeld, & Boulding, 2001], *Intellectual Property and Unfair Competition in a Nutshell* [McManis, 2000], *Intellectual Property-Patents, Trademarks, and Copyright in a Nutshell* [Miller & Davis, 2000], and *Mass Communication Law: Cases and Comment* [Gillmor, Barron, & Simon, 1998].

THE CHANGING NATURE OF LAWS AFFECTING THE MEDIA

Media managers must expect that the media industry landscape will change dramatically and regularly in the future. They will make decisions pitting the business interests of their owners against the public interest. Recent events demonstrate how laws, rules, and regulations affecting the media change often.

For example, the Telecommunications Act of 1996 changed the broadcast, cable, and telephony industries by eliminating or changing radio and TV station ownership limits, extending broadcast license terms, simplifying the license renewal process, deregulating cable rates, and increasing fines for obscenity. By 1997, the Supreme Court struck down a provision of the Telecommunications Act. The Communications Decency Act of 1996 had imposed criminal penalties for transmitting indecent or patently offensive material over computer networks to minors (Childs, 1997; Mauro, 1997).

Section 202(h) of the Telecommunications Act of 1996 requires the Federal Communications Commission (FCC) to review its media ownership rules every 2 years (*www.fcc.gov/mb/policy/own.html*). (An outline of existing rules can be found at the FCC's Web site [*www.fcc.gov/ownership*] and the Media Access Project's Web site [*www.mediaaccess.org/programs/diversity*].) Ownership rules are a major industry concern because relaxing them would allow media companies to buy a variety of media outlets and gain economies of scale in news operations, for example. Yet having a limited number of media owners could result in too few companies controlling the flow of information, including news and entertainment, thus hampering the robust marketplace of ideas (Hickey, 2002).

The ownership rules "have been at the center of a legal and political firestorm" (Dreazen, 2002, p. A2). The FCC is undertaking a wide-ranging review of the major ownership rules including: (a) the TV ownership limit, whereby one broadcaster's stations cannot reach more than 35% of U.S. viewers; (b) the TV duopoly rule, which limits the number of stations a company can own in the same market; (c) the cross-ownership rules, which limits ownership of radio and TV stations, as well as newspapers and TV stations in a single market; and (d) the dual-network rule, which prohibits companies from owning more than one of the four major networks (Dreazen, 2002; Halonen, 2002a, 2002b).

The Supreme Court ruled in *Associated Press v. U.S.* (1945) that the widest possible dissemination of information from diverse and opposing sources was central to public welfare. Hickey (2002) said if media ownership rules are eliminated or relaxed further, fewer companies could control the content of news and entertainment programming. The Media Access Project (*www.mediaaccess.org*) identified the results of radio consolidation after the passage of the Telecommunications Act of 1996. The number of radio owners declined 25% by 2001. In 1996, Westinghouse owned 85 stations and was the largest radio owner. By 2001, Clear Channel was the largest owner with about 1,200 stations. In a few years, individual owners could own 4,000 stations or more.

Hickey (2002) identified potential problems with joint ownership of newspapers and TV stations in the same market. The number of independent newspaper owners would likely decrease, reducing the number of diverse news voices. These jointly owned newspapers and stations could be unlikely to investigate each other, self-censoring themselves to protect their owners' interests.

Hickey (2002) said coverage of merger issues is inadequate because the companies that will profit from deregulation own news organizations. He identified the worst-case scenario that could stem from eliminating media ownership rules:

> ... some transnational company that knows little and cares less about your community, and whose main allegiance is to its stockholders and advertisers, will own your local daily and weekly newspapers, all your television and radio stations, the cable system, the Internet service provider, several of the national networks that serve you, your local video stores and movie houses, many of the magazines and books you read, and all of the sports teams in your area. That would allow endless cross-promotions of the owner's interests, and probably very little hard news about anything having negative impact on advertisers or on the company itself. Everything you read or see, every opinion, every image, and every jot of information would arrive through one corporate filter (p. 54).

Owners, publishers, and general or station managers, as well as editors, news directors, and reporters, must expect to face thorny decisions regarding ownership issues. Managerial decisions that support a diversified information marketplace could result in difficult, potentially job-threatening, and legally complex consequences. Yet the future of a strong, independent, and free press is at stake.

GENERAL AREAS OF LEGAL CONCERN

Antitrust

The Supreme Court affirmed in *Associated Press v. United States* (1945) that antitrust laws apply to the media. The Newspaper Preservation Act (NPA) of 1970 gives certain daily newspapers a limited exemption from antitrust laws. Two newspapers within a market may form a joint operating agreement (JOA) when one is in probable danger of financial failure. In 2001, about 1 year after *The Denver Post* and *Rocky Mountain News* merged their business operations, the News narrowed its losses 34% to $15.9 million. The News had lost $24.1 million in 2000 (Accola, 2002).

Under a JOA, the newspapers' advertising, circulation, production, and administrative departments are merged, whereas their editorial departments are kept separate. Proposed JOAs must be approved by the U.S. Attorney General, although administrative hearings are often held before a decision is made. Readers interested in additional information on antitrust might read Gillmor, Barron, and Simon (1998) and Lacy and Simon (1992).

Libel

Carter, Dee, and Zuckman (2000) said libel and slander are the publication by one person of a defamatory statement that identifies the person defamed and is made to that person and at least one other individual, who reasonably understand that the statement is defamatory. Defamatory statements injure the reputation or create an ill opinion of an organization or living person, and they expose one to public shame, ridicule, and/or hatred.

Defamatory statements include words like *murderer, cheat,* or *thief.* Typical defamation categories are dishonesty, being accused of a crime, engaging in immoral behavior, professional incompetence or misconduct, financial irresponsibility, or engaging in child or substance abuse. Trade libel includes making disparaging statements about a product or service. Defamation is generally governed by state laws, but is subject to the limitations imposed by the First Amendment (Barron & Dienes, 2000; Carter, Dee, & Zuckman, 2000; Goldstein, 2002; for a more detailed explanation of libel, consult Gillmor, Barron, & Simon [1998] or the most recent *AP Stylebook*).

Libel includes more permanent types of communications, such as printed material, photographs, paintings, motion pictures, and signboards, whereas slander includes less tangible forms like the spoken word, gestures, and sign language. The only complete and unconditional defense to a libel civil action is that the facts stated are provably true. A second defense is absolute or qualified privilege. *Absolute privilege* means that certain people in certain circumstances can make libelous comments without fear of being sued. These include most public records and official proceedings, judicial proceedings, and legislative proceedings. To win a libel case, a public official or figure must prove actual malice or that the reporter or editor acted with reckless disregard or knew the published facts were false. A private person must show that the reporter or editor was negligent or did not act with due diligence (Carter, Dee, & Zuckman, 2000).

McKee (2002) said name-calling, sophomoric comments, and/or comments made in bad taste are not necessarily libel when discussing an issue of public interest. Two morning talk-show hosts and their producer ribbed an employee of another station who was an unsuccessful contestant on the TV show, "Who Wants to Marry a Multimillionaire?" She was ridiculed for competing with 50 other women for a $35,000 wedding ring, a new car, and the chance to marry a complete stranger. The hosts called the contestant a *chicken butt, big skank,* and *local loser,* but these comments were not found to constitute libel. Still, prudent media managers must consider whether to encourage employees to publish or broadcast these kinds of comments.

Potentially serious problems may arise regarding libel and online publication in the future. Online publishers could be sued for defamation anywhere an online article is read. A serious chilling effect may result as publishers might avoid posting material that could potentially offend someone on their Web sites. Media managers may have to check the libel statutes in various localities before publishing stories online that could potentially defame people in those areas. Further, U.S. courts are generally viewed as more protective of free speech rights than courts in other nations. Any media outlet that publishes material potentially harming the reputation of a non-U.S. citizen should have its counsel review libel and defamation laws in that person's nation before publication (Kaplan, 2002).

Advise reporters and editors that the plaintiff in a libel case will inquire about their state of mind when trying to prove they were reckless or knew what they were publishing was false. Tell employees to keep memos in their files demonstrating how care was taken and why they believed the story was fair and accurate. Have at least one newsroom supervisor keep current on state and federal libel developments. Instruct reporters to keep careful notes, have more than one source and/or obtain supporting documents for potentially libelous statements, and obtain the appropriate court documents (such as complaints, cease-and-desist orders, and judgments) when allegations are made. Repeat words like *alleged* and *allegation* in a story when legal action is pending. Avoid publishing a story based on an official's intent to charge or investigate. It may be better to wait until charges are filed. Finally, have a lawyer review potentially libelous stories before publication (Gillmor et al., 1998; Goldstein, 2002).

Although prudence and care make good sense, always consider whether the public interest is best served by publication or broadcast. Lawyers may evaluate the cost of a lawsuit rather than its chances for success or whether self-censorship serves the public. A media manager may have to take a stand against a frivolous lawsuit intended to discourage free speech.

Privacy

The right of privacy encompasses the right to live one's private life free from publicity (Keeton, 1984). Privacy entitles an individual to prevent the use of or interference with personal and intimate aspects of life. Such invasions presumably have a negative effect on a person's psychological well-being (Gillmor, Barron, & Simon, 1998).

Carter, Dee, and Zuckman (2000) identified the four aspects of privacy: (a) appropriation of another person's name or likeness, (b) unreasonable intrusion on another person's seclusion, (c) placing another person in a false light before the public, and (d) unreasonable publicity about another person's private life. The right to privacy is forfeited when a person is voluntarily or involuntarily involved in a news event. A journalist is typically protected when writing about someone involved in a matter of legitimate public interest. Yet unreasonable publication of material with no current newsworthiness that reveals embarrassing private facts is typically unprotected. News managers should exercise care, discretion, and good taste when considering whether to publish a story on a private person.

Carter, Dee, and Zuckman (2000) said federal law prohibits the interception of conversations carried over a wire and nonwire conversations where privacy is expected. In 1994, this protection was extended to cellular and wireless communication. Federal law prohibits unauthorized access or tampering with information storage facilities for electronic communications services. Journalists who wiretap a phone conversation, bug a room where a meeting is held, or access a private phone mail system may be liable.

A manager should be familiar with state privacy laws, ensure that at least one newsroom supervisor keeps up with federal and state privacy statues, and educate editors and reporters about them. In some states, it is legal for reporters to conceal audiotape recorders when talking to news sources, yet other states outlaw concealed audio recording. It is illegal to use a hidden video camera to record people without their consent in some states (Carter, Dee, & Zuckman, 2000).

The use of computerized records and Internet access appears likely to intensify the conflict between open access to records and individual privacy. Delta and Matsuura (2002) said any firm that captures and uses personal data regarding Internet users or their activities should disclose how those data would be used in advance. Firms should develop clear personal data, consumer communications, and disclosure privacy policies. Ensure that once the policies are implemented, they are applied rigorously and disclosed consistently with all legal requirements. Require a valid legal order before customer information is disclosed and notify customers of such orders before disclosing their data. That allows customers to challenge the release of information before it occurs.

Protecting privacy raises special concerns for marketers or others targeting or creating Web pages for children on the Internet. The Children's Online Privacy Protection Act requires those who knowingly collect personal information from children younger than 13 years old to obtain verifiable consent from the child's parent or guardian and provide an on-line description of its privacy policies and practices before collecting that information. Delta and Matsuura (2002 see p. App. 1–2) said such privacy policies must, at minimum, identify the types of information to be collected, describe how that information will be used, and identify all third parties who have access to that information. (More information and Internet links on protecting the privacy of children are found in the Regulatory and Self-Regulatory Electronic Resources section at the end of this chapter.)

PREVENTING LEGAL PROBLEMS

There are general principles and procedures that media managers can institute to minimize legal problems. Generally all communications and agreements among supervisors, employees, and those outside the organization should be documented. The following section on performance evaluation provides documentation guidelines that can be adapted and applied to other areas.

Performance Management and Evaluation

One of the first things a new manager must do is discover whether employees know how their performance is measured. It is important to remember that any document a manager prepares about an employee could potentially be used as evidence in a trial. Zachary (2000) said performance evaluations could lead to wrongful discharge, libel, defamation, discrimination, and/or intentional infliction of emotional distress lawsuits.

Regular, formal communication from supervisors with their employees about performance is simply good business practice. Documenting performance problems using factual information supports a firm's legitimate, nondiscriminatory reasons for rewarding, disciplining, or firing an employee. Try to standardize performance criteria and measurement across the organization, if possible, to enable comparisons between employees in various departments and demonstrate that standards and procedures are applied consistently (Fentin, 2002; How to Align, 2002; How to Remake, 2002; Two Ways, 2002; Zachary, 2000).

Notify employees and educate them about how to prepare for evaluations long before they occur. Develop organizational goals, allowing managers, supervisors, and employees to participate in setting them. Meet with your employees to discuss the written goals, performance measurements, and deadlines of evaluations. Explain what rewards may be given for exceptional performance and the penalties for unsatisfactory performance. When finalized, communicate goals to supervisors and employees and incorporate them into performance evaluations (How to Align, 2002). This maximizes the likelihood of achieving organizational goals and provides objective performance criteria that apply equally to all employees.

Give every employee a copy of the instructions and forms used to evaluate their performance. Include in writing that there are no valid oral employee agreements in all application forms, employee manuals, and Web sites (Thompson, 2002). That way managers and employees know that promises made verbally are not binding. Post all forms, manuals, and employment documents on the company's Web site and inform all employees when any revisions are made. Employees should not be surprised when new criteria are used or new managers with new expectations evaluate them (Two Ways, 2002).

Conduct formal, written evaluations of all employees annually on objective criteria such as their ability to perform essential job skills. State such expectations clearly and directly on performance evaluation forms. Consider including feedback from managers as well as employees' peers and staff (Fentin, 2002; Hinkle, Hensley, Shanor, & Martin, 2002; How to Align, 2002; How to Remake, 2002; Two Ways, 2002).

Use specific measures with specific criteria to avoid the halo effect of giving high evaluations overall to favorite employees or those who perform well only in a few areas (How to Remake, 2002). Include several measurement options on evaluation forms such as *outstanding, very good, good, needs improvement, unsatisfactory, not observed,* and *not applicable.* A manager rating a reporter's performance could rate each of the following job duties and skills using these options: (a) story accuracy; (b) ability to meet deadlines; (c) newsgathering skills; (d) ability to suggest and develop story ideas; (e) ability to develop sources; (f) level of awareness and knowledge of the assigned beat and community; (g) breadth of coverage, including coverage of minorities and minority viewpoints; (h) writing skills, including story organization, importance, style, and word selection; (i) ability to communicate and work with the public, supervisors, and other staff members; (j) ability to respond to constructive criticism or feedback; and (k) overall performance (including other relevant factors, accomplishments, or areas for improvement not covered in a through k). Using measurement options to rate performance allows managers to distinguish objectively between employees performing at the highest, satisfactory, and unsatisfactory levels as well as those performing at the highest levels on some tasks, but unsatisfactorily at other tasks (Fentin, 2002; Skoler, Abbott, & Presser, 2002; Two Tools, 2002).

Skoler, Abbott, and Presser (2002) said to update job descriptions annually. Ask specific questions to develop new descriptions like (How to Remake, 2002; Two Tools, 2002): (a) Why was the job created? (b) How should a person doing this job spend his or her time? (c) What are the three most important duties of this position? (d) What does it take to succeed at this job? and (e) What is the easiest way to determine whether this job is done well?

Then develop a preliminary job description, allowing all affected employees and supervisors to agree or disagree with the list of job duties and suggest revisions in writing. Have all appropriate supervisors and employees acknowledge in writing that they reviewed and received the final job description after it is approved. This educates all parties about job duties, helps prevent inaccurate impressions about what a job entails, and assists employees and supervisors in dealing with disputes over job duties during or after performance evaluations (Hinkle, Hensley, Shanor, & Martin, 2002).

Managers should provide specific comments and examples in performance reviews. State performance accurately, clearly, and concisely because it is in everyone's best interest to do so (Fentin, 2002; Skoler, Abbott, & Presser, 2002). Managers might decide on a central message for the evaluation and then support that appraisal when completing the evaluation form. Provide objective, quantifiable, and factual information. Include descriptions of incidents in performance evaluations where employees acted above or below expectations to avoid subjective judgments based on personality or sympathy rather than performance (How to Remake, 2002; Two Tools, 2002).

If an evaluation reveals that an employee lacks necessary job skills, provide and document training in those skills. Document and offer continuous feedback to every employee who performs below expectations. Also consider how employees achieved results. For example, if one account executive surpasses sales goals using unethical, inappropriate, or counterproductive methods, do not reward the behavior (How to Align, 2002).

Treat performance problems consistently across evaluations to avoid discrimination claims. For example, if two employees are often tardy, document and address tardiness the same way in both evaluations. Consistency in evaluation helps protect a firm from wrongful discharge actions (Hinkle, Hensley, Shanor, & Martin, 2002; How to Align, 2002; How to Remake, 2002; Skoler, Abbott, & Presser, 2002; Two Tools, 2002).

Ideally, a performance evaluation enables a manager to set goals for the employee to accomplish before the next review. These goals could include problems, or below-par performance to eliminate, as well as accomplishments to achieve. Include a written acknowledgment signed by the employee and supervisor to work toward those goals. Allow the employee to sign a different form acknowledging disagreement with the evaluation and/or goals. Give the dissatisfied employee an opportunity to respond. This is fair to employees and prevents a later claim that they were unaware of the evaluation (Hinkle, Hensley, Shanor, & Martin, 2002; Skoler, Abbott, & Presser, 2002).

Training Managers to Conduct Performance Evaluations

Another important aspect of performance evaluation is to effectively train managers how to conduct them. Hinkle, Hensley, Shanor, and Martin (2002) and Skoler, Abbott, and Presser (2002) said employers should provide clear instructions to performance evaluators, train them to eliminate bias, and monitor the process while evaluations occur. Performance appraisal training usually takes about a day and includes various practice exercises on the typical evaluation errors that managers make. Provide clear, written instructions explaining the purpose and importance of evaluations, acceptable work behaviors, results to be expected for each employee, and why they should be fair, honest, and accurate. Emphasize firmly and repeatedly during training that stereotyping or bias is not tolerated. Include information about dealing with potential wrongful termination or equal employment opportunity problems.

Train all managers on the proper way to conduct evaluations and common errors to avoid. For example, instruct managers to avoid rating employees who resemble them or who they like more highly than other employees. Resist the tendency to rate all employees in the middle of the scale, especially when performance clearly deserves a lower or higher rating. Be careful not to rate an employee against peers rather than objective job standards. Avoid attributing employee failures to factors they control and successes to external factors. Resist the tendency to give recent minor events more importance than major events that occurred months earlier. Instead continually keep notes in a file of employee performance throughout the evaluation period to refer back to when conducting the evaluation (Hinkle, Hensley, Shanor, & Martin, 2002; How to Remake, 2002; Skoler, Abbott, & Presser, 2002; Two Tools, 2002; Zachary, 2000).

Avoid vague comments like, "Jane's performance is improving" or "Joe needs to work harder." State exactly why performance is improving or identify the nature of the performance problem factually. For example, say the employee was tardy 15 times during the evaluation period. Do not speculate about the causes of performance problems to avoid legal pitfalls (Hinkle, Hensley, Shanor, & Martin, 2002; How to Remake, 2002; Skoler, Abbott, & Presser, 2002; Two Tools, 2002).

A manager who cannot be honest with employees cannot generate positive results, lacks credibility, and potentially creates legal problems. Sometimes a manager genuinely likes and does not wish to upset an employee by a poor evaluation. Pairing a poor rating with an unnecessary positive comment to spare the employee's feelings is unwise. Refrain from tempering bad with good (or vice versa) because it makes evaluations seem arbitrary (Hinkle, Hensley, Shanor, & Martin, 2002; Skoler, Abbott, & Presser, 2002; Zachary, 2000).

Identify supervisors who try to avoid confronting personnel problems. Avoiding unpleasant confrontations in the hope that future performance will improve if good ratings or positive reinforcement is given now can create legal problems for a firm. Excessive leniency falsely raises and then deflates an employee's expectations. More important, employees who are unaware of their shortcomings cannot correct their deficiencies (Hinkle, Hensley, Shanor, & Martin, 2002; Skoler, Abbott, & Presser, 2002; Zachary, 2000).

Have all supervisors sign a form acknowledging they read all job descriptions and reviewed and complied with all performance evaluation guidelines and instructions every time they conduct evaluations. Place each form in the manager's personnel file. Establish central monitoring of performance reviews to ensure managers rate employees consistently and bias does not creep into the process. Have each manager's supervisor review evaluations before they are given to employees. Train these upper managers to look for potential legal problems, inconsistencies in employee ratings, inappropriate or personal comments, and unintended meanings in the evaluations of lower level managers they review (Hinkle, Hensley, Shanor, & Martin, 2002; How to Align, 2002; How to Remake, 2002; Skoler, Abbott, & Presser, 2002; Two Tools, 2002).

Require managers to initiate performance conversations to ensure a continuing dialogue. All written performance evaluations, especially unfavorable ones, should be followed by face-to-face conversations with the employee. Two managers should be present. Require the employee to acknowledge in writing that she or he received the written performance evaluation and the meeting was held to discuss it. Managers should document what they discussed and file the notes with the evaluation. Allow employees who disagree with an evaluation to make written comments and appeal within an appropriate time period (Fentin, 2002; Skoler, Abbott, & Presser, 2002; Two Ways, 2002).

Progressive Discipline

Managers must be familiar with appropriate procedures for disciplining and, if necessary, firing employees when unsatisfactory evaluations occur. Using progressive discipline (or using an oral warning, written warning, then dismissal) gives employees a fair chance to correct performance before termination and provides documentation for employers who must fire employees for legitimate, nondiscriminatory reasons (Fentin, 2002). Wrongful-termination lawsuits may result from a failure to document progressive discipline. A progressive discipline system should begin with recruitment and continue through orientation, training, performance evaluation, and supervision (Falcone, 1997).

Fentin (2002) and Falcone (1997) provided documentation guidelines for implementing progressive discipline. Begin with private, informal counseling about the unsatisfactory performance or behavior. The manager should document the conversation, including when it took place and what was discussed, and place a memo in the employee's personnel file.

A verbal warning is typically the next step. Two managers (e.g., the employee's direct supervisor and the head of that department) should meet in private with the employee, discuss the performance problems, provide specific steps for correcting them, and give goals and deadlines to complete the corrections. The two supervisors and the employee sign a notice documenting that the employee received the verbal warning. Only other employees who actually need to know about the warning to conduct their jobs are informed, but directed to keep it private. That way the employee's privacy is protected and the company does not risk defamation charges.

If the verbal warning fails, give the employee a written warning based on objective performance criteria that include specific examples about the problem or apparent inability to perform at minimum standards. The document should explain why the performance was unsatisfactory, suggest a way to improve, establish a disciplinary time period for improvement, and outline the consequences of failing to improve. For nonprobationary workers, the disciplinary period might be 30 days for a poor performer's work, 60 days for an underachieving sales person, or 90 days for a tardiness or absenteeism problem. Again hold the meeting in private with two managers present. Both must witness the employee signing the written warning to acknowledge its receipt. Both must document what was said in the meeting and place the notes, a copy of the written warning, the signed acknowledgment, and all related materials in the employee's file.

Give the employee the opportunity to respond verbally and in writing. Use the same type of document for any employee who makes a similar infraction to ensure consistency of discipline. If one employee received a reprimand or discipline for a particular infraction, all employees making the same infraction should receive the same discipline.

Falcone (1997) provided examples of how to write up progressive disciplinary actions. For excessive tardiness, a first written warning might state:

- On April 12, 2003, you had your third instance of tardiness during the previous 2-month period when you arrived 35 minutes late to work. This written warning is to notify you that continued tardiness could result in disciplinary action and, ultimately, termination of your job. You are now being placed on a 90-day disciplinary period during which you must arrive at work on time or further disciplinary actions, possibly resulting in termination, will occur. This 90-day disciplinary period begins today, April 12, 2003. If you are tardy two more times, you will be given a final written warning before termination.

A second written warning might state:

- On May 17, you had your fifth instance of tardiness overall and your second instance of tardiness since your 90-day tardiness disciplinary period went into effect on April 12, 2003. You arrived 20 minutes late to work. You were given a written warning for your third incident. This notice is to be considered your final written warning for tardiness. If you are late for work again, you will be dismissed.

The third written warning might state:

- On May 23, 2003, you had your sixth instance of tardiness in a 3-month period when you arrived 30 minutes late to work. You were given a written warning for your third incident and a final written warning for your fifth incident. It is clear that you have not taken your former warnings seriously. We are waiving our right to dismiss you. If you have one additional incidence of unexcused tardiness in the next 90 days, you will be dismissed from work. If you successfully complete the 90-day disciplinary period, your tardiness and attendance record will continue to be monitored closely. Any further violations will be dealt with very seriously and could be grounds for dismissal.

Preventing Problems When Terminating Employment

Fentin (2002) said that several supervisors (e.g., the direct supervisor of the employee, the head of that supervisor's department, the supervisor of all departments, and/or the head of the firm) should have a meeting before firing an employee to establish whether progressive discipline was followed fairly and correctly. This protects the employee from being fired unfairly by a biased or incompetent manager and protects the firm against a wrongful termination suit. Having the meeting prevents the employee from hearing different reasons for being fired from different managers.

Managers might ask the following questions in the meeting to ensure that a termination is fair (Baxter, 1983b): What is the employee's overall record? Are there any mitigating factors that might explain or excuse the employee's misconduct or unsatisfactory performance? Are any statutory problems involved (e.g., regarding race, age, gender, etc.)? Were any job security representations made to the employee? If yes, is the termination consistent with those representations? Are there any public policy concerns? Has the employee received progressive discipline? Is the termination justified? Does it fit the offense?

Have two managers present to document the entire conversation when an employee is terminated. Both should record as much of what the employee says as possible. Require the employee to conduct an exit interview with an ombudsman or independent manager not involved in the termination. Have the independent manager document the exit interview in as much detail as possible. Exit interviews provide an early warning of potential harassment or discrimination claims and/or management problems that need to be addressed (Fentin, 2002).

Although it is difficult to fire someone without due process, on-the-spot firings are warranted when an employee breaks the law, engages in substance abuse on company property, or engages in illegal conduct, gross insubordination, or negligence. If there is any doubt, a manager can suspend an employee until an investigation of the conduct is completed. This allows time to speak to an attorney versed in labor law. Previous disciplinary actions may also be examined to ensure disciplinary actions are fair (Falcone, 1997).

Employers must be conscious of how they fire employees to minimize the employee's frustration, anger, and embarrassment. Tell employees privately why the person is being fired as candidly as possible. Be firm yet compassionate without being apologetic. An apologetic demeanor may suggest the employer feels guilty and thus imply wrongdoing to the fired employee. Limit the amount of information provided to prospective employers calling for reference checks on fired employees. Provide only the fact and dates of employment and the positions held. Avoid providing negative information because the former employee may sue if such information is publicized (Baxter, 1983a, 1983b; Zachary, 2000).

The Need for Documentation

These detailed performance evaluation, progressive discipline, and termination procedures show the objective and consistent written procedures to develop for dealing with potential legal problems. Managers and their attorneys should review important transactions to identify potential pitfalls. Then include clauses spelling out details of possible concern in all contracts. For example, contracts with freelancers should be in writing and signed by both parties. Include fees and expenses, the work's appropriate subject matter, and what its finished form should be (Rauch, 1991).

Document communications with outside individuals such as the public, interviewees, news sources, business contacts, advertisers, freelance writers, photographers, and artists. Establish complaint procedures because irate advertisers, public or private persons who are the subject of stories, readers, listeners, and/or viewers contact media firms regularly. Train employees to treat all complaints seriously. Instruct them to be polite and conciliatory, even if they believe the complaint is baseless, because courteous treatment often defuses a situation. Have employees tell a complainant that they are writing down the facts for internal investigation and then do so, without admitting anything, interrupting, or passing blame. Then bring the complaint to the appropriate supervisor's attention, ensuring that a possibly defensive employee cannot complicate the situation by acting alone. The supervisor should determine whether the complaint has merit and then send a letter confirming the complaint was received that day, providing an explanation, proposing a solution, or providing a deadline by which the complainant will be contacted.

Use different procedures for a serious complaint, when a lawsuit is threatened, and when the complainant is an attorney. Instruct employees not to admit anything and immediately refer the matter to top management, along with all available documentation. Top management must then contact an attorney before responding and allow the attorney to handle the problem when necessary. In any event, employees must feel comfortable about reporting complaints to supervisors, especially complaints caused by their own error or misconduct. If a retraction or letter of apology is needed, an attorney must review it before dissemination. A retraction could repeat the offense and be viewed as an admission of wrongdoing (Rauch, 1991).

Media organizations should publicize their policies internally and have training sessions regarding appropriate procedures and behavior. Never assume that all employees have the judgment and experience to deal with legal and ethical dilemmas; even long-term employees can lose their cool. The best way to prevent legal and ethical concerns is to anticipate common problems and prepare for them. The media provide information to the public; such organizations must never forget the legal and ethical responsibilities that accompany this role.

Understanding and Preventing Discrimination

Title VII of the amended Civil Rights Act of 1964 proscribes employment discrimination (or treating an employee unfairly or unfavorably) based on race, religion, gender, or national origin. Prohibited actions include refusing to hire employees based on race or gender, providing unequal conditions of employment, and providing unequal pay for the same job (Lacy & Simon, 1992).

McGill (2002) reported that American newspapers became less diverse in 2000. More persons of color left newspapers than joined them, dropping from

11.85% to 11.64% of employees. At the same time, the percentage of people of color in the U.S. population reached 30%. What does the inability to attract and retain sufficient numbers of people of color say about an industry that reports on discrimination in other firms?

Consider how divergent the views of people of color and their coworkers are. Seventy-three percent of African-American journalists felt that African-Americans were not as likely to be considered for career opportunities, yet only 2% of newsroom managers felt that way. Perhaps this is why 78% of African-American journalists felt managers had unrealistic perceptions of them, whereas only 24% of managers felt that way (McGill, 2002). These beliefs of journalists of color demonstrate why it is so important to implement fair and consistent performance evaluations.

McGill (2002) said such perceptual discrepancies indicate that separate cultures have evolved in newsrooms. In one culture, White managers and journalists think opportunities for advancement are equal. In another culture, managers and journalists of color perceive that different standards are being applied to different types of people. Such perceptions are reinforced when people within the White male management culture talk mostly to others in that same culture, neglecting interaction with people in other cultures. People from different cultures must be able to communicate their differing perceptions with each other in a supportive environment.

The primary reasons journalists of color give for leaving the profession were consistent over time: lack of professional challenge and lack of advancement opportunities. Although pay, quality of the work environment, interpersonal relationships, and other factors are important, advancement and challenges must be equally available to journalists of color to retain them. Promotions bring the new duties and challenges that journalists of color desire yet feel they must work harder and longer than White employees to get. Unfortunately, most journalists of color leave the newspaper profession feeling disillusioned and disappointed—a far cry from the high ideals they held at the beginning of their careers (McGill, 2002).

McGill (2002) said managers must find ways to promote more journalists of color into professionally challenging positions. Such promotions signal an organizational culture change to other employees of color who perceive the same advancement opportunities for themselves. Managers must communicate more effectively with people of color and be open to their different perceptions. White Americans and Americans of color found they lived in two divergent worlds and held very different perceptions during the O.J. Simpson trial.

Many of the same types of issues discussed here regarding persons of color also apply to female employees (see the "Female Workplace" section in chap. 2). For example, women are paid less than men for the same jobs and receive fewer management opportunities. Managers must understand these different cultures exist and create a positive climate conducive to open communications, fair and equitable promotions, as well as a productive work environment and job satisfaction for employees of all colors and genders. Not only is this the right thing to do, it will also encourage women and employees of color to remain in media industries and prevent incidents of discrimination.

Using Arbitration to Avoid Legal Problems

Managers can review the nonprofit American Arbitration Association's (AAA) Web site (*http://www.adr.org*) to develop and implement arbitration or mediation of disputes. The AAA defines *arbitration* as submitting a dispute to one or more impartial persons for a final and binding decision. *Mediation* is a process where a neutral party who lacks the authority to make a binding decision assists the disagreeing parties in reaching their own settlement.

A media firm could develop a dispute resolution plan to include in employee handbooks and personnel manuals. The plan could be used to settle sexual harassment, discrimination, or wrongful termination disputes. Several practical guides, including the *Beginner's Guide to ADR* and *A Guide to Mediation and Arbitration for Business People*, are found on the AAA's rules and procedures link.

Protecting Employee Health and Safety

The terrorist attacks of September 11, 2001, changed how media firms approach employee security. Media managers must update security procedures at primary (e.g., main office downtown) and secondary locations (e.g., suburban or regional bureaus, sales offices, printing plants, transmission towers, etc.) to ensure employees are safe and avoid legal problems. Establish responsibility and procedures for continually monitoring and updating security.

Advise employees to consider their personal safety when doing their jobs. If an employee feels uncomfortable covering a story or doing the job, best judgment should be exercised to avoid unnecessary risk (Maucker, 2001). Publicize all safety policies in employee manuals and Web sites.

The Federal Bureau of Investigation (FBI) posts information about terrorist threats and advice for enhancing security on its Web site (*www.fbi.gov*). Media managers should adopt the FBI's advice regarding suspicious letters and packages (FBI Advisory, 2001). Train employees to look for mail or parcels with no return address, excessive postage, misspelled words, incorrect titles, or addressed only to a title, an incorrect title with a name, protruding wires, lopsided or uneven sides or centers, rigid or bulky exteriors, excessive tape or string, a strange odor, and items with external stains or crystallization.

Handle suspicious mail carefully without shaking or bumping it, isolate it from other employees, leave it unopened without smelling or tasting it, and then call 911. If the piece is opened and a bomb threat exists, evacuate the building immediately, call 911, and contact the nearest FBI office. If radiological contamination is suspected, limit exposure by isolating and not handling the item, shielding everyone from it, evacuating the area, and calling 911 and the nearest FBI office. If chemical or biological contamination is suspected, isolate the item while minimizing its handling, wash hands with soap and warm water, and call 911 and the nearest FBI office (FBI Advisory, 2001).

Media firms have set up mail screening locations away from their main facilities where sorters wear gloves, masks, protective eyewear, and/or protective clothing. Isolate suspicious mail for examination later in a secure environment and bag it immediately to limit contamination. Employees who may be contaminated should be stripped privately, cleaned, and dressed in a protective suit. Quarantine other employees who had contact with the contaminated employee or mail. Shut down the ventilation system and lock down the area or floor until the contamination threat is over (Maucker, 2001).

Media firms hired additional security personnel to guard building entrances and exits as well as primary corridors. Take digital photos of all employees, enabling security guards to access a picture of any employee at a building entrance if security questions arise. Other firms adopted employee ID badges or cards that double as keys for opening doors. Employees must wear identification prominently and at all times when at work.

Access to media facilities is often restricted, and employees must escort visitors. Emergency numbers are publicized and drills are held to familiarize employees with exits, stairwells, and evacuation procedures. One newspaper formed two newsroom SWAT teams who volunteered to be on call at all times and keep their cars stocked with food and water (Maucker, 2001).

Develop a system to inform employees in other departments and locations when a potential threat occurs. The goal is to spread accurate information quickly to prevent injury or death. Train employees in evacuation procedures and e-mail, intercom, and telephone communication systems. Develop additional low-tech communication procedures in case e-mail and phone systems are disrupted. Suspicious packages or items could be quickly scanned or photographed digitally and then e-mailed to all employees to promptly alert others to potential danger.

Develop a contingency plan for relocating operations, implementing backup publishing or broadcasting, and dealing with an attack. For example, if an attack occurs, have daily conference calls with company management to share information, concerns, and stress communication. Have the firm's communications office issue regular news and security updates to employees. Hold regular employee forums to explain what is happening and security precautions to observe (Maucker, 2001).

Finally, media outlets might advise readers or viewers against sending anonymous or unmarked mail to avoid complaints or lawsuits from failing to respond.

Tell the public to include a name, address, telephone number, and/or e-mail address in all correspondence (Maucker, 2001). Implementing procedures like these minimizes potential risks for employees and potential legal actions resulting from sabotage, disasters, or disgruntled members of the public.

Managers face a much larger variety of health and safety concerns on the job than discussed here. The importance of keeping up with regulations (such as the Americans With Disabilities Act) and consulting with the appropriate legal expert for advice cannot be overemphasized.

Avoiding Problems Related to Pornography and Obscenity

Evolving technology has created new legal problems for media managers regarding pornography. Media firms creating or sponsoring Web sites, bulletin boards, and chat rooms must exercise care when loading material to and from their sites, allowing third-party access, selling materials online, and allowing e-mail to be transmitted. Obscenity is not protected by the First Amendment, and child pornography is unprotected so remove both immediately if found anywhere on a site (Delta & Matsuura, 2002).

Special problems arise because the Internet "knows no borders," yet obscenity is defined by contemporary community standards. Never assume that sexual materials are not obscene in some jurisdiction and forbid the posting of such materials. Ensure that employees who operate and maintain computer systems are aware of who accesses the firm's Web site.

Delta and Matsuura (2002; see Appendix 12) advised firms to monitor the content of Web sites, bulletin boards, and chat rooms and enact subscriber agreements that permit a firm to monitor and remove inappropriate content. Have subscribers, content providers, and others with access sign contracts or complete opt-in agreements that they will not upload sexual or other objectionable material. Ensure that employees with the responsibility monitor all Web content closely and carefully and report all questionable material to the appropriate manager as soon as it is found. Such employees should be informed of what types of material to immediately delete when discovered.

Problems Related to Electronic Access to Government Information

Media organizations may obtain government information using the Freedom of Information Act (FOIA), which established a process for requesting information from federal agencies. The FOIA did not address electronic data, but was subsequently interpreted to provide access to computer records. FOIA obligations apply when existing search engines at a federal agency can retrieve the requested data using a reasonable effort. The form in which electronic records are disclosed is not specified, and another equivalent medium may be used. Courts have found microfiche and paper to be equivalent forms to computer records (Delta & Matsuura, 2002).

Another access issue is whether software that a federal agency developed can be obtained using FOIA procedures. A significant factor is whether access to the software is needed to use the requested electronic records. When the federal agency intended the database or software for public sale, the FOIA will not prevent it. This issue is likely to arise as more federal data and software are generated and their economic value is recognized (Delta & Matsuura, 2002). Hale (2001) said that, although media organizations can afford the costs of accessing databases, the public would be unable to afford such fees.

Under the FOIA, e-mail messages that are considered public records are subject to disclosure requirements. Archived, printed, or readily accessible e-mail messages are more likely to be treated as public records. Messages akin to personal and confidential telephone conversations are unlikely to be subject to disclosure (Delta & Matsuura, 2002). Managers should recognize that e-mail documents are considered records for litigation purposes and establish disclosure and retention policies at their media firms (Frayer, 2002).

Access issues also involve safety and security. After the September 11, 2001, terrorist attacks, federal agencies removed information from Internet sites that might help terrorists plan future actions. Pipeline-mapping data were removed from the Department of Transportation's site, information about hazardous material sites was taken off the Environmental Protection Agency's site, and a study on potential chemical terrorism was eliminated by the Centers for Disease Control (Zipp, 2002). Future media managers will be faced with this question: Is publishing this sensitive material worth possibly jeopardizing public safety?

Media managers and employees may find themselves in the minority when taking a stand for access. In October 2001, Attorney General John Ashcroft directed federal agencies to resist FOIA requests when they find a sound legal basis for doing so. Federal agencies were formerly under a presumption of disclosure, resisting release only when the requested documents could potentially harm a legal interest. The newer, more restrictive standard was instituted to safeguard national security, protect sensitive commercial information, and protect personal privacy (Zipp, 2002). These additional protections lay the foundation for potential abuses of freedom of access in the future.

Unpopular journalistic stands for open access are found in the public arena as well. A Florida law passed after the death of stock-car racer Dale Earnhardt makes autopsy photos private—to be released only by a judge's order. A judge decided that releasing the autopsy photos would invade the privacy of Earnhardt's widow and sealed them at her request. The Orlando Sentinel tried in court to unseal the photos. The resulting protest from racing fans led legislators to make all autopsy photos private (Zipp, 2002). The media must educate the public about the need to protect access to government information before access erodes further.

Deception in Advertising

Managers may need to train employees to clear or review advertising to determine whether it is deceptive or offensive to the audience. Sections 5 and 12 of the Federal Trade Commission (FTC) Act of 1914 give the FTC the power to regulate deceptive advertising and other unfair acts or practices. If an advertiser is injured by a competitor's misleading ad, it may sue under Section 43(1) of the Lanham Act, which provides protection for trademarks. *Deception* under the Lanham Act is defined as any false or misleading description or representation of fact (Gillmor, Barron, & Simon, 1998; Preston, 1994, 1996).

The current FTC definition of *deception* is: (a) There must be a representation, omission, or practice that is likely to mislead the consumer; (b) the representation, omission, or practice is examined from the perspective of a consumer acting reasonably in the circumstances to the consumer's detriment; and (c) the representation, omission, or practice must be a material one (Policy Statement of Deception, 1983). Richards (1990) said, "regulable deceptiveness results only if purchase behavior of a substantial number of people is likely to be affected" (p. 24).

Deceptive claims or practices include false verbal or written statements, misleading price claims, selling dangerous or defective products without adequate disclosures, not delivering promised services, and failing to meet warranty obligations. The FTC considers whether the entire ad is likely to mislead reasonable consumers so even if all of an ad's claims are true, if the general impression of the ad is false, it still may be deceptive (Policy Statement on Deception, 1983; Preston, 1994).

The FTC said certain practices are not likely to deceive reasonable consumers. For example, misrepresentations about inexpensive products that are evaluated easily and purchased frequently by consumers are of less concern because these advertisers depend on repeat sales for survival. The FTC usually does not pursue cases based on puffery or correctly stated and honestly held opinions about a product, or obvious exaggerations about the product or its qualities (e.g., the best or greatest; Policy Statement on Deception, 1983; Preston, 1996).

Newspapers, magazines, broadcast stations, cable channels, Internet sites, and so on can screen ads prior to public dissemination to ensure they are not deceptive or offensive. Media outlets may establish their own clearance codes on how to review ads for deceptive content and avoid offending their particular audiences. The FTC provides its Advertising Policy Statements and Guidance (*www.ftc.gov/bcp/guides/guides.htm*) and Screening Advertisements: A Guide for the Media (*www.ftc.gov/bcp/conline/pubs/buspubs/adscreen.htm*) to educate managers about effectively reviewing ads for misleading content.

REGULATORY AND SELF-REGULATORY
ONLINE RESOURCES FOR MANAGERS

There are many other Web sites with useful information for media managers. The Internet Law Library provides access to U.S. federal and state laws, as well as some international laws and treaties (*http://www.lawguru.com/ilawlib/*). The U.S. Code can be searched online (*uscode.house.gov/usc.htm*). Most federal agencies are accessed at The Federal Web Navigator (*lawdbase.law.villanova. edu/fedweb/*).

Federal Web sites can be examined for specific advice of interest to media managers. The U.S. Equal Opportunity Commission (*http://www.eeoc.gov*) has a quick start link where employers can learn about federal equal employment laws (*www.eeoc.gov/qs-employers.html*) and a link for laws, regulations, and policy guidance (*www.eeoc.gov/policy/index.html*). The Federal Emergency Management Agency (*www.fema.gov*) offers advice for planning and preparing for disasters (*www.fema.gov/library/prepandprev.shtm*).

The Society of Professional Journalists (SPJ; *http://www.spj.org*) has an FOIA Resource Center (*www.spj.org/foia.asp*) to help journalists and nonjournalists in obtaining information from federal and local governments. The SPJ's diversity link (*www.spj.org/diversity.asp*) offers expertise on civil rights, gay/lesbian issues, and gender issues.

The National Association of Black Journalists (NABJ; *http://www.nabj.org*) provides information about issues concerning journalists of color and a Media Resource Center (*www.nabj.org/html/mediarsrcs.html*). The Asian American Journalists Association (AAJA; *www.aaja.org*) includes a link on Guides for Covering Arab Americans and South Asians as well as a media watch and industry news reports. The National Association of Hispanic Journalists (NAHJ; *www.nahj.org*) provides a link to purchase its Latinos in the United States: A Resource Guide for Journalists and explain its mission and goals (*www.nahj.org/ mission.html*). The Native American Journalists Association (NAJA; *www.naja. org*) publishes its downloadable Reading Red Report on Native Americans in the News (*www.naja.com/red.html*). The National Lesbian & Gay Journalists Association (*www.nlgja.org*) offers HIV/Aids information links for journalists (*www.nlgja.org/news/aidslinks.html*). The Detroit Free Press published 100 Questions and Answers About Arab Americans: A Journalist's Guide (*www. freep.com/jobspage/arabs.htm*).

The Reporters Committee for Freedom of the Press (*http://www.rcfp.org*) reports on legal actions regarding press freedoms and has links to the First Amendment Handbook and the News Media & The Law. The Libel Defense Resource Center (*www.ldrc.com*) monitors First Amendment rights in libel, privacy, and other legal areas. Editor & Publisher (*www.editorandpublisher.com*) has legal articles and a database (*www.editorandpublisher.com/editorandpublisher/ business_resources/medialinks.jsp*).

The Newspaper Association of America (NAA; *http://www.naa.org*) provides information on the newspaper industry and publishes Presstime (*www.naa.org/presstime/*) and TechNews (*www.naa.org/technews/*) magazines online. The NAA has a Government and Legal Affairs link with information on employee relations, government affairs, legal affairs, and postal affairs, as well as links to the White House, U.S. House of Representatives, and U.S. Senate.

The Radio-Television News Director's Association (*http://www.rtnda.org*) has Freedom of Information and Research links and publishes its Code of Ethics online (*www.rtnda.org/ethics/coe.shtml*). The National Association of Broadcasters (*www.nab.org*) includes links entitled Legal & Regulatory Affairs, Science & Technology and Research & Information. Electronic communications managers can stay abreast of the Federal Communications Commissions' (FCC; *www.fcc.gov*) activities and priority issues. There also is a media ownership link (*www.fcc.gov/ownership/*), a continuing priority issue for the FCC.

Columbia Journalism Review (CJR; *http://www.cjr.org*) provides Resource Guides and reports on a variety of subjects (*www.cjr.org/resources*). CJR provides Who Owns What, a guide to what major media companies own (*www.cjr.org/owners/*). The National Press Photographer's Association's (NPPA; *www.nppa.org*) Critical Incident Response Team (*www.nppa.org/services/cirt/ default.htm*) provides information on how to deal with traumatic incidents on the job.

The Federal Trade Commission (FTC; *http://www.ftc.gov*) provides information about the FTC in general as well as news releases discussing recent advertising deception cases and consumer and business publications (*www.ftc.gov/ftc/consumer.htm*). The FTC publicizes its privacy initiatives (*www.ftc.gov/privacy/index.html*) online. It has a Kidz Privacy page (*www.ftc.gov/bcp/conline/edcams/kidzprivacy/index.html*) with downloadable information on how to comply with the Children's Online Privacy Protection Act (*www.ftc.gov/bcp/conline/edcams/kidzprivacy/biz.htm*). These links provide good advice on developing Web pages that safeguard the online privacy of children.

The Consumer Product Safety Commission (CPSC; *www.cpsc.gov*) provides information about product safety and recalls. The CPSC Kid's Page (*www.cpsc.gov/kids/kidsafety/index.html*) includes safety tips and provides a good example of a public service home page for children.

The Council of Better Business Bureaus (CBBB; *http://www.bbb.org*) reviews dispute resolution as well as how to advertise legally and ethically for local and national advertisers and agencies. The CBBB's Business Guidance page (*www.bbb.org/subpages/bizsubpg.asp*) has links to its self-regulatory programs on online privacy, online reliability, and advertising. Surfing the CBBB's Advertising Review Programs (*www.bbb.org/subpages/adsubpg.asp*) enables managers to keep current with its national advertising self-regulatory bodies, the National Advertising Division (NAD), and the National Advertising Review Board (NARB). The NAD investigates the truthfulness and accuracy of national advertising. The NARB is the appeals board for advertisers or challengers who disagree with NAD decisions. For local advertisers and others, the CBBB's advertising guidelines provide information for advertisers and agencies to use when questions arise as to whether an ad claim or technique is ethical.

The Children's Advertising Review Unit (CARU; *http://www.caru.org*) of the CBBB reviews advertising directed to children. It publishes the CARU Self-Regulatory Guidelines for Children's Advertising online (*www.caru.org/carusubpgs/ guidepg.asp*) to provide advice on advertising to children ethically and accurately. CARU's Safe Harbor Program (*www.caru.org/carusubpgs/harborpg.asp*) offers information on protecting the privacy of children online.

The American Advertising Federation (*http://www.aaf.org*) has a government affairs link with information on advertising regulation and self-regulation. The American Association of Advertising Agencies (AAAA; *www.aaaa.org*) includes a Washington Scene link with government reports and recommendations regarding advertising. Search for the AAAA's Standards of Practice to guide advertisers and agencies at its Web site. The Public Relations Society of America (*www.prsa.org*) provides background information on the public relations industry (*www.prsa.org/_Resources/main/*) and publishes its Code of Ethics and Professional Standards (*www.prsa.org/_About/ethics/*) online.

The Direct Marketing Association (DMA; *http://www.the-dma.org*) has ethical guidelines for direct marketers (*www.the-dma.org/library/guidelines*). The DMA offers information about privacy issues (*www.the-dma.org/library/privacy/ index.shtml*) and government affairs (*www.the-dma.org/government/index. shtml*). The Interactive Advertising Bureau (IAB; *www.iab.net*) provides research and advice about online advertising. It publishes standards, including those for interactive advertising units (*www.iab.net/iab_banner_standards/ bannersource. html*). The IAB has a privacy link that includes guidelines, a resource center, and its privacy policy (*www.iab.net/privacy/index.html*).

There are many other individuals, organizations, and agencies online that provide information, research, and/or alternative viewpoints of the various media industries and their influence on society. Cornell University's Legal Information Institute (*http://www.law.cornell.edu/*) includes information on Supreme Court decisions and legal events in the news. The American Arbitration Association (*http://www.adr.org/index2.1.jsp*) provides information and guidelines (*www.adr.org/index2.1.jsp?JSPssid=13758&JSPaid=32229*) as well as state-specific rules (*www.adr.org/index2.1.jsp?JSPssid=13807*) on conflict management and dispute resolution.

The U.S. Census Bureau (*http://www.census.gov*) provides demographic profiles (*www.census.gov/Press-Release/www/2002/demoprofiles.html*) and a search engine (*www.census.gov/main/www/srchtool.html*) to find specific data. The Centers for Disease Control and Prevention (*www.cdc.gov*) offers statistical information and reports (*www.cdc.gov/scientific.htm*). The Pew Research Center (*http://people-press.org*) provides a forum for ideas as well as research and datasets on the media and public policy.

Commercial Alert (*www.commercialalert.org*) aims to protect the public and children from exploitation by the commercial culture. Adbusters (*www. adbusters.org*) offers a critical perspective on advertising. The Center for Media Literacy (*www.medialit.org*) aims to teach children and adults about the media that surround them and has links to media literacy and media-related sites (*www.medialit.org/othersites.html*). The Media Research Center (*www.mrc.org*) offers the perspective of those who believe the media has a liberal bias.

The Poynter Institute (*http://www.pointer.org*) provides many links and information on being a better journalist. A Journalist's Guide to the Internet (*reporter.umd.edu*) offers a variety of legal and regulatory links. JournalismNet (*www.journalismnet.com*) has a variety of media and journalism-related links.

SUMMARY

Media law, regulation, and self-regulation are obviously complex and involve much more than what was discussed in this chapter. Prudent media managers should review the sources cited in this chapter, as well as other appropriate sources and counsel, to keep abreast of the ever-changing laws, ethical standards, and professional and ethical issues affecting media firms. Managers who fail to keep up with the law risk legal problems and lawsuits.

INTRODUCTION

Although cases with Internet components are included here, Delta and Matsuura (2002) provided a good resource for developing your own case or learning more about legal issues regarding the Internet. Delta and Matsuura (2002) included appendixes with advice on handling a variety of Internet legal concerns for managers such as Guidelines for Handling Personal Data (p. App. 1-1), Electronic Records Management Checklist (p. App. 2-1), Network Use and Security Guidelines (p. App. 3-1), Web Site Notice/Disclaimer Checklist (p. App. 4-1), Checklist for Link Licenses (p. App. 5-1), World Wide Web Site Development Agreement (p. App. 6-1), Model Electronic Data Interchange Trading Partner Agreement and Commentary (p. App. 7-1), E-Commerce Business Practice Guidelines (p. App. 8-1), On-Line Content Management Checklist (p. App. 9-1), Guidelines for Managing On-Line Conflicts (p. App. 10-1), Avoiding Problems Caused by Obscene and Indecent Materials (p. App. 12-1), and Minimizing Potential Liability from Internet Operations (p. App. 14-1).

Professors and students are encouraged to read these appendixes and discuss the major problems and solutions for Web page development and implementation by media organizations. For example, students could read the appendixes, examine the Web site of a prominent local or national media outlet assigned by the professor, and discuss in the next class whether the outlet has any existing or potential legal problems with its Web site. Have students read these appendixes and then search databases like ABI Inform/ProQuest and Lexis-Nexis Academic Universe to find examples of media firms having Internet legal difficulties. Each student could write a paper explaining the case, how the outlet handled the Internet legal problem correctly or incorrectly, what the outlet should have done and could do in the future to correct and prevent such problems, and write an outline or fact sheet showing other media managers how to deal with the problem. Each student could bring in their papers and fact sheets to turn in and discuss in class to develop overall guidelines for dealing with common Internet legal problems. Students could use a real-life problem found in the database search to develop an original case with an outline of correct answers. The case could be developed together as a class or written individually by students.

Because laws involving the Internet and other aspects of the media change often and regularly, students and professors could look for new sources of advice. Look for guidelines or appendixes similar to those developed by Delta and Matsuura (2002). These new sources also could be used in the ways described previously.

Case 6.1
Developing Counterterrorism Plans and Procedures

Develop a plan and procedures for protecting employee health and safety in the event of a terrorist attack. Select a media outlet in the nearest major city (that does not already have such a plan on its Web site) and develop a plan and procedures. If possible, have your professor arrange a visit to a major media outlet to learn about security procedures. Start by rereading the section of the chapter on employee health and safety. Then read the following online sources, making notes or printing sections that state and describe what procedures to implement in an emergency or terrorist attack. Review the FEMA Fact Sheet: Terrorism (*http://www.fema.gov/hazards/terrorism/terrorf.shtm*) and Backgrounder: Terrorism (*www.fema.gov/hazards/terrorism/terror.shtm*). Review the CDC's Fact Sheets Facts About Anthrax (*www.bt.cdc.gov/DocumentsApp/FactSheet/Anthrax/about.asp*) and Updated Information About How to Recognize and Handle a Suspicious Package or Envelope (*www.bt.cdc.gov/DocumentsApp/Anthrax/10312001/han50.asp*). Go to the FBI's press room (*www.fbi.gov/pressrel/pressrel01.htm*) to download "What to do if you receive a suspicious letter or package" dated October 12, 2001 (*http://www.fbi.gov/pressrel/pressrel01/mail3. pdf*).

Go to FEMA's outline of the Emergency Management Guide for Business and Industry (*http://www.fema.gov/library/bizindex.shtm*) or review the longer version (*www.fema.gov/library/biz1.shtm*). You might review the Office of Emergency Preparedness Web site (*http://ndms.dhhs.gov/index.html*) and the FBI's Terrorism page (*www.fbi.gov/terrorinfo/terrorism.htm*). Also review the CDC's Public Health Emergency Preparedness and Response page (*www.bt.cdc.gov/*), including the Emergency Response (*www.bt.cdc.gov/EmContact/index.asp*) and Preparation and Planning (*www.bt.cdc.gov/EmContact/index.asp*) to see if any links there would be useful. Check out the NPPA's Critical Incident Response Team (*www.nppa.org/services/cirt/default.htm*) page for information on how to deal with traumatic incidents on the job.

Conduct a search of major electronic databases such as ABI Inform/ProQuest, Lexis-Nexis Academic Universe, or Ebsco. Search the Internet for examples of such plans developed by media outlets.

ASSIGNMENT

Develop a terrorism response plan that includes the major components deemed vital by the online sources noted earlier as well as any other sources you find. Write a plan that includes, but is not limited to, all of the following sections. Be sure to include important guidelines or advice not listed next.

1. Describe the new security procedures to be implemented at the media outlet's primary and secondary locations to help prevent terrorist attacks, disasters, or emergencies. Explain how security procedures will be monitored and updated as needed. These include, but are not limited to, entrance and access to primary and secondary locations, employee identification, security inside the buildings, how to identify suspicious persons, procedures for processing mail and packages, radiological contamination, chemical or biological contamination, bomb threats or discovery of a bomb, and so on.

2. Describe what to include in a training program (e.g., emergency or evacuation drills, what to do if a bomb is detected, etc.), who should implement it, and why. Explain how often to conduct training and why. Discuss ways to make guidelines on responding to crises easily available to employees at a moment's notice.

3. Designate a primary and secondary employee (e.g., use a specific job title listed on the outlet's Web site or typically found in the type of media outlet you are using) from each major department (e.g., news, sales, circulation, production, etc.) who should handle responses to the attack in that department and ensure enough first aid, food, and water provisions are on hand. Establish a chain of command and rules to follow in each department in the event that the primary and secondary employees are incapacitated or killed during the attack.

4. Describe the procedures to follow in the event of an attack (e.g., evacuation, etc.), including the specific procedures to follow in the case of anticipated major types of attacks (e.g., bombing, anthrax, etc.).

5. Describe the essential first aid, medical, and counseling knowledge needed to deal with injury or trauma during or after an attack. Identify the kind of training needed and provide resources and information on the subjects for employees to locate quickly during an emergency or attack.

6. Explain the communication system or procedures to use within departments, between departments, and between locations in the event of an attack, both high- and low-tech, should power be lost or equipment fail.

7. Develop a list of local and national contacts for each major type of terrorism emergency situation and the order in which to contact each (e.g., call 911, call the FBI, etc.).

8. Develop a contingency plan for relocating operations, including backup publishing, broadcasting plans, and so on.

9. Develop a plan for dealing with the public or how to advise the public about proper ways to mail or contact the media outlet.

10. Develop a company policy regarding employee safety and decide where and how to publicize it. Provide enough detail and examples to make it easy for employees to apply in real-life situations. For example, give examples of when employees should consider their personal safety, when they might feel uncomfortable covering a story or doing their jobs, and the types of best judgment to exercise to avoid unnecessary risk or danger while performing job duties.

11. Develop a plan or policies for the other major considerations you found in your research on terrorism and emergency preparedness.

Case 6.2
The Case of the Poorly Performing Salesperson

Ed Markham, the African-American sales manager at WCTV, was considering how to handle a problem with one of his salespersons, Jane Folsom who was White. Ed was promoted to sales manager 3 months ago after working at WCTV for 2 years. He earned his promotion by exceeding sales goals every month after his first on the job. He developed a research report using secondary data like MRI and the Lifestyle Market Analyst to analyze the market. His former boss praised the report, gave a copy to all salespersons, and included a summary of it in the rate card. When his former boss left for a new job in a larger market, he recommended Ed as his replacement.

Jane had been a salesperson at WCTV for 2 years. For almost 2 years, she had exceeded sales quotas about as much as Ed had. For the past 3 months, she had not met sales quotas. After his second month as sales manager, Ed talked to Jane about her performance. She attributed her below-average performance to the closing of a major advertiser, Anthony's Fashions. This local clothing store closed because several major retailers, including J.C. Penneys and Dillards, had opened at the local mall.

Ed listened to Jane's explanation and then suggested ways to obtain new clients. He asked Jane whether she had set personal sales goals, set up a prospect file of new and inactive advertisers as well as existing businesses that were potential clients, came up with research and data on the market to use in presentations and reports to clients, came up with new ideas or opportunities to advertise for clients, or asked her clients about their needs and goals (Shaver, 1995). Jane said no, she simply telephoned or visited her clients regularly to see if they wanted to run ads.

Ed also asked Jane why several of her clients had not paid their bills. He explained that a salesperson must check out a client's ability to pay before running a schedule. Jane replied that she was not aware of that fact and no one had ever trained her to sell. She had sold time for a radio station before, but that was all the training she had. Ed's predecessor had just hired her and cut her loose.

Ed gave Jane a memo after their first meeting a month ago asking her to focus on sales training for the next month. First, she should read Shaver's (1995) *Making the Sale! How to Sell Media With Marketing.* He gave her a copy, told her to read it, and asked her to contact him if she had any questions. After reading the book, he told her that she should establish written personal sales goals, begin to develop a prospect file (with two new and two inactive clients), and develop three ideas for new advertising opportunities for existing clients. In the memo, Ed told Jane that he would not hold her to sales performance standards that month. He wanted Jane to focus on doing the background work he assigned to help her improve her future sales performance.

At the meeting a month later, Ed discovered Jane had made only a half-hearted attempt at training. For example, she had not developed a prospect file; she told him she had no idea how to do it. Ed asked her why she had not contacted him to set up a meeting to discuss questions she had about the book or completing the assignments, as noted in his memo. She said she had forgotten. Asked specific questions about Shaver's (1995) sales book, she was unable to respond, suggesting she had not read it.

Ed asked Jane to read the book again, and scheduled a meeting with her to discuss the book. Ed instructed Jane to have a written memo ready for the next meeting that identified the assistance or training she needed to accomplish the tasks he had set for her the previous month. "Base your needs assessment memo on the Shaver book and be prepared to discuss the book fully," he told her. Ed said he would send her a memo about their meeting, outlining what he had verbally asked her to do during the next month as well as the consequences of not completing these tasks. Ed told her, "Jane, if you don't start to make a serious effort in participating in your training, and ultimately improving your sales performance, your job here could be in jeopardy."

Ed's gut feeling was that something else was bothering Jane. He wondered why she had gone from exceeding sales quotas to below-average sales performance. He was surprised an employee would respond half heartedly to a written notice of unsatisfactory job performance. He wondered if there was another reasons she was not responding to his attempts to help her. Ed wanted Jane to succeed because he thought she was a good salesperson despite her apparent lack of formal training and recent performance. He wanted to give her a fair chance to improve, but knew he would have to fire her if she did not take her training seriously and improve her performance. He wondered how to be fair to her while protecting the station. He had never faced this kind of problem before. Welcome to management, he told himself.

ASSIGNMENT

Review the chapter and answer the following questions.

1. Were Ed's actions in working with Jane fair and appropriate thus far? Why or why not?
2. Are there any other steps Ed should take now in dealing with Jane and this situation? If yes, explain them in detail.
3. What do you think may be the reason for Jane's sudden poor performance?
4. How can Ed discover whether there is another reason for Jane's apparent unresponsiveness to his efforts to help her improve her performance without incurring any legal liability? Should he take steps to find out? Why or why not?
5. What steps should Ed take to identify the training Jane may need? Why?
6. How can Ed determine fairly whether Jane simply lacks adequate sales training without opening his station to a wrongful termination or other lawsuit? Explain your answer and provide examples of what Ed should do.
7. How should Ed document the steps he takes to train or, if necessary, discipline Jane? Why?
8. With what other resources or persons should Ed consult regarding Jane? Why?
9. How should he use these resources? What should he do? Why?
10. How should Ed respond to today's meeting with Jane? To answer this question, write a sample memo from Ed to Jane about today's meeting.
11. Write a sample memo for Ed assuming that Jane does not respond satisfactorily to the meeting scheduled for 1 month from now.

12. Write a sample memo for Ed, assuming Jane does respond satisfactorily to the meeting 1 month from now.
13. What other present or future steps or actions do you recommend to Ed? Why?

Case 6.3
Privacy Analysis of a Web Site Directed to Children (or Adults)

Select a media outlet or advertiser's home page on the Internet intended for or targeted to children. Examine the site fully. Carefully review all privacy statements, policies, procedures, or descriptions included in the Web site.

(Note. This case could be adapted to analyze the privacy of Web sites intended for adults. For example, substitute sites having advice regarding children discussed later in this case with those from the chapter for adults, such as reviewing the FTC's privacy initiatives [*www.ftc.gov/privacy/index.html*] online instead of its Kidz Page. Other online resources to use instead of the ones for children noted later include the DMA's ethical guidelines for direct marketers [*www. the-dma.org/library/guidelines/*] and information about privacy issues [*www. the-dma.org/library/privacy/index.shtml*] and government affairs [*www. the-dma. org/government/index.shtml*]. The IAB's privacy link [*www.iab.net/privacy/ index.html*] also could be used for adults. NAA's Electronic Publishing link on its home page [*www.naa.org*] has information about online privacy for newspaper Web sites [e.g., see the article at *www.naa.org/ artpage.cfm?AID= 4099&SID=107*].)

Consider how effective the Web site's privacy policies are in protecting the privacy of children (or adults). Use the following information and sources to assess privacy effectiveness. Delta and Matsuura (2002) described procedures to protect children on the Internet: (a) those knowingly collecting personal information online from children younger than 13 years of age must obtain verifiable consent from a child's parent or guardian before collecting the information; and (b) provide privacy policies and practices before collecting information identifying the type of information to be collected, describe how the information will be used, and identify all third parties who will have access to the information.

Delta and Matsuura (2002, Appendix 1—Personal Data Privacy, pp. App. 1-1 to 1-2) provided guidelines for developing personal data privacy policies for children and adults:

1. Description of data—Tell individuals clearly about the type of personal data to be collected.
2. Description of uses/users—Identify the intended uses of personal data as well as who will be using the data.

3. Security measures—Describe and implement the security measures to be used to protect personal data from unauthorized uses or access.

4. Accuracy—Describe how individuals can review their personal data, challenge it, or correct it.

5. Special measures for safeguarding children—Describe and implement special procedures to prevent the misuse of personal data about or obtained from children. Provide disclosures of how and by whom such data will be used. Provide a way for parental authorization to be obtained and monitored.

6. Oversight and audit procedures—Describe and implement methods to monitor the effectiveness of privacy measures and procedures. Neutral third parties should conduct audits, and the results should be made available to the public on request.

7. Contracts with data users—Enter into contracts with other parties who will use the personal data you collect online. Include specific provisions in the contracts about the obligations of the party using the data to protect it and limit its use.

Now review advice and requirements for protecting the privacy of children online including the FTC's Kidz Privacy page (*www.ftc.gov/bcp/conline/ edcams/kidzprivacy/index.html*). (Substitute other privacy links from the chapter or those you find regarding adults if you are reviewing a Web site for persons age 18 or older.) Download and review the information on how to comply with the Children's Online Privacy Protection Act (*www.ftc.gov/bcp/conline/edcams/ kidzprivacy/biz.htm*). Also review the CARU's Self-Regulatory Guidelines for Children's Advertising online (*www.caru.org/carusubpgs/guidepg.asp*) and Safe Harbor Program (*www.caru.org/carusubpgs/harborpg.asp*). Then scroll completely through and read, but do not complete, the Children's Privacy Policy Generator at the DMA's Web site (*http://www.the-dma.org/library/privacy/ childrensppg.shtml*). Try to find other sources regarding online privacy and review them as well.

ASSIGNMENT

After reviewing these sites and any other information you find, review again the commercial home page for children (or adults) you selected. Evaluate whether it follows the online guidelines for advertising to children (or the appropriate guidelines for adults). You may combine the principles noted in all of the advisory or self-regulatory guidelines listed or select one set of advisory or self-regulatory guidelines for your analysis. Prepare a report that includes the following.

Questions to Answer if Evaluating a Web Site for Children

1. Does the company indicate the age group to which the page is targeted? If not, to which age group does the home page seem to be targeted?
2. Did the company or marketers appear to take advantage of the typical targeted child's age, knowledge, sophistication, and maturity unfairly or unethically when developing the Web site? Why or why not?
3. Are the company's privacy policies and practices notices prominently displayed and easy to find and read for the targeted age group?
4. Are the company's privacy policies complete and appropriate? Provide details and explain why or why not.
5. Is it easy for the targeted age group to understand they are being asked to disclose personal information (if applicable)? Has an opt-out mechanism to avoid submitting personal information been provided? Is it easy for the target group to understand and use the opt-out mechanism? In your opinion, is it pressure-free or are children encouraged too strongly or unethically to get a free gift or something else for providing personal information?
6. Is there a clear, appropriate, and easy way for parental authorization to be obtained and monitored? Are parents notified independently and separately from the child? Does it appear easy for children to circumvent the system, pretend to be their parents, and authorize or provide consent themselves?
7. Is there a mechanism, easily understood by the typical targeted child, for avoiding future e-mail messages from the advertiser or company? Did you receive any unsolicited e-mail after surfing the site? Was there a mechanism appropriate for the target group in the unsolicited e-mail for refusing future e-mails?
8. Whenever purchase or personal information is sought, is there a prominent message that is easily understood by the target group asking them to seek a parent or guardian's permission before doing so? Also is there a mechanism for canceling the purchase, after the fact, by the parent or guardian?
9. Were there any other guidelines or practices that the advertiser or media outlet violated or executed well? What were these guidelines or practices? Why did the company execute them well or violate them?
10. Overall, do you think the advertiser or media outlet complied with the regulatory and self-regulatory guidelines regarding online privacy protection for children? Why or why not?
11. Generally speaking, do you think the regulatory and self-regulatory guidelines are an effective way to protect the privacy rights of children surfing the Web? Why or why not?

Questions to Answer if Evaluating a Web Site for Adults

1. Are the company's privacy policies and practices prominently displayed and easy to access, find, and read?

2. Are the company's privacy policies complete and appropriate? Provide details and explain why or why not.

3. Is it easy for a visitor to understand they are being asked to disclose personal information (if applicable)? Is an opt-out mechanism to avoid submitting personal information provided?

4. Is there a mechanism for avoiding future e-mail messages from the advertiser or company? Did you receive any unsolicited e-mail after surfing the site? Is there a mechanism in the unsolicited e-mail for refusing future e-mails?

5. Is there any inappropriate, offensive, or objectionable content on the site? If yes, what possible legal problems or ramifications exist?

6. Were there any other guidelines or practices that the advertiser or media outlet violated or executed well? What were these guidelines or practices? Why did the company execute them well or violate them?

7. Overall, do you think the advertiser or media outlet complied with the appropriate legal advice and/or self-regulatory guidelines regarding online privacy protection? Why or why not?

8. Generally speaking, do you think self-regulatory guidelines are an effective way to protect the privacy rights of adults surfing the Web? Why or why not? Provide examples to explain your answer.

Case 6.4
Reviewing and Analyzing Freedom of
Information Resources and Issues

Select a state of interest and review online and other available sources to discover its information access laws if any. Conduct a database search in ABI Inform/ProQuest or Lexis-Nexis Academic Universe to find recent cases or issues regarding access to information in your state of interest or any state or national freedom of information legislation, issues, cases, or debates. For example, see if any access issues or cases involving national security have arisen. Have there been any abuses of access in the name of protecting national security? Have any other cases involving celebrities or public figures like the Dale Earnhardt case arisen? Is there a new category of type of access issue that has emerged recently?

Visit the nearest law library to review copies of the access laws in your state of interest. Contact the appropriate government agency or office for more information about access in your area. (If your research into state access to information becomes too difficult, research access at the federal government level. Access most federal agencies at the Federal Web Navigator [*lawdbase.law. villanova.edu/fedweb/*] and examine their online postings and instructions regarding access and freedom of information requests.)

Then conduct an online review of FOIA sites. Check out the SPJ's FOIA Resource Center (*http://www.spj.org/foia.asp*) and The Internet Law Library (*www.lawguru.com/ilawlib/*). Review other sources that may have articles and information on access. For example, try searching the Reporters Committee for Freedom of the Press site (*www.rcfp.org*) and its Tapping Officials' Secrets page (*www.reporterscommittee.org/tapping2001/index.cgi*) for information on your state of interest. *Editor & Publisher* (*www.editorandpublisher.com*), the NAA's Web site (*www.naa.org*), and the RTNDA's (*www.rtnda.org*) Freedom of Information link with information on access (*www.rtnda.org/foi/atp.shtml*) are good sites to explore. Also try Cornell University's Legal Information Institute (*www.law.cornell.edu*), A Journalist's Guide to the Internet (*reporter.umd.edu/*), including the Records and FOIA link (*reporter.umd.edu/records.htm*), and any other FOIA resources or links you find.

ASSIGNMENT

Develop a report, including but not limited to the following questions, which could be used by reporters or others as a guide to understanding the FOIA, the major issues surrounding it, and for requesting government documents.

1. What laws, if any, are applicable in the state you selected?
2. What are the major contemporary issues regarding access to government information in your state and nationally? Identify and describe each type of issue, both national and state, and provide a description and example of each.
3. What are the general techniques for obtaining documents from the appropriate state government or federal entities?
4. What are common problems or pitfalls to avoid when attempting to gain access to government documents?
5. Why may erosion of access to government information occur in the future? What can media outlets or organizations do to preserve and protect access to information?
6. What other important information or advice did you find in your research? Identify and explain each factor here.

7

PLANNING

Any manager who wants to make effective decisions must be certain those decisions are closely aligned with the current business opportunities, unique resources, and strengths of the media company. Planning is done in cycles with careful timing and resource allocation part of the process. Media companies continue to write and follow mission plans, but the time frames for review have been adjusted because of rapid technological changes, recent economic downturns, as well as the events of September 11, 2001.

For example, one large media company changed from reviewing budgets on a 3- to 5-year cycle to a twice-annual review, allowing much closer monitoring of consumer and advertising fluctuations. Other managers report that, although mission statements were formerly posted everywhere to signal their connection to business decisions, now there is less discussion and more debate about actions than they have heard in 20 years. "Things have been changing so fast, that we all recognize we are in a dynamic time for our business, and there are change agents everywhere," says one manager. Although time frames and response rates may have accelerated, the process of planning remains stable.

STEPS IN PLANNING

The planning process for media companies is pragmatic and generally takes three forms: (a) strategic, (b) intermediate, and (c) short-run planning. Strategic planning involves allocating resources to achieve the firm's long-term goals. These plans can cover 1 to 10 years, but are usually developed for a 3- to 5-year period. They represent the ways a company expects to carry out its mission.

Intermediate plans generally cover 6 months to 2 years and provide reinforcement or correction data for long-term goals. Because of current economic uncertainties, many media companies find it challenging to remain proactive rather than reactive to market fluctuations affecting customers and product demands. Successful companies adjust nimbly to environmental changes, avoiding distractions from their strategic planning goals due to temporary fluctuations.

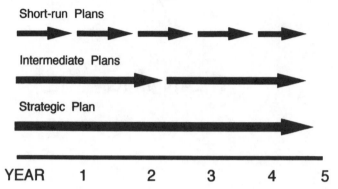

FIG. 7.1.   Relationship among strategic, intermediate, and short-run planning.

Short-run planning involves a few weeks up to a year. This type of plan allocates resources on a day-to-day or month-to-month basis. Figure 7.1 shows how the three plans fit together. The strategic plan fulfills the firm's mission and overall general goals. The intermediate plan involves the general way in which the strategic plan is pursued, and the short-run plan is how the strategic plan works on a day-to-day basis.

Common Characteristics of Planning

All three types of planning have commonalities, although the time period, responsible parties, and actual steps vary. Media companies have general organizational goals or fairly abstract statements of what they hope to achieve within given areas of performance. These goals are derived from the media firm's mission statement, which reflects its business domain and may include statements about its role outside its primary business markets.

The mission statements for public media companies are written for legal and business clarity. Most managers could not recite them word for word, but do have a pragmatic understanding of how the statements guide decision making and resource allocations. One vice president for circulation says his medium-size urban newspaper in the southeast looks at planning on a rolling, 5-year cycle that provides a "fundamental road map without a lot of explicit detail. But it is a road map where all the departments get together and come to consensus so that we're moving in a general direction" (personal communication, April 19, 2002).

If managers were asked what their newspaper's mission is for the next 5 years, there would be a variety of answers, but everyone would acknowledge they are focused on increasing readership. "And that's been a change in the industry over the last couple of years. I mean, it used to be growing circulation, growing penetration—but over the last couple or three years it has really transitioned to readership, which is a really more accurate reflection of our measurement in the marketplace" (personal communication, April 19, 2002).

His newspaper's mission also focuses on content, and all managerial plans emphasize the importance of the product for the community. It is a public service-based vision that translates into a more targeted effort at specific zoning of news content. He sees both the readership and content goals as parallel planning priorities, adding that, "if you do a good job with the content, the readership will grow" (personal communication, April 19, 2002).

Planning Tools

To assess progress, an organization must have specific operational definitions for measurement. For example, the goal of increasing viewership among long-term residents of the community could be operationalized as increasing ratings by two points during the next 6 months among audience members who have lived in the area of dominant influence (ADI) for more than 10 years. The operational definition must specify in measurable terms the group to be affected (people who have lived in the ADI or market area for more than 10 years), a time period during which the change is expected (next 6 months), and a measurable level of performance that is being sought (two ratings points).

Planning without well-defined goals is like attending a potluck dinner where the diner may enjoy the meal, but by chance rather than culinary design. Every plan involves preparation. The better the preparation is, the greater the chances of reaching the goals. Preparation is simply the collection of information about the goals and possible alternatives for achieving them. The goals that fit the mission and can be operationally achieved are the ones followed by the organization.

All planning includes procedures for carrying out the plan. The procedures outline mechanisms for analysis, information collection, and monitoring that assist in developing and executing plans. Of course knowing what tools are available for planning is not the same as knowing how to apply those tools. Application is perfected through experience, practice, and reflection.

Finally, all planning involves assessment to provide tangible evidence of the process. The steps for achieving goals and the time frame and resources necessary for carrying out the plan are identified. Results are compared against goals for assessment purposes. Now the three major planning documents are covered in detail.

STRATEGIC PLANNING

Strategic planning is the long-term process by which an organization pursues its mission and tries to reach its goals. If an organization participates in two or more of the three traditional media markets—information, advertising, and intellectual—the strategic plan must explicitly address these markets and explain the relationship among them. A TV station cannot make plans for the advertising market without including the information market where viewers are attracted.

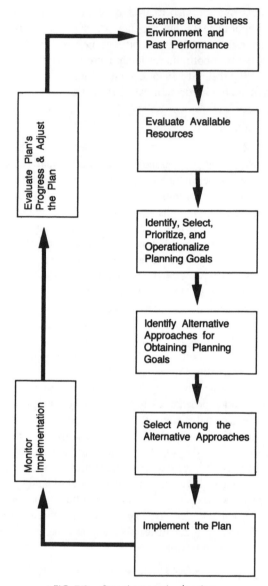

FIG. 7.2.   Steps in strategic planning.

A newspaper cannot plan for the information market without examining the role it plays in the intellectual market.

Smith et al. (1985) used the term *strategic management* in lieu of *strategic planning* because the traditional concept of strategic planning did not include control of the plan as it was implemented. They said strategic management includes: (a) analyzing the environment, (b) determining objectives, (c) analyzing strategic alternatives, (d) selecting strategy alternatives, (e) implementing the strategies, and (f) evaluating and controlling performance.

Combining these approaches plus adding control to planning results in a more refined approach to strategic thinking, which includes the following steps (see Fig. 7.2):

1. Examine the business environment and past performance.
2. Evaluate available resources.
3. Identify, select, prioritize, and operationalize planning goals.
4. Identify alternative approaches for obtaining goals.
5. Select from among the alternative approaches.
6. Implement the plan.
7. Monitor implementation.
8. Evaluate the plan's progress and adjust the plan.

Collection and analysis of information are part of these eight steps in strategic planning. Plans for the future must be grounded in experience and an understanding of current market conditions. Environmental factors affect how media companies approach their planning. Economic downturns have forced companies to adjust the time frame for strategic planning.

The market analysis is the primary method of evaluating the business environment. The internal examination involves how well the firm accomplished its goals in the past and why. Failure to reach goals could have resulted from any number of problems inside the firm, including inappropriate goals, goals set too high, poor analysis of data, inadequate resources, or poor performance.

Technology Resources

Technology in the last 5 years provided a dynamic way for managers to be closer to customers (whether they are advertisers or subscribers). For example, turnaround time has been greatly reduced for solving and responding to problems. Building technology options into the planning process is essential for media companies. One vice president of circulation for a newspaper says, "Technology has allowed us to put out a better product because we have improved deadlines for later news, have better distribution networks, and have greater ability to zone" (personal communication, April 19, 2002).

Many traditional media companies consider the Internet and online services as complementary products and plan accordingly. They cross-sell advertising, readers, viewers, and listeners. They sort regular subscribers so that sports enthusiasts receive e-mail alerts about special sales on sports equipment or offer additional discounts to customers who respond to cross-promotions on the Web. "We see the Internet as a way to grow our customer base as well as maintain and retain what we have. It has improved our customer relationship management," says a media manager (personal communication, April 19, 2002).

The Internet provided media companies with tools to build and retain customer relationships that are dynamic and not dependent on subscribers reporting problems to service departments. For example, subscribers can be sorted into regularly contacted groups. Within 2 weeks of subscribing, a new customer might receive an electronic welcome packet with coupons, special offers, and notices of presales at the retailers they identified as favorites. The next e-mail contact might thank the customer for being loyal and invite comments on the quality of service. The third contact might announce a special payment option for quality customers. Later on in the relationship, the subscriber might be identified as a preferred customer who has won two free tickets to a concert the media company is sponsoring.

Such timed, consistent, and planned targeting is attractive, allowing customers to be sorted and contacts adjusted according to demographics, lifestyle variables, geography, or customer longevity. Advertisers are easily built into the plan. The media company thus facilitates dynamic and multidimensional relationships among the medium, subscribers, and advertisers.

Evaluate Available Resources

A manager must evaluate at-hand resources to ensure that goals can be met. At-hand resources include the company's name and reputation, personnel, plant and equipment, and finances. At-hand means the resources are held currently by the firm or can be easily borrowed. Thus, financial resources also include an organization's credit.

Evaluating available resources is important because resources determine whether goals can be achieved. Although resources can be changed from one form to another, the process does not always occur as quickly as management would like. If a large metropolitan TV station needs an experienced award-winning anchor, it will take time to recruit such an anchor. The uncertainty of time necessitates good resource planning based on accurate evaluation of which anchors are good prospects.

As the strategic plan develops, evaluation reveals whether the resources needed to achieve the plan's goals are currently available in the form necessary. When the organization lacks the resources in the appropriate form needed by the plan, the plan must include ways to acquire new or convert current resources. If the needed resources are not and cannot be made available, the goals associated with those resources should be reconsidered or abandoned.

Setting Goals

No guidelines exist for the number of goals a firm needs to identify or select. However, all of the selected goals should be obtainable and consistent with the firm's general goals and mission. Each goal requires resources that are relatively fixed. The more goals a firm pursues, the more competition there is inside the organization for resources. For example, a small Ohio newspaper group might select the following goals:

1. Add daily newspapers until the group has papers in markets that make up 20% of the circulation in Ohio (information market goal).
2. Increase by 3% the penetration of existing markets (information market goal).
3. Increase by 2% revenue from national advertising (advertising market goal).
4. Increase by 5% the column inches of display advertising that run in the papers (advertising market goal).
5. Increase by 10% the column inches and percentage of the news hole devoted to letters to the editor and guest columns (intellectual market goal).

The goals listed for the information and advertising markets conceivably could compete for resources. The acquisition of newspapers costs money, as will efforts to increase penetration. The penetration goal involves additional spending for the circulation and news departments, as well as to promote the changes from the increased spending.

All five goals would consume resources and initially compete. However, as the plan goes into effect, achieving some goals generates revenue, which can then be applied to meeting other goals. Timing is important to consider because not all goals have to be reached at the same time. Some are set for the second or third year of the plan, and some are made contingent on reaching others.

Alternative Approaches

Almost all long-term goals are reached with more than one approach and often require multiple approaches. For example, a radio station that wants to increase its share of listeners can alter its music format and promote itself in a number of ways. The aim is to select the most efficient and effective ways to reach or surpass the goals. The ability to select the best approach depends on how exhaustive the analysis procedure is. Often management settles for a less than optimal plan to achieve a goal because all ideas were not identified in the decision-making stage.

Brainstorming is a commonly used technique for generating ideas. It applies two basic principles of creative thinking: A positive attitude is established, which means criticism is withheld until after ideas are developed, and unusual ideas are encouraged even if they seem impractical (Whiting, 1995).

Assessing alternatives includes eliminating impractical or improbable ones. Improbability and impracticality are based on any number of characteristics, including approaches with high risk, high environmental uncertainty, and high resource needs. The list of approaches is then pared to a manageable number of three to six good alternatives for achieving the goals. Comparison of alternative plans can be as formal or informal as management likes. From these comparisons, efficiency and effectiveness are determined. Efficiency is measured by the amount of resources needed to reach a goal, and the most efficient approach is the one that achieves the goal with the smallest expenditure of resources. Effectiveness is the probability that the approaches achieve the goals of the plan.

INTERMEDIATE PLANNING

Intermediate planning requires a marketing plan, a financial plan, and a human resources plan. The three must be coordinated with each other as well as with the overall strategic plan.

Marketing Plan

A marketing plan deals with the marketing mix, which includes product, place, price, and promotion (the four Ps). The marketing mix is applicable to the information, advertising, and intellectual markets. Although they are interrelated, each should have a marketing plan of its own. The product is simply what is sold or given to a consumer in exchange for time or money. In the information and intellectual markets, the product is information and ideas. In the advertising market, it is the potential attention of consumers to advertising information. The value of the advertising exposure depends on the number of viewers, readers, or listeners as well as the types of people paying the attention.

In most organizations, the product decision is based on the location of older products in their life cycle. Buzzell and Cook (1969) discussed five stages of a product's life cycle:

1. Infancy is when a product enters the market. Sales are low.
2. Growth occurs when the product matures as to whom and where it will sell. Sales grow rapidly if the product finds its niche in the marketplace.
3. Approaching maturity is when the established product begins to battle competitors over market share. Sales continue to grow, but at a slower rate.
4. Maturity occurs when a product finds its place in its category. Competition continues and sales grow much more slowly than earlier stages.
5. Decline is the final stage when consumers lose interest in the product and sales begin to decline.

With most media products, *place* is an important consideration. News commodities such as newspapers and newscasts are aimed at specific geographic areas. The content reflects this aim. A society's size, geography, social aspects, cultural characteristic, and political nature affect the places for which news products are designed. Place is also related to price in the United States. Some parts of the country have higher and lower standards of living than others. The same book would face a lower demand due to price in one region than in another.

Place also affects the process and cost of distributing the media product. The cost of delivering a newspaper increases as one moves away from the production site. The cost of distributing a broadcast TV program is basically the same within the signal's range. If the station wants to distribute the program elsewhere, satellite transmission would increase costs.

Price affects demand and determines how much revenue the firm takes in. Pricing is a difficult process because the joint nature of most media commodities creates extreme uncertainty. Managers are afraid to overprice in one type of market because it reduces demand in another. Increasing a magazine's subscription price might reduce circulation, which could affect the price charged to advertisers.

The traditional way to price existing products is to look at inflation, examine competitors' prices, add on additional expenses that have developed, estimate the impact of price on demand, and state the price with a profit goal in mind. The traditional way to price new products is to calculate production and distribution costs and add a desired profit margin.

The final P in the marketing mix is promotion. Promotion involves persuading people to use the product. Promotion includes advertising, public relations, and promotional activities.

Financial Plan

Budgets are the yearly plan of the organization. They cover expected sources of money and predicted expenses. The budget must reflect the priorities of the strategic plan or the mission of the organization will not be accomplished.

The strategic plan includes general budgetary priorities, whereas the intermediate plan reflects details for acquisitions as well as distribution of assets. Intermediate plans generally include documentation for all anticipated expenditures so that company accountants can anticipate and predict losses and gains connected to the intermediate plan.

Human Resources Plan

Employee planning involves the development of the talents, skills, and aspirations of people within an organization. The well-designed human resources plan analyzes the talents and skills a firm currently has compared with future needs. The key areas for manipulation and adjustment in human resources plans include: (a) work flows (which are connected to efficiency, control, and job description issues), (b) staff choices, (c) staff sizes (including how hiring freezes, terminations, and early retirements will be handled), (d) performance appraisals, (e) training and development, (f) compensation, (g) employee relations (including top–down/bottom–up communication, feedback, etc.), (h) employee rights (including ethical codes/enforcement as well as discipline), and (i) international management (including the use of expatriates, country nationals, or other staffing needs).

Say a newspaper plans to move most classified sales to its online product to update ads in a more timely fashion and offer links to customers. Managers have to assess whether to make the transition with current advertising staff (who are skilled in writing and selling advertising, but not in technology) or hire technology-skilled workers (who need training in advertising sales and copy writing). A third possibility is to hire recent college graduates from advertising programs (who have both sets of skills, but little experience).

All the choices are rational, but there are different costs and benefits associated with each alternative. Even more important, the decision should connect to a clear technology priority in the company's mission. That way training programs, recruiting efforts, and employee assessment procedures are proactive and suggestive of an appropriate decision connected to decisions managers are making in other departments.

SHORT-RUN PLANNING

Just as intermediate plans serve as maps for the strategic plan, short-run plans are ways to meet the goals of the intermediate plans. However, short-run planning is most vulnerable to becoming reactive.

Managers responding to temporary environmental or business fluctuations must assess how long the effects of the changes will be a factor and whether those changes can be ignored until stability returns. A firm with an inflexible strategic plan has the most difficulty in responding to change. Such a firm is most vulnerable to following a fatal path that drains resources, fails to address immediate opportunities, and is overcome by more alert competitors.

However, a firm with an ambiguous mission may invest too early in a new product or service, or it may prematurely abandon an idea that just needs time and effort to succeed. Constant and consistent assessment is critical with short-run planning.

STRATEGIC PLANNING FOR INTERNATIONAL MARKETS

Moving into international markets affects a media company's long-term strategic plan. New issues arise that must be carefully considered within the context of the overall planning process discussed earlier. Planning for international operations is becoming increasingly important for media corporations. Over the years, there was a handful of multinational media corporations and media products such as films and TV programs exported to foreign audiences. However, during the 1980s and 1990s, the internationalization of the media industry grew dramatically.

In 1980, no major media player was based outside North America (Compaine & Gomery, 2000). By 1998, few U.S.-based firms were major global media. However, the United States was attracting interest from international media such as Murdoch's News Corporation, which is based in Australia and has interests in Europe and Asia. News Corp.'s major properties include magazines, broadcast TV, cable networks, film production and distribution, and book publishing. The United States is also attracting interest from Bertelsmann (a Germany-based leader in recorded music and book publishing), Reed-Elsevier (a Dutch–English joint venture with interests in magazines and electronic info services), Pearson PLC (book publishing) and EMI Group (recorded music leader), both based in London, and Softbank (magazines and electronic info services) in Japan (Compaine & Gomery, 2000).

During the same period that foreign companies were investing in the U.S. media, communication companies in the United States were buying or starting companies overseas. The economics of media production make global operations desirable. Once a company creates a media product such as a TV program, film, or magazine, it costs almost nothing to distribute it to more people (U.S. Department of Commerce, 1993). Moreover, each additional person who sees a program or magazine spreads the costs of producing it more widely, thereby increasing the media company's profit.

Despite these economics, media companies interested in international expansion face significant barriers. Most nations, including the United States have had laws limiting or forbidding foreign ownership of media companies. Such laws protect domestic media industries from foreign competition and concerns that foreign owners might influence content and public opinion in times of war or national crisis. Restrictions on foreign ownership generally were most stringent for telephone systems, TV, and radio stations. Magazine companies and book publishers tended to be less regulated so foreign ownership was more common in these media sectors.

Many countries also restrict media imports. Europe and Canada have had strict quotas on the importation of U.S.-produced films and TV programming (Gershon, 1997). Critics of imported media fear the sheer volume of relatively inexpensive U.S. film and TV products will inhibit domestic activity. Plus, the values shown in these U.S. films and TV may undermine national cultures and values—a process known as *cultural imperialism*.

Expanding Markets

In the 1980s and early 1990s, a number of factors came together to encourage Western countries to open media markets to foreign investment. Improved communication and transportation technologies made it easier for corporations to expand into new markets, so companies in many industries around the world began to globalize their operations.

Multinational companies need highly developed information-transfer systems such as computer networks, sophisticated telephone systems, and databases to run expanded operations (U.S. House of Representatives 1980, 1981a, 1981b). That need puts pressure on governments to deregulate their domestic telecommunications industries to provide consumers and businesses access to the latest technologies and services regardless of whether they are provided by domestic or foreign-owned providers.

Concurrently, there was a movement to reduce trade barriers between nations because free international trade creates greater economic efficiencies, helps business, and provides consumers with more product choices for lower prices. The need for access to the best communication technology and services, and the desire to reduce trade barriers in general, led many developed nations to reevaluate their media ownership limits. Trade agreements signed during the period, including the European Union agreement between European nations (Gershon, 1997) and the North American Free Trade Agreement (NAFTA) among the United States, Canada, and Mexico, included specific provisions to encourage the opening of media markets to foreign trade and investment.

Changes in the international economy and business environment pressured developed countries to make it easier for media companies to operate internationally just as changes within the media industry encouraged media firms to take that step. The growth of the global economy encouraged many media companies to buy media operations in foreign countries where it was allowed.

Finally, media companies invested overseas or developed joint ventures with foreign partners to get around the limitations some nations placed on the foreign import of media products. Overseas investment became a way to maintain and increase foreign exports (Carveth, 1992; Gershon, 1997). As media globalization continues, it becomes increasingly likely that professionals in all types of media will work for a company having overseas holdings or owned by a foreign company. Thus, ambitious media managers must prepare to meet the planning challenges and opportunities presented across cultures and borders.

Business Record

As with domestic companies, strategic planning for international media operations begins with examining the business environment and past performances of the country or countries where a firm is considering investing. The questions raised, however, are somewhat different than those a manager faces when examining a home market and company. Numerous factors influence a decision about where to invest, including the strength of the local economy, regulatory environment for media, language and cultural differences that may affect how media are received, and what advertising might be sold to support the media product. These factors also affect which media product(s) are developed.

Media products are generally luxury items. If most of a country's residents live a meager existence with little or no disposable income, the market for media products is generally weak. Advertisers are not interested in reaching consumers with little potential buying power. In contrast, countries with strong economies generally have highly developed media markets and stiff advertising competition. A manager engaged in international strategic planning must balance analysis of the country's economic conditions against what is known about the competition.

Just as when Eastern Europe was opened, media managers can spot countries that lack a strong economy or media industry, but are showing signs of growth in both areas. Media corporations from Europe and North America invested heavily in Eastern European countries after the Eastern Bloc collapsed in 1989. Ownership of large segments of Eastern Europe's print media passed into the hands of foreign companies (Hollifield, 1993; Sukosd, 1992).

Other opportunities arise when developed countries deregulate or privatize media sectors. Germany had two publicly operated TV networks until 1984 when it permitted commercial broadcasting, which expanded rapidly. Although German companies largely control commercial TV there, some foreign media enterprises such as the News Corporation Ltd. and Walt Disney Co. have holdings in German TV (Holtz-Bacha, 1996).

Regulatory Restrictions

Media managers must carefully evaluate national regulatory environments. Other nations may require media companies that buy foreign media to share partial ownership with domestic partners. Media content and copyright regulations can be troublesome. Some countries have not signed international copyright agreements and others do not enforce international copyright laws, making production or distribution of media products there particularly vulnerable. A media company entering these countries may have difficulty protecting its publications or programs from illegal copying or pirating. Pirating is already widespread in the recording and software industries.

These economic and regulatory decisions impact what media products a company should attempt to produce and/or sell overseas. If a market's economy is weak due to a potential audience's limited disposable income, develop publications or programs that give audiences useful information such as home repair or sewing rather than unnecessary fashion or gossip programming. Content regulations could also affect a media manager's choice of what to produce. Great Britain, for example, has more restrictions than the United States on what media can report about criminal justice proceedings and official secrets. Some photographs and magazine advertisements depicting women in United States would be deemed pornography in some Middle Eastern countries. Such regulations can make it more difficult to produce content and sell advertising overseas.

Education, Culture, and Language

Educational, cultural, and language differences also affect product and market choices. A publishing company manager must consider literacy rates because most of a country's population must read to be a thriving market for magazines, books, and newspapers. If only a small percentage of the population is computer literate or has access to computers, online media services are not likely to be successful.

Cultural differences are critical as well. By nature, media mirror and influence the culture in which they are created and sold. That is why so many countries worry about cultural imperialism from foreign-produced media.

A media manager must thoroughly understand the local culture of the country where a company plans to invest. Cultural differences influence how media content and advertisers are received. For example, humor is culturally based, playing off subtle situations or words familiar to people in one culture, but not their neighbors over the border. Humorous content does not tend to travel well.

Media content is language based so it must be available in the local language to reach an overseas audience. This means dubbing films and video or adding subtitles. Publications must be translated, which is difficult and has a high risk of error, or produced locally by native speakers in the overseas market. Successful ad campaigns or product names may not translate well into other languages.

English has become the dominant language of the new electronic media. Yet that means non-English speakers cannot access English-based electronic media content and advertisements. Some countries fear the growing importance of new media and its domination by English will undermine local languages. Certain governments require electronic content and media products offered locally to be in their national language. So media companies and advertisers making their content available to international audiences must have it translated or dubbed.

Evaluate Resources

Several important issues surface when evaluating available resources to support international expansion. The manager must decide what the company's primary goal is because that answer will influence other answers to key decisions about internationalizing operations. Other issues include whether the firm should enter the foreign market by taking its own product in or acquiring existing media companies there. Another concern is how the new venture is financed and how much financial risk the company wants to incur. Those issues raise questions of whether the investment should be managed through a wholly owned subsidiary, partnership, strategic alliance, licensing, or other ownership structure. The company then decides how to organize and manage the new venture and find the human resources necessary for success.

The first issue is establishing the primary goal for overseas operations. Bartlett and Ghoshal (1989, 1990) identified four primary models (international, multinational, global, and transnational) for managing cross-border operations and the goals that drive those models.

Four Models

The *international* model defines companies that use overseas operations to distribute their domestic products in foreign markets. Thus, the overseas operation is seen as secondary to the company's main purpose. Human resources control and most knowledge needed to produce the product of the foreign office stay with company headquarters. Information flows one way from company headquarters to the overseas operation, which is expected to return little to the parent company besides profits (Bartlett & Ghoshal, 1989, 1990). One example of the international model is TV companies that establish overseas joint ventures to skirt import quotas on domestically produced programming.

The *multinational* company places more emphasis on foreign operations, using its subsidiaries to develop different products for different markets. It modifies its strategies and management practices to maximize efficiency in each country where it operates. The emphasis is on producing local products that are specifically tailored to local markets. In multinational companies, managers are often hired locally and operate with a fair amount of independence from company headquarters in making daily decisions.

A multinational company might be seen as a series of semi-independent but affiliated national companies with similar but distinct product lines (Bartlett & Ghoshal, 1989, 1990). This strategy maximizes the relevance of the company's products to its local audience, but lessens the company's ability to capture economies of scale. Newspaper companies based outside the United States that own many U.S. newspapers are an example of this model. Each newspaper is produced for a local audience. Only some of the copy from any given newspaper is shared with other U.S. papers. Even less is of interest to newspapers in the home country.

Global companies view the entire world as their market, designing and producing products to be sold universally. Global companies maximize production efficiencies, assuming consumers in all nations want basically the same things. Most management planning and decision making are made in worldwide headquarters, although production may be scattered around the globe (Bartlett & Ghoshal, 1989, 1990). Magazine publishers often take this approach, publishing magazines reproduced by one company in multiple countries with only minor adjustments to content and translation.

The U.S. film and TV industries take a global approach to film production. In recent decades, the large budgets required to make films made it necessary for Hollywood producers to take foreign film markets into account. Overseas audiences can make the difference in profit margins. Foreign audiences have thus become more than a secondary market to Hollywood studios, producing films with global popularity in mind. However, Carveth (1992) and Turow (1992) suggested this may be changing. European audiences are increasingly interested in films with European content, which may eventually move the film industry to adopt the transnational model.

The *transnational* model of international management began to emerge in the mid-1980s and 1990s. It merges the best of the other models while becoming more responsive to consumers' increasing demands that products be at least somewhat localized. The transnational company is neither centralized in the home market or global headquarters nor decentralized in all of its outlying operations. Instead different subsidiaries are assigned different specialties and given the resources and responsibilities to produce them. This makes the company flexible and responsive in meeting local needs while still being able to combine the efforts of its different overseas operations to gain efficiencies in production and economies of scale.

Nationality is deliberately downplayed because the organization recruits on a worldwide or regional basis for the best people to fill management positions. Managers are dynamic employees who identify with organizational goals rather than provincial ones. Corporate managers will share planning data with overseas subsidiaries. These operations constantly scan their local environments for new product ideas, new markets, and new efficiencies to share with corporate operations around the globe (Bartlett & Ghoshal, 1989, 1990). This two-way learning process is a key distinguishing element of the transnational model. The truly transnational manager recognizes that a primary benefit of operating in worldwide markets is the ability to learn from the people in those markets and gain new ideas for better products and better ways to do business.

The recording industry fits the transnational model in some respects. Burnett (1992) said a handful of multinational media companies control the worldwide recording industry—up to 80% of the market in some countries. As consolidation in the industry increased, so did the number of new artists and diversity of music available to consumers. Burnett said this is due to the multinationals' strategy of affiliating with small semi-independent recording labels worldwide, which then search their local music scenes for new talent. These small labels constantly introduce new music and artists to market locally and regionally. The multinationals then distribute more widely if they believe the sound has wider appeal.

Entering Markets

After a media company sets its goals for international expansion, it decides how to enter its chosen foreign market. There are two basic approaches: start its own overseas operations or acquire an existing media company in that country. If the primary goal is to be an international company and use its overseas operations as a secondary market for existing products, it is unlikely to enter a foreign market by buying another company and its product line.

However, multinational, global, or transnational operations might be accomplished through start-ups or acquisitions. Acquisitions allow the buyer to enter the new market with an already established product, reducing the risk of the investment. Much of the globalization that took place during the 1980s and 1990s was accomplished through media mergers and acquisitions.

Next, the new venture's ownership structure is planned. As with domestic operations, the ownership structure directly affects its available sources of capital. The simplest approach is to set up a wholly owned subsidiary overseas or a company the parent company owns and operates entirely. This simplifies decision making and leaves little room for misunderstandings among co-owners from different countries.

However, running a wholly owned subsidiary means the parent company cannot learn about the new market from a local co-owner or another company with expertise there. The company must shoulder all the financial burden of the foreign investment. This burden can be considerable due to additional travel, shipping, and communication costs between the subsidiary and headquarters. As a result, it usually takes several years for a foreign investment to become profitable.

Partnerships

Another option is to set up a joint venture or strategic alliance with one or more partners. In this arrangement, partners share decision making as well as the risks, costs, and ultimately the success of the foreign investment when it becomes profitable. Many countries require foreign-owned media companies operating within their borders to have at least one local partner. Strategic alliances with local producers also are a means for foreign media companies to gain access to restricted media markets. Having a local partner is particularly valuable because the partner provides contacts (with government, industry, and clients), advice on developing culturally appropriate and attractive content, and helps the new venture avoid the inevitable mistakes of doing business in a new environment.

There are significant advantages to joint ventures even when the partner is not a local company. Strategic alliances help companies share knowledge, tap new innovations, and share the costs of technology development, especially in technology-intensive media specialties. However, the disadvantages include the disagreements that arise over strategies and decision-making authority. There can be culturally based misunderstandings among partners from different countries. A company could use the alliance to gain proprietary knowledge of the dominant partner's product line, later dissolving the joint venture to use that knowledge to compete against its former partner. Finally, if one partner is financially weaker than the other, problems can arise if the new subsidiary performs below expectations and must be subsidized longer than planned.

A third approach to overseas investment is licensing, where a media company sells another company the rights to produce specific media products in a foreign market. The company buying the rights assumes all risks of making a successful entry into the new market. The parent company usually supplies the concept, graphics, and design elements, whereas the company that buys the license is responsible for product translation, production, and distribution. Television programs such as "Wheel of Fortune" and "America's Funniest Home Videos" and magazines have been licensed to European and overseas media companies.

A licensing arrangement allows the seller to widen the distribution of its publication or programming with minimal risk and financial investment. The licensee, in turn, gains the rights to a proven and successful media product, making it easier to find an audience and advertisers. Yet license fees greatly reduce the direct gain the creating company receives from having its product in a new overseas market. The licensor loses control over production of its publication or program, making it difficult to ensure that high standards of quality are maintained. If the licensee fails in the new market, it may be difficult for the creating company to reenter the market with that publication or program using a different licensee or another arrangement.

In summary, once a company evaluates the business environment, performance of a potential overseas market, and the resources available for its expansion, the planning process becomes more similar to domestic strategic planning. Planning goals are refined further and operationalized. Alternative approaches are selected to meet, implement, monitor, evaluate, and adjust the plan and goals. Each of these steps, however, is carried out in the context of the company's original internationalization goals, its analysis of the target country's business environment, its decisions about how its foreign operations are structured, and the effects those structures have on available resources.

INTERNATIONAL INTERMEDIATE PLANNING

When the company enters the intermediate planning process, managers face additional issues specific to transborder media management. Particular attention is paid to the product or service aspect of the overseas marketing plan.

International Marketing

Again the economy, regulatory environment, and culture affects a media company's choice of the publications, programs, or other services to distribute. Cultural factors are carefully analyzed even after a media firm decides to distribute a particular product. Often differences are so subtle they are difficult for a nonnative manager to recognize, but those differences can signal success or failure for the new foreign venture.

Say a magazine or TV program features recipes or cooking tips. The producers must ensure the recipes are adapted for local tastes and the necessary ingredients are locally available. Home repair and other how-to publications or programs must consider local needs and locally available products and tools. Those teaching people to build decks and patios are useless where the majority of a country's population live in apartments in cities, as is the case in many European nations. Advertisements must be screened to avoid offending local mores or insulting readers and viewers.

Even the company logos, program set designs, and so on must be carefully reevaluated in the foreign market. Color is culturally significant and can signal different things in different countries. For example, white is the color of mourning in the Middle East.

Place is also an issue because transportation and communication infrastructures of many countries are less developed than in the United States. The target country's infrastructure is examined to see how easily the product can be distributed outside of urban areas. The investing firm must decide whether the costs of widespread distribution are acceptable.

The promotion process also changes because promotional slogans and even the publication or program's name may not translate well into other languages. Common U.S. promotional strategies such as event sponsorship may not be possible or acceptable for increasing audiences overseas. It is difficult if not impossible to collect ratings and readership data, making it hard to do target marketing. Hence, the media manager must carefully research possible promotional strategies when developing a marketing plan for another country.

Human Resources Issues

The human resources plan addresses how to acquire and develop, as well as where to find, the employees needed to manage the foreign operation and produce the media content. Existing managers or key personnel may be sent to oversee the new cross-border operation. This *ethnocentric* approach ensures that staff is familiar with the company's goals. These managers are unfamiliar with and have few or no contacts in the new market. It can also be difficult to find Americans who are qualified to work overseas. Fewer Americans speak a second language and lived or traveled extensively in other countries than employees found in other regions of the world.

With the *polycentric* model, employees are hired locally for the new foreign office or existing management and personnel are left in place. A large measure of corporate control is forfeited. The foreign managers and employees have local contacts, but they need training and time to assimilate corporate expectations.

Among transnational companies, the *geocentric* model is a third approach to personnel management. For example, a New Zealand executive might manage a U.S. office for a German parent company, or a Japanese national might run a subsidiary in India for a British corporation. Companies make long-term commitments to these multifaceted, international managers. They are groomed carefully for top leadership positions where their international outlook, expertise, and experience can be used to guide the transnational organization. Ambitious future managers must expect increased competition for top jobs as companies look worldwide for the most talented, capable, and adaptable individuals.

Staff Choices

When an organization determines a human resources plan, it considers the availability of local talent. Illiteracy and training may be a major concern for a firm considering a property in a developing nation. A firm having a global vision is concerned about hiring locals who focus on their own unit rather than the organization as a whole. Production raises issues if the media product requires managers with broader experience and a sophisticated understanding of the links in the process. Managers with less product-specific knowledge are desired for a primarily stand-alone product with little interdependence across units. A nation's political stability is a factor. Expatriates are favored when the risk of government intervention or terrorism exists. Expatriates are less susceptible to local political forces and provide assurance that overall organizational goals are upheld.

Finally, significant cultural differences affect managerial selection. If language, religion, and customs are different, expatriates who are good interpreters or transition agents between the home and host country make good choices. Cultural barriers are lowest for U.S. companies in Europe, Canada, Australia, and

New Zealand, with midrange barriers in Latin America and greatest barriers in Asia, the Middle East, and Africa.

Yet U.S. expatriates can fail to complete assignments. It is estimated that 20% to 40% return prematurely—a failure rate three to four times that of European and Asian companies. Failures are costly because "premature returnees cost $98,000 to $294,000 each in 2000 dollars, which translates into $3.8 billion per year in direct costs to U.S. firms" (Gomez-Mejia, Balkin, & Cardy, 2001, p. 561). Other intangibles such as business disruptions, pauses in leadership, and missed business opportunities are connected to failures.

Financial Planning Abroad

Most financial planning is done during the initial strategic planning process for overseas market entry. Details of how the new venture is capitalized during its first few years are worked out as the venture is set up and ownership structure is established. The initial financial plan may be reconsidered if unexpected difficulties are encountered. Overseas operations are generally expensive to run due to higher travel and communication costs. New start-up ventures often take several years to become profitable under the best of circumstances; when investing overseas, it can take even longer.

Several factors could alter intermediate financial projections and require emergency funding for the new venture. Economic downturns are harder to anticipate and can throw off initial financial plans if they occur. Hiring a local staff may create greater than expected training costs because the staff must learn new ways of working, even if the parent company buys an existing media company. New equipment costs and legal expenses may soar as the parent company negotiates in an unfamiliar legal and regulatory environment. Foreign-produced media content may not be accepted locally due to cultural differences and will need adjustment.

Assessment

Finally, managers must establish a company benchmark during intermediate planning to measure the new venture's financial success. For some firms, a new venture is a success if it generates enough revenue to cover its expenses during the intermediate planning period. For other firms, a venture is profitable when it also covers the parent company's additional overhead, such as travel, communication, training, and management oversight. Others consider a new venture profitable only if the parent company's initial investment and start-up expenses are repaid and its operating costs and management overhead are covered.

Probably the most difficult situation is when the new venture does not meet the parent company's financial benchmarks during the intermediate planning process. The manager then decides whether the long-term potential benefits justify maintaining an unprofitable overseas media operation. The manager must rethink how the overseas investment is structured, how it is managed, and the products it produces. Sometimes a struggling media venture is rescued by changing partners, managers, the product mix, or by changing and relaunching an established product. Sometimes the only viable decision is to abandon a market and focus company efforts on other products or countries.

Technology Impacts

Converging media technologies eroded the distinctions between the telephone, computer, TV, radio, newspaper, magazine, and book industries. Convergence and increased competition, combined with reduced revenues and profits, pressured media companies to expand internationally (Turow, 1992), often by developing profitable synergies or distributing the same content or concepts through different media products. A story idea was cross-marketed by a multimedia conglomerate through its book publishing and film studios while the movie soundtrack was sold through its record company. These synergies also were realized by acquisition of and investment in other lines of business often to gain experience overseas. Media technology manufacturers also wanted to gain control of popular films or music to ensure such entertainment features were distributed in formats compatible with their technologies (Carveth, 1992; Gershon, 1997; Turow, 1992).

By 2002, signs of disenchantment with new and converging media emerged. The forced departure of Thomas Middelhoff as head of Germany's Bertelsmann in July 2002 sent a chilling signal to international online media developers. AOL TIME WARNER INC. and Vivendi Universal SA joined Middelhoff, an international technology visionary who invested in Web-music upstart Napster, in heavy investments in media technology. All were sharply withdrawing to their core traditional media businesses by 2002. Over the next decade, an interesting set of models should emerge as technology becomes less of an experimental toy and more of an integral strategic planning tool for companies that want an international presence and solid profits.

SUMMARY

Planning is the essence of good management. It is much like decision making in that its success depends on the adequate collection and analysis of information. The planning process should involve people from all organizational levels. Planning takes three basic forms: strategic, intermediate, and short run. Strategic is long-range planning, usually involving 3 to 5 years. Intermediate planning often involves 6 months to 2 years. Short-run planning involves a week to a year.

Investing overseas often entails more risk than expanding a media company's business in its own home market. Yet in today's global economy, overseas investments are becoming more common and important to the long-term well-being of media corporations. International operations provide access to larger audiences and more advertisers, and they tap new technologies, new ideas, and new artists or producers from countries beyond a firm's home market. Having subsidiaries in other countries balances a company's finances as a downturn in one country's economy may be partially offset by an upsurge or stability in the economy of another. Finally, the multinational media corporation often has resources and economies of scale that can give it advantages in head-to-head competition against other strictly domestic media operations.

Thus, the pace of media globalization is increasingly rapid. Future media managers must have foreign language skills, multicultural knowledge, and a global outlook. Media executives of the 21st century must understand the complex issues that arise when managing media ventures in different countries, have the skills to anticipate those challenges, and possess the knowledge and ability to plan strategically for success in the global media economy.

ACKNOWLEDGMENTS

The author wishes to thank the Sam Houston State University Journalism Program and Yvette Keener, student assistant, for their support and assistance during the writing of this chapter.

Case 7.1
Connecting Online and Traditional Media:
Not Always an Easy Planning Task

Sheila was promoted 3 months ago to vice president of interactive media at a medium-size newspaper in the west. Her new responsibilities include coordinating strategic planning for the entire organization. Next month she is scheduled to present a 3- to 5-year strategic plan for integrating online classified advertising with traditional newspaper classified advertising to the newspaper's executive board.

Sheila was promoted primarily because she used technology to open new markets for her company. Ten years ago, she started at the newspaper in part-time classified advertising sales taking orders over the phone. Within a year, she convinced the advertising director to experiment with online ads, and after a few years built up a small department. In 1997, she was named director of new media. Her primary goal then was to have the largest possible database of classified ad listings. She started her campaign with car dealers and real estate firms. "We knew the vast majority of car dealers and real estate companies only ran a portion of their listings in the printed newspaper. We began to offer packages to run *all* their listings online," she said.

Next, Sheila created a Web site for each advertiser and then merged their listings into the newspaper's search program. At first she did all the work herself, but then added a programmer, two production people, and one salesperson. Today she has $18\frac{1}{2}$ full-time employees, including four salespeople, three sales support staff to help with ad creation, and two programmers. The rest are producers who function as news journalists. They manage two Web sites. One is a regional portal with partnerships that serves as a repository for all the newspaper's classified ads. The other site is devoted to a news product that contains most of the daily newspaper's contents plus four or five local stories updated throughout the day. The online news product has increased overall readership as well as the number of times the same people visit the company's server.

Marketing Potential

The goal for the classified advertising Web site is to have the largest number of listings possible. "If people want to see a full inventory of local jobs, cars or houses available in the region, we want them to think of us and our Web site as the place to come," Sheila says. Recently she focused her attention on increasing online job advertisements. Hiring is down because of economic factors. However, Sheila knows local employers still have jobs to advertise because she assigned most of her staff to interview local businesses.

From the staff research, she learned there were businesses wanting to advertise jobs, but not the traditional way. In the past, businesses with jobs to fill hired a recruiting firm to place ads in the newspaper for a fee, sort through applicants, and schedule interviews with the most qualified applicants. The recruiting firm also received a commission from the newspaper for every ad it placed. The relationship between the newspaper and recruiting firms was closer than the one between the newspaper and businesses. Sheila learned the newspaper advertising staff did not contact businesses directly, but relied totally on recruiting firms to bring classified job ads to the paper. Several local recruiting firms folded in the past year, and the newspaper's classified job listings dropped 10%. During this same period, the online job listing service, Monster.com, drew over 14% of local adults to its Web site. The newspaper's advertising manager said recruiting firms claimed online services like Monster.com were unpopular with local businesses because they draw too many resumes and unqualified applicants.

Sheila would not stake her company's competitive advantage on providing fewer resumes and applicants than online services. While acknowledging that online services can draw resumes from people who are clearly not qualified, she knew electronic formats allow easy and almost instantaneous sorting. She could offer job listings at about a tenth of the cost of recruiting firms. She sees Monster.com and similar services as strong competitors for local job listings. She had 10 staff members make personal contact with local employers to find out how they recruit using the Internet. She found that businesses do not care how many resumes or unqualified applicants they receive because their human resources software filters and then matches qualified people with job openings. They even archive applicants who are perfect for jobs opening soon. They do not want the newspaper or a recruiting firm to screen for them.

Competitive Advantages

Sheila thinks her online service offers local employers at least three unique advantages. The first is the combined distribution channels of the newspaper and Web site. Half of the 200,000 people who visit her Web site never check the newspaper for employment ads. Other people only read the newspaper and never do an Internet job search. Unlike online sources, she offers high visibility in two media.

Second, she offers local customer service—something the newspaper had turned over to recruiting firms. She admits it is old fashioned, but such personal attention worked well in the automotive and real estate classified markets. It is a service that national online providers cannot duplicate. If there is a problem, the local businessperson "can march right down here and talk to me about it."

Third, a local online service delivers better quality applicants. She is testing to confirm this. Early findings show applicants who use a newspaper Web site have higher demographics than random responders from a larger area.

Financial Concerns

Whereas the newspaper uses a rigid rate card, Sheila printed an online rate card once in 1995 that cost $5,000 for a nice design and folder, but it was outdated in a month so she never printed another. In general, Sheila does better by tailoring and customizing to the advertiser, especially for banner ads and sponsorships. Job posting rates and packages are published online and the online rates are nominal (compared with the newspaper). An interesting Internet dynamic is there are no marginal costs when adding one ad or job posting online versus adding 20 or 100. "There's no difference to us," Sheila says.

Sheila's online operation is similar to TV and radio stations that provide clients with a list of things they can do or the overall value of an ad. Selling online banner advertising space is like buying time on radio stations. If you call a month in advance, when much radio time is available, it costs one price, but if you call at the last minute, the price goes up because there is little time left. Sheila tracks how much banner space is available on both Web sites (the classified ad site and news site) and prices according to availability when customers inquire.

In addition to job, car, and real estate ads, Sheila's online site caters to small independent companies like Nosey Neighbor, which offers public records searches (for criminal checks, financial backgrounds, employment histories, etc.). Sheila's online classified ad site also attracts smaller advertisers who find the traditional newspaper too expensive. Sheila is certain online classified advertising can be a major contributor to the company's profits. First, she must develop a flexible plan that can handle the dynamics of an online medium without losing the traditional revenue generated by newspaper classified advertising.

Human Resources Issues

Sheila is excited about the prospects of online advertising, but concerned about the conflict between her online salespeople and the newspaper salespeople. Until recently, the online and newspaper salespeople were not even in the same building. About 8 months ago, Sheila moved two online salespeople into the same building as the newspaper's advertising staff. There were mixed results from the forced interaction. The newspaper sales staff said the online advertising people are cannibalizing their revenue. "That's in spite of the fact that we're just one drop in the bucket," said Sheila, pointing out that if the newspaper Web site was not capturing the online advertising revenue, a competitor would be stealing the business from the company.

Incentives are also an issue because they are higher for newspaper salespeople than online salespeople. It is hard for Sheila to develop a competitive incentive package for her sales staff because the revenue overall is smaller (than for the newspaper). She wants to keep a decent online profit margin.

In addition, there are serious job skill differences between Sheila's staff and the newspaper's staff. Some newspaper salespeople are unfamiliar with online ads and do not even use the Internet. Because they do not use it, they are skeptical about how many customers use, although her Web site gets significantly more traffic than readership figures show for the entire newspaper.

> Sheila said, We have trouble conversing. Even in the simplest ways—it's so easy to have misunderstandings in terms of terminology and things. I have actively encouraged our print counterparts to hire people with Internet experience. We will not make progress if the technology-savvy people are in some small department off to the side and don't have any chance at career advancement. They'll leave and go someplace other than newspapers. I think it's really important for us to take the skills they have and integrate them and the technology into the heart of the newspaper.

There will come a time when the vice president of advertising will be somebody who started off in the Internet.

Staffing is a major concern. How do we train people? How do we plan for future hiring and integration of the two staffs (online and printed newspaper)? These are questions Sheila must answer in her strategic plan. Sheila was an English major who taught herself to use the Internet. Early media technology staff were generalists and company entrepreneurs. They would sell ads, make callbacks, work on the Web site—do it all. However, to achieve real excellence, we need people who specialize, Sheila says.

Connecting Mission to Action

Sheila's biggest challenge is figuring out how to integrate the online business into the established functional organizational setting where separations among the newsroom, advertising department, circulation department, and production exist. Online products are much more cross-functional. They must be flexible and able to change rapidly, Sheila says. Fitting the online business into the traditional top–down organizational structure of a newspaper is difficult.

Sheila knows her strategic plan must be tied to the company's mission statement: "It is the mission of this newspaper to provide a timely, convenient, ethical and accurate product of excellence and public service designed to inform, entertain, and enlighten readers living in our community and region."

ASSIGNMENT

Using the information in the chapter and the case, write Sheila's 3- to 5-year strategic plan for integrating online and newspaper classified advertising. She will present it to the company's executive committee in 1 month.

1. Be sure to clarify how the mission statement guides the strategic plan. The strategic plan should include an analysis of: the business environment, past business performance, available resources, identification of goals, preferred as well as alternative ways to meet the goals, implementation plans, and evaluation/assessment tools.
2. Prepare an intermediate plan including marketing, financial, and human resources components designed to support the strategic plan.
3. Design a short-run plan that outlines the steps to take and how resources are allocated during the first few weeks of the plan's initiation.

8

MARKET ANALYSIS

A market is where customers buy goods, and services are supplied and sold by businesses. A market analysis defines the opportunities a business has in a particular market or with a particular product and the short- and long-term threats it may face. It is a critical component of strategic media management and is inextricably interwoven with planning and marketing research.

There are two ways to view the market analysis process: (a) as a formal project a media manager undertakes before the company makes a major new investment, launches a new product, or changes its overall business strategy; and (b) as part of the daily routine of media managers at all organizational levels. Managers at all organizational levels must constantly scan the competitive environment for changes in the structure of their markets, the demand for their products, and the nature of the competition they face. Each manager must identify opportunities to exploit or new, emerging competitive threats. Media managers who do not actively and continually analyze their market are almost guaranteed to face competitive problems they never saw coming.

Market analysis is a useful skill for self-employed media professionals such as freelance writers and independent producers. When executives listen to independents pitch an idea for a book or TV series, they want to hear specific details about how it will earn revenue for the firm (e.g., they want the concept pitched as a market analysis). What is the target audience and how large and valuable is it to advertisers or financiers? What similar concepts already exist to compete with the proposed project? How will it fit with the mix of films, books, or series that the company already produces? What will it cost to produce? What is the production/distribution company's return on investment likely to be?

Even media professionals such as reporters benefit from understanding the market analysis process. A reporter who wants to launch a major investigative project or visit China to write about a special museum exhibit of Chinese art is wise to propose the project to the editor in market analysis terms. What will the project cost in time and money? How will it position the newspaper or TV station in relationship to its direct competitors? What will the return on investment be in terms of circulation or ratings, promotional opportunities, journalistic awards, or reputation in the market? The reporter who gathered the data and analyzed such issues before pitching the idea has a much better chance of gaining project approval than one who walks into the editor's office and says, "Hey, Boss! I had a great idea this morning!"

So how is a market analysis conducted? A market is typically defined by geography and product. Geography is the physical location where the product is sold, so a newspaper's geographic market is the area where the paper is distributed through home delivery or newsstand sales. A radio station's geographic market is the area reached by its broadcast signal. Whereas broadcast and print outlets have carefully defined local geographic markets, other types of media companies, such as film, TV, online, book, and magazine producers, see the entire world as their geographic market, selecting and developing content accordingly.

Product refers to the type of product a company sells. A market analysis for a product includes demand for that product and the number of competitors selling that product or substitutes for it in the firm's geographic market. For media companies, analyzing the product aspect of their markets is more complicated than for most industries because media products are joint commodities.

Said another way, media companies work in a dual-product market or sell the same product into two different markets at the same time. They sell content to audiences and sell those audiences to advertisers. The advertisers buy advertising messages specifically targeted to the types of audiences the content attracts. For media companies, an analysis of their product market includes more than just a look at the demand and competition for the content they produce. It must also examine the advertising market, audiences in their geographic market, and how desirable those audiences are to potential advertisers.

Recently media economists identified a third element besides product and geography to define media markets: the investment market for media companies (Albarran, 1996). This third element is growing in importance as media managers compete with other media companies and industries to attract investors. Decisions are often based on how likely an investment or project will affect the company's stock price or overall value. A media company may not invest in or develop a product that could help its competitive position in the long term if management thinks the move could harm its position in investment markets in the short term.

This chapter provides an overview of the market analysis process. It outlines the elements of product, geographic, and investment markets that media managers need to monitor. The ways those elements are evaluated in the media industry also are discussed.

THE PROCESS OF MARKET ANALYSIS

The market analysis process consists of carefully examining three types of factors: external conditions, internal conditions, and financial conditions (Stevens, Sherwood, & Dunn, 1993). External conditions include long-term trends such as market growth, demand for the product, political/regulatory conditions and technological trends, as well as more specific factors in a given market such as market structure, access to distribution channels, target market, and the market's economic and sociological environments. Internal conditions include the company's mission, objectives, capabilities, current products, and resources. Financial conditions include revenue estimates, cost estimates, return on investment, and intangible benefits. In practice, these factors overlap and mutually influence one another. However, the categories provide a useful framework for trying to make sense out of a complex process.

External Conditions

Most discussions of market analysis focus on external conditions. This is because there are more external factors to consider, which managers view as more complex and less controllable than internal or financial considerations. The specific external conditions that a manager examines in a market analysis vary from situation to situation. Yet in a media market analysis, there are common issues that need to be addressed. Some issues involve forecasting key long-term trends, whereas others involve analyzing specific elements of market conditions.

Forecasting Important Long-Term Trends

Trends in Market Growth and Development.   The first question asked in a market analysis is: What are the overall trends and developments in the market for the product? This can be a difficult question for media managers to answer. Consumer demand for media products has steadily increased in recent decades. However, because of increased competition, audience fragmentation, and changing consumer tastes, demand for some media products decreased. Between 1993 and 1998, the average number of hours that Americans listened to radio fell 3% and should decline further by 2003 (U.S. Census Bureau, 2000). In the newspaper industry between 1964 and 1997, average weekday readership in the U.S. adult population fell from 79.9% to 54.9% (Newspaper Association of America, 1999). In contrast, the average number of hours Americans spent watching TV increased in the 1990s. Yet the number of channels available to viewers increased even faster, so the average audience size for individual channels, networks, and programs fell sharply (Adams & Eastman, 2002).

Although such long-term trends appear discouraging, they do not mean that media products are poor investments or media managers should not consider entering these or other markets. Even more important, a trend at the national level may not apply to a specific geographic market. A market analysis should look at both national and local trends.

Another area of trend forecasting critical to media managers is demographics. Data from the 2000 census showed that fewer than 70% of the U.S. population identified themselves as White only, non-Hispanic. The economic power of minority communities grew significantly in recent decades. Additionally, in the early 21st century, the United States was undergoing the largest wave of immigration in its history, creating large populations for whom English was a second language. These trends meant that the audience for U.S. mass media became much less of a mass with more demand for diversity in media content.

In addition to changes in the population makeup, lifestyle changes also affect the market for media products. Since the 1970s, women have entered the U.S. workforce in large numbers; by 2001, 60% of all women worked outside the home (U.S. Census Bureau, 2001). This one change relates to several major trends that emerged in media markets over the same period: Demand for daytime TV programming declined. Drive time and workplace listening increased in importance for radio as the in home daytime audience declined.

As women moved into the workforce and the average number of hours Americans spent working increased over the past few decades, demand for newspapers shifted from evening to morning deliveries. By the end of the 1990s, the same trend appeared in TV news. Ratings for early evening TV newscasts declined. Women who did not work outside the home dominated the audience because fewer people in the labor force were home by 5:30 p.m. By the end of the 1990s, much of the competition for local TV news audiences shifted to the early morning daypart (5 a.m.–7 a.m.), when the mass audience was home preparing for the workday. These examples illustrate the importance of considering both demographic and lifestyle trends in media market analyses.

Trends in Product Demand.   Demand measures the quantity of a product people will buy at a particular price. Demand is a function of the price of the product, the price of substitutes and complements for the product, the income of consumers, and consumer taste (Stigler, 1952).

Price.   Price is negatively related to demand for most products and services. As prices go up, demand goes down and vice versa. The relationship between the change in price and demand is called *elasticity of demand*, and it varies from product to product. When the price of a product increases 1%, if demand decreases more than 1%, demand for the product is said to be *elastic*. If demand decreases less than 1% when the price rises 1%, demand for the product is *inelastic*. If price and demand change at the same rate, the product is said to have *unit elasticity*.

Elasticity of demand is a measure of how sensitive demand is to changes in price or economic conditions. Media managers need to understand the nature of the demand for their products because it directly affects their ability to set prices.

For example, if demand for a product is inelastic, then a price increase will likely result in higher revenues because demand will fall more slowly than the price rises. However, if product demand is elastic, then a price increase can actually cost the company money by causing a decrease in the total revenues that the company generates from sales.

For example, consider the case of a city magazine entitled *Downtown*, which has a circulation of 100,000 per month. If the subscription price is $1 per copy, *Downtown* will generate $100,000 per month in circulation revenue. If demand for the magazine is inelastic, when management increases the cover price to $1.25, the company will actually increase its monthly circulation revenue to $112,500 even if the number of subscribers falls to 90,000 because of the price increase. The gain in revenue from the price increase will be greater than the loss in revenue from the drop in circulation.

However, because media is a joint commodity, the market analyst must consider the impact of the circulation loss on advertising. Advertisers buy space based on circulation size, and advertising rates usually fall when circulation falls. Thus, advertising revenues may also decline if the price increase causes a drop in demand for subscriptions. If a 10% decline in *Downtown*'s circulation caused a 10% drop in advertising revenue, then the gain in circulation revenue from the price increase would not make up for the loss in advertising revenue from the fall in advertising rates. Price elasticity in both the advertising and audience markets are considered when a media company changes prices in one.

The concept of elasticity of demand is also used to measure effects that changes in the overall health of the economy have on demand for a product. In the media industry, demand for advertising time and space tends to be sensitive to the state of the economy. The number of ads a company buys is optional, and advertising is generally one of the first budget lines companies cut when sales dip. As a result, the media industry is highly vulnerable to national and local economic swings, and even a slight downturn could result in hiring freezes or layoffs at the local newspaper, radio, or TV station.

On the consumer side, demand for media products is relatively inelastic, although it varies from product to product. Free over-the-air radio and TV are largely immune to price and the economy because consumers pay nothing to receive them. Demand for expensive premium channels and digital services for cable are more sensitive to swings in price and the economy than the demand for basic cable services.

Price elasticity is often related to the number of available substitute products. The greater the availability of comparable products, the greater the price elasticity for all of them.

Price of Substitutes and Complements.   A *substitute* is a product that can be used in place of another product. Pay per view is a substitute product for both movie rentals and the theater. A *complement* is a product purchased to use with another product. Videotapes are a complement product to VCRs, which are useless without them.

If the price of substitute products is significantly lower and the *utility*—the usefulness or satisfaction that the consumer gets from the substitute is comparable—then demand for the original product falls. If the prices of complementary products are too high, then demand for the product falls. If the average cost of a DVD rental were $25 a night, there would be little demand for DVD players.

Consumer Income. A person's demand for products is related to income. As a person's income rises, there is more discretionary money to spend on optional goods and services such as information and entertainment. Demand for media products varies widely across individuals. Those who use information directly in their work, such as business managers, financial advisers, and teachers, tend to spend a higher percentage of their income on information products because it is a professional investment. Most people, however, make the majority of media expenditures for entertainment. In general, an increase in income would be expected to generate increased demand for media products, but the relationship may not be proportionate.

Consumer income also affects demand in the advertising side of the market for media products. Advertisers generally prefer to reach audience members with higher incomes because those individuals have more discretionary income available to spend on products—both necessities and luxuries. Thus, populations with higher average incomes are more attractive to advertisers than those with lower incomes. Advertisers are often willing to pay higher rates to reach high-income audiences.

Consumer Tastes. Consumer taste is a general concept that covers questions of why audiences select the products they do. There are few theories that predict changes in consumer taste, but from an economic standpoint it can be said that consumers must find *utility* in a product to be willing to buy it.

Utility is the usefulness or satisfaction that a consumer derives from using something. Many products that media companies thought were sure things failed because consumers did not find them useful. In the 1980s and early 1990s, for example, ordering pizza online was promoted as a reason for subscribing to Videotext and online services, but consumers found it easier to use the phone.

Consumer tastes are changeable and difficult to predict. Yet research on information use (Lacy & Simon, 1993), uses and gratifications (Severin & Tankard, 1992), and dependency theory identified some general ways that people use media. These uses include surveillance, decision making, diversion, social-cultural interactions, and self-understanding.

Surveillance includes monitoring the environment to identify new useful or interesting information. Decision making involves conscious information-seeking behaviors with the goal of deciding on a course of action. Diversion includes using media products for entertainment or distraction. Social-cultural interaction includes using information or media to establish common ground with others. Discussing a news or sports story at the office or, for teenagers, being informed about the current hot pop star help establish bonds with other people and may be a source of power within a social or professional group. Self-understanding is the use of media or information to develop personal value systems or philosophies or improve the ability to manage one's life.

Forecasting consumer demand is always difficult. Yet attention to the concept of utility and to what is known about how and why people use media is an important step in market analysis.

Trends in Political/Regulatory Conditions. Telecommunications industries such as broadcasting and cable are subject to government regulation. Because regulatory policies change over time, a market analysis must consider the current state of regulation in both the product and geo-graphic markets and any looming changes. For example, in 1996, the Telecommunications Act removed the limit on the number of radio stations one company could own nationwide. That regulatory change set off a wave of radio consolidation that made it difficult for small radio companies to survive in large markets. In another example, an increase in the price of postage can dramatically raise distribution costs and reduce profits for weekly newspapers, magazines, and newsletters.

Media companies are increasingly looking to foreign markets for future growth. Cable networks are frequently distributed by satellite and local cable systems in countries around the world. For media products having global market potential, such as cable networks and TV programs, a market analysis must include an examination of international trade regulations, and national and regional regulations governing foreign ownership of media, or the sale and distribution of foreign-produced media content. Additionally, a market analysis conducted before investing overseas would examine the regulations that might affect business conditions in a local market, just as is done in a domestic market. Those regulations would include such things as wage and hour laws, tax laws, business restrictions, and so on.

Technology Forecasting. The media industry is one of the industries most affected by emerging technologies in recent decades (Day & Schoemaker, 2000). Thus, market analyses must take account of the opportunities and threats that new technologies may pose. In the early 1980s, the development of the videotape recorder threatened to siphon off audiences from movie theaters and TV. Over the long term, VCRs and their new competitors, DVDs, proved to be a problem for TV networks, but a financial opportunity for Hollywood. Film studios gained a new revenue source in movie rentals and sales while TV lost audiences to movie rentals and recorded programming.

In the 1990s, the Internet created new competition for the newspaper industry. It allowed TV and radio stations to offer print versions of their newscasts to online readers and provided a new classified advertising medium—a critical newspaper revenue source. Napster and other online providers threatened music industry sales by making it easy for users to copy and share music over the Internet. The turn of the 21st century saw local radio station managers anxiously forecasting the effect satellite radio would have on their markets while TV executives warned consumers that using digital recorders to zap TV ads could mean the end of free over-the-air TV (Kempner, 2002).

Experts predict that the pace of communication technology innovation will continue to accelerate. Media managers need to constantly monitor these technological developments for their potential as business opportunities and threats. No market analysis is complete without careful consideration of the emerging innovations that will influence the media market sector of interest.

Analyzing Specific Factors in the Market

A market analysis includes a careful examination of the specific conditions that affect success in a given product or geographic market. Among the conditions to consider are market structure, existing technologies, nature of the target market, and the market's economic and sociological environments.

Market Structure. When managers analyze the market in which they operate, an important consideration is market structure. Market structure analysis is conducted for both product and geographic markets, but it is perhaps easiest to understand when described in the context of the geographic market. Market structure consists of six elements: (a) seller concentration, (b) buyer concentration, (c) barriers to entry, (d) product differentiation, (e) cost structures, and (f) vertical integration. Each of these elements is considered separately.

Seller Concentration. Seller concentration is a measure of the number of competitors in the market. If there are too many competitors, it is difficult for new companies to enter the market and earn enough money to survive. This is one of the challenges facing online media companies. There are more than 2 billion Web sites available to audiences, and many sell advertising. Consequently, it is difficult to attract a large enough audience to any given Web site to make it attractive to advertisers. The tremendous competition for those advertisers interested in buying space online drives down online advertising rates.

However, it can be just as difficult, if not more difficult, to enter a highly concentrated market where there are only a few sellers or perhaps even just one seller. Sellers in concentrated markets tend to have tremendous market power and can capture economies of scale that smaller companies cannot realize. This gives larger companies a production–cost advantage to reduce prices below what their smaller competitors can afford.

The optimal number of competitors in a market depends on the size of the market and demand for the product. Analyzing seller concentration is not simple because different types of media are substitute products for one another for both consumers and advertisers. Someone analyzing the radio market in a particular town cannot just examine other radio stations. They must also consider the number of newspapers, magazines, TV stations, cable and satellite channels, and movie theaters, as well as the local level of online use. These media all compete for the audience's time and attention. A person who is watching TV cannot effectively listen to radio at the same time. A person who is reading the print version of the newspaper cannot be online simultaneously. Indeed, in the battle for audiences in recent decades, the greatest competition among media companies has been for consumers' time, not their money.

Measuring seller concentration as it relates to advertisers is even more complicated. Besides the media already listed, there are other competitors for advertising. Outdoor advertising companies, direct mail companies, and sports arenas, to name a few, also compete for advertising.

Since 1996, changes in the U.S. broadcast industry have made seller concentration even more difficult to assess. Broadcast industry consolidation means that in many markets, although there are still numerous radio stations on the dial, many are owned by the same company, located in the same building, and managed by the same management team. Companies owning clusters of radio stations or, more recently, two TV stations in the same market can capture economies of scale that give them a competitive advantage. Typically, they offer bundled, multistation advertising packages at a discounted price. For advertising clients, bundling is less expensive and more efficient because they can buy time on multiple stations with one deal.

Nor can the media market analyst ignore the effects of media consolidation at another level. If a major corporation owns a media outlet, it generally has more resources available to it than a media company that is independently owned or owned by a smaller company. For example, a radio station with a corporate owner that holds 1,000 stations across the United States almost certainly has more financing and expertise available to it than a station owned by a local family or church. In business, this is known as having *deep pockets*, and a market analysis should look at the number of competitors in the market that have significant corporate resources available to them.

Buyer Concentration. This is a measure of the number of buyers in the marketplace for the product. For media companies, the most important element of buyer concentration is the number and type of potential advertisers in a market. Not all businesses are potential advertisers. Companies that buy mass media advertising generally do direct-to-consumer sales, such as automobile dealers or fast-food restaurants. Local manufacturers, government agencies, and business-to-business suppliers are generally not potential advertisers except in specialized media such as business and legal newspapers.

Having too little buyer concentration in a market means there are many advertisers and each buys only a little time or space. In such a market, it costs the media company more to locate and negotiate with so many small customers than it can recover in revenues from the sales. The company could not survive over the long term. This is a problem facing firms that sell advertising space online.

The more common problem in media markets, however, is too much buyer concentration. There may be only a few major advertising clients in a rural media market, representing a large percentage of the revenue earned by local media companies. Where buyer concentration is high, an advertiser gains tremendous power in negotiating advertising rates and other benefits such as positive news coverage of their business. The media company complies because it cannot afford to lose the client. Thus, a media market analysis considers the number and quality of potential buyers as they relate to the number of sellers in the same market.

Barriers to Entry.   A barrier to entry is anything that makes it difficult for a new competitor to enter the market. Although barriers to entry vary by industry, three common barriers in the media industry are high fixed costs, government regulation, and the market power of existing sellers.

Fixed costs are those a company incurs to produce one unit of its product. Said another way, they are the costs a company pays just to be in business. A company has little ability to adjust or control fixed costs. Fixed costs include the building the business is in, utilities, insurance, personnel and equipment needed to run the operation, and technologies needed to produce and distribute the product. Daily newspapers have higher fixed costs than TV stations because they need more employees and high-cost printing presses to operate. Television stations have higher fixed costs than radio stations because again TV requires more people and equipment.

High fixed costs in an industry are an entry barrier because a tremendous amount of investment capital is needed to begin operations and stay in business until the company generates profits. Generally, it takes at least several years before a new media operation becomes profitable. The higher the fixed costs, the longer it takes to reach profitability, the more money the investors risk on the venture, and the less likely the new company will survive long enough to become established in the market.

Government regulations are another barrier to entry. U.S. broadcasters must obtain a license from the federal government to operate. Cable system operators often have franchise agreements with local governments to provide service to the community and use public rights of way for their cables.

Antitrust laws limit the amount of market power one company can attain and limit the number and type of media outlets that one company can own in a single geographic market. Both serve as a barrier to entry and as a means to lower barriers to entry. Such laws are entry barriers for large corporations that already have substantial market power because the laws require such companies to get government approval for additional acquisitions. For example, after announcing their plans for a merger in 2000, AOL and Time Warner had to gain approval from the European Union and the U.S. Justice Department before they could actually complete the deal.

By limiting the amount of market power that any one company can attain, antitrust laws lower entry barriers for smaller companies. When a big company has too much market power, it can control the factors that influence product demand and squeeze smaller companies out of the market. For example, a national media company with holdings in several industry sectors might give more radio air play on its stations nationwide to recording artists who book with its concert-promotions subsidiary than it gives to artists who sign with a competitor. This makes it difficult for independent concert promoters to book artists, particularly top artists. The assumption behind antitrust laws is that consumers are best served by having many sellers in a market, which enhances product innovation and reduces prices.

Although most market analyses concentrate on the number and type of barriers that make market entry difficult, the complete absence of barriers becomes a barrier to entry in its own right. The online media industry faces just this challenge. With low fixed costs, no government regulation, and few content companies with significant power in the online market, there are virtually no barriers to entry to becoming an online content provider. Anyone who can afford a computer, server, and telephone line can develop a Web site and enter the market. The result is a market with more than 2 billion Web sites, a highly fragmented audience, and insufficient buyer and seller power. As a result, relatively few online content providers can develop profitable businesses.

Product Differentiation. Product differentiation is a measure of the amount of difference between the products that sellers are offering in the market. Media companies are often accused of failing to offer consumers much product differentiation. When "Who Wants to be a Millionaire?" became a big hit for ABC in the summer of 1999, almost every network launched its own version of the game show in primetime during that fall season. Similarly, the success of the reality show "Survivor" spawned a tidal wave of sequels and spin-offs.

For the market analyst, the question is whether the project being proposed is too similar or too different from what is already in the market. If it is too similar, consumers are unlikely to buy it because it has little utility for them. If the product is too different, the company producing it takes a much greater risk because managers will have little ability to judge the likely market for the product until the company makes a substantial investment.

The economics of information products makes product differentiation a serious issue for media companies. In most industries such as automobile manufacturing or fashion retailing, producers can limit their initial investment in a wholly new concept by producing and test marketing a prototype. If the test marketing shows the new product is likely to be popular, the company can give the go-ahead to its manufacturing operations and increase its investment. If the test market shows the product probably will fail, the manufacturer limits its losses by canceling production plans.

Such risk-limitation strategies are much less possible for media companies (Priest, 1994). A book publisher has to buy the rights to a book, pay the author, go through the editing process, and print at least a limited run of copies before it can judge how well the book sells. A film studio has to invest almost the full cost of producing a film before it has anything to show to test audiences. At that point, options for change are limited. The studio may be able to re-shoot and edit a sad ending into a happy ending in response to test-audience feedback, but if the audience rejects the entire film, production costs have already been incurred and the investment is a loss.

Sequels and spin-offs are the media industry's response to this dilemma of product-differentiation risk. If the first film or TV series was successful, the sequel is almost guaranteed to have a built-in fan base even if its potential audience is smaller. An entirely new film or TV series runs the risk of having virtually no audience at all. Talent such as successful writers, directors, and performers who already are popular with audiences also helps reduce risk. These realities of information economics make media companies reluctant to invest in new talent, new storylines, and avant-garde production approaches. This reduces the product differentiation or choice available to consumers and is a barrier to entry to those trying to break into the industry.

When media companies offer too little product differentiation, failure follows. In 1999, most of the game-show spin-offs of "Millionaire" were ratings failures and were cancelled by their networks at the end of the fall season. Audiences might have loved watching a game show one night a week, but they apparently were not enthusiastic about having a primetime schedule full of them.

Media market analysts' difficult challenge is maximizing product differentiation while minimizing risk. One strategy increasingly used in the media industry is to look for products or concepts that were successful in limited geographic markets and then introduce versions of them into new areas. In the early 1980s, the concept of local weekly business newspapers was launched in a few Midwest cities to provide local businesses with in-depth coverage of their markets. The concept was immediately successful. By the end of the decade, such papers were found in large and mid-size cities across the United States and around the world. Similarly, "Millionaire" originally was a British program, but by 2001, versions of it were being shown in at least 64 countries around the world.

Brand identification is another important aspect of product differentiation to consider in market analysis (Aaker, 1995). Consumers tend to develop brand loyalty over time so having a recognizable brand is an advantage, particularly against new market competitors. Brand identification has long been a major marketing focus for consumer product managers. Only in the mid-1990s did media managers begin trying to develop clear brand identities for their stations, networks, and publications to differentiate their products (Jacobs & Klein, 2002).

Cost Structures. Cost structures are the total production costs in a particular market and include both fixed and variable costs. The importance of fixed costs has been addressed. However, for media companies, personnel costs are generally one of the largest budget lines. In large-market TV stations, compensation costs are around 40% of total expenditures and as much as 50% for small-market stations (National Association of Broadcasters, 2001).

Personnel are a variable cost to some degree because media companies have at least some control over the number of people they hire. Yet the media industry is personnel dependent. Information and entertainment products are creative products. Their quality and appeal depend on the talents and creativity of the people who develop them. Media companies may opt to hire employees at the lowest costs possible, but it is likely to affect product quality and success. Additionally, if one competitor pays its employees at below-market levels, it is likely to lose its employee talent to competitors. Consequently, one of the important variables a media-market analysis must include is an examination of the availability and cost of the personnel needed to succeed in a given market.

Vertical Integration. Vertical integration is when a company owns the companies that it buys its inputs from or those to which it sells its final products. In the media industry, a newspaper company that also owns a newsprint manufacturing company is an example of vertical integration. Similarly, a cable multiple system operator (MSO) having ownership stakes in various cable networks is vertically integrated.

Vertical integration is a form of market power. It is difficult for new competitors to enter markets where existing sellers are highly vertically integrated. Having access to distribution channels is necessary for any product to succeed (Pearce & Robinson, 1997). In media industries, vertical integration allows some content creators to get access to media distribution channels while closing others out of the market. For example, in 1995, the Financial Syndication rules preventing broadcast TV networks from owning the primetime programming they aired were eliminated. In the absence of the Fin-Syn rules, many networks now fill their primetime schedules with series made by their own studios. That makes it harder for independent producers to survive in the primetime entertainment market. Similarly, more cable networks compete for carriage on local cable systems than there are channels available. The networks that are at least partly owned by the major MSOs have a much better chance of being picked up than independent networks. A cable network not given carriage by MSOs or satellite TV service providers has no access to distribution channels and thus no way to reach its market.

Access to Distribution Channels: Existing Technologies.   Another element of analyzing access to distribution channels is examining technologies of market production and distribution. A market analysis should examine the nature, quality, and location of the technologies being used.

The analysis of a local media market might include information about whether the newspaper owned its own press or contracted its printing to another company; the type of press used; the press' capacity in terms of volume, color, and reproduction quality; how old it was; and when it would need to be replaced. For broadcast stations, technology issues center around band, dial, and channel position; power of the transmitter; and height and location of its tower.

In radio, an AM station's signal generally travels farther than an FM station's signal, which travels line of sight. Yet the sound quality of an AM signal is less. A high-powered AM station may be heard over hundreds or even thousands of miles at night, but a weaker FM station is a better source for listening to music. Likewise a radio station that has a license for a dial position in the middle of the spectrum is more likely to be found by listeners scanning the band than one with a license for a dial position at the end of the band. In contrast, cable networks that are in the basic tier or lower numbered channels are more likely to be seen by viewers who are surfing with the remote than those placed on high-numbered channels such as the 80s or 100s.

The power of broadcast stations' transmitters is also an issue. Radio stations with licenses for high-wattage transmitters have a larger potential audience than those with low-wattage transmitters because the more powerful transmitters reach larger areas. Where a great deal of difference in the power of two stations exists, it is unlikely the station with the weaker transmitter will have higher ratings than the more powerful station because of the smaller size of its potential audience. Tower height and location are important for FM stations, but less so for AM stations. Because FM signals travel line of sight, if two FM stations have transmitters of the same power, but one has a taller tower or built its tower on a hill, its signal will reach farther.

Tower location, power, and whether a station is licensed for VHF or UHF transmission are also important for broadcast TV stations. These issues of signal reach are becoming less important because more than 60% of the U.S. audience receives TV through cable or satellite providers. What is important is the capacity and subscription rate of the local cable system, particularly for UHF stations.

Also of increasing importance is the adoption rate for high-definition TV sets among area consumers and whether the local cable system can carry the HDTV signals stations are required to broadcast. If the TV station is broadcasting HDTV, but the local cable system is not carrying the signal, the TV station loses access to the distribution channel to about 60% of its market. Likewise, if the station is broadcasting in HDTV, but consumers fail to buy the sets, the station is cut off from its distribution channel.

The technology questions in a market analysis for cable companies include channel capacity, homes passed, and digital capacity. Cable operations require major capital investments. When a local system reaches its channel capacity, it may require a significant investment to expand the number of channels offered to compete with satellite TV providers. Any new, important technological development, such as the introduction of digital, can force cable systems to undertake an expensive reconstruction of their infrastructure. The number of *homes passed*, a measure of the cable system's potential market, is important because a system cannot offer service to someone whose home is not passed by its infrastructure. So a market analysis compares the number of homes the cable service provider passes and the number of households in the market.

New media companies are particularly dependent on technology for distribution. In the late 1990s, a number of promising digital companies failed because their products required broadband distribution, and the rollout of broadband Internet access in the United States was much slower than expected. The market for online products depends wholly on the degree to which the target market audience adopts computer and online technologies. For such products as Video-on-Demand or graphic-intensive interactive multimedia games, broadband is required for effective distribution. The costs of broadband services remain high, and U.S. consumer adoption has been slow. Technological limitations make broadband services difficult to access in large areas of the country.

Where an online product is designed for a global market, regional and national differences in technology adoption are included in the market analysis. Scandinavian countries have the highest levels of individual adoption of online technologies in the world, making them a good market for online media products. Adoption levels in South America and Africa are much lower. Such technological and sociological issues demonstrate why a market analysis addresses whether access to the necessary distribution channels is available so the media product can actually reach audiences and advertisers.

The Target Market.   A market analysis must include an analysis of the target market. For media companies, not all audiences are created equal. Some types of audiences are more desirable to advertisers than others, which means that they are also more desirable as target markets for media companies. For example, 18 to 49-year-old women are the most desirable target market because they tend to make most household buying decisions. They have more income to spend and appear willing to experiment with new products or brands.

Critics say the focus on providing content primarily for the demographic groups advertisers prefer means that large population segments are not served by media. Media companies largely ignored ethnic minorities over the years because relatively few advertisers specifically targeted them as potential customers. That has changed recently as cable networks designed for specific ethnic groups were launched, and Spanish-language TV and radio is one of the fastest growing formats in the United States.

As media competition increased, media companies started narrowcasting or targeting audience groups more and more narrowly. The Fox network emphasized programming for younger viewers. The mass-audience broadcast and cable networks began offering more programming targeted to ethnic minorities. Cable networks targeting people with disabilities started to appear.

Some media such as radio are called *lifestyle media* because their content closely relates to the lifestyles of the audience they attract. *Urban* radio attracts an ethnically diverse, younger, urban listener, whereas *Oldies* draws the suburban Baby Boom generation. Selecting a radio format is, in effect, selecting a target audience, which has direct consequences for the station's potential ratings and revenues. Newspaper managers and advertisers know the demographic and psychographic profiles of business page readers differ from the profiles of lifestyle section readers. Advertisers buy space in those sections accordingly.

Advertisers buy media targeting a narrow demographic to know exactly the audiences they reach and most are potential customers. The advertiser willingly pays a higher advertising rate for a comparatively smaller audience. When advertisers buy time or space in daily newspapers and broadcast networks targeting a mass audience, they know they are reaching a larger audience with many people who are not potential customers. Specialized media also may attract advertisers that mass media cannot. Business newspapers sell space to business-to-business advertisers, such as office equipment and furniture companies that are unlikely to buy much space in the mass media.

The target audience is analyzed in a market analysis to identify the audience and advertisers that existing media companies pursue. Other available or underserved audiences in the market are examined to consider whether advertisers exist to reach those groups. A careful target market analysis examines potential advertisers in the market that are unlikely to buy advertising in a mass-audience medium because they may be an untapped business opportunity.

Economic and Sociological Conditions.   The final elements to include in an analysis of external market conditions are the economic and sociological conditions in the geographic area. The key economic elements include the unemployment rate, how it compares to state and national averages, the long-term growth trends in area, and the diversity of business and industry in the economy.

A market having a higher than average unemployment rate is of concern for a market analyst, particularly if the rate represents a long-term trend and not just a temporary increase. High unemployment means people in the market have less disposable income. A city or region that is not growing is less desirable because a lack of local economic growth makes it harder to increase the media company's revenues and value. An area heavily dominated by a single industry is also less desirable because a downturn in that industry can lead to a sharp economic decline. Of greater concern is an area where a single company provides most of the jobs. The loss of that company would be devastating.

Demographics and psychographics are the sociological elements a media market analyst examines. Demographics define target markets and describe people in terms of age, race, gender, education level, and income. Psychographics describe lifestyle, culture, and values. Demographic factors are important to advertisers so understanding market demographics is crucial for market analysts. Psychographics are important too because a town dominated by a politically conservative population is fundamentally different from a politically liberal town. A market with a large, affluent population of corporate executives has different media needs and tastes than a community of farm families. Understanding such differences is critical to making successful decisions about content. Content that succeeds in Berkeley, California, may not be popular in Albany, Georgia.

Internal Conditions.   Examining internal conditions is a self-examination process for a firm to determine whether it has the internal resources needed to invest in and launch a new product or move into a new market successfully. One technique for analyzing internal conditions is the SWOT analysis, which stands for Strengths, Weaknesses, Opportunities, and Threats (Pearce & Robinson, 1997). A SWOT analysis examines the company's mission statements, goals, organizational structure, leadership, personnel and financial resources, organizational and professional cultures, and existing product mix and markets.

In a SWOT analysis, the analyst asks whether the proposed investment is consistent with a firm's mission statement and goals. How will the new venture fit into the current organizational structure? Is the new market geographically proximate, or does taking on the new business create the need for new office space or communication and management infrastructure? Can the company's leadership assume the added responsibilities or are they already managing all they can handle? Do they have the expertise to handle this line of business or market? If not, is it possible to hire that expertise? How does the new product fit into the existing product mix? Running a media company does not mean that company will succeed in running a retail operation, such as a media firm launching retail sales using E-commerce operations on its Web site.

A critical question is whether the company has the financial resources to make the investment and sustain it as long as necessary to become profitable. Less obvious is whether the new project is a good mix with the company's existing organizational and professional cultures. Different types of professions and organizations have different cultures. Culture clashes are a major source of organizational tension and often cited in failed corporate mergers. Following the AOL and Time Warner merger, there was open conflict between AOL executives, who operated out of a centralized, fast-moving, interactive culture, and Time Warner executives, who worked autonomously, each running a division with little input from others (Munk, 2002). Cultural clashes also exist between two companies in the same business having different products. A radio station with a hip-hop format has a different internal culture than one with a classical music format. These differences need to be examined, understood, and managed.

The company's position in its existing markets is also a carefully examined internal condition. Is it in a strong position? Is it a market leader? Is it facing serious competitive threats or an eroding market? If the company is in a strong position, then it is probably a good time to make new investments. Investing might be more difficult if the firm faces serious competitive threats in its existing markets. Yet if the company's business is eroding, it may be difficult but advantageous to move into new products with a better long-term future.

Once data are gathered on internal conditions, the analyst uses them to view the company's strengths and weaknesses in relation to the proposed new project. A strength in one set of circumstances may become a weakness if conditions change and vice versa. A sophisticated analysis considers how the company would perform under different scenarios if the project goes forward, as well as what new opportunities or threats the investment offers. Most projects provide both opportunities and threats to examine carefully and honestly.

Finally, the analysis of internal conditions must account for the proposed project's effect on the investment market (Aaker, 1995). Management must consider how the investment or new product could affect the company's short- and long-term financial performance because it affects the company's value to owners and investors. A drop in a publicly held company's stock price brings its top executive under fire from major stockholders and financial analysts. Owners of private firms also expect the value of their holdings to grow over the long term.

Financial Conditions.   The final market analysis element to estimate is the financial costs and returns resulting from the project or investment. The revenues to forecast include: (a) those generated by the new project, (b) the expected long-term ROI or return on investment, (c) the capital available to finance it, and (d) possible intangible benefits to the company. If purchasing an existing property, data are available to help estimate revenues and costs based on previous performance. If a media company is considering something like a new business start-up, format change, or buyout of another company, revenue and cost data may be unavailable or a poor guide to the future.

An analyst examines current and future costs to forecast how long it takes for the firm's revenues to exceed costs or to profit from the investment or product. Planned operational changes, the investment those changes require, and current and future market economics are considered to estimate when the breakeven point should be reached. Executives must ensure the firm can sustain losses long enough for the new operation to establish itself. All too often companies are forced to abandon promising projects because they lack the finances to sustain them until the market develops.

Return on investment (ROI) measures how much profit an owner makes relative to the amount of investment required to make that return. Firms seek the highest return on investment possible. When a company compares two competing investment options, it usually invests in the one having the highest ROI potential. A good investment decision requires an estimate of the likely ROI.

If the project requires a substantial investment, the availability and cost of financing must be examined. Firms usually finance investments in three ways: revenue, borrowing, or expanding ownership. All three methods have risks.

When using revenue, a firm pays for the project out of the money it generates from existing business. This reduces profits at least temporarily and can put pressure on a publicly held company's stock price. Borrowing involves taking on debt and is usually used for long-term investments. Borrowed money must be repaid with interest, which is the cost of financing. Careful attention is paid when taking out loans because financing costs must be paid out of revenues. The company will fail if the combination of operating costs and debt service exceed the company's revenues over a long period of time.

Expanding ownership is a way to finance a company by bringing in investors. Multiple investors can increase the costs and complexity of corporate decisions by necessitating negotiation among the owners or battles for corporate control. If the company sells stock publicly, it faces a host of new state and federal securities regulations to comply with and increasing operating costs. Management face new pressures to continuously maximize shareholder value through the stock price, affecting the range of future options for the company.

The intangible elements of a financial analysis are even more difficult to evaluate and calculate. Investments and new products also return value in the form of public relations, reputation, and prestige. Over the long term, an enhanced reputation may generate additional business, thus returning revenues and profits. Yet there is no guarantee that actual financial returns will result, and they are difficult, if not impossible, to measure. Nevertheless, they are often used to justify major investments and should be considered.

SUMMARY

A market analysis is a careful, critical consideration of the factors that may affect a company's success in a competitive environment. When undertaken as a formal project, it is generally done to evaluate the potential for a new investment or product. Effective media executives constantly scan the competitive environment where they work, analyzing it for unrealized opportunities and emerging threats. Authors, producers, or reporters who seek support for a project idea must also understand the market analysis process because executives generally want projects pitched in those terms.

The specific issues involved in a market analysis vary from project to project. Yet the process generally includes an examination of external, internal, and financial conditions. This entails careful evaluation of: (a) long-term market trends and developments; (b) the actual conditions in the product or geographic market; (c) the proposed project's compatibility with the firm's mission, objectives, capabilities, and current business; and (d) the project's effect on the firm's long-term financial performance.

A market analysis serves several critical functions. It helps managers effectively monitor the competitive environment in which they operate, take advantage of new opportunities or deal with emerging threats, and make better short- and long-term business decisions. The ability to effectively evaluate the market is a critical skill for media industry managers, whether they are producers in the newsroom or top-level corporate executives.

Case 8.1
A Market Analysis for McLauren Communications

You and your colleagues are senior analysts with RCR Media Consulting and Brokerage Co. Sarah McLaren, owner of a small radio station group called McLaren Communications, has contacted RCR. Ms. McLaren is aware of two radio stations in two different, but comparably sized, markets that are going up for sale. She only has the capital to buy one. She hired RCR to conduct a market analysis of the two stations and recommend which of the two—if either—to buy.

McLaren Communications currently owns five radio stations in three small markets, all size 200+. All five of the company's current holdings are in the midwest plains states. Two of the stations are AM News Talk stations. The other three are FM. One has a country format, and the other two are Classic Rock.

McLaren Communications' company mission statement says: "McLaren Communications is a strong, positive commercial enterprise that succeeds through serving its communities with high-quality information and entertainment programming that reflect strong community values." Ms. McLaren's stated objective is to see the company grow and diversify into different types of media. It is also her stated goal to manage her media companies to reflect her own strong traditional values, deep religious commitment, and socially conservative outlook.

The current annual revenues of McLaren Communications are $10 million. The company has a net profit margin of only 1%, small by broadcast standards, but not unusual for small market radio. Ms. McLaren is the owner and chief executive officer (CEO) of McLaren Radio. Although she has a great deal of media experience, she is relatively new to radio. Five years ago, she sold the nine small-town weekly newspapers she owned to venture into radio. She brought her newspaper management team with her, expanding it by bringing in the general manager of one of the radio stations she acquired.

McLaren Communications has already done its own analysis of financial conditions and determined it has the resources to buy one of the two stations. Specific financial data for the two stations will not be available until McLaren Communications opens negotiations with the owners. The preliminary market analysis that she is hiring RCR to conduct should provide some insight into what types of short- and long-term revenue and profitability she might expect from the properties based on the markets they are in, the competition they face, and the prospects for growth. She told RCR that she does not expect specific financial figures, but rather a general description of which property is likely to generate the best ROI in the short and long term based on publicly available information.

ASSIGNMENT

The president of RCR assigns you to conduct the market analysis of McLauren Communication's proposed acquisitions. The two stations up for sale are WSAC-FM in Midtown and KSNT-FM in Areaville. Your job is to write a thorough, detailed market analysis, concluding with a firm recommendation about which radio station to buy and why, provided you decide to recommend that McLauren Communications buy one at all. Your report should include a step-by-step discussion of the critical factors that a market analysis includes, as well as: (a) a comparison of those factors between the two markets under consideration, (b) an analysis of what you think those factors will mean in terms of the stations' short- and long-term performances and why, and (c) a final recommendation as to which station McLaren Communications should buy, if either one, and why you are making that recommendation based on the factors you identified in your market analysis.

In addition to the data provided, you may conduct your own research, particularly to forecast trends. Sources to consult may include: Statistical Abstracts of the United States (available in print and online), National Association of Broadcasters Web Site, and current books, trade publications and journal articles on the radio industry, including Veronis & Suhler Communications Industry Forecast and Investing in Radio.

Midtown[1]

Midtown is a small community in a small state in the northeast United States located 1 hour from two different major metropolitan areas. Some signals from media based in those cities reach Midtown. Historically, the community was affluent, reflected by the high median income the town reported in past years. Yet most of the affluent community members are in the high-tech and financial services industries, which were hit hard in recent years by layoffs. Many jobs in the high-tech sector were in the dot.com industry. Currently, unemployment is high and has not yet shown up in median income figures.

It will take several years to recover the lost high-tech jobs, and many executives from that industry are leaving the area to find positions elsewhere. City officials expect in the next few years the community will see a slight decline in population and median income. How long the downturn will last is not predictable.

Midtown is primarily a suburban bedroom community for larger urban areas nearby. More than 50% of the population commutes into the nearby cities to work, reflected in the average travel time to work. The audience is in cars during the critical "Drive Time" radio daypart.

During the 1990s, dot.com entrepreneurs set up operations and became an important part of the Midtown economy. A few still survive. The community has a vibrant retail sector that draws customers from nearby communities. The strength of the retail sector is reflected in the high retail sales figures relative to the population size. Besides retail and the few tech companies that remain, Midtown is primarily a residential community.

Midtown is completely hemmed in by other incorporated communities and is unable to expand geographically. The communities immediately surrounding it have industrial economies and solid blue-collar populations, whereas Midtown is a white-collar island in the area. Midtown is located in the middle of the state, halfway between the northern Appalachian Mountains and the Atlantic Ocean. The local terrain is rolling and hilly.

---

[1] All persons, stations, communities, media companies, and data in this case study are completely fictitious. Any similarity to actual individuals or companies is purely coincidental.

Lifestyle scales identify Midtown's residents as being "2nd City Society" or "upscale executive and young upscale white-collar; affluent retirees." Much of the recent ex-urban migration out of the cities settled in tonier communities either along the mountains or the sea, now considered to be largely "Elite Suburbs" (superrich, executive, upscale white-collar couples) or "Urban Uptown" (elite, upscale, bohemian singles and couples). Politically, the community is moderately conservative, but not particularly religious.

Areaville

Areaville is a mid-size community in the Pacific Northwest that is rapidly transforming itself from a farming town to a small city. Located 90 minutes from a major urban area, a range of hills between the two communities blocks most of the city's radio and TV signals from reaching Areaville, although some TV signals are carried on the Areaville cable system. It is 3 hours from the sea in a valley dotted with orchards, farms, and small lakes.

Historically, the community was solidly middle class, grounded in farming and diversified small industry. Recently, Areaville benefited from an ex-urban migration from the nearby city and Southern California, which increased the local population's affluence. The lifestyle of the area is attracting media and entertainment professionals who want to leave California. They are moving in to live and commute back to Southern California for projects. As a result, both in Areaville and the nearby city a vibrant new industry of small media production companies is springing up as Hollywood discovers the region is a good place to live and do business. Labor and production costs are much lower than in Southern California, resulting in a steady growth rate throughout the 1990s and an unemployment rate lower than the national average of 5.6%. Yet the larger economy remains diversified, demonstrated by the area's occupational profile. Despite the changes, the community remains solidly middle class. The city is in an isolated valley, and no natural features exist to limit its physical expansion.

Sociologically the community is ethnically diverse. Its psychographic profile is a mix of mid-level white-collar couples and middle-class blue-collar families, with a scattering of rural farm and ranch families and elite ex-urban executives seeking small-town life. The community is politically liberal with strong support for such issues as immigration rights and the environment. Outdoor activities are popular. Areaville's size and distance from other urban centers means the average commute for residents is quite short, and a substantial percentage use alternative systems such as bicycles and public transportation.

Community Profiles

	Midtown	Areaville
Market size		
Radio market size	193	175
Television size	91	87
Population		
Total population	174,400	396,487
Total households	72,500	94,700
Households by income	%	%
Under $19,999	8.2	15.4
$20,000–39,999	11.1	20.9
$40,000–74,999	22.6	28.6
$75,000–99,999	14.8	13.9
$100,000+	43.3	21.2
Median income	$87,059	$55,253
Unemployment rate	7.2%	4.2%
Ethnic population	%	%
White	92.5	75.4
African American	2.4	8.3
Hispanic	4.5	11.1
Asian	0.6	5.2
Education	%	%
Grades 0–11	15.1	11.9
High school grad	26.7	28.7
College 1–3 years	23.3	31.8
College 4+ years	34.9	27.6
Occupation	%	%
Managerial	35.5	20.5
Technical	33.5	25.7
Service worker	9.4	15.5
Farm worker	1.2	9.0
Precision production	10.6	11.3
Operator	9.8	18.0
Transportation to work	%	%
Public	12.4	0.8
Driving	75.9	70.3
Carpool	6.4	12.6
Other	5.3	16.3
Average travel time (min.)	60	15
Retail sales data	**$ (000)**	**$ (000)**
Total retail sales	3,373,986	3,446,047
Retail expenditure per household	57,687	33,789
Grocery, food, & beverage	878,118	881,351
Restaurants & bars	320,581	324,586

Community Profiles (continued)

	Midtown	Areaville
General retail & clothing	800,037	810,222
Motor vehicles and parts	783,146	798,543
Building supplies	319,548	323,456
Health & personal care	153,247	150,672
Furniture, appliances, & electronics	119,309	123,428
Radio: time spent listening (TSL) (Mon.–Sun. 6 a.m.–Mid.)	**(Min.)**	**(Min.)**
Persons 12+ (min.)	17:30	18:30
Men 18–34	16:30	19:30
Men 25–54	18:45	21:30
Men 35–64	20:15	21:15
Women 18–34	18:30	17:15
Women 25–54	19:00	18:00
Women 35–64	17:45	17:00

Midtown Cable

Owner: National MSO Cable.*
Channel capacity: 80 Channels
Available channels: 5
1 Channel of local programming
Technology: Digital
Homes passed: 69,897
Subscribers: 35,400

Midtown Print Media

Local Daily: Midtown Daily Register. Distributed mornings, Monday-Sunday. Circulation 59,658. Owner: Major Group Newspapers.*

Midtown City Life. Monthly city and lifestyle magazine. Circulation 5,000. Owner: Major Group Newspapers.*

Two city dailies for the nearby metropolitan areas also are distributed in Midtown.

Areaville Cable

Owner: National MSO Cable*
Channel capacity: 100 Channels
Available channels: 2

---

* Denotes a major media group: More than 150 radio stations nationwide; 15% or more of the total TV viewing audience nationwide; 10% or more of the local cable systems nationwide; 15+ daily newspapers nationwide.

Midtown Radio Stations

Rank 12+ 6 a.m. Mid.	Call Letters	Dial Position	Format	AQH Share	Owner	Inside/Outside Metro Area	Watts	Ant. High
1	WVAD-FM	98.3	Hot Adult Contemporary	14.3	Jayson Media	In	1,300	140
2	WGGR-FM	99.9	Adult Contemporary	8.0	Big Group*	Out	27,500	204
3	WSSS-FM	95.1	Album-Oriented Rock	7.9	Toms Radio	In	29,500	194
4	WDGF-FM	101.1	Oldies	4.2	Smith Radio*	Out	6,800	404
5	WRUF-AM	660	All Sports	3.9	CPU Radio	In	50,000	
6	WBAT-FM	100.5	Oldies	3.5	Big Group*	In	900	186
7	WWAR-FM	92.5	Country	3.4	Smith Radio*	Out	17,000	268
8	WNBB-AM	770	News Talk Information	2.5	CPU Radio	In	50,000	
9	WATH-FM	104.7	Pop Contemporary Hit	1.9	State Commun.	Out	7,400	381
9	WCOL-FM	102.9	Oldies	1.9	Smith Radio*	In	19,500	247
11	WMLC-AM	940	Nostalgia	1.8	Jayson Media	In	680	
12	WSAC-FM	105.5	Pop Contemporary Hit	1.7	Seascape Media	In	16,500	173
13	WSEA-FM	101.3	Country	1.2	Seascape Media	Out	10,000	326
14	WQYQ-FM	93.7	Rhythmic Oldies	1.0	CRC Radio	Out	21,000	238
14	WZRT-FM	97.3	Pop Contemporary Hit	1.0	State Commun.	In	6,000	473
16	WSTS-FM	100.7	Urban	0.8	CPU Radio	Out	50,000	152

* Denotes a major media group: More than 150 radio stations nationwide; 15% or more of the total TV viewing audience nationwide; 10% or more of the local cable systems nationwide; 15+ daily newspapers nationwide.

Midtown Television

Rank (Evening News)	Call Letters	Channel	Network	Owner
1	WCTV-TV	2	NBC	Ligon Communications*
2	WRDV-TV	11	CBS	Parker Television*
3	WQQT-TV	6	Fox	Byers Media
4	WNBB-TV	4	ABC	Claude Communications*
7	WPBS-TV	7	PBS	Midtown Unified School District

* Denotes a major media group: More than 150 radio stations nationwide; 15% or more of the total TV viewing audience nationwide; 10% or more of the local cable systems nationwide; 15+ daily newspapers nationwide.

3 Channels of local programming
Technology: Digital
Homes passed: 83,450
Subscribers: 58,415

Areaville Newspapers

Areaville News Herald. Distributed mornings, Monday-Sunday. Circulation 73,589. Owner: Terrell Family Media.

Case 8.2
A Market Analysis for CPU Radio Group

Selecting Potential Radio Formats

CPU Radio Group in Midtown hired RCR Media Consulting to examine the performance of WSTS–FM, the lowest rated station in Midtown. Use the data descriptions in Case 8.1 and your own research on current radio listening trends to do a market analysis on potential radio formats for WSTS–FM in Midtown.

ASSIGNMENT

Make a recommendation to the executives of CPU about programming options to consider for WSTS–FM. Answer the following questions:

1. What are three radio programming options that CPU Inc. managers might want to consider as possible formats for WSTS-FM?

Areaville Radio

Rank 12+ 6 a.m. –Mid.	Call Letters	Dial Position	Format	AQH Share	Owner	Inside/Outside Metro Area	Watts	Ant. High (mtrs)
1	KKID-AM	1240	News Talk Information	10.0	Big Group*	In	1,000	
2	KHRH-FM	96.9	Country	8.3	Smith Radio*	In	100,000	177
3	KSPK-FM	102.7	Pop Contemporary Hit	7.6	Big Group*	In	100,000	131
4	KBRZ-FM	106.3	Album-Oriented Rock	6.7	R Squared*	In	3,000	65
5	KSWT-AM	1400	News Talk Information	5.6	Big Group*	In	670	
6	KCOW-FM	105.3	Oldies	5.0	Big Group*	In	3,000	100
7	KKRN-FM	107.3	Hot Adult Contemporary	4.9	Smith Radio*	In	100,000	168
8	KJNK-FM	98.1	Country	4.3	R Squared*	In	100,000	299
9	KCRP-FM	104.1	Pop Contemporary Hit	4.2	Areaville Radio Inc.	In	31,000	187
10	KQTE-FM	97.7	Rhythmic Contemporary Hit	3.6	Big Group*	Out	100,000	297
11	KNEE-FM	95.1	Classic Rock	3.3	Johnson Radio	In	50,000	87
12	KRNN-FM	96.1	Adult Contemporary	1.8	Areaville Radio	In	100,000	430
12	KMRY-AM	1480	All Sports	1.8	Smith Radio*	In	1,000	
13	KWRM-AM	590	Album-Oriented Rock	1.6	Wyatt Radio	Out	5,000	
14	KSNT-FM	98.5	Urban	1.0	Areaville Radio	In	100,000	358

* Denotes a major media group: More than 150 radio stations nationwide; 15% or more of the total TV viewing audience nationwide; 10% or more of the local cable systems nationwide; 15+ daily newspapers nationwide.

Areaville TV

Rank (Evening News)	Call Letters	Channel	Network	Owner
1	KSTC–TV	2	CBS	Big Group Television*
2	KDCR–TV	11	ABC	Terrell Family Media
3	KRVW–TV	6	NBC	RMR Television*
4	KRSS–TV	4	Fox	Pictures Communications*
5	KUCT–TV	9	WB	Jones Communications*
6	KRCR–TV	13	UPN	Jones Communications*
7	KPBS–TV	8	PBS	University of Areaville

* Denotes a major media group: More than 150 radio stations nationwide; 15% or more of the total TV viewing audience nationwide; 10% or more of the local cable systems nationwide; 15+ daily newspapers nationwide.

2. Discuss in detail the pros and cons of each of those options in the context of the Midtown media market.
3. What are the current listening trends nationwide for the three radio formats you are proposing for WSTS-FM? What might the implications of those trends be for your recommendations?
4. Which of the three are you most strongly recommending to CPU and why? Be sure to argue your case.

Case 8.3
Options for Conducting a Market Analysis

Option A. Select a local newspaper, magazine, radio station, local cable system operator, TV station, or Web company. Conduct a market analysis of its position in the market. Write your report for a potential investor, including a detailed analysis of the media company you have selected and its market. Address the issues outlined in the chapter. Make a buy/do not buy recommendation to the investor based on your market analysis and argue for your recommendation based on your analysis.

Option B. Conduct a market analysis of a selected community and the media already serving it. Try to identify an available market niche for media in the community that is not being met. Write your market analysis as a business plan for that media opportunity. Discuss each of the important factors in a market analysis in detail.

Option C. Identify a major project that you would like to pursue: an important long-term investigative news story, a film idea, a TV series, and so on. Do a detailed market analysis for your project addressing the important factors that need to be considered. Then take one of the two following actions:

1. Use the market analysis process to identify a real media company that might support your project. Describe in detail the market factors for that company that are relevant to your project idea. Explain carefully why you think your project might be appropriate for that company to support based on the analyses you have done for your project idea and for your target investor.
2. Imagine you are an employee in a real media company, such as a local newspaper or TV station that might be interested in your project. Use the market analysis process to identify that company's market. Develop an effective approach to use with your supervisor in that company to gain support for your idea. Base your pitch on the market analysis you conducted for your project and the company. Explain to your supervisor how the company's market position will be improved if you are allowed to pursue your idea.

Sources you may want to consult as you do your research include: Bacon's Media Directories, Blair's Television and Cable Factbook, Broadcasting and Cable Yearbook, the community's Web site, and the local Chamber of Commerce.

Current books, trade publications, and journal articles on the media industry sector of interest may be useful including: Editor and Publisher Yearbook, Investing in Radio, Investing in Television, National Association of Broadcasters Web site, National Association of Broadcasters Television Financial Report, Standard Rate & Data, Statistical Abstracts of the United States (available in print and online), and Veronis & Suhler Communications Industry Forecast.

There are many other resources, directories, fact books, and sources of information that could provide you with valuable information for a market analysis. Ask your librarian for help in locating them.

MARKETING AND RESEARCH

This chapter enables the reader to develop a broad perspective on marketing and research. Many marketing decisions, research questions, methods, and information gathered are common across media organizations. The basic types of research questions and methods used by media organizations are discussed. Major providers of media research and online research resources are presented.

With the increasing competitiveness of the media industry, marketing and research activities are central to the job of media management. Marketing activities revolve around decisions about the marketing mix or four Ps—*product, pricing, placement* (distribution), and *promotion*. To make these decisions, managers need answers to questions about their customers. For media managers, the two types of customers are consumers (readers, viewers, or listeners) and advertisers. One way media managers use research is to develop profiles of their consumers to market their space or time to advertisers.

MARKETING AND ADVERTISING IN TODAY'S MEDIA ENVIRONMENT

Marketing is the "process of planning and executing the conception, pricing, promotion, and distribution of ideas, goods, and services to create exchanges that satisfy individual and organizational objectives" (AMA Board, 1985, p. 1). Marketers consider the correct blend and emphasis of marketing mix elements needed to attract and satisfy their primary customers or target segments. These marketing mix decisions are crucial to determining the message content and media placement of advertising. Advertising's role in the marketing mix is to communicate the value a brand, product, service, or media outlet has to offer to the desired target segment.

Major advertisers use integrated brand promotions (IBP) and/or integrated marketing communications (IMC) for promotional planning. IBP is

> the use of various promotional tools, including advertising, in a coordinated manner to build and maintain brand awareness, identity and preference. When marketers combine contests, a Web site, event sponsorship, and point-of-purchase

displays with advertising, this creates an integrated brand promotion. (O'Guinn, Allen, & Semenik, 2003, p. 13)

IMC is "the process of using promotional tools in a unified way so that a synergistic communication effect is created" (O'Guinn, Allen, & Semenik, 2003, p. 37).

The growth of cable, direct satellite channels, and the Internet resulted in the fragmentation of mass media audiences. The primetime (or 8–11 p.m. Eastern time) audience shares for the four major TV networks declined from 72% a decade ago to 46% in 2002 (Green, 2002). IBP and IMC increased in importance because advertisers must define and attract smaller, more precise segments of consumers who share similar characteristics. A result of fragmentation is that advertisers consider a wider range of options for advertising placement including traditional, nontraditional, and specialized media.

Traditional mass media such as radio, TV, newspapers, and magazines deliver larger audiences (e.g., for popular primetime programming and major sporting events like the Super Bowl) and special audiences attracted to certain editorial content (e.g., sports fans to the sports section of a daily newspaper). Nontraditional media include the Internet, TV screens in airport waiting areas, posters at public events, and grocery store cart or floor advertising. Specialized media include direct mail, billboards, subway posters or car cards on buses, and FSIs or free-standing inserts in newspapers. Other specialized or niche media attract audiences with special interests, such as professionals (e.g., physicians and attorneys) using traditional media and films, trade shows, convention exhibits, tapes, and CDs. Media managers must realize that advertisers now consider many competitors when deciding where to place advertisements (O'Guinn, Allen, & Seminik, 2003; Sissors & Baron, 2002).

Positioning is designing a brand so it occupies a distinctive and valued place in the target consumer's mind relative to other brands (O'Guinn, Allen, & Seminik, 2003, p. 212). Positioning develops a perceptual space or how a brand (or newspaper, station, or Web site) is perceived on a variety of dimensions, such as quality or social display value. For example, *The New York Times* positions itself as a high-quality, in-depth, informative paper for educated, sophisticated, and affluent readers. Advertisers communicate the position of the brand or product— media or otherwise—using advertising, IBP, and/or IMC to create the desired image in the minds of consumers it targets.

The content of media outlets is developed to attract a specifically defined target audience, just as manufacturers create products designed to attract a target segment of consumers. Often media products are designed for audiences that advertisers desire to reach (e.g., the TV program "Friends" targets young adult viewers). In this case, the advertiser and media manager target the same audience, and the media manager also targets the advertiser by targeting the advertiser's audience. Alternatively, the media manager may accept the audience attracted by the editorial content of the media vehicle and then find advertisers interested in targeting that audience.

Over the past 50 years, the development of marketing, IBP, IMC, and positioning created the need for a new organizational function—marketing research. Marketing research enables media managers to discover their audience's needs and wants and determine how best to meet them. The chapter discusses the marketing research process, how to develop and design research, and the major media research companies.

THE MARKETING RESEARCH PROCESS

It is important to conduct research systematically and objectively to ensure the quality of the information obtained. No manager wants to spend tens or hundreds of thousands of dollars gathering information unless it accurately reflects reality. *Systematic* research is well planned and organized. All the details are outlined in advance of data collection. *Objective* research is void of bias. Research bias appears in many forms, but often results from a researcher's preconceived desires or expectations for the outcome of the research study.

Stages of Marketing Research

The process of marketing research is similar to the research process in other areas of study. There are eight stages to the process.

Research Question. This stage is also referred to as setting research objectives. The research question may be about a particular problem, such as: Why do consumers buy one product rather than another? or Which newspaper design do readers prefer? Some researchers prefer to set objectives rather than state questions. For example, the second question phrased as an objective is: Determine the newspaper design readers prefer.

Secondary Research Review. A researcher reviews the available information on a topic of interest before conducting research. Often enough data are available to save the time and money necessary for a new research study. Secondary research is often used by media managers and is discussed later in the chapter.

Primary Research Design. The researcher develops a plan or *design* for the study. Will the study be qualitative and use intuitive data collection, or quantitative and use specific measurement techniques like surveys? What type of quantitative or qualitative research would be best? Why? The design for the study is driven by the research questions.

Data-Collection Procedure.   The specific data needed to answer the research question are identified and a plan is created to appropriately collect the data.

Sampling Design.   Due to financial and time constraints, researchers study a subset of the population of interest. This smaller group is called a *sample* and must be representative of the population of concern. A design for obtaining a representative sample must be outlined.

Data Collection.   The data are collected. Often this is the most time-consuming and costly part of a research study.

Data Processing and Analysis.   Data are typically edited or verified before being analyzed. Verification reviews the data for completeness and bias. Then the data are interpreted or analyzed and entered into a computer program.

Report Writing.   The final stage is to write a report that clearly details the study, the results obtained, and how the results answer the research question(s).

TYPES OF RESEARCH AND RESEARCH QUESTIONS

Media managers must understand certain basic research concepts to develop objective and systematic research or assess whether a research firm is needed. Media research examines variables or factors, defined as phenomena or events measured or manipulated, such as the characteristics of a newspaper's readers or TV program's viewers. Independent variables are varied systematically by the researcher to see how they affect dependent variables or what the researcher wishes to explain. For example, do full- or half-page ads (independent variable = ad size) attract more readership (dependent variable = number of readers who recall information from each different ad size). The values of the dependent variable are not manipulated, but rather measured or observed. Reliability or a reliable measure is dependable, stable, and consistently gives the same answer over time. Validity or a valid measure actually measures what it is designed to measure (Wimmer & Dominick, 2003). A manager considers all these factors when evaluating the quality of research.

The type of research problem suggests which method to use. Having knowledge of research methods enables managers to decide between competing research proposals submitted by outside suppliers (including evaluating the research design, methods, questionnaires, and sampling techniques used) or design and implement research inhouse. Managers also must understand and interpret research findings to use the results effectively.

Consider three issues before designing a research study. First, how much is already known about the problem at hand? Second, how much information is needed about each audience member? Third, how important is it that the study results are generalizable or applicable to other people and situations? The answers to these questions direct the researcher to some types of research and not others. The following is a discussion of the different categories of research available and some considerations for choosing any of them. (For more information on research methods, conducting research and analyzing research see sources like Williams & Monge [2001]; Wimmer & Dominick [2003].)

Primary Versus Secondary Research

Primary research is conducted for the specific purpose at hand. It is designed by the researcher to answer the specific question posed and is likely to provide the needed information. Secondary research is conducted for purposes other than the researcher's specific purpose. Secondary research is often cheaper and easier to collect than primary research, more quickly accessible, and provides sufficient, if not perfect, information. For example, many TV stations and advertisers use Nielsen ratings books to evaluate TV program audiences.

Media managers often use secondary research, especially syndicated research. Syndicated research is used to answer research questions about the audience (e.g., a publication's readership or the surfers of a Web site), the effectiveness of an advertising message (message or evaluative research), and the placement of advertising by advertisers (advertising activity or media planning research). Syndicated research is conducted on an ongoing basis by a specialized firm to serve a group of companies in the industry, rather than contracted to meet the needs of one company. Major providers of syndicated research include Nielsen, Arbitron, Mediamark Research Inc., and Simmons Market Research Bureau.

Exploratory, Descriptive, and Causal Research

Exploratory research is conducted when a researcher approaches a relatively new topic and little information is available to guide the study. Research questions may not be well defined, and there may be many issues of interest that cannot be narrowed down for study. As such, exploratory research identifies key variables, issues, or ideas that help the researcher better understand the general problem and define more specific research questions.

A TV network might be interested in developing a new type of reality show to attract a younger audience but still maintain adult interest. Researchers might test program concepts by speaking to small numbers of parents and children in a focus group. This would allow for free thinking and reveal important ideas that programmers failed to envision. The exploratory research would identify directions for developing the new program and define a more focused set of research questions to study. Exploratory research used to generate advertising messages is called *developmental advertising research* (O'Guinn, Allen, & Semenik, 2003).

Descriptive research describes a group of people or a situation in detail across a set of variables defined in the research questions. A local newspaper interested in updating its comics section might analyze which strips satisfy reader interest and which to safely drop without losing readers. The newspaper could poll its readers to identify how many read each strip and if replacement comics exist that are preferred. Descriptive research is useful for identifying audience segmenting characteristics and estimating the actual sizes of those segments.

Most of the questions that managers ask are inherently causal in nature. When a manager considers strategic options, he or she is really asking, Which of these strategies will create or cause the outcome I desire? Only causal research can answer questions that specifically pose a question about a strategy causing an observable effect on an outcome—typically audience behavior. A broadcast programming executive expects the decision of when to air a program to affect the size and characteristics of that program's audience and the programs appearing before and after it.

Causal research is difficult and expensive. It requires research to be accumulated over time, allowing for multiple causes to be examined and for competing theories (as to why behavior occurs) to be controlled. No single research project can establish causality. Because business decisions often do not allow time for causal research, media managers usually accept the ability to reliably predict behavior as a replacement for understanding causal relationships.

Designs for Data Collection

Once the researcher defines the problem, reviews secondary data, and decides that primary data collection is necessary, a study design is developed. Exploratory research typically uses *qualitative research* designs that do not rely on the measurement of variables, but use subjective or intuitive data collection or analysis (Wimmer & Dominick, 2003). Qualitative research provides a relatively quick insight on a problem to plan further action. Qualitative research typically uses small convenience samples, rather than large representative samples, so it is not used as a basis for risky decisions. Qualitative research techniques include *focus group* and *depth interview* techniques.

A focus group usually consists of 8 to 12 people who represent the population of concern and is facilitated by a trained moderator. Focus groups provide an open-ended response situation where synergy among the participants enhances the generation of ideas. Discussions typically last between 1 1/2 and 2 hours. Information collected during a focus group is valuable, but it cannot be generalized to the greater population with confidence due to the small sample size and the unique nature of interaction.

Depth interviews are often unstructured personal interviews where a trained interviewer probes the subject's behaviors and feelings for up to 2 hours. They generate a great deal of information, often unexpected, for any one individual. However, their problems include small sample size, limited generalizability, and higher cost than focus groups and other data-collection methods.

Descriptive research is often conducted using *quantitative* methods or a description of a phenomenon involving the specific measurement of variables via such methods as surveys or observational methods (Wimmer & Dominick, 2003). Quantitative methods use larger, randomly collected samples, allowing researchers to generalize the results to other people and situations. The survey or self-report method asks people to report their behaviors, attitudes, opinions, and characteristics relevant to the managerial problem. A survey consists of administering a questionnaire specially designed to answer the research questions. The questionnaire is administered face to face through a phone interview or Web site, or it is mailed or e-mailed to subjects. Results are then compiled to describe the research problem and potential outcomes.

Surveys are often cross-sectional or performed at one moment in time. A longitudinal study is used when data need to be collected at more than one point in time to evaluate the research question. For example, the NPD Group (*www.npd.com*) collects information from its Online Panel of more than 900,000 worldwide members who agreed to participate in NPD surveys. NFO World Group (*www.nfow.com*) maintains a large interactive community online panel called NFO InDepth Interactive.

Observation does not rely on self-reports, but observes consumer behavior using obtrusive (known to the observed individual) or unobtrusive (unknown to the observed individual) methods. Some widely used observational data-collection methods include scanner data and tracking of Internet users' surfing behavior. Scanner data are used at point-of-purchase sites such as grocery stores to collect information on purchase behavior. Many grocery chains provide preferred customer cards that are scanned each time a purchase is made. The customer receives a coupon, discount, or other reward when the card is used. Because the customer provided demographic information to the grocer to receive the card, the list of purchases is associated with that individual's demographic profile.

Content analysis provides an objective and systematic means to investigate media content. It is used to describe message composition and content. For example, content analysis is often used to examine typography, layout, and makeup in newspapers and magazines. It is used to study how the media portray minority groups, differences in news coverage, and the level of violence in TV programming.

The ability of descriptive research to accurately describe a large population relies on two elements of research. First, the sample studied must be randomly selected from the larger population the sample represents to prevent biases related to income, gender, ethnic background, and so on. Every subject should have an equal chance of being selected so no group or age is overrepresented.

Random sampling allows researchers to reduce and estimate the probability that the biases exist. Second, a large sample size is needed because the larger a random sample, the less likely it is to be biased. Most samples should be larger than 400, and a sample of more than 1,000 works well for representing millions of people.

Causal research is performed using laboratory experiments when control over extraneous conditions is important and feasible. For example, the same newspaper lifestyle section is tested, whereby one group of individuals reads one version and a second group reads a second version in a controlled setting without disruptions. This makes it more likely that different reactions to the two sections are due to the lifestyle content and not some external factor. However, exposure to the lifestyle section in a laboratory setting is contrived and may differ from reading it at home, resulting in a different or less than natural reaction to the section.

Field experiments are conducted in natural settings to minimize the disadvantages of experiments. For example, delivering one version to residents in one geographic region of a city and a second version in another region tests two versions of a newspaper lifestyle section. Readers' reactions are monitored in both regions to discover which section was preferred more by which readers. Real-life conditions are present, yet a field experiment lacks researcher control, allowing many factors to influence the outcome. The researcher may never be sure that the readers' reactions varied only because of differences in the two lifestyle sections.

An experimental design isolates the cause–effect relationship between the managerial factor of concern (the independent variable) and the desired audience behavioral outcome (the dependent variable) to have internal validity. When an experiment has internal validity, the probability is high that only the independent variable caused the dependent variable to change. An experiment has external validity if its results can be generalized to other situations and people. To increase the likelihood of external validity, randomly select the sample used in the experiment from the larger population.

You cannot have perfect internal and external validity in the same experiment. Internal validity requires control over all factors extraneous to the independent and dependent variables of concern. Controlled lab situations enhance internal validity, but decrease external validity by removing outside factors. External validity requires that extraneous variables not be controlled as in field experiments. However, once extraneous variables are allowed to fluctuate, internal validity suffers. There is always a trade-off between internal and external validity, so the research objectives should guide the balance between the two.

Basic Versus Applied Research

Basic research identifies general principles of practice and answers general questions for media managers. For example, a question such as, "Which type of advertising strategy creates a more positive attitude toward the advertised brand: comparative or single-sided?" is best answered using a basic research approach. This question appears specific, but it is general because the results of a study designed to answer this question could provide information to apply to a variety of brands, product categories, or advertising media. Basic research helps a manager develop principles of practice to use over time.

Applied research is conducted to obtain information for a specific decision in a unique situation. For example, an online newspaper in New York might conduct a study to identify its readers' reactions to either publishing in a commemorative edition archival photos of the Brooklyn Dodgers and New York Giants baseball teams or making the photos available online. Applied research takes fewer resources than basic research and answers the specific question at hand, but is of limited use in other situations.

TYPES OF APPLIED MEDIA RESEARCH

Media companies ask similar applied research questions regardless of the nature of the company. The following discusses five basic types of applied media research, including how the information gained is used by advertisers and how it is used to market the media company.

Audience Research: Secondary Data

Audience research examines the characteristics of present and potential target audiences. A company can perform primary audience research or use the many secondary, syndicated sources of audience data. Audience research often identifies the demographic, geographic, and psychographic characteristics of potential audiences. Demographic characteristics include age, education, gender, race, marital status, occupation, and income. Audiences are segmented by geographics including region of the country, state, city, or neighborhood. Geodemographic segmentation uses data from the U.S. Census Bureau and zip codes to identify neighborhoods around the country that share demographic characteristics (O'Guinn, Allen, & Semenik, 2003).

Psychographics describe the individual's lifestyle, activities, interests, and opinions. The VALS 2 (for values and lifestyles) typology divides audience members into eight categories based on demographic and psychographic profiles; it categorizes consumers by resources (including age, income, education, intelligence, self-confidence, health, and energy level) and self-orientation (or motivated by principles or idealized criteria, status, or products that demonstrate success, or action or a desire for activity, variety, and risk taking). The VALS 2 typology and survey are located online (*www.sric-bi.com/VALS/*). The Lifestyle Market Analyst (*www.srds.com/frontMatter/ips/lifestyle*) provides demographic and psychographic data for cities and counties nationwide and lifestyle profiles of more than 70 consumer interest groups.

Managers of media outlets should learn how advertisers use secondary data to develop effective ways to sell time or space to advertisers. Advertisers and media planners analyze secondary data to decide how to spend an advertising budget, how much their competitors spend in major media, how many in the target audience should see the ad, and where and when to place the ads to effectively reach the targeted audience. The media planner analyzes secondary data to select vehicles where to place the ads (e.g., *The New York Times* is a vehicle in the newspaper medium). The media buyer purchases time and space in the vehicles that efficiently reach the target audience. Media firms use these same secondary data to identify their audiences and those of competing media outlets.

Using Audience Research.   Simmons Market Research Bureau (SMRB; *www.smrb.com*) and Mediamark Research Inc. (MRI; *www.mri.com* and *www. mriplus.com*) report usage rates of national media and brands to identify heavy, medium, and light users of a product. The information allows advertisers and media managers to define a target segment by demographics, geographics, and media usage habits. A Public Broadcasting System (PBS) station manager could use MRI data to identify and describe the target segment of major contributors (or adults donating $50 or more to public TV—see Table 9.1). The population base column and total row show there are 199,438,000 adults in the U.S. Column A, and the total row show the projected estimate of 6,066,000 adults who contributed $50 or more to public TV in the last 12 months. Column A and the Graduated College row show an estimated 2,882,000 of major contributors to public TV are college graduates. Column B and the Graduated College row show that 47.5% of major contributors are college graduates (or 2,882,000 major contributors who are college graduates/6,066,000 major contributors in the U.S. = 47.5%). Column C and the Graduated College row show that 6.4% of college graduates are major contributors to public TV (or 2,882,000 major contributors who are college graduates/44,940,000 U.S. college graduates = 6.4%). (An asterisk next to a column indicates fewer than 50 subjects responded, so consider these results cautiously.)

Column D and the Graduated College row show an index of 211 for major contributors who are college graduates. Many secondary research reports use indexes so they are now explained. An index shows a relationship between two percentages, as shown in the following formula for calculating index numbers:

$$\text{Index Number} = \frac{\text{Percentage of consumers in a demographic segment}}{\text{Percentage of population in the same segment}} \times 100$$

TABLE 9.1
MRI Data on Major Contributors to Public TV

Contributed $50 Or More Past 12 Months to Public Broadcast Television Report Base: Adults Mediamark Recreation Volume— Spring 2000 Copyright 2000, Mediamark Research Inc. (Add 000 to end of numbers in Pop. & A Columns) * Sample size for this item is less than 50	* Population Base: Adults (000)	* A Contr. $50 or More (000)	B Percentage Down	C Percentage Across	D Index
Total	199438	6066	100	3	100
Demographics					
Men	95691	2617	43.1	2.7	90
Women	103747	3449	56.9	3.3	109
Graduated college	44940	2882	47.5	6.4	211
Attended college	52878	1276	21	2.4	79
Graduated high school	66360	1298	21.4	2	64
Did not graduate high school	35260	610	10.1	1.7	57
*18–24	25691*	164	2.7	0.6	21
25–34	39066	553	9.1	1.4	47
35–44	44791	1149	18.9	2.6	84
45–54	34774	1568	25.9	4.5	148
55–64	22711	1264	20.8	5.6	183
65 or over	32404	1368	22.6	4.2	139
Professional	20825	1045	17.2	5	165
Executive/Admin./Managerial	19692	1205	19.9	6.1	201
Clerical/Sales/Technical	37625	860	14.2	2.3	75
H/D Income $75,000 or more	48259	3065	50.5	6.4	209
H/D Income $60,000–$74,999	22279	571	9.4	2.6	84
H/D Income $50,000–$59,999	19004	476	7.8	2.5	82
H/D Income $40,000–$49,999	21816	510	8.4	2.3	77
H/D Income $30,000–$39,999	24055	420	6.9	1.7	57
H/D Income $20,000–$29,999	25327	411	6.8	1.6	53
H/D Income $10,000–$19,999	24406	444	7.3	1.8	60
*H/D Income Less than $10,000	14292*	168	2.8	1.2	39
Marital Status: Married	114055	4385	72.3	3.8	126
Household size: 1 Person	26674	752	12.4	2.8	93
Household size: 2 Persons	68888	2592	42.7	3.8	124
Household size: 3 or More	103876	2722	44.9	2.6	86
*Any Child in HH: Under 2 years	15224*	230	3.8	1.5	50
Any Child in HH: 2–5 Years	29840	602	9.9	2	66
Any Child in HH: 6–11 Years	40268	899	14.8	2.2	73
Any Child in HH: 12–17 Years	39005	946	15.6	2.4	80
Geographics					
Marketing Reg.: New England	10172	496	8.2	4.9	160
Marketing Reg.: Mid-Atlantic	32601	1066	17.6	3.3	107

TABLE 9.1
Continued

Marketing Reg.: East Central	26616	667	11	2.5	82
Marketing Reg.: West Central	30192	782	12.9	2.6	85
Marketing Reg.: Southeast	38789	866	14.3	2.2	73
Marketing Reg.: Southwest	22644	628	10.4	2.8	91
Marketing Reg.: Pacific	38424	1561	25.7	4.1	134
MSA Central City	67669	1875	30.9	2.8	91
MSA Suburban	93169	3337	55	3.6	118
Non-MSA	38599	854	14.1	2.2	73
Magazine Reading					
*American Way	1108*	52	0.9	4.7	155
Architectural Digest	4368	321	5.3	7.4	242
*Atlantic Monthly	998*	164	2.7	16.5	542
*Audubon	1546*	170	2.8	11	362
*Barron's	1127*	94	1.6	8.4	275
Bon Appetit	5268	379	6.3	7.2	237
*Delta's SKY Magazine	2465*	116	1.9	4.7	154
Family Circle	21086	737	12.1	3.5	115
Forbes	4472	299	4.9	6.7	220
Fortune	3722	281	4.6	7.5	248
Gourmet	4724	320	5.3	6.8	222
*Hemispheres (United)	1507*	116	1.9	7.7	254
*Kiplinger's Personal Finance	2969*	194	3.2	6.5	215
*Los Angeles Times Magazine	3582*	211	3.5	5.9	194
Martha Stewart Living	10491	497	8.2	4.7	156
*Metropolitan Home	2548*	167	2.8	6.6	216
Modern Maturity	15117	676	11.1	4.5	147
Money	7507	490	8.1	6.5	215
National Geographic	30258	1369	22.6	4.5	149
National Geographic Traveler	4310	270	4.5	6.3	206
Newsweek	19130	1038	17.1	5.4	178
*New York Magazine	1074*	87	1.4	8.1	266
New York Times (Daily)	2769	319	5.3	11.5	379
New York Times (Sunday)	3939	379	6.3	9.6	317
The New Yorker	2767	337	5.6	12.2	401
*Northwest World Traveler	1517*	143	2.4	9.4	309
People	34469	1037	17.1	3	99
Reader's Digest	44264	1515	25	3.4	113
Smithsonian	7060	630	10.4	8.9	293
*Southwest Spirit	1878*	135	2.2	7.2	237
Sports Illustrated	20833	487	8	2.3	77
Time	21663	1084	17.9	5	165
Travel & Leisure	4783	312	5.1	6.5	215
TV Guide	32692	741	12.2	2.3	75
U.S. News & World Report	10070	585	9.6	5.8	191

TABLE 9.1
Continued

Contributed $50 Or More Past 12 Months to Public Broadcast Television Report Base: Adults Mediamark Recreation Volume— Spring 2000 Copyright 2000, Mediamark Research Inc. (Add 000 to end of numbers in Pop. & A Columns) * Sample size for this item is less than 50	* Population Base: Adults (000)	* A Contr. $50 or More (000)	B Percentage Down	C Percentage Across	D Index
Wall Street Journal	3588	391	6.4	10.9	358
*Washington Post (Sunday)	2536*	162	2.7	6.4	210
*Working Mother	2430*	137	2.3	5.6	185

So the 211 index represents the 47.5% of major contributors who are college graduates divided by 22.5% of all U.S. adults who are college graduates (or 44,940,000 adult U.S. college graduates divided by the total of 199,438,000 adults in the United States) or:

$$211 = \frac{47.5\% \text{ of major contributors are college graduates}}{22.5\% \text{ of U.S. adults are college graduates}} \times 100$$

Sissors and Baron (2002) said indexes provide a common method for comparison. An index of 100 is equal to the average, 150 is 50% above average, and 70 is 30% below average. So the 211 index tells us that college graduates are 111% more likely than the average U.S. adult to be major public TV contributors. Index numbers are viewed as central tendencies such as averages or means. An index, like an average, describes the group as a whole rather than one person.

Demographic or other characteristics having indexes over 100 are not necessarily the best to select. Consider segment size, level of use or consumption, and other primary or secondary research when selecting a target segment. Sometimes several categories of the same demographic or characteristic are included in the target segment. For example, the 55 to 64 age group has the highest index of 183 and comprises 20.8% of major contributors. Yet if the manager only targeted 55- to 64-year-olds, most major contributors from the target segment would be omitted. By adding major contributors ages 45 to 54 (25.9%) and 65 and older (22.6%), the target segment size is increased to 69.3% of all major contributors (or 20.8 + 25.9 + 22.6—only add mutually exclusive categories within the same characteristic such as age when using MRI; Sissors & Baron, 2002).

Which characteristics best exemplify the national target segment of major contributors to public TV? The MRI data in Table 9.1 suggest major contributors are college graduates ages 45 and older who have annual household incomes of $75,000 or more. They tend to be married, but have no children at home, work in administrative or professional occupations, and live in the suburbs of major cities. Major contributors appear most likely to live in the New England and Pacific marketing regions. Although these are national data, a local public TV manager could conduct research to assess whether these demographic characteristics hold true locally. For example, the station's printed or online contribution forms could include a brief demographic and media usage questionnaire for obtaining local data.

Managers of media outlets should understand reach and frequency because advertisers and media planners use these concepts when developing media schedules or plans. Reach refers to the percentage of the target segment exposed to a vehicle, ad, or program at least once in a given period. Reach is a measure of dispersion or how widely the message is received. Frequency is a measure of repetition and refers to how often the audience segment is reached on average. An advertiser may select a particular medium or combination of media based on whether the product is sold to the public at large or a specialized segment (such as major contributors to public TV).

Advertisers and media planners also consider cost per thousand (CPM) when making advertising placement decisions. CPM is the cost to deliver 1,000 people or households to an advertiser. It is an estimate of media efficiency for reaching the desired segment. CPMs are used for intermedia (or comparing different media) and intramedia (or comparisons among vehicles in the same class like newspapers or magazines) comparisons. Although intermedia comparisons are made to select among different media classes, remember these media are not directly comparable in terms of how the audience is measured and commercial impact. Intramedia CPMs compare ads of the same sizes and types (e.g., compare full-page, four-color ads among magazines or compare 30-second ads among primetime TV shows). The basic CPM formulas are as follows (Sissors & Baron, 2002).

For Newspapers

$$CPM = \frac{\text{Cost of ad} \times 1000}{\text{Circulation}}$$

For Print Vehicles When Audience Data Are Available

$$CPM = \frac{\text{Cost of one page black \& white ad (or appropriate size and color)} \times 1000}{\text{Number of prospects (or readers in the target segment) reached}}$$

For Broadcast Media (Based on Audience or Households Reached by a Given Program or in a Given Daypart or Standard Broadcast Daytime Period

$$CPM = \frac{\text{Cost of 1 unit of time (e.g., :30-Second spot)} \times 1000}{\text{Number of households or persons reached by a given program, daypart or time period}}$$

Advertisers and media planners evaluate factors including CPMs, reach, frequency, indexes, number and percentage of target readers, and target subsegments to select the most effective mix of vehicles to reach as many different members of the target segment as possible. A media planner considering where to place ads for a firm that wants to inform major contributors of its sponsorship of PBS programs could use the MRI data to select particular vehicles. Which combination of publications appears to best reach major contributors to public TV? An estimated 5.6% or 337,000 of major contributors read *The New Yorker* with an index of 401. *Smithsonian* with an index of 293 reaches 10.4% or 630,000 major contributors and probably broadens reach because of its different geographic dispersion. By adding *The Wall Street Journal* with an index of 358 that reaches 6.4% or 391,000 major contributors to the media schedule, the planner extends reach to business executives and those with an interest in business. By adding *Bon Appetit* with an index of 237 and readership of 6.3% or 379,000, the planner reaches major contributors with epicurean interests. Obviously some major contributors may subscribe to more than one of these vehicles, increasing the frequency of exposure to the ad or campaign.

CPMs help ensure that the media plan or schedule is as cost-efficient as possible in reaching the desired target segment. Assume that the advertiser gave the media planner a limited budget so choices must be made on maximizing reach among various target subsegments. The media planner decides a business-oriented magazine is needed because many in the target audience work in administrative occupations. *Forbes* with an index of 220 reaches 299,000 or 4.9% of major contributors (see *www.forbes.com, www.forbes.com/fdc/advertise.shtml*, or *www.forbesmedia.com* for rate cards, an editorial calendar, demographic information, and advertiser information). Major contributors comprise 6.7% of readers of *Forbes*, which charges about $77,760 for one full-page, four-color ad. *Fortune* with an index of 248 reaches 281,000 or 4.6% of major contributors (*www.fortune.com* or see the print media kit at *www.fortune.com/indexw.jhtml? channel=/html/mediakit.html*). Major contributors comprise 7.5% of readers of *Fortune*, which charges about $78,200 for one full-page, four-color ad. Yet how do these vehicles stack up in terms of cost efficiency? The intramedia CPMs for a full-page, four-color ad in each business magazine vehicle are the following.

Forbes CPM

$$\text{Full-Page, 4-C ad} = \frac{\$77,760 \times 1000}{299,000 \text{ major contributors reached}} = \$260.06$$

Fortune CPM

$$\text{Full-Page, 4-C ad} = \frac{\$78,200 \times 1000}{281,000 \text{ major contributors reached}} = \$278.29$$

Assuming there are no other important reasons for using either magazine, the CPM analysis suggests *Forbes* is the more cost-efficient buy. The cost to reach 1,000 major contributors is $18.23 less than if *Fortune* were used. Although *Forbes* has a lower index (220 vs. 248 for *Fortune*), it actually reaches more major contributors than *Fortune*. So if reach is a major goal in the media plan, *Forbes* is selected because it is a more cost-efficient buy, reaches more major contributors, and the ad costs less than an ad of the same size and type in *Fortune*.

Advertisers and media planners analyze the viewing and listening levels of various programs on different stations and channels to decide which broadcast vehicles best reach the target segment. In many markets, the level of program viewing and listening, as well as demographic and other data, are measured four times each year by Nielsen (*www.nielsenmedia.com*) or Arbitron (*www.arbitron.com*) during the *sweeps* periods. Arbitron and Nielsen assign stations to only one viewing or listening market area where they receive the largest audience share. Nielsen calls these nonoverlapping, mutually exclusive market areas comprised of counties grouped around cities or towns, designated market areas (DMAs). Each county or parish in the continental United States is assigned to only one DMA. Households using TV (HUT) or persons using TV (PUT) is the total percentage of homes (or persons) in a DMA watching TV during any daypart, such as morning, primetime, and late night or after 11:30 p.m. Eastern time (Sissors & Barron, 2002).

Broadcast managers are concerned with sweeps results because the price of advertising time is based on ratings and shares. A TV *rating* is the number of households (or persons) who watch a TV show divided by all TVHH or TV households (or persons) in that market area having a TV set. Ratings measure overall reach. A *share* is the estimated percentage of HUTs or PUTs during a specified time period that is watching a program. A *share* is the number of households (or persons) watching a particular program divided by the total number of households (or persons) with TV sets actually turned on during the time the program is aired. Shares are always larger than ratings because there is never a time when every single household has a TV on. Shares measure comparative performance from program to program, station to station, and network to network.

Shares are helpful for evaluating how one program fares against its competition and whether it has gained or lost audience members over different times of the year. A program's rating depends on its popularity and the daypart when it airs. The rating of a show that airs during the day is normally much smaller than a primetime show airing between 8:00 and 11:00 p.m. Eastern time. Yet that daytime show may have a higher share of viewers using TV in its time period or daypart. HUTs and PUTs are lower in the summer when fewer people watch TV and higher in the winter when more time is spent indoors watching. If

TABLE 9.2
Using Ratings and Shares
Sweeps Period

	February 2002	May 2002	July 2002	November 2002
ABC Action 2 News				
Rating	15	15	16	20
Share	25	28.8	33.3	35.7
NBC Ch. 7				
Hometown News				
Rating	25	23	21	21
Share	41.6	44.2	43.8	37.5
CBS Ch. 12 News				
You Can Use				
Rating	8	7	7	7
Share	13.3	13.5	14.6	12.5
Port City				
HUT Levels 6–6:30 p.m.	60	52	48	56

you looked only at ratings, you would miss the differences in viewing levels at various times of year (Sissors & Baron, 2002; see also Nielsen's home page for the definitions of terms like *rating* at *www.nielsenmedia.com/terms.htm*; national ratings and shares are found online at *http://tv.yahoo.com/nielsen*).

Media managers must identify the population base on which a rating is based. Cable channels may report ratings as a percentage of their own coverage rather than the total United States to make a stronger sales pitch to advertisers. Assume a cable channel reaches 15 million homes and has a program watched in 1,500,000 homes. The cable channel may report a rating of 10 for the program based on the channel's coverage area (or 1.5 million/15 million) rather than a rating of 1.4 based on all U.S. TV households (or 1.5 million/105.5 million USTVHH). Some Internet Web sites do the same and express audience size as a percentage of Internet users rather than the U.S. population (Sissors & Baron, 2002).

Ratings and shares are used in a local DMA to analyze the performance of local programs. The general manager at the ABC-affiliated station in the Port City DMA is analyzing the performance of her 6 p.m. newscast. She may conduct primary research if the analysis suggests her investment in a new anchor and equipment may be affecting the ratings. From Table 9.2, it appears that her newscast's audience size increased over the past year, especially in July. Had she considered only ratings, she would miss that her audience share increased in May, although the rating did not increase due to a smaller HUT level. (Shares for each sweeps period do not add up to the HUT levels because some local viewers were watching other local stations and cable channels from 6:00–6:30 p.m.)

Advertisers, media planners, and broadcast managers use the cost per point (CPP), which "measures the cost of one household or demographic rating point in a given market" (Sissors & Baron, 2002, p. 54). A CPP is an estimate of the dollars required to deliver one rating point (or one percentage of the audience) of any DMA. The formula is:

$$CPP = \frac{Cost\ of\ a\ commercial}{Rating}$$

SQAD (*www.sqad.com*) is a media cost forecasting company that provides CPPs and CPMs for TV and radio market areas nationwide. So a media planner having a SQAD report and ratings books can estimate the cost of ads and media plans, as well as evaluate the cost efficiency of shows in different markets. Managers use CPMs to compare different vehicles' efficiencies while they calculate a broadcast media plan via CPP (Sissors & Baron, 2002).

Although measurement methods are expected to change continually as new technologies are developed, broadcast media usage is measured using diaries (surveys), meters (observation), and telephone surveys. Diaries are booklets in which viewers and listeners write the stations they watch or listen to and when. National TV audiences are measured using people meters that automatically register the channel numbers tuned in, day of week, and time of day. Sample household members push a button to indicate when they view. Meters and diaries measure local TV viewing in about 50 large markets. The other local TV and radio markets are measured using diaries. Nielsen is experimenting with measuring more local markets using people meters. Arbitron is experimenting with the personal people meter (PPM) that automatically records consumers' media exposure using a pagerlike device (Crupi, 2002; Hall, 2001; Wang, 2002). The most important periods for measuring ratings, called *sweeps*, occur in February, May, July, and November (Sissors & Baron, 2002; Wimmer & Dominick, 2003).

One commonly used telephone survey method is day-after recall, where respondents are called to determine their listening and viewing activities of the previous day. With the coincidental method, households are called at random during the time period of interest, and respondents are asked what they are watching or listening to at that time. This method might be used to obtain immediate feedback about the success of primetime or special programming.

Managers must consider measurement limitations when evaluating audience data. Subjects may not be careful or honest when reporting viewing and listening habits. A meter records only which channel is tuned in and when the respondent pushed the button—it does not necessarily record whether anyone stayed in the room to watch. The problems with PPMs include limited sample sizes due to high cost, difficulties in recruiting participants because installing a people meter is invasive, and subjects tiring of pushing buttons. The diary method does not work well because subjects watch more channels at shorter intervals, resulting in smaller ratings and viewer confusion (Ephron & Gray, 2001). Diary reports tend to underestimate cable audiences (Hall, 2001). Concerns were raised about the estimated audience sizes generated from Nielsen's diaries and static people meter (Wang, 2002) and Arbitron's trial of its portable people meter (PPM; Crupi, 2002).

Magazine and newspaper audiences are often measured using three techniques: recent-reading and frequency-of-reading of magazines and yesterday-reading for newspapers. With recent-reading, a subject is shown more than 200 cards with the logos of magazines, each card one at a time, and asked whether the magazine was read or looked at in the past month or other publication period. Frequency-of-reading is measured by showing a list of about 50 magazine logos or cover pictures and asking the number of copies of each magazine that a subject read out of the last four issues. Yesterday-reading is measured by asking a selected sample which newspapers they read yesterday (Sissors & Baron, 2002).

Nielsen/Net Ratings (*www.nielsennetratings.com*) measures visits to Web sites. Nielsen places software on the computers of a nationally representative sample of about 60,000 subjects to record all sites they visit. Data gathered include the number of unique visitors to a site, how deeply they go into the site, how long they stay on each page, and how often they return. ABC Interactive (ABCi; *www.abcinteractiveaudits.com*) conducts audits for Web sites, search engines, and Internet broadcasters and posts audit reports online in its report library. The Interactive Advertising Bureau (*www.iab.net*) evaluates and recommends guidelines, standards, and practices for interactive media.

Many companies (listed in Table 9.3) provide information about consumers and their product and media usage habits to advertisers and advertising agencies. Print and electronic managers also use some of these same sources. Various sources are available to newspaper managers seeking secondary information (see Table 9.4). A number of companies provide information about or research services for radio, TV, and/or cable broadcasters (see Table 9.5) as well as Internet and out-of-home media organizations (see Table 9.6).

Audience Research: Primary Data Collection

A media manager may conduct a primary audience research study to answer questions unanswered by syndicated data. The major types of research used by newspaper managers include circulation, readership, and advertising studies.

Circulation Studies.   Geography is important to local newspaper managers because it defines the area where readers are attracted. Circulation studies reveal the newspaper's market share, market share of competing media, existing circulation patterns, and areas of potential circulation growth. A newspaper manager then conducts a situation or market analysis to determine which areas to target for increasing circulation.

Readership Studies.   Readership studies describe the people who live in the target areas. They often include questions about demographics, psychographics,

TABLE 9.3
Sources of Advertising Research

Source	Service
Mediamark Research Inc. (MRI; *www.mri.com*)	Provides demographic and media usage information for light, medium, and heavy users of many product categories.
Simmons Market Research Bureau (SMRB; *www.smrb.com*)	Provides demographic and media usage information for light, medium, and heavy users of many product categories. Also provides reports on kids, teens, Hispanics, and other segments.
SRDS or Standard Rate and Data Service (*www.srds.com*)	Provides media rates and data in a variety of books on the major media and the Lifestyle Market Analyst and Hispanic Media & Market Source.
CMR (Competitive Media Reporting) (*www.cmr.com*)	Provides advertising expenditure information for ten major media. Downloadable R&D Briefings are available at the Online Data link.
SCANTRACK (*www.acnielsen.com*)	Provides scanner-based sales and marketing information to monitor sales, evaluate price, and promotion effectiveness. AC Nielsen has a representative and demographically balanced Worldwide Consumer Panel tracking consumer purchase behavior and shopping patterns across all retail types.
Information Resources (*www.infores.com*)	Provides sales and marketing research such as store tracking and electronic point-of-sale consumer purchases around the world. Offers U.S. and European panel data.
Scarborough Research (*www.scarborough.com*)	Provides local market consumer shopping patterns and demographic, lifestyle, and media usage information. Provides a syndicated study to print media, electronic media, new media, outdoor media, sports teams and leagues, agencies, advertisers, and yellow pages on local, regional, and national levels.
Harris Interactive (*www.harrisblackintl.com*)	Provides predictive, custom, and strategic market research, consulting, and The Harris Poll. Conducts Internet market research.
Gallup and Robinson (*www.gallup-robinson.com*)	Provides ad copy testing, tracking studies, concept testing, claims substantiation, spokesperson testing, event sponsorship, international testing, custom, and media research and services.

TABLE 9.3
Continued

Source	Service
NFO World Group (*www.nfow.com*)	Provides research and consumer panel data for product development, brand management, market evaluation, pricing, customer satisfaction, distribution, and advertising effectiveness. Offers Internet-based research and maintains an interactive consumer panel community.
NPD Group (*www.npd.com*) (*www.npdor.com*)	Provides market data such as sales volume and trends, market share, pricing, point-of sale tracking, and consumer behavior. NPD's Online Panel allows surveying of demographic and geographic segments.
RoperASW (*www.roper.com*)	Provides research on consumer lifestyles, values, attitudes, and market behavior as well as Starch Ad Readership scores.
Opinion Research Corporation (*www.opinionresearch.com*)	Provides public opinion, marketing, and social research.
J.D. Power and Associates (*www.jdpower.com*)	Provides customer satisfaction studies, market research, analysis, and forecasting.
Hoover's Inc. (*www.hoovers.com*)	Provides information on companies, industries, and market intelligence.
Market Facts (*www.marketfacts.com*)	Provides marketing research consulting and information to consumer packaged goods companies and other sectors including telecommunications, technology, and business-to-business markets.
Sales and Marketing Management (*www.salesandmarketing.com*)	Provides data for effective buying income, population, buying power, and retail sales in its *Survey of Buying Power*.
Advertising Research Foundation (ARF; *www.arfsite.org*)	The professional organization for the advertising, marketing, and media research field. Publishes the *Journal of Advertising Research*.
Advertising World (*www.advertising.utexas.edu/world*)	The University of Texas at Austin Advertising Department's comprehensive site of advertising industry links.
Advertising Media Internet Center (*www.amic.com*)	Provides media and rate information as well as secondary research on print, broadcast, and the Internet.
AdTrack (*www.usatoday.com/money/index/ad001.htm*)	Weekly *USA Today* and Harris Interactive poll that tracks the effectiveness of advertising campaigns.

TABLE 9.4

Sources of Print Research

Source	Service
Newspaper Association of America (NAA; *www.naa.org*) (*www.newspaperlinks.com*)	Provides data about the newspaper industry, newspaper advertising. Publishes Facts About Newspapers report and has data online.
Magazine Publishers of America (MPA; *www.magazine.org*)	Provides data and information online about the magazine industry and magazine readership including the *Magazine Handbook*.
MPA Publishers Information Bureau (*www.magazine.org/pib*)	Provides information and data online including advertising revenues, pages, and historical trends. Tracks the amount and type of consumer magazine advertising.
Standard Rate and Data Service (SRDS; *www.srds.com*)	Publishes the *Business Publication Advertising Source, Consumer Magazine Advertising Source, Newspaper Advertising Source, Community Publications Advertising Source, Circulation 2002*, and *Print Media Production Source* providing rates and data on various publication types.
Audit Bureau of Circulation (ABC; *www.accessabc.com*)	Audits and verifies the circulation of newspapers, magazines, business and farm publications, the Internet, and trade shows.
BPA International (*www.bpai.com*)	Audits and verifies circulation of trade print publications, newspapers, trade shows, industry databases, Web site traffic, and wireless communications.
Verified Audit Circulation (VAC; *www.verifiedaudit.com*)	Provides circulation data for free and paid community newspapers including TMCs, shopping guides, alternative newsweeklies, special interest, ethnic, and niche publications as well as trade and consumer magazines and yellow pages directories.
Competitive Media Reporting (CMR; *www.cmr.com*)	Provides advertising expenditure information for 10 major media including major print media.
Mendelsohn Media Research (*www.mmrsurveys.com/ mhomefrm.htm*)	Provides custom and syndicated advertising and media research including the Affluent Survey and Affluent Travel Survey as well as subscriber studies, editorial surveys, and print media evaluations.
RoperASW (*www.roper.com/products/ starch.html*)	Provides Starch Ad Readership scores by measuring 25,000 ads in over 400 magazine issues.
Pulse Research (*www.pulseresearch.com*)	Provides research and marketing services for daily and weekly newspapers, shoppers, and

TABLE 9.4
Continued

Source	Service
	other special interest publications. Offers market research for planning and developing a Web site targeting local market areas.
Editor and Publisher (*www.editorandpublisher.com*)	Publishes the Market Guide of descriptive information on daily newspaper markets including demographic, retail sales, income levels, shopping, industries, and other data. Publishes the International Yearbook with listings of all dailies Worldwide and U.S. and Canadian community, special interest, and weekly papers.
Folio (*www.foliomag.com*)	Provides information and articles about the magazine industry for magazine management.
MRI+ (*www.mriplus.com*)	Provides a searchable database of magazine rate, audience, and editorial data.

TABLE 9.5
Sources of Broadcast Research

Source	Service
Television Bureau of Advertising (TVB; *www.tvb.org*)	Publishes TV facts online with information about ad revenue, TV trends, TV basics, station times sales, TVHH by market, and political advertising.
Cabletelevision Advertising Bureau (CAB; *www.cabletvadbureau.com*)	Publishes excerpts from Cable TV Facts online including information on advertising revenues and shares. Publishes online Cable Network Profiles with audience data on major cable networks.
The Cable Center (*www.cablecenter.org/index.cfm*)	Provides background information about the cable industry and its history.
Magness Institute (*www.cablecenter.org/education/magness/index.cfm*)	Conducts telecommunications research and provides educational opportunities for cable industry professionals worldwide.
Radio Advertising Bureau (RAB; *www.rab.com*) (*www.rab.com/station/mediafact*)	Provides information about radio advertising, publishes the Media Fact Book online, and has a Research link with some radio information available to the public.
National Association of Broadcasters (NAB; *www.nab.org*)	Industry association that works on broadcast issues. Provides some information and research online.

TABLE 9.5
Continued

Arbitron (*www.arbitron.com*)	Provides audience data for radio, cable outdoor, and the Internet. Surveys retail, media, and product patterns of local market consumers. Developing the Portable People Meter for radio, TV, and cable ratings. In a joint venture with Scarborough Research, it provides media and marketing research services to broadcast TV, magazine, newspaper, and online industries.
Nielsen Media Research (*www.nielsenmedia.com*)	Provides TV audience measurement and related services worldwide. The National People Meter service provides audience estimates for broadcast networks, cable networks, Spanish language networks, and national syndicators. Provides local ratings estimates for TV stations, regional cable networks, MSOs, cable interconnects, and Spanish-language stations. Provides Monitor-Plus with competitive advertising intelligence information as well as Internet usage and advertising information.
SQAD (*www.sqad.com*)	Provides CPPS and CPMs for local market radio and TV for various demographic segments. National data include network TV, cable, syndication, and Internet research.
Marketing Evaluations/TVQ (*www.qscores.com*)	Provides qualitative ratings of broadcast and cable programs, performers, characters and licensed properties, brand names, and sports personalities. Has a People Panel used for Q scores, diary studies, product tests, telephone surveys, attitude, and usage tracking and for screening concepts.
FMR Associates, Inc. (*www.fmrassociates.com*)	Provides radio research, perceptual research services, EARS music and program testing, MusicTrac Call-Out Research, media research, and market research services. Conducts research for noncommercial broadcasters like the Corporation for Public Broadcasting and National Public Radio.
Frank N. Magid Associates Inc. (*www.magid.com*)	Provides broadcast consulting and research services as well as online, E-commerce, and media convergence research and strategy.
Standard Rate and Data Service (*www.srds.com*)	Publishes the *Radio Advertising Source* and *TV & Cable Source* with data and advertising rates.

TABLE 9.5
Continued

Source	Service
CMR (Competitive Media Reporting) (*www.cmr.com*)	Provides advertising expenditure information for 10 major media including major broadcast media.
Broadcasting and Cable Yearbook (*www.bowker.com*)	Provides information on radio, TV, and cable including listings on all radio and TV stations, multiple system cable operators, independent owners, suppliers of industry services, station ownership, trade shows, and associations and market statistics.
Media Rating Council (*www.mrc.htsp.com*)	Develops standards and reviews rating methodology to ensure data are credible.

TABLE 9.6
Internet and Other Research Sources

Source	Service
Internet and Out-of-Home Sources	
Interactive Advertising Bureau (*www.iab.net*)	Evaluates and recommends standards and practices, fields research on Internet advertising effectiveness. Provides IAB's Advertising ABCs and other advice and data online on Internet advertising. Has standard Internet ad sizes and types online.
Association for Interactive Media (*www.imarketing.org*)	Provides information on the commercial use of e-mail marketing, e-tailing, e-commerce, online marketing, and interactive TV.
Information Technology Association of America (*www.itaa.org*)	Provides information on the information technology industry including computers, software, telecommunications, Internet, and online services.
The Open Group (*www.ema.org*) (*www.opengroup.org/finder-a.htm*)	Provides information and advice on achieving boundaryless information flow.
Internet Society (*www.isoc.org*) (*www.isoc.org/internet*)	Provides information on the Internet and is the home for Internet infrastructure standards.
Outdoor Advertising, Association of America (OAAA; *www.oaaa.org*)	Provides information about the outdoor medium. Links include Facts & Figures and Research.

TABLE 9.6
Continued

Direct Marketing Association (*www.the-dma.org*)	Provides information on direct, database, and interactive marketing. The DMA Library has a Research and Statistics link.
Electronic Retailing Association (*www.era.org*)	Provides information on the electronic retailing industry including infomercials and online sales. Provides an Industry Facts & Figures link.
Point of Purchase Advertising International (www.popai.org) (*www.popai.com/frames/ homepopaina_fr.html*)	Provides information on point-of-purchase (P-O-P) advertising.
Promotional Products Association International (*www.ppa.org*)	Provides information on products imprinted with a firm's name, logo, or message including clothing or merchandise. The Resources & Technology link includes research.
Yellow Pages Integrated Media Association (*www.yppa.org*)	Provides information and data on print and electronic yellow pages industry.
ABC Interactive (ABCi; (*www.abcinteractiveaudits.com*) (*www.abcinteractiveaudits.com/reportlib/ site_bytes.html*) (*www.abcinteractiveaudits.com/ reportlib/avail_info.html*)	Audits and verifies Web site traffic, ad delivery, search engines, e-mail and e-mail ad delivery, and Internet broadcasters. Provides audits online—see addresses at left.
Standard Rate and Data Service (*www.srds.com*)	Publishes the Interactive Advertising Source, Out-of-Home Advertising Source, Direct Marketing List Source, and Technology Media Source.
Nielsen/Net Ratings (*www.nielsennetratings.com*)	Provides measurements of Web site visits.
AdZone Research, Inc. (*www.adzoneinteractive.com*)	Provides Internet ad activity data for sites worldwide by advertiser, brand, industry, date range, impressions, geographic location, and expenditures. Monitors banner ads, text ads, interstitials, keywords, links, buttons, pop-ups, and hover ads.
Traffic Audit Bureau for Media Measurement (TAB) (*www.tabonline.com*)	Provides circulation data or means to measure out-of-home media including posters, bulletins, and shelter and truck advertising.

TABLE 9.6
Continued

Source	Service
Internet Advertising Resource Guide (*www.admedia.org*)	Advertising site developed by Dr. Hairong Li at Michigan State Univ. The Research link lists many sites.
Netacceptable (*marketing.tenagra.com/ net-acceptable.html*)	Provides links on unacceptable and appropriate Internet advertising.
Digitrends.net (*www.digitrends.net*)	Provides information for interactive marketers.
Selected Government Data and Information Sources	
U.S. Census Bureau (*www.census.gov*) (*http://factfinder.census.gov/home/ en/acsdata.html*)	Provides demographic and economic data on U.S. market areas. The American Community Survey (address at left) and American Factfinder link have useful information.
National Archives and Records Administration (*www.nara.gov* or *www.archives.gov*)	NARA's Research Room link provides a starting point for searches.
Other Research Links	
ITS (Information Technology Services) at Univ. of Texas-Austin Statistical Support (*www.utexas.edu/cc/stat*)	Provides links to General and Specific Statistics and answers to questions about using statistics.
Open Directory Project DMOZ-Directory Mozilla (*dmoz.org/Science/Math/Statistics/*)	Provides an open directory of links developed by volunteers and hosted and sponsored by Netscape Communication Corp.
Statistics.com (*www.statistics.com*)	Commercial site that provides links to data sources.

and media usage to discover who reads the newspaper, why, the sections they prefer, and the benefits they obtain from reading it. A large metropolitan newspaper might develop a lifestyle section appealing to upper income city residents who are moving to a particular zip code. A small town newspaper might increase soccer coverage in the sports section when research shows many local children and parents participate in soccer.

Studies incorporating demographics, psychographics, and media usage are used to measure the audience characteristics of competing media. Information about who exclusively reads each local daily, weekly, and shopper; who reads a combination of these publications and why; and how these and other publications are used may reveal untapped readership segments.

Advertising Studies. The media manager or media representative sells media space to media buyers using a media kit. A media kit positions the media product as an ideal vehicle for the advertiser. Media outlets may conduct research to accurately describe the demographic and psychographic composition of their audiences. Industry groups provide advertising advice and data for media kits (see Tables 9.3, 9.4, 9.5, and 9.6). The Chamber of Commerce, other local economic development offices, or state agencies concerned with economic development provide market information. State or regional press associations may compile primary and secondary market information. Include CPM data in media kits or make them available to advertisers.

Many vehicles with online sites include a media kit, rate card, and information on their audiences. MRI+ (*www.mriplus.com*) consolidates searchable databases used to evaluate magazines that include information used in media kits when one registers with the free service. Many media outlets list media kits on their Web sites, including Forbes (*www.forbes.com/fdc/advertise.shtml* or *www. forbesmedia.com*) and Fortune (*www.fortune.com/indexw.jhtml?channel=/html/ mediakit.html*).

Advertisers purchase data on their own and competitors' past and present media activity from Competitive Media Reporting (CMR; *www.cmr.com*). CMR provides the Multi-Media Service (*www.cmr.com/products/multimedia.html*) that reports ad spending in 10 major media: consumer magazines, Sunday magazines, newspapers, outdoor, network TV, spot TV, syndicated TV, cable TV, network radio, and national spot radio. The Company/Brand $, Class/Brand $, and Ad $ Summary reports detail spending in these media by industries, parent companies, and brands. Media managers use these data to identify a desired advertiser's buying patterns and gain insight into media buys.

Positioning research includes studies of audience perceptions to discover a brand or product's unique attribute (or combination of attributes) to better meet consumers' needs. Positioning research diagnoses why audiences are not attracted to a product and includes other factors such as how a product compares to competitors. It often uses exploratory and descriptive methods such as focus groups or surveys. Identifying consumer habits, lifestyles, behaviors, and desires through primary target segment research provides the information basis for product positioning.

For media organizations, positioning concerns the audience's image of the media outlet or company, or the *product* in this case. A new cable network's name is critical to its successful positioning because it may be the only information the audience hears about it. At the media content level, studies of audience reactions to and preferences for broadcast and cable programming, news and magazine articles and format, and the structure and content of Web sites are critical to maintaining audience commitment. A manager conducts a mail or telephone survey, focus group, or personal interviews to determine whether the local community favors the news talent and newscast. Results may be used to determine local news anchor changes.

Media Content: Evaluative, Formative, and Summative Research

Evaluative research determines how well the media content conveys what it is intended to convey. Causal research methods such as experiments are often used to conduct this research. Advertisers and their advertising agencies use evaluative research to test messages before (pretesting) and after (posttesting) ads are conveyed to the general public.

Test marketing evaluates audience tastes for broadcast and cable programming, print editorial content, Web site structure and content, and advertising. An ad might be aired in one market before it airs nationally to project what its effect on consumer behavior might be. Ads might be shown in two different markets or on a two-way cable system in one city, with subscribers in one part of the city seeing one version of a program or commercial and those living in another area seeing another version. Results of a random telephone survey reveal which program version earned higher ratings or which commercial spurred more sales.

With formative research, production companies and TV networks pretest programming and advertisers pretest ads before committing full resources to them. Concept testing assesses a program's potential popularity or the potential effectiveness of an ad's key selling concept before exposure to the general public. A concept is tested by having subjects read a one-page program summary or showing them a mock-up of a commercial made using slides and an audiotape. Subjects may be invited to a theater to view a pilot program. After viewing, they report their feelings about the program to help network executives determine how popular various characters and endings might be (Wimmer & Dominick, 2003).

Summative research examines whether the appropriate message is conveyed to the target market. This allows the media or advertising manager to evaluate whether the media or advertising content objectives were actually accomplished. Summative research can be performed in the field during a campaign or purchased as secondary data. For example, RoperASW (*www.roper.com*) offers Starch Ad Readership (*www.roper.com/products/starch.html*), measuring about 25,000 ads in more than 400 magazine issues to develop readership scores. Scores include the percentage of readers who saw the ad and read the copy. Ads are ranked against others in the same issue and product category to assess how the ad performs over time and against competitors.

SUMMARY

All media managers must understand research from a broad perspective to use it effectively. It is important to understand research methods and concepts like variables, reliability, and validity to conduct or effectively assess research.

Before designing a research study, three issues are considered. First, how much is already known about the problem at hand? Second, how much information is needed about each audience member? Third, how important is it that the study results are generalizable to other people and situations? The answers to these questions direct the researcher to some types of research and not to others.

Advertising, print, broadcast, cable, and online managers use similar kinds of data, research sources, and research techniques in different ways. Media outlet managers must comprehend how advertisers use audience data and media planning concepts such as indexes, reach, frequency, CPMs, and CPPs to select media vehicles for advertising buys. Understanding how advertisers and agencies use these concepts helps a manager sell advertising time or space effectively.

Some of the research categories that are important to effective media management are primary, secondary, syndicated, exploratory, descriptive, and causal research. Applied research methods include audience, positioning, formative, and summative research. Data-collection designs available to the researcher include focus groups, in-depth interviews, surveys, and experiments. By collecting information about the consumer, the media manager makes more informed strategic decisions and thus markets the media vehicle more effectively to advertisers.

Case 9.1
The Case of the Ratings Increase

Sue Al-Matrouk, general manager of WPRT-TV 2 in Port City, was delighted to receive the latest sweeps report showing the ratings and shares for Action News at 6 p.m. appeared to increase over the past four sweeps periods (see Table 9.2). She wondered whether the increase was due to the investment she had made in a new anchor, new set, and equipment like the Doppler radar, news helicopter, and remote truck. It was expensive to retain the news helicopter so she would cut that expense if it was not a factor in the ratings increase. Yet her news director, John Small, said he had received a great deal of positive feedback about it. Perhaps she could share the cost of the helicopter with another media outlet. She also wondered whether the new promotional campaign by promotions director Janice Biaggi had had an effect.

Sue noted the ratings and shares of the long-standing newscast leader in the market, NBC's "Hometown News," appeared to be declining since May. She wanted to know why this was happening. The CBS "News You Can Use" newscast remained solidly in third position and could be losing viewers. She wondered whether these changes were due to improvements in her newscast, factors related to the competing newscasts, other factors in the market, or a combination of all these factors. She planned to call Robert Howard, her station's group owner, to inform him of the ratings increase and ask him to support a research project to find out what contributed to the newscast's success.

Avery Atkin, sales manager at WPRT, came into her office with a big smile on his face. "In all my years in this market I've never seen a book like this. I've never seen us so close to Hometown News. We may have the best sales quarter ever after my team and I go out and sell advertising based on this book." Sue replied, "I'm excited too. I'm really proud of our team because all the hard work paid off. And I know you and the sales staff will do a great job selling us based on this book. But I want to be sure we stay on this upward track. We may be poised here to overtake and pass Hometown News and I don't want to squander this opportunity." Avery replied, "Yeah, this is great, but we really do need to understand why this is happening so we can keep it up."

Just then John and Janice came in also looking quite happy. Sue said, "Good news sure travels fast. Great job, gang! I know how hard you've worked and I'm so proud of what we've accomplished." Janice said, "Thanks! Yeah, this is great. I just want to keep this train on the track, so to speak." "Thanks and me, too," said John. "I've been in the news business too long to sit on my laurels."

Sue thought for a moment and said, "Let's plan to have a meeting tomorrow. I want each of you to tell me why you think this is happening and what we need to do to maintain this success. I also want each of you to propose ideas and objectives for a research study. We need some good research to plan and maintain this success in the future. I think Robert will support a study and might even give us some extra money if we give him a good research proposal."

ASSIGNMENT

1. Evaluate the ratings, shares, and HUTS in Table 9.2 carefully. Write a paragraph or two explaining what these ratings and shares appear to suggest about each station's performance and why. Explain whether it appears viewership for each station is increasing, declining, or staying the same and why.
2. How much confidence do you have in your answers to Question 1? What do the ratings and share data really reveal? Do the data in Table 9.2 tell us why the ratings and shares of the station have changed? Why or why not?
3. Write a few detailed paragraphs that answer the following questions. How can Sue determine whether the ratings and shares for her 6 p.m. newscast are improving due to the investments she's made in talent and equipment? Can she answer this question? Why or why not? What can Sue realistically do to get ideas about why viewership of her newscast may be increasing?
4. What type of research study should each of the following managers propose to Sue? What type of research study is needed to determine external

factors that may be having an effect? Name and describe the research objectives, type of study, or research, methods, and data analysis techniques to use, and so on, to answer Questions 4a through 4d.

   a. What type of research study should the news director propose? Why?

   b. What type of research study should the sales manager propose? Why?

   c. What type of research study should the promotions manager propose? Why?

   d. What type of research study should be developed to discover what other factors (e.g., changes in the other stations' newscasts, etc.) may have an influence?

5. Using your answers to Question 4, design a research plan for Sue to present to the station's owner. For what type of research study or studies should Sue contract? What type of study or studies could Sue contract for that would serve the needs and meet the research objectives of news, promotions, and sales and examine external factors? Should she contract for more than one study? If yes, which ones should she contract for and in what order?

Case 9.2
Evaluating Contributors to Public TV

Assume you are the general manager of the public TV station in your city or the nearest major city. You just completed your latest fundraising campaign and are unsatisfied with the results. You want to discover why your fundraising campaign was not as successful as you had anticipated. Review the Mediamark data for all contributors to public TV nationwide (see Table 9.7). Evaluate Simmons or more recent Mediamark data if available. If the SRDS Lifestyle Market Analyst (LMA) is available in your library, review data on the relevant demographic segment profiles (e.g., 45 to 64 years old, income $75,000 and over, and any other relevant categories you find). Evaluate any other available data about the target segment of contributors to public TV.

Review the census data for demographic and economic information about your city or the nearest major city. Try to find out who major individual and business contributors might be. If the LMA report is available in your library, review data for your city or the nearest major city in the Market Profiles section. Look for other sources of secondary or syndicated media research that provide information about your city or market.

Review Tables 9.3, 9.4, 9.5, and 9.6 to see if any of these sources are available in your library. Check for other sources of secondary or syndicated media research reports on the public TV contributors target segment, your city or market, and evaluate any appropriate data available. In other words, conduct a thorough

TABLE 9.7

MRI Data on All Contributors to Public TV

Contributed to Public Broadcast Television in Past 12 Months— Report Base: Adults Mediamark Recreation Volume— Spring 2000 Copyright 2000, Mediamark Research Inc. (Add 000 to end of numbers in Pop. & A Columns) * Sample size for this item is less than 50	* Popu- lation Base: Adults (000)	* A Contr. to Public TV (000)	B Percent- age Down	C Percent- age Across	D Index
Total	199438	17219	100	8.6	100
Men	95691	7877	45.7	8.2	95
Women	103747	9342	54.3	9	104
Graduated College	44940	7034	40.9	15.7	181
Attended College	52878	4233	24.6	8	93
Graduated High School	66360	4204	24.4	6.3	73
Did not Graduate High School	35260	1748	10.2	5	57
18–24	25691	668	3.9	2.6	30
25–34	39066	1979	11.5	5.1	59
35–44	44791	3433	19.9	7.7	89
45–54	34774	3945	22.9	11.3	131
55–64	22711	2729	15.8	12	139
65 or over	32404	4464	25.9	13.8	160
Employed Full Time	113259	9351	54.3	8.3	96
Professional	20825	2707	15.7	13	151
Executive/Admin./Managerial	19692	2741	15.9	13.9	161
Clerical/Sales/Technical	37625	2606	15.1	6.9	80
Precision/Crafts/Repair	14305	679	3.9	4.7	55
H/D Income $75,000 or more	48259	6838	39.7	14.2	164
H/D Income $60,000–$74,999	22279	1757	10.2	7.9	91
H/D Income $50,000–$59,999	19004	1451	8.4	7.6	88
H/D Income $40,000–$49,999	21816	1662	9.7	7.6	88
H/D Income $30,000–$39,999	24055	1688	9.8	7	81
H/D Income $20,000–$29,999	25327	1794	10.4	7.1	82
H/D Income $10,000–$19,999	24406	1363	7.9	5.6	65
H/D Income Less than $10,000	14292	667	3.9	4.7	54
Census Region: Northeast	39250	3858	22.4	9.8	114
Census Region: North Central	46071	4381	25.4	9.5	110
Census Region: South	70545	4966	28.8	7	82
Census Region: West	43573	4014	23.3	9.2	107
Marketing Reg.: New England	10172	1340	7.8	13.2	153
Marketing Reg.: Mid-Atlantic	32601	3051	17.7	9.4	108
Marketing Reg.: East Central	26616	2182	12.7	8.2	95
Marketing Reg.: West Central	30192	2844	16.5	9.4	109
Marketing Reg.: Southeast	38789	2667	15.5	6.9	80

TABLE 9.7
Continued

Marketing Reg.: Southwest	22644	1558	9	6.9	80
Marketing Reg.: Pacific	38424	3577	20.8	9.3	108
MSA Central City	67669	5952	34.6	8.8	102
MSA Suburban	93169	8548	49.6	9.2	106
Non-MSA	38599	2719	15.8	7	82
Marital Status: Married	114055	11668	67.8	10.2	118
Household size: 1 Person	26674	2412	14	9	105
Household size: 2 Persons	68888	7175	41.7	10.4	121
Household size: 3 or More	103876	7632	44.3	7.3	85
Any Child in HH: Under 2 years	15224	842	4.9	5.5	64
Any Child in HH: 2–5 Years	29840	1779	10.3	6	69
Any Child in HH: 6–11 Years	40268	2688	15.6	6.7	77
Any Child in HH: 12–17 Years	39005	2946	17.1	7.6	87
Home Owned	139215	13899	80.7	10	116
*Have Cable TV	1487*	90	0.5	6.1	70
Have Pay TV	19507	1472	8.5	7.5	87
Heavy Cable Viewing (15+ Hrs)	21039	1415	8.2	6.7	78
*A&E Television Network	3493*	288	1.7	8.2	95
American Movie Classics	19371	1521	8.8	7.9	91
Cartoon Network	23637	1624	9.4	6.9	80
CMT (Country Music TV)	13764	1006	5.8	7.3	85
CNBC	46017	3780	22	8.2	95
CNN	21341	1565	9.1	7.3	85
Comedy Central	13122	855	5	6.5	75
Court TV	47833	3584	20.8	7.5	87
The Discovery Channel	21949	1398	8.1	6.4	74
E! Entertainment Television	60645	5729	33.3	9.4	109
ESPN	20535	1666	9.7	8.1	94
ESPN2	16341	1927	11.2	11.8	137
Fox Family Channel	2968	413	2.4	13.9	161
Fox News Channel	4107	223	1.3	5.4	63
Game Show Network	4368	708	4.1	16.2	188
*Headline CNN News	1259*	187	1.1	14.8	172
History Channel	1546	326	1.9	21.1	245
Home & Garden TV	22695	2211	12.8	9.7	113
Lifetime	40824	3028	17.6	7.4	86
MSNBC News	25937	2821	16.4	10.9	126
MTV	25752	1186	6.9	4.6	53
Nick at Nite	19507	1472	8.5	7.5	87
Nickelodeon	21039	1415	8.2	6.7	78
Sci-Fi Channel	19371	1521	8.8	7.9	91
TBS	50814	3677	21.4	7.2	84
The Travel Channel	10078	1007	5.8	10	116
TLC (The Learning Channel)	31998	2618	15.2	8.2	95

TABLE 9.7
Continued

Contributed to Public Broadcast Television in Past 12 Months—Report Base: Adults Mediamark Recreation Volume—Spring 2000 Copyright 2000, Mediamark Research Inc. (Add 000 to end of numbers in Pop. & A Columns) * Sample size for this item is less than 50	* Population Base: Adults (000)	* A Contr. to Public TV (000)	B Percentage Down	C Percentage Across	D Index
TNN (The Nashville Network)	23637	1624	9.4	6.9	80
Turner Classic Movies	13764	1006	5.8	7.3	85
TNT (Turner Netw. Television)	46017	3780	22	8.2	95
TV Land	13122	855	5	6.5	75
USA Network	47833	3584	20.8	7.5	87
VH1	21949	1398	8.1	6.4	74
The Weather Channel	60645	5729	33.3	9.4	109
WGN-TV	20535	1666	9.7	8.1	94
Access Internet Magazine	16341	1927	11.2	11.8	137
American Legion	2968	413	2.4	13.9	161
American Rifleman	4107	223	1.3	5.4	63
*American Way	1108*	184	1.1	16.6	193
Architectural Digest	4368	708	4.1	16.2	188
Atlantic Monthly	998	271	1.6	27.1	314
Audubon	1546	326	1.9	21.1	245
Automobile	3867	293	1.7	7.6	88
Barron's	1127	271	1.6	24.1	279
Better Homes & Gardens	33591	3523	20.5	10.5	121
Bon Appetit	5268	888	5.2	16.9	195
Business Week	4263	700	4.1	16.4	190
Catholic Digest	2577	366	2.1	14.2	165
Chicago Tribune Magazine	2765	446	2.6	16.1	187
Conde Nast Traveler	2571	406	2.4	15.8	183
Consumer Reports	15863	2170	12.6	13.7	158
Consumers Digest	6318	719	4.2	11.4	132
*Continental	1519*	192	1.1	12.6	146
Cooking Light	6536	864	5	13.2	153
Cosmopolitan	15472	995	5.8	6.4	74
Delta's SKY Magazine	2465	324	1.9	13.1	152
Discover	6209	615	3.6	9.9	115
Ebony	10588	801	4.6	7.6	88
Elle	3783	283	1.6	7.5	87
Entertainment Weekly	8161	638	3.7	7.8	91
Essence	7067	627	3.6	8.9	103
Family Circle	21086	2033	11.8	9.6	112

TABLE 9.7
Continued

Field & Stream	11069	553	3.2	5	58
Flower & Garden	5224	466	2.7	8.9	103
Food & Wine	4195	619	3.6	14.8	171
Forbes	4472	686	4	15.3	178
Fortune	3722	553	3.2	14.9	172
Glamour	10826	610	3.5	5.6	65
Golf Digest	5759	649	3.8	11.3	131
Golf Magazine	5856	785	4.6	13.4	155
*Golf World	1447*	212	1.2	14.7	170
Good Housekeeping	23312	2085	12.1	8.9	104
Gourmet	4724	693	4	14.7	170
GQ (Gentlemen's Quarterly)	6195	404	2.3	6.5	75
Harper's Bazaar	2799	337	2	12	139
Health	5490	512	3	9.3	108
Hemispheres (United)	1507	252	1.5	16.7	194
Home	3936	292	1.7	7.4	86
House & Garden	11292	1162	6.7	10.3	119
House Beautiful	6351	919	5.3	14.5	168
In Style	4941	491	2.9	9.9	115
*Inc.	1728*	224	1.3	13	150
Jet	7997	492	2.9	6.2	71
Kiplinger's Personal Finance	2969	568	3.3	19.1	221
Ladies' Home Journal	14507	1431	8.3	9.9	114
Los Angeles Times Magazine	3582	518	3	14.5	168
Macworld	1912	305	1.8	15.9	185
Mademoiselle	5147	398	2.3	7.7	90
Martha Stewart Living	10491	1290	7.5	12.3	142
Men's Fitness	4931	425	2.5	8.6	100
Men's Health	7819	830	4.8	10.6	123
*Men's Journal	1787*	178	1	9.9	115
Metropolitan Home	2548	449	2.6	17.6	204
Midwest Living	2546	383	2.2	15	174
Modern Maturity	15117	2397	13.9	15.9	184
Money	7507	1146	6.7	15.3	177
Motor Trend	6599	475	2.8	7.2	83
Muscle & Fitness	6960	431	2.5	6.2	72
Mutual Funds	2711	300	1.7	11.1	128
National Enquirer	12133	753	4.4	6.2	72
National Geographic	30258	3612	21	11.9	138
National Geographic Traveler	4310	676	3.9	15.7	182
Natural History	1533	357	2.1	23.3	270
Newsweek	19130	2606	15.1	13.6	158
*New York Magazine	1074*	165	1	15.4	178
New York Times (Daily)	2769	629	3.7	22.7	263

TABLE 9.7
Continued

Contributed to Public Broadcast Television in Past 12 Months— Report Base: Adults Mediamark Recreation Volume— Spring 2000 Copyright 2000, Mediamark Research Inc. (Add 000 to end of numbers in Pop. & A Columns) * Sample size for this item is less than 50	* Popu- lation Base: Adults (000)	* A Contr. to Public TV (000)	B Percent- age Down	C Percent- age Across	D Index
New York Times (Sunday)	3939	887	5.2	22.5	261
The New Yorker	2767	650	3.8	23.5	272
*Northwest World Traveler	1517*	260	1.5	17.1	198
Organic Gardening	3480	511	3	14.7	170
Outdoor Life	5365	415	2.4	7.7	90
Parade	79858	8542	49.6	10.7	124
Parenting	9612	539	3.1	5.6	65
Parents' Magazine	12424	709	4.1	5.7	66
PC Magazine	6647	749	4.4	11.3	131
PC World	6553	692	4	10.6	122
People	34469	3083	17.9	8.9	104
Popular Mechanics	8389	790	4.6	9.4	109
Popular Science	5962	576	3.3	9.7	112
Prevention	9684	1124	6.5	11.6	134
Psychology Today	3035	297	1.7	9.8	113
Reader's Digest	44264	4611	26.8	10.4	121
Redbook	9797	778	4.5	7.9	92
Road & Track	4772	450	2.6	9.4	109
Rolling Stone	8445	459	2.7	5.4	63
Scientific American	3086	455	2.6	14.7	171
Self	4096	488	2.8	11.9	138
Sesame Street Parents	4841	350	2	7.2	84
Seventeen	8069	493	2.9	6.1	71
Shape	4533	378	2.2	8.3	97
*Ski	1348*	189	1.1	14	162
*Skiing	1009*	97	0.6	9.6	112
Smart Money	2914	484	2.8	16.6	192
Smithsonian	7060	1375	8	19.5	226
Soap Opera Digest	6820	420	2.4	6.2	71
*Soap Opera Weekly	4614*	174	1	3.8	44
Southern Living	12621	1345	7.8	10.7	123
*Southwest Spirit	1878*	378	2.2	20.1	233
Sports Illustrated	20833	1586	9.2	7.6	88
*Star	7169*	329	1.9	4.6	53
Sunset	4402	782	4.5	17.8	206
*Teen	4940*	339	2	6.9	79

TABLE 9.7
Continued

*Tennis	1015*	185	1.1	18.3	212
*Texas Monthly	1854*	204	1.2	11	127
Time	21663	2780	16.1	12.8	149
Town & Country	2918	416	2.4	14.3	165
Traditional Home	2869	313	1.8	10.9	126
Travel & Leisure	4783	781	4.5	16.3	189
TV Guide	32692	2217	12.9	6.8	79
U.S. News & World Report	10070	1397	8.1	13.9	161
USA Today	4374	480	2.8	11	127
USA Weekend	44966	4541	26.4	10.1	117
Vanity Fair	4866	506	2.9	10.4	120
Victoria	2637	408	2.4	15.5	179
Vogue	8953	714	4.1	8	92
*Walking Magazine	2084*	286	1.7	13.7	159
Wall Street Journal	3588	800	4.6	22.3	258
Washington Post (Sunday)	2536	381	2.2	15	174
Woman's Day	19781	1612	9.4	8.2	94
Woman's World	7782	654	3.8	8.4	97
*Working Mother	2430*	228	1.3	9.4	109
*Working Woman	2409*	300	1.7	12.5	144
Yankee	2688	472	2.7	17.5	203

secondary research review on contributors to public TV and your market or city. (Note. Published sources of secondary or syndicated research tend to have instructions on how to use and interpret their data at the beginning or end of the report or in a separate pamphlet or publication that may accompany the report. Some include instructions, advice, or answers to frequently asked questions [FAQs] on their Web sites.)

ASSIGNMENT

Write a report detailing the primary target segment of contributors to public TV nationwide, including demographics, geographics, psychographics, and any other information you find. Identify and describe the major potential corporate contributors or supporters in your city (including the major companies and industries located there). Then write a proposal for a research project to assess why your most recent fundraising campaign was unsuccessful and whether local contributors have similar characteristics to contributors nationally. Include each of the following sections in your final report and research proposal.

1. Provide a description and analysis of the target segment of contributors to public TV. Include all major characteristics including demographics, geographics, and psychographics. If possible, identify how many persons or

households appear to be in the major public TV contributors target segment (e.g., the number of households in your city headed by persons 45 to 64 years old having incomes of $75,000 and over from the LMA). Write a detailed and concise report on the target segment of national public TV contributors.

2. Provide a detailed, yet concise description of your market area or major city. Provide information about the city's major economic conditions, industries, characteristics, and so on. The goal is to describe your city accurately, describe local economic conditions, and identify major local industries, companies, and so on (and identify and describe potential corporate contributors in the next question).

3. Provide a detailed, yet concise description of potential corporate contributors. Identify the major companies and industries in your city, and describe how and why each might be persuaded to contribute to or support your local public TV station.

4. Write a research proposal to discover why your most recent fundraising campaign was not as successful as hoped and the characteristics of present and potential local individual contributors (or whether they are similar to the national target segment of individuals who contribute to public TV). Develop a part of your research proposal to discover the major local companies and industries who have/have not contributed to the local public TV station and why.

Your research proposal should discuss the major aspects of the marketing research process, including research questions, a secondary research review, primary research design, data-collection procedures, sampling design, data collection, data processing and analysis, report writing, and potential research firms to contact about conducting the study. Identify local or national research firms you might hire to conduct the research you propose. Explain why the research company or companies are qualified and appropriate choices for the type of study you propose to conduct. Identify which research company is the best to hire to conduct your research and why. Provide an appendix in your report that includes examples of the types of questions to ask individual and corporate contributors in your study.

Case 9.3
Developing A New Magazine

Assume you work at a major national magazine publishing firm. Your task is to develop a proposal for a new magazine. Your magazine may have a national audience or be targeted to a certain region (e.g., *Southern Living, Midwest Living*), state (e.g., *Texas Monthly*), or city. You may propose a general interest magazine or one tailored to a certain interest segment (e.g., *Field & Stream, Gourmet*, etc.). Your primary criteria are that a significant and viable audience segment and group of major advertisers exist to support the magazine. You must provide supportive data that are realistic and suggest the magazine you propose could survive and prosper.

You might begin by evaluating data such as magazine launches by category, growth of magazines by category, number of magazines by category, and number of editorial pages by subject at the Magazine Publishers of America (MPA) home page (*www.magazine.org*). MPA publishes the Magazine Handbook with a variety of useful data available for downloading (*http://www.magazine.org/resources/downloads/MPA_Handbook_01.pdf*). MPA's Publishers Information Bureau (*www.magazine.org/pib*) provides information about advertising revenue, historical trends, pages, and so on online. If your library has the appropriate Standard Rate and Data Service publication (e.g., SRDS Consumer Magazine Advertising Source or Business Publication Advertising Source), review it to see which magazines already exist in the categories you are considering, what their editorial descriptions are, their regular features and sections, who they target, how much they charge for advertising, and so on. *Folio* (*www.foliomag.com*) provides information about new launches, magazine advertising, and other industry insights that may be helpful in developing a magazine proposal. Advertising industry publications like *Advertising Age* (*www.adage.com*) often publish articles or data about magazines. Conduct a search on ABI Inform/ProQuest, Lexis-Nexis Academic Universe, or Ebsco to find other articles and data on magazine launches and the magazine industry.

Once you have narrowed your ideas to a few categories, evaluate the relevant data in Mediamark, Simmons, and the SRDS Lifestyle Market Analyst (LMA) if available. For example, if you are considering a magazine targeted to dog owners, check dog food product sales data in Mediamark and/or Simmons. Then review the demographics, geographics, and media usage data for people who buy dog food. These reports contain the brand names of major companies in the category (e.g., major dog food companies like Purina and Iams and the brands they make). Write down those company and brand names and look in CMR's Ad $ Summary if it is available in your campus library (it lists brands and parent companies plus the amount they spent in major media during the past year alphabetically in the brand index; also check for spending data for the category in the volume). Check to see which major advertisers advertised in magazines and copy the names and amounts of those that did. Conduct a search of those major advertisers in ABI Inform/ProQuest, Lexis-Nexis Academic Universe, or Ebsco to find out how much they spent and in which magazines they advertised.

Then review the LMA lifestyle segment Own A Dog (or the appropriate segment for the type of magazine you propose). There you will find demographic data on dog owners (or your lifestyle segment) nationwide and information about the other lifestyle activities they enjoy. This helps you identify potential features or sections and other potential advertisers for your proposed magazine. Review the instructions at the front of the LMA volume to see whether there is other information of interest. If you are thinking about proposing a city magazine, check out the LMA demographic and psychographic data from the market profiles section to get ideas and data to help justify your choices of sections and features to offer. Then visit a local library, bookstore, or newsstand to review copies of existing magazines in your proposed category. Check their Web sites. Review their sections, advertisers, rate information, and so on. Also search the Advertising Media Internet Center (*www.amic.com*) and MRI + online database (*www.mriplus. com*) if desired (you will need to register to use these sites).

In other words, find and evaluate as much information, research, and data as possible to develop a thorough magazine proposal and a comprehensive understanding of the category in which you wish to launch your magazine. Ask your professor for suggestions of available information sources or databases to use. Try to think of any other sources of data or information. Conduct a comprehensive search for sources in your campus library using databases and online search engines like Google or Yahoo. Review Tables 9.3 through 9.6 for other sources to explore. Use your imagination to develop original and useful information to include in your proposal.

ASSIGNMENT

After conducting a thorough and detailed information search, write a proposal to start a new magazine. You must support your proposed magazine and recommendations with information and data. Your proposal must include each of the following sections.

1. A title and overall description of the proposed magazine, including its editorial mission and descriptions, features and sections, types of articles to include, and so on. Explain why you propose the title you selected. Provide as much detail as you can about the proposed magazine and its content. Provide data and information to support why you selected the magazine, magazine type, and magazine category you selected for your proposal. Explain how and why it is different from other existing magazines in the category. Identify the unfilled niche or position it fills. Make a strong case based on actual recent data and information.

2. Identify and describe your target segment of readers in as much detail as possible. Provide an estimate of the number of potential readers or subscribers nationwide (e.g., the number of persons or households owning a dog from the LMA) or in your region, state, or city of interest. Provide as much detail as possible about the major characteristics of your target segment of potential subscribers or readers, including demographics, geographics, psychographics, and so on. Explain how and why your proposed magazine will be of interest to your target segment. Explain how and why it matches them and their interests. Provide information and data to support your recommendations.

3. Identify and describe a minimum of five potential advertising categories and examples of advertisers in each (e.g., dog food advertisers like Purina and Iams for a dog magazine, etc.). Provide data on how much is spent in magazine advertising in the category. If possible, provide data for how advertising spending in the category increased over the past 5 years or decade (this information may be available in CMR's Ad $ Summary). Provide information about how much each company/brand that advertises in magazines spent (or spent on advertising in general if specific magazine data are unavailable). If possible, identify the magazines in which these advertisers have placed ads. Explain why your proposed magazine will be an attractive advertising vehicle for these advertisers, providing as much detail, data, and support as you can.

Case 9.4
Developing an Online Media Kit

Assume you work for a major daily, weekly, ethnic, or community newspaper in your town or the nearest city. Your job is to develop data to include in an online media kit for that paper. Begin by reviewing the Web page and newspaper media kits for major newspapers like *The New York Times* (*http://nytadvertising. nytimes.com/adonis/html/open/adhome.shtml* and *http://www.nytimes.com/ adinfo/*), *USA Today* (*www.usatoday.com/ads/usat/inside_usat.htm*), *Chicago Tribune* (*www.tribuneinteractive.com/chicago/mediakit/home.htm*), and the *Tampa Tribune/* TBO.com/WFLA News Channel 8 (*http://clients.tbo.com*) to review a site with media kits for multiple media outlets and its rates and Advertiser Information Guide (*http://tampatrib.com/tribhelp/rates/*).

Then review pertinent information about interactive marketing and advertising at the Interactive Advertising Bureau's (*www.iab.net*) Web site, including Advertising ABCs (*www.iab.net/advertise/adsource.html*), which describes ways of advertising and sizes and types of Internet ads or Interactive Marketing Units (*www.iab.net/iab_banner_standards/bannersource.html*), and Measuring Success (*www.iab.net/measuringsuccess/index.html*). Also review the Electronic Publishing link at the Newspaper Association of America's home page (*http://www.naa.org*). Review articles like "Reaching Out: Newspaper Sites Add Audience" (*www.naa.org/artpage.cfm?AID=4342&SID=103*) that provide background information and research data to use in a media kit.

Next review the Web sites of the existing major media outlets in your city (e.g., those for TV stations, radio stations, cable outlets, magazines, and/or other newspaper sites). Review the types of information and data they include as well as how they describe the benefits of advertising in each medium or vehicle. Develop your own list of pros and cons from surfing these Web sites. Obtain ideas for what to include, what not to include, what to do, and what not to do in the Web site you are developing for the paper.

Review Tables 9.4, 9.5, and 9.6 for other possible sources of information. For example, you could visit the Television Bureau of Advertising (*www.tvb.org*), Cabletelevision Advertising Bureau (*www.cabletvadbureau.com*), and Radio Advertising Bureau (*www.rab.com*) Web sites to see the kinds of information used in broadcast media kits. Use your imagination to find other sources of information for developing a media kit.

ASSIGNMENT

Develop a preliminary media kit for your paper that includes the following sections. Provide details, data, and specific information where possible. Develop a final proposal that the paper's Web designer can use to build the Web page.

1. About the paper: Provide background information about the paper, its mission, and descriptions of major pages or features on the site.
2. Editorial sections and descriptions: Provide a brief overview of each section of the paper and the kinds of articles often found in each section. Identify whether each section targets any specific or special reader segments.
3. Editorial calendar: Provide an editorial calendar showing when special issues will be published during the year (if available or applicable).
4. Audience data: Provide an audience profile of readers including demographics, psychographics, and all other information available. Provide any information you have on reader loyalty, how long readers visit the site, and so on.
5. Comparative data on other local media and media outlets: Provide any information that identifies the advantages of advertising on the paper's new Web site versus the Web sites of other media outlets. Explain why advertisers should advertise on your paper's site rather than or in addition to other local Web sites.
6. Rate information: Provide information about rates, advertising acceptability standards (or the what ads the paper will/will not accept for publication), and other information for selling the site not included in Number 7.
7. Advertising units: Review the IAB's Interactive Marketing Units (*www.iab.net/iab_banner_standards/bannersource.html*) and recommend the types of banner, skyscraper, rectangle, and/or pop-up ads to offer for sale to advertisers. Justify and support your choices.
8. Obtaining reader information: Provide ideas and suggestions for implementing ways to obtain demographic, psychographic, or other information from readers. For example, should you require readers to register when first visiting your site and obtain demographic and other information then? What other ways could you collect information for your media kit online

that respect the privacy of your readers? What exact information should you try to collect (e.g., age, income, zip code, education, etc.) and why?

9. Other recommendations: Provide any other advice or guidance to the Web page designer for developing an online media kit for the paper. Provide any other data, design advice, methods, resources, and so on that might be helpful in designing a site that is useful to advertisers.

Case 9.5
Dealing With Cable Customer Dissatisfaction

You are the manager of the cable system in your city (or the nearest city). You are concerned about the constant complaints from customers regarding service. You received 20 letters this week alone; you shudder to think how many complaints the receptionist received by phone. You are also concerned because the local city government is beginning to make noise about the poor level of service the cable company provides.

You decide to conduct a survey of subscribers to identify the major service problems and how they might be solved. You have never conducted a survey and cannot afford to hire a research firm. You must design a study that can be conducted by you and your employees.

ASSIGNMENT

Prepare a report describing how you could design and conduct such a survey from scratch using only company employees and resources. Include the following in your report:

1. Identify and describe the appropriate method to use to conduct the survey and how it can be handled inhouse. In other words, what kind of survey can be handled by local cable employees and why?

2. Discuss the sources of free or low-cost information to consult for developing your consumer survey. Explain how these sources can be used and why they are appropriate for this situation.

3. Explain how questions for the questionnaire will be developed. In other words, how can you find out what the major problems are before you conduct the survey? How can you decide which questions to include in the survey and why? How can you allow for employee input on which questions to include? How can you allow for community input on which questions to include?

4. Provide examples of the types of questions that accurately measure what your major service problems are.
5. Suggest other questions to include, if any, besides questions regarding the problems and their solutions. Describe the other types of questions to include and explain why they are needed.
6. Make a decision regarding the kind of survey to conduct. Explain and support your decision.

10

BUDGETING AND DECISION MAKING

Managers use several types of information to make decisions. This chapter discusses how media managers use accounting information for planning and controlling organizational behavior. Most people think of accounting as indecipherable columns of numbers representing debits and credits. Indeed, accounting information is often presented in annual reports and budgets as rows and columns of dollars and cents. Yet without accounting information, managers would lack the necessary information to plan and evaluate performance; organizations would have poorly defined goals, if they were to have goals at all; and managerial learning and organizational growth might never occur. Consequently, accounting provides essential information for the day-to-day activities and long-term growth and survival of organizations.

Managers can select from a wide range of accounting information. The information a manager selects to use for decisions depends on several factors, including the manager's level in the organization, the long- or short-term nature of the decision, the organization's size and complexity, and the nature of the firm. Regardless of the types of accounting information available, one form of information managers use extensively is the budget. Thus, the main focus of this chapter is on how managers develop and use budgets in planning and controlling the functions of a media organization.

TYPES OF ACCOUNTING INFORMATION

Accounting activities are divided into financial accounting and managerial accounting. Financial accounting provides information about an organization's health to outsiders. Managerial accounting provides information about the day-to-day operation of the company for managers to use in planning and budgeting. Although both are related to managing an organization, this chapter concentrates primarily on managerial accounting.

Financial Accounting Information

Financial accounting refers to the preparation of materials, such as annual reports, for use primarily by individuals external to the organization. The general public, regulatory agencies, owners, investors, creditors, taxing authorities, and industry associations use such materials. For example, a public media company's annual report may reveal the culture and values of that organization. The annual report's cover design, letter to shareholders, and information about planned investments and acquisitions reveal what management considers important to the firm's long-term success.

A balance sheet also reveals a great deal of information about a company. Let us consider how to analyze a balance sheet using an example for a fictitious broadcast group with seven TV and two radio stations called Callas Communication (see Table 10.1). The long-term objective of Callas Communications is primarily to acquire more TV stations and, if possible, other media and communications-related properties in the future. Another goal is to identify and acquire stations that have the potential for substantial long-term appreciation and profitability. Callas' management looks for personnel who can aggressively manage these stations to maximize profits, allowing the company to purchase more stations. Callas' seven TV stations are network affiliates of ABC, CBS, NBC, or Fox.

This background information is important for evaluating Callas' balance sheet, which reflects the financial status of a corporation by listing its assets and liabilities. It serves as a stop-action photograph of a company on a given date. When a series of balance sheets are examined together, they reveal how the company behaved across time.

The balance sheet is divided into major sections called *assets, liabilities*, and *shareholder's equity*. Assets are resources that a company owns or that are owed to a company. Liabilities are amounts of money that are owed by the company in some form to a person or organization. Both assets and liabilities take many forms, but the total assets minus the total liabilities reveal the company's financial health. The difference between assets and liabilities is shareholder's equity, which represents the value of the company that belongs to the owners. The balance sheet gets its name from the fact that assets must always equal liabilities and shareholder's equity. Several of the terms in the balance sheet shown in Table 10.1 need defining.

Assets.   Current assets include money or other resources that are easily converted to money. For example, accounts receivable include money owed the company for services or products rendered. Inventories are those objects that can be sold readily for cash.

Investments and other assets are resources that come from investing other resources. Property, plant, and equipment include land, buildings, and equipment owned by the company. Because large media organizations, such as daily

TABLE 10.1
Consolidated Balance Sheets for Callas Communications

	December 31	
	2001	*2002*
Assets		
Current assets		
Cash and cash equivalents	$76,098	$444,602
Accounts receivable, less allowance for doubtful accounts ($505,759 in 2001 and $391,910 in 2002)	20,869,263	21,645,960
Film contract rights	4,650,692	5,021,280
Other current assets	3,083,819	7,827,972
Total current assets	28,679,872	34,939,814
Property and equipment, net	25,705,700	26,849,615
Film contract rights and other noncurrent assets	2,980,489	3,427,662
Deferred financing fees less accumulated amortization ($2,947,833 in 2001 and $4,049,724 in 2002)	11,879,623	11,345,329
Intangible assets		
Goodwill	60,154,095	60,962,282
Network affiliations	198,353,310	198,353,310
Broadcast licenses	54,317,488	54,317,488
	312,824,893	313,633,080
Depreciation	(20,373,673)	(28,144,992)
Net intangible assets	$292,451,220	$285,488,088
	$361,696,904	$362,050,508
Liabilities and stockholders equity (deficit)		
Current liabilities:		
Accounts payable	4,228,495	3,213,571
Accrued interest	4,476,488	4,857,102
Other accrued liabilities	2,800,052	3,598,027
Film contract rights payable and other current liabilities	5,556,854	7,662,692
Total current liabilities	17,061,889	19,331,392
Long-term debt	272,719,996	281,248,667
Film contract rights payable	2,935,627	2,706,742
Deferred tax liability and ther noncurrent liabilities	25,495,392	24,881,817
Commitments		
Redeemable preferred stock	36,390,000	36,390,000
Stockholders equity (deficit)		
Common	67,173	69,425
Additional capital	37,491,361	36,437,716
Accumulated deficit	(29,272,158)	(36,300,728)

TABLE 10.1
Continued

	December 31	
	2001	2002
Assets		
Less: unearned compensation	(1,192,376)	(2,005,023)
Note receivable from officer		(709,500)
Total stockholders equity (Deficit)	7,094,000	(2,508,110)
	$361,696,904	$362,050,508

newspapers and TV stations, require a large fixed investment, this category is often a large portion of assets for these firms. In contrast, magazines, weekly newspapers, and Web sites have much lower fixed investments. Depreciation represents the value of property, plant, and equipment used up in the organization's operation. If a newspaper or TV station buys a computer system, a certain percentage of that system's cost becomes depreciation each year until the value reaches zero. One can look at property, plant, and equipment as investments in future production. Because that investment is used for production, it declines in value, which must be represented on the balance sheet.

Goodwill, publication, and *broadcast rights* represent the value of any legal rights a company has to publish or broadcast and the value of how people feel about the company. Goodwill is the value of the company's reputation. A problem with these categories is that they are hard to measure. Quite often a company will figure its liabilities and owner equity, and the difference between these two and its assets will be goodwill. Just as equipment depreciates, goodwill has a limited life. People who watch TV stations have viewing preferences that change, especially with multiple viewing options due to direct satellite, cable, and VCR and DVD players. Goodwill for these people ends. This loss of goodwill is amortized and placed in the balance sheet to show the loss of this asset.

In reviewing Callas' balance sheet, much of the company's assets are listed as intangible assets, especially network affiliations. It appears that Callas may have simply listed the difference between assets and liabilities as intangible assets. Given the aggressive acquisition stance Callas takes, one would expect to see a large amount under intangible assets and liabilities in the balance sheet.

Anyone considering an investment in Callas is wise to be cautious. Callas' stations are all VHF network-affiliated stations. Network affiliations are valuable because there are a limited number of very high-frequency (VHF) channels available in each market. Television stations broadcasting on the VHF band have had a competitive advantage over ultrahigh-frequency (UHF) stations. This advantage has diminished as viewing options increase. The major networks' share of the national viewing audience has declined steadily. Such a high reliance on intangible assets may indicate a company in, or potentially in, financial trouble.

Liabilities and Shareholder's Equity. Current liabilities are debts due within a relatively short period of time. Besides the typical short-term debts, such as salaries, a company like Callas has interest payments on the high level of debt the company carries given its goals of acquiring media properties. Also note the long-term debt or noncurrent liabilities. These are liabilities that extend for 1 year or more. For example, if a company sells bonds, the amount owed the bondholders would be noncurrent liabilities.

The large amount listed under long-term debt also indicates the company's long-term goal of acquiring properties. For example, during the past year, Callas acquired a radio station for approximately $6 million in cash and assumed certain liabilities. The purchase price and liabilities are reflected in the long-term debt column for 2002. A TV station acquisition the previous year is reflected in the 2001 long-term debt. Obviously the owners and stockholders believe that these station purchases will pay off over the long term; otherwise they would be unwilling to acquire so much debt.

This debt is reflected in the shareholder's or stockholder's equity section, which shows a deficit. Shareholder's or stockholder's equity represents the resources of the company that belong to the owners in one way or another. For example, if the company had earned a profit, any retained earnings listed would be the amount of profit that remains in the control of the company's managers.

In the case of Callas Communications, both preferred (voting) and common (nonvoting) stocks are listed under liabilities. Should the company ever liquidate, the holders of preferred stock would be compensated first. Presently the stockholders' equity is a deficit, so anyone considering an investment in Callas must be cautious.

Although outsiders generally use a balance sheet to evaluate a company's financial position, a series of balance sheets can also help managers. They are not so much generators of information for decision making as they are warning signals. By monitoring the balance sheets across time, managers can sense whether the company's financial position is improving or deteriorating.

If the ratio of assets to liabilities is increasing, the company is doing well. If the ratio is declining, it could be doing better. In reviewing Callas' balance sheets for 2001 and 2002, it appears the company could be doing better because intangible assets increased slightly in 2002. However, liabilities increased even more than assets, and the stockholders' equity showed a deficit.

Another item to note is the "Note receivable from officer" listing under stockholders' equity. The company made a personal loan to an officer of the company with an annual interest rate of 8%. Other stockholders or potential investors might legitimately question the wisdom of making personal loans to officers from company funds. Such a loan may indicate that the company uses questionable accounting practices. During 2001 and 2002, making loans to officers became part of the scandals involving Enron, WorldCom, and several other large corporations. Even George W. Bush benefited from a corporate loan before he became president.

MANAGERIAL ACCOUNTING INFORMATION

Managerial accounting emphasizes the accounting information needs of the manager for day-to-day decisions. Budgets and income statements are developed to aid managers in assessing whether organizational goals are being met. Budgets and income statements are the accounting information formats most frequently used by managers.

Budgets and Income Statements

A *budget* is a statement of the planned use and acquisition of financial resources for meeting specific goals during a particular period of time. Budgets quantify the objectives and specific goals of the manager's department or company. Budgets provide direction for decision making and are an integral part of the planning process. Consequently, budgets are used as detailed and coordinated plans for the future.

Budgets also set performance standards or criteria for evaluation. An income statement is generated at the end of the budgeted time period. The *income statement* reflects the actual expenditures and revenues for each category listed in the budget for the time period. A comparison of the budget and income statement for the same time period allows the manager to evaluate the unit's performance and provides necessary information for controlling the department's functions.

Annual budgets are prepared for the business and each of its departments. Each budget is subdivided into 12 monthly periods. The budget for the business is called the *profit* or *master budget plan*; departmental budgets are called *operating budgets*. Long-range budgets also are developed, but typically only at the level of the business as a whole.

Table 10.2 illustrates a master budget plan for radio station KHIT–FM, which was recently purchased by Callas Communications. KHIT is a top-40 hit music station serving a geographic area with a population of about 300,000. The area includes a major state university and several smaller colleges with a combined student population of about 60,000. KHIT's market serves as a regional medical center and has an automotive manufacturing plant and regional recording studio. A major regional discount grocery retailer maintains its headquarters here, as well as a national insurance and investments company. The area's median income, excluding students, is about $45,000.

The summarized master budget plan displayed in Table 10.2 reflects the budget for the business as a whole. The actual profit plan would include operating budgets from each department. The budget is comprised of expenses, which are the costs associated with running the radio station, and revenues, which are the sources of income for the station. Table 10.2 shows the proposed allocation of financial resources to the various departments in the radio station as expenses, as well as the revenues expected from specific sources for the coming year.

TABLE 10.2

KHIT–FM Budget

Station Revenue and Expense Items	Dollars
Revenues	
National/regional advertising	200,000
Local advertising	850,000
Total projected sales	1,050,000
Agency and rep commissions	(100,500)
Other revenue	50,000
Total projected net revenue	999,500
Expenses	
Departmental operating expenses	
Engineering	38,000
Program production	145,000
News	30,000
Sales	184,000
Advertising and promotion	70,000
General administration	300,000
Nonoperating expenses	
Depreciation	53,000
Interest	17,000
Total expenses	837,000
Pretax profit	162,500

The major source of revenue is generated from the selling of airtime for advertising. The advertising revenue is categorized by geographic source. Local advertising accounts for 81% of the station's sales revenues, and national/regional advertising accounts for 19% of revenues. Total expected revenue is calculated by subtracting the sales representatives' commissions, which depend on the amount of sales. Miscellaneous additional revenue is added to calculate the projected total revenue for the coming year.

Projected operating expenses are itemized by department and indicate each department's forecasted financial needs. The two types of expenses itemized in the budget are operating and nonoperating expenses. Operating expenses include the day-to-day costs of running the radio station. The operating expenses of a radio station might include the cost of using an outside news service, music license fees, subscribing to an audience ratings service, and employee compensation.

Nonoperating expenses include other costs not incurred from operating the station, such as equipment depreciation and interest to be paid on any outstanding loans. Depreciation is a common nonoperating expense because equipment loses its value and eventually needs to be replaced.

The departmental operating and nonoperating expenses are summed to calculate the projected total expenditures for the coming year. Total expenses are

TABLE 10.3
Annual Budget for Radio Station KHIT

Station Revenue and Expense Items	Dollars This Year	Dollars Last Year Actual
Revenues		
National/regional advertising	200,000	190,000
Local advertising	850,000	775,000
Total projected sales	1,050,000	965,000
Agency and rep commissions	(100,500)	(95,000)
Other revenue	50,000	40,000
Total projected net revenue	999,500	910,000
Expenses		
Departmental operating expenses		
Engineering	38,000	35,000
Program production	145,000	130,000
News	30,000	30,000
Sales	184,000	180,000
Advertising and promotion	70,000	55,000
General administration	300,000	298,000
Nonoperating expenses		
Depreciation	53,000	50,000
Interest	17,000	15,400
Total expenses	837,000	793,400
Pretax profit	162,500	116,600

subtracted from total net revenues to calculate the projected business profit before paying taxes. For KHIT, the expected profit for the coming year is $162,500.

Table 10.3 shows this year's budget in comparison with the previous year's income statement for radio station KHIT. A comparison of last year's actual expenses with the projected figures developed by the new owner shows some important differences. For example, more revenue is expected from local and national advertising sales and other revenue. A spending increase is planned for program production, engineering, advertising, and promotion. These figures reflect the planning and decision-making activities of several managers at KHIT.

The new sales manager, new general manager, and existing programming director developed the budget for the coming year over the course of 3 months of discussions, data gathering, and decision making. Callas Communications brought in two new managers from other stations with track records of increasing revenues. The company purchased the station because management felt a strong additional profit potential was likely given the large student population and diversified economy in the market.

Presently, the economy is strong in the market, so the new managers want to take advantage of this quickly. The auto manufacturing industry often experienced downturns, so profits must be increased quickly to improve performance before another downturn begins. Also the new managers want to educate local and national advertisers about why increasing their advertising budgets would help their businesses. The new sales manager had successfully retrained sales personnel before to increase sales and develop new accounts. The revenue projections were based on this manager's previous successes.

The general manager felt another strategy should be developed to increase profit during the coming year to satisfy the owners. Several general strategies might be utilized: (a) the staff could work harder to maintain existing advertising revenues, (b) costs could be cut, or (c) other types of revenue could be sought.

The sales manager was already working on the first solution. The second solution of cost cutting would improve the situation in the short run, but the long-run consequences could affect the station's ratings negatively, thereby reducing advertising revenues in the future. Budget amounts were increased slightly for engineering, program production, sales, advertising, promotion, and general administration to maintain the station's quality. These increases were judged to be the smallest possible to maintain quality and cover planned projects for the coming year. The news department budget was not increased because management felt the station's 18- to 44-year-old core audience listened because of the station's music selections, not its news coverage. The general manager also noted that she would work with all department heads to trim the budget where possible without sacrificing quality.

The programming head, who was retained by Callas, proposed an idea to generate additional revenue. The station would put its morning and afternoon drive-time programs on its Web site. People who missed a program or wanted to listen to one they enjoyed again could listen to the station's most popular DJs at times other than drive time. The highest paid DJs work during drive times, but people might listen to them at other times too.

By running the afternoon and morning shows again and leaving them online for up to a week, advertisers could have additional exposure. For a small increase in the price of the drive-time ads, they would be left on the Web site version. If the advertiser did not want this option, the ads would be removed by editing. The initial cost of doing this could be relatively low—computer software and time editing the audio files. However, over time, there might be greater cost. At the next contract negotiations, the DJs might want additional money for reusing their material. Also there are issues concerning the use of music on the Internet. The 2002 ruling about music royalties set a rate of .14 cents per song for commercial stations for Internet-only Webcast compared with .07 cents per song when distributed by broadcast or simulcast (Hanson, 2002). It is not clear which rate would apply to archived programs, but KHIT might have to edit out the music and leave the jokes and talk.

The budget developed for KHIT's coming year represents the desired future status of the radio station based on the decisions of the management team that prepared the budget, keeping the owner's goals in mind. The budget provides spending guidelines for the department heads and sets performance expectations for the sales staff. In particular, this budget sets a criterion for evaluating the short-range decision to promote the station through the archiving of drive-time programming. If the archiving generates additional revenues of at least $10,000 and advertising sales are increased as projected, KHIT might continue the practice past the next year. If the outlined expectations were not met, the radio station would probably drop the strategy for the next year.

The example of radio station KHIT illustrates how annual budgets are developed and used for short-range planning and routine decision making. Long-range budgets are used for plans of 5 years or more and cover more nonroutine decisions. Whether a manager makes a fairly routine, short-range decision or a nonroutine, long-range decision is often a function of the manager's level in the organization. The types of budget information a manager needs and uses for decision making are affected by the long- or short-term nature of the decision.

The steps in the decision-making process are reviewed to explain how managers use budgets. Two important aspects of the process also are discussed: how short- versus long-range decisions affect the use of information and how the differences in organizational levels affect managerial decision making.

MANAGERIAL DECISION MAKING

Managerial decision making, like most decision making, consists of six stages, as shown by the decision-making wheel in chapter 1 (this volume). Collecting and analyzing information plays the central role in this process, but managers at different organizational levels collect and use information differently.

The case of KHIT illustrates this process. The sales manager identified the possible increases in advertising revenue through discussions with sales personnel and advertisers, and by evaluating local and national economic indicators. The sales manager viewed the opportunity from the perspective of how it would affect the department during the coming year. The general manager, in contrast, specified the overall organizational goal of increasing profits in comparison with last year. The sales manager informed the general manager of the opportunity to improve sales performance through training and mentoring the sales staff. The general, sales, and program managers reviewed several strategies and selected the archiving strategy because it appeared to be a relatively cost-effective way to increase profits. Yet all managers were involved to ensure that the organizational and departmental perspectives were considered.

This example also demonstrates how the budget is used for implementing the solution. The income statement is used to monitor the solution because it provides information about the performance of the solution. Both can be reviewed to refine the solution in future years. All three managers understand that if profits are not increased in the next year or two, all may lose their jobs.

Long- Versus Short-Range Decisions

Short-range decisions are often routine decisions—the type that a manager has some degree of experience in making on a regular basis. Because of the manager's experience with a routine decision, information about alternative strategies, and the results of those strategies is accumulated. As a result, routine decisions usually involve less risk, and the decision outcomes are more predictable than in nonroutine decisions.

Routine decisions are evaluated within some short period of time, perhaps a few months. So if short-range decisions have unexpected negative consequences or do not produce the expected results, changes can be made quickly to minimize the impact of the undesired outcomes.

Nonroutine decisions are made infrequently and have long-range effects and consequences. Such consequences are difficult to anticipate. For example, the decision to invest resources in new equipment, such as a new system of computers for a newspaper, has the short-range consequence of increasing costs during the fiscal year of the purchase. However, the long-range consequences may be more difficult to determine and forecast. For example, desired long-range outcomes would increase writer productivity and efficiency in the production of the paper. Yet an unanticipated, long-range consequence of using video display terminals was repetitive motion injury, which could have been avoided by purchasing ergonomic furniture and materials. Hence, background research is needed to evaluate the likelihood of those outcomes and predict the value added to the paper in the long run.

Managers should also evaluate problems to see whether an unexpected and more cost-effective solution may be found. For example, newspapers are finding ways to reduce the cost of serving advertisers. These include cheaper and faster ways to make color proofs and the use of election tearsheets to show that ads have run. Some newspapers have purchased high-end color copies for making page and ad proofs. Such copiers cost $50,000 or more, but can print a proof in 3 to 4 minutes for $0.37, rather than 20 to 30 minutes for $7 (Toner, 1997). Newspapers can also send e-mails with hyperlinks to their advertisers, and the hyperlink allows the advertiser to see and print the ad (Goodman, 2002). Newspaper managers can keep up with such innovations by reviewing *Presstime* each month. Managers in other media firms can check their trade publications each month for similar cost-saving ideas.

Unexpected, long-run negative results of decisions are even more difficult to predict than expected positive long-range outcomes. A contemporary concern is whether the Internet will draw readers away from newspapers. Many papers publish online editions to retain readers and prevent erosion of classified advertising. Yet publishing online may discourage some potential subscribers from buying a subscription. Newspaper managers must keep abreast of trends to ensure that readers and revenues are not lost to the Internet.

The fact that future outcomes must be predicted makes long-range decision making more difficult than short-range decision making. Long-range decisions often involve some large investment of capital and inventory, making the decision even riskier. Because newsprint expenses alone represent 15% to 20% of a newspaper's advertising budget (Rudder, 1997), newspapers try to buy extra newsprint when prices are down and less newsprint when prices are high. This affects their newsprint inventory. A company that can accurately predict variations in newsprint prices will increase profits. Those that miscalculate will pay more for newsprint and reduce profits.

Long-range decisions most often occur at higher levels in organizations, and shorter range decisions occur at middle and lower levels. Higher level management personnel make the riskier decisions and take responsibility for decisions that affect the entire organization. Middle and lower level management make decisions that are more routine, less risky, and result in consequences that directly influence their departments. The level of decision making and the nature of the decision affect the type of information the manager needs for the decision-making process. Indeed, the type of budget information managers use and evaluate varies based on these same factors.

Levels of Planning, Decision Making, and Information Needs

The nature of planning and decision making varies with the organization level at which each process occurs. At the highest levels of management, decisions are made determining the firm's policies and general guidelines for evaluating the company's performance. This is what the owners of Callas Communications do. The information that top management uses is often summarized and future oriented. For example, information about future market share, economic indicators, and other market performance measures are forecasted and used by upper level management to predict revenue and profit goals for the coming year.

Middle-level management typically deals with using resources efficiently and effectively. At this level, managers need information to develop operating budgets. Often decisions need to be made about investing in new equipment, services, or people. For example, a newspaper's managing editor might decide to buy a new advice column about the Internet if readers indicate an interest in this service and information.

Lower level management deals with more structured, routine tasks and uses information from inside the organization. Decision rules are communicated, preferably in verbal and written form. The information used is detailed and typically unambiguous. At this managerial level, information is not necessarily forecasted for future concerns. For example, KHIT's programming director must decide when DJs will take vacations.

DEVELOPING THE MASTER BUDGET PLAN
AND DEPARTMENTAL BUDGETS

Developing budgets is one part of the planning process where decisions are made about the available resources for achieving goals. Generating the master budget plan for the entire business can take some time—usually 3 to 6 months—depending on the size, nature, and complexity of the organization. Managers at all levels of the organization participate in the effective development of the master budget plan. At the highest level, a budget committee might consist of the company president, controller, vice president of sales, and vice president in charge of production. In a media organization, the budget committee includes the top manager, controller, and all department heads. This committee establishes budget goals for the company that directly affect the budgeting at the departmental level. The budget committee also reviews and approves departmental budgets.

A budget director reports directly to the controller and coordinates budgets at the departmental level. The budget director prepares a timetable for the development and approval of all operating budgets and works with managers in the development of each departmental budget. The master budget plan is assembled and submitted to the budget committee and then the board of directors for approval. Finally, the budget director is responsible for preparing and distributing performance reports based on the previous year's budget to the budget committee and department managers.

Forecasting

A key element of generating budgets is forecasting. Forecasting is an effort to predict future events and trends and anticipate their implications for the company. Granger (1980) listed three types: event-outcome forecasts, event-timing forecasts, and time-series forecasts. With event-outcome forecasts, a manager tries to predict the consequences of an event. For example, how will the closing of the regional recording studio in town affect KHIT–FM? With event-timing forecasts, a manager attempts to predict when a specific event will take place. For example, if a growing city has only one network-affiliated TV station, that station's management would be interested in knowing when a second network affiliate might enter the market. With time-series forecasting, a manager attempts to predict the effects of a series of phenomena on the business. For example, what effects will the listing of employment notices on the Internet by individual companies have on a newspaper's classified ad linage?

The benefits of accurate forecasting seem obvious given the central role of information in decision making. However, accurate forecasting is not easy. So many factors can change, and the possibility of measurement errors is so great, that accurate long-range forecasting is as much an art as a science.

Despite the limitations, however, budgeting requires some forecasting. Kreitner (1986) listed three types of forecasting: informed judgment, surveys, and trend analysis. Informed judgment involves the forecasting of events and trends by an individual or group based on knowledge of the topic being forecast. Informed judgment is used extensively in the creation of most short-term budgets. Surveys are efforts to anticipate the future by asking questions of a sample of people who represent a larger group. The idea is to draw conclusions about the future of the larger group based on comments from a small percentage of that group.

Trend analysis extends historical trends found in data about the past into the future, with some alterations based on assumptions of change. Because everything changes to a degree, all trend analysis must address key factors that shape the event being forecast. For example, if KHIT's advertising staff is extending trends in advertising sales, the staff needs to specify assumptions about changes in overall business sales. The staff might assume, based on predictions by government economists, that retail sales in their market would increase 5% during the next year. Using this figure, the staff could come up with an estimate of retail sales. From this figure, they could estimate their revenue during the next year by applying the percentage of local retail sales that they have received as advertising revenue during the past 5 years.

KHIT's staff might also use the trade press and Internet resources to review economic indicators. For example, *Advertising Age, Broadcasting, Presstime,* and other trade publications typically carry articles about actual and projected advertising expenditures. Economic information may be found at the Census Bureau's home page (*http://www.census.gov/econ/www/index.html*).

All budgeting requires some forecasting. It is important to deal explicitly with assumptions about the changing economic environment. Otherwise a station will underestimate revenues in a booming economy and overestimate revenues in an economic downturn. Two principles tend to hold true: The longer the time range a budget covers, the more important forecasting becomes, and the longer the range a budget covers, the harder it is to forecast accurately. This, in effect, is the forecasting dilemma. The only solution is to invest in several forecasting methods for the long range and hire competent forecasters.

Departmental Operating Budgets

Although forecasting plays a role in the annual departmental budget, the need for extensive forecasting is minimized by the data from previous years' income statements and budgets and from the expertise of the people within the departments. Informed judgment plays a key role, although this should be bolstered by available data in the marketplace.

The department budget is the central document for controlling the finances of an organization, and it plays a direct or an indirect role in most decisions.

TABLE 10.4

Operating Budget and Income Statement for the News/Editorial
Department of an 80,000 Circulation Daily Newspaper

Item	This Year ($)	Last Year ($)
Payroll		
Salaries	3,500,000	3,395,000
Overtime	40,000	40,000
Correspondents and freelancers	80,000	75,000
Office supplies	60,000	45,000
Research materials		
Computer time	120,000	100,000
Books, magazines, newspapers	1,000	5,000
Travel	40,000	50,000
Photography	40,000	38,000
News services	164,000	160,000
Syndicated material	124,000	120,000
Other news/editorial	75,000	75,000
Total	4,244,000	4,103,000

Table 10.4 shows the newsroom budget for a daily newspaper with a circulation of 80,000. The departmental operating budget is set up on an annual basis, with at least monthly updates on past spending and resources that remain available.

All budgets are broken down into categories of expenses considered to be important in running the business. Which expense categories are important varies from medium to medium and from company to company. At the newspaper represented in Table 10.4, payroll is divided into salaries for full-time employees, overtime paid to full-time employees, and money used to pay part-time employees called *correspondents* and *freelancers*. A larger newspaper might list photography salaries separately from those of writers and editors. It might also differentiate between regular part-time employees (correspondents) and irregular part-time employees (freelancers). The important consideration is that budget categories and subcategories reveal how the money is being spent within the department in a way that allows for decision making.

The amount of money allocated to a budget category reflects its relative importance in reaching the department's goals. For instance, management at the newspaper represented in Table 10.4 decided to spend more on an online research database service this year. The cost of this online database is shared with other departments at the newspaper. Resources were cut for books, magazines, and newspapers because some of these materials will now be available through the online database. Expenditures for travel were also cut to help pay for the database. The correspondents and freelancers expenditure was increased so the paper can hire someone to train employees to use the online database and hire temporary help when big stories break.

The importance of budget items can change across time to reflect the organization's long-term plans. The commitment to using the online database is seen in increased payroll and office supply expenditures. The paper's management plans to reward employees who use the database effectively, and additional office supply purchases of paper and an additional printer are in the budget. However, a plan that would increase profit by controlling costs would reveal payroll reductions or keep them stable as revenues increase.

The operating budget can be thought of as an ideal for the year's spending. Yet with news media, the ideal rarely happens. This is why managers often end up shifting money from one category to another and may even get additional resources from the top management of the media organization. When world-changing events such as those on September 11, 2001, happen, news organizations will ignore the operating budget. Money will have to be shifted and new resources found. Often revenue will be forgone as newspapers run more pages and TV news goes to 24-hour coverage. A budget is a map, but detours are expected. A quality news operation will often require deviations from the budget to accomplish important company goals.

Budgeting Methods

The department heads are usually in charge of generating their department operating budgets. They are most familiar with their department's needs. Yet they are not as familiar with the business environment as the employees who maintain contact with those outside the organization. The reporters, camera crews, salespeople, and receptionists are the ones who deal with news sources, readers, listeners, viewers, and advertisers. For this reason, the department heads' informed judgment must reflect their workers' experience.

Budgeting methods involve two considerations: flow of information and assumed starting point of the budget. The flow of information can be upward, downward, or both. Upward flow means the information goes from employees to the managers. Downward flow is the reverse, and both means a two-way flow occurs.

In the departmental budgeting process, information must flow both ways to generate an effective budget. Managers need information from employees to understand what they need to do their jobs effectively. At the same time, workers need to understand the budgetary constraints that face their organization so they do not squander resources.

Although this flow of information is greatest during the budgeting period, it should continue all year long. The budget is a starting point. Actual expenditures must be compared to the budget throughout the year. Employees need to know how expenditures compare to the budget process throughout the year. This is especially true of journalists. A journalist who understands the budget and can argue for a big story within its constraints is more likely to have management's support than one who does not understand what a particular story request means to the department's budget.

The second consideration is the assumed starting point of the budget. Typically, it is assumed that last year's operating budget reflects the needs of the department. The previous year's funding levels become the starting point for this year's budget. This approach is similar to trend analysis because it assumes the trend represents what is needed. The shortcoming is that it perpetuates any miscalculations or errors from previous budgets.

An alternative starting point is called *zero-based budgeting*, which assumes that every budget starts at zero and managers must justify all expenditures. It is easier to identify inefficiencies or wastefulness using this method. However, the process is far more time-consuming than basing expenditures on last year's operating budget.

An example of how the two might come into play can be found in Table 10.4. Suppose the editor finds in the income statement that only $73,000 was spent last year on correspondents and freelancers, which was $2,000 less than budgeted. The new budget could start with the $75,000 in last year's budget, although that amount is not needed based on last year's performance. An additional $5,000 is added because of inflation and the expectation that the local university basketball team will go to the NCAA tournament. Using this method, the request for $80,000 is probably more than what will be used.

If zero-based budgeting is used, the editor has to justify the $80,000, which would be hard to do based on last year's performance. Most likely, the amount needed for correspondents would be the same as the previous year ($73,000), plus the $5,000 figure, which would equal $78,000. However, the editor might have to shift money from other places if unexpected events require more freelance hours.

Despite the seeming appeal of zero-based budgeting to the overall organization, it is not a commonly used process in media organizations. First, the increased demand on time is a problem for many managers who already have too many responsibilities or who do not enjoy dealing with numbers. This latter problem is especially true in newsrooms where many people consider themselves to be *word* and not *number* people. Second, this approach takes power away from departmental managers. Money is power, and departments can become adversarial rather than cooperative as they compete for budgets. Many of those who have power do not like to risk giving it up, which is what zero-based budgeting can do. In effect, individual managers' goals can interfere with what is best for the organization.

Some compromise between the two assumptions is best. Justifying budget items is an important process in identifying areas that no longer need as many resources; this allows the shifting of resources to new areas. As shown in Table 10.4, resources could be shifted from books, magazines, and papers to computer time on the online database. However, the time requirements to justify all budget items would overburden many smaller organizations. If the budget director actively identifies areas that are waning in importance within departments, the department heads can deal with these categories without having to totally justify all budget items.

SUMMARY

Accounting practices fall into two categories: financial and managerial. Financial accounting is used primarily by those outside the organization and is typified by the balance sheet. The balance sheet is a picture of the assets and liabilities of an organization at a given point in time. It summarizes the organization's financial well-being.

Managerial accounting is aimed at generating information for decisions. The most important forms of managerial accounting are budgets and income statements. A budget is the plan for how the organization will spend money during a given time period. The income statement is a summary of how money was spent in previous time periods. The master budget plan covers the entire organization, whereas the departmental operating budget deals with the plans for the individual departments within the organization.

Forecasting plays an important role in budgeting. The longer the period covered by a budget, the more important and difficult accurate forecasting becomes.

The information flow for budgeting within an organization should be upward and downward through the organization structure. It is also important to consider whether last year's budgeted expenses are the appropriate starting point for creating next year's budget or whether all managers should start at zero in making up their budgets. Usually a compromise between the two approaches is best.

Case 10.1
Analyzing the Performance of a Media Company

Obtain a copy of an annual report for a public media company, such as Gannett, Knight Ridder, or AOL-Time Warner, from the Web. This can be done by entering the URL for the company's site or entering the company's name in a search engine. Review the annual report for information about the company, paying special attention to the balance sheet and any accompanying explanations.

ASSIGNMENT

Write a report analyzing the company's annual report. Discuss whether the company seems to be in good financial health and why. Also discuss whether the company's expenditures and performance over the past year seem prudent. You may use a variety of other information about the company's history. Answer all of the following questions in your report.

1. Does the company seem to be managed well financially speaking? Why or why not?
2. Did the company appear to operate profitably? Why or why not? (If the company reported a deficit, explain whether it seems to be indicative of a problem, or whether it simply represents something like a one-time major purchase that should contribute to the long-term good of the company.)
3. Do the major expenditures or purchases mentioned in the report seem reasonable given the company's goals? Why or why not? (Be sure to identify the major expenditures and their amounts when answering this question. Also note whether no major expenditures are listed in the report.)
4. Do you see any accounting practices or items in the report that appear questionable or representative of poor accounting practices? If yes, identify these practices or items and explain why you think they are questionable.
5. Would you recommend that someone invest in this company? Why or why not?
6. What other ideas, impressions, or comments do you have after analyzing this company's performance?

Case 10.2
Forecasting Advertising Sales

Select a local newspaper, magazine, broadcast station, cable company, Web site, or any other local media outlet. Try to predict whether advertising sales will increase or decrease for that media outlet over the next year. Review Shaver (1995), especially chapter 5, or another media sales book for ideas on completing this assignment. Shaver mentioned other data sources besides those listed here.

To get started, contact the local Chamber of Commerce to get information about economic indicators. Review any local business publications or the business section of your local newspaper for information about the market's economy or business openings or closings. Review relevant national trade or industry publications for information about trends in or forecasts of advertising sales.

Also review online sources like the Census Bureau's economic page (*http://www.census.gov/econ/www/index.html*). Visit the online home pages for trade or industry publications and conduct online searches for forecasting or advertising sales articles or data. For example, visit *Advertising Age* (*www.adage. com*) or *ADWEEK* (*www.adweek.com*). Access the Newspaper Association of America for information on newspapers (*www.naa.org*). Review *Broadcasting &*

Cable online (*www.broadcastingcable.com* or *www.tvinsite.com*). Ask your professor for other online sources.

ASSIGNMENT

Write a report indicating whether advertising sales should increase or decrease for your media outlet over the next year. Include the following sections in your report.

1. Discuss the overall economic indicators for your market. For example, are many new businesses opening in the market? Are many businesses closing? What is the market's unemployment level? What are the largest employers in the market? What are the major retail centers and how successful are they? Are there any major positive or negative economic events expected in your market? If yes, how might they affect advertising sales?
2. Are advertising sales in general expected to increase or decrease during the coming year? Why?
3. Identify the types of firms, products, or services for which advertising should increase or decrease during the coming year. Explain why these increases or decreases are predicted.
4. Explain whether your media outlet can expect advertising sales to increase over the coming year and why. Provide suggestions for new clients to approach. Provide ideas for other ways to generate additional revenue through advertising sales based on your research.

Case 10.3
Forecasting to Purchase a Radio Station

Develop a report forecasting economic conditions in a particular market for each of the next 3 years. The report should include, at minimum, the following types of economic activities: employment, manufacturing, retail sales, local taxes, housing sales, and advertising expenditures. The purpose of the report is to decide whether Callas Communications should purchase a radio station in the market selected. Recall that Callas' long-term objective is primarily to acquire more TV stations and, if possible, other media and communications-related properties. Callas seeks to identify and acquire stations that have the potential for substantial long-term appreciation and profitability.

Select a market to study that can be researched through the library or online economic resources. Collect data about each of the areas listed previously, at minimum, from the past 5 years. Interview people who are knowledgeable about market economic indicators, including economists, businesspeople, local government economic development staff, employees from local media advertising departments, government officials, and business reporters. Review local business publications or the business section of the local newspaper for information about economic predictions or indicators. Also review the online sources mentioned in Case 10.2.

ASSIGNMENT

Prepare a three- to five-page report that forecasts economic activity in the selected market. The report should discuss the economic indicators just listed for each of the next 3 years. Conclude the report by predicting the strength of the market's economy during the 3-year period and whether the economy will be strong enough to warrant Callas' purchase of a radio station there.

Case 10.4
Analyzing a Budget

Select a student newspaper, radio, or TV station. Ask the director for a copy of the media outlet's budget preferably from the last several years. Review the budget to see the outlet's mission statement or goals and how expenses have changed over time. Have the director visit the class to discuss the budgeting process, including major purchases made during the budgeting period reviewed.

ASSIGNMENT

Write a report assessing the outlet's budgeting process. Answer all of the following questions in the report. Be prepared to share the report with the media outlet's budget director.

1. Does the outlet use last year's budget as the starting point for the annual budgeting process, zero-based budgeting, or both? Should the outlet change its starting point? Why or why not?
2. Which items or categories in the budget have the largest allocations? Why?
3. Do the categories of expenses in the budget seem complete? Do additional categories need to be added? Why or why not?

4. Does it appear that one or more categories of expenses have changed in importance over time? Why?
5. Which employees are involved in the budget development process at the media outlet? Should other employees be involved? Why or why not?
6. How does information flow during the budgeting process at the outlet: upward, downward, or both? Should the flow of information be changed? Why or why not?
7. Does the media outlet seem to be trying to fulfill organizational goals through its budgeting process and actual budget allocations? Why or why not?
8. Does the media outlet have a good, effective budgeting process? Why or why not?

Case 10.5
Cutting the Budget at KHIT–FM

The general manager at KHIT–FM just informed the sales and programming managers that employees of the local automotive company will go on strike tomorrow. The strike is expected to last several weeks, possibly several months, creating a major problem in the local economy. It is estimated that overall retail expenditures will drop half a percent for every week the employees are on strike.

The general manager wants to retain plans for placing archived audio online because top management at Callas Communications agrees that it represents a strong profit venture. Other ways to maintain profitability must be found.

Review Tables 10.2 and 10.3, the master budget plan for KHIT–FM. (The nonoperating expenses shown there are fixed and cannot be changed.) Also review the information about KHIT–FM discussed in this chapter. Consider other ways to cut the budget or develop additional sources of revenue given the impending strike. Try to estimate the amount of advertising revenues that KHIT–FM may lose due to the strike.

ASSIGNMENT

Create a new budget to meet the profitability requirements of Callas. Make suggestions as to which parts of the budget may be cut and explain why. Write a report that answers all of the following questions.

1. How much advertising revenue may be lost due to the strike? How was the estimate calculated?
2. How should KHIT–FM respond to the possible strike? Which budget categories should be cut (and by how much) or eliminated if the strike lasts for several weeks or months? Why?

3. What additional sources of revenue might the station tap? Explain ideas for generating additional revenue for the station given the impending strike.
4. Present a new budget for KHIT using the format shown in Table 10.2.
5. Explain why the new budget will allow the station to meet its profit goal for next year (or increase pretax profits by $10,000 from $162,500 to $172,500).

EXTENDED CASE STUDIES

INTRODUCTION

Newspapers across the country are facing a loss of readers, especially among younger Americans, and must continue to develop new ways to use and profit from the Internet. Media organizations of all kinds face budget cuts and layoffs. Future managers must consider strategies to handle such difficult situations without making matters worse. The extended case studies feature fictitious characters at fictitious media organizations facing fictitious situations. However, both extended cases are based on real-life events and represent the kinds of problems and issues that media managers face on the job.

Extended Case 1 encompasses concepts covered throughout the book. It can be used as a major end-of-the-semester assignment, an assignment to cover certain course segments or several chapters (e.g., assign Questions 1 and 2 after covering chaps. 1, 2, 3, 4, and 6 in class), or an assignment encompassing one or a few chapters (e.g., assign only Question 5 after covering chap. 6 or assign only Question 8 after covering chaps. 5 and 6). One or more questions can be assigned from it only once during the semester. It can also be used in a holistic and comprehensive approach to dealing with organizational problems by assigning different questions from the case at several points during the semester. Using the holistic approach allows students to see how changes in one area of the firm affect other departments or decisions in that same organization.

Extended Case 1 also can be used for individual and/or group assignments so students learn and apply the individual and group decision-making aspects covered in the book. For example, have students work individually on one question in the case. Then have them work in teams on several questions in the case at midterm. Have teams work on all or many of the case's questions as a final course project. The goal is to give professors and students the most flexibility in using the case to allow for different teaching and learning styles.

Many sources are included in Extended Case 1 to aid students and professors. The goal is to teach students to locate, assess, and analyze a variety of data. That is why the case directs you to select a major city close to you. Professors often already have data about nearby cities or media markets that can be used for this case. This allows professors to tailor the case to meet their own learning goals and use material they already have.

Professors are also urged to examine the sources included in the case and select those most appropriate to their goals and teaching styles. After publication, some of the Internet addresses in the case could change or disappear. Students could find the number and types of sources in the case overwhelming if they receive little or no guidance in using them.

For example, if the course is taught in a computer lab (or could be for a short period of time), the class as a whole could take a day or week to conduct an Internet and database search to locate information to share. Different search objectives could be assigned to different students or teams in the class. If useful articles are found in the database searches (e.g., ABI Inform/ProQuest, Lexis-Nexis, Ebsco), students could e-mail them to the professor, who could then give e-mail or hard copies to the entire class. If useful Internet sites are found, the addresses could be shared with the class as well. By dividing the major search goals and sharing what is found, much information to use in working on the case can be obtained quickly.

Extended Case 2 provides information and practice in dealing with the difficult problems of restructuring and layoffs. It provides a different type of major case, allowing students to deal with a more focused, yet still comprehensive and vexing management situation. Students must consider the managerial, organizational, structural, legal, ethical, and human consequences of the decisions they make.

In summary, one goal in both extended cases is to give students a chance to consider major problems they are likely to face at various points in their careers. A second goal is to provide a variety of real-life situations to apply theory, research, and data analysis. A third goal is to give students a better perspective on how smaller problems seemingly unique to one department or situation are interrelated with, and not necessarily independent of, larger more complex organizational problems.

Extended Case 1
The Case of Change at a Newspaper

Coy Parker, the White managing editor of the *Metropolis Morning Herald*, faced some serious problems. He had just met with Jackson Tenkiller, his publisher who was a member of the Aniwaya or Wolf clan of the Cherokee nation about the paper's declining readership. Jackson worried that circulation continued to decline among younger adults and said a plan was needed to deal with the readership problem.

> We've got to stop this decline before it gets much worse. We need to find out why we're losing readers and can't attract younger readers. Once we find that out,

I want to investigate the types of content to change or add to the paper and Web site, what new sections or types of stories we might develop, and what else we can do to attract new readers and retain the old ones. Our Web page isn't generating any meaningful reader interest or revenue for us. We've got to find new ways to use it.

Jackson said, "While we're trying to figure that out, MegaMedia wants us to create more synergy among its media properties owned locally. We need to use all outlets to cross-promote each other." The MegaMedia Company was a large national group that owned newspapers, TV and radio stations, magazines, outdoor/billboard, and electronic information and publishing firms. Locally, Mega-Media owned the *Metropolis Morning Herald*, the local NBC-affiliated TV station, an all-news talk AM station, and a top-40 hit FM radio station.

MegaMedia had purchased a server-based newsroom for its media outlets in the market to share. Any video or digital photograph that was shot in the field or came in by satellite would go directly into the server. Videotape would no longer be needed, and content could be easily adapted for print, broadcast, or streaming on the Internet. Several reporters and employees could view and edit a story at their desktops while it was being edited elsewhere (Hudson, 2002). MegaMedia's eventual goal was to be the multimedia news leader in Metropolis, but felt this new technology could ease cross-promotion among its various local outlets. The main server and equipment were housed at the local NBC TV station, but were accessible by e-mail and the Internet to the other locally owned outlets. Editing stations were located at the TV station, radio stations, Internet office, and newspaper newsroom.

Buying server-based newsroom technology was part of MegaMedia's long-term goal of developing partnerships to share news content and promotional opportunities to reach a broader audience in Metropolis (Fuquay, 2002). Each outlet could eventually share story-planning budgets. Presently the TV station's meteorologist appeared on the newspaper's weather page. *Herald* reporters, editors, and columnists were occasional guests on the news-talk radio station and TV newscasts. Jackson said,

MegaMedia knows convergence or partnerships between newspapers, television, radio and online sites are becoming more common. About 100 media partnerships exist already, though most are promotional. Only a dozen or so share news reports and resources. But if we worked together the newspaper could break stories online or on radio or TV, or vice versa. MegaMedia's top management feels we could attract younger viewers and listeners to the newspaper for more in-depth coverage of important local stories using cross-promotion.

Jackson had other ideas to consider too.

There was an article in The Quill about how the *Orlando Sentinel* is trying to attract the Spanish-speaking community (Orlando Sentinel Reaches, 2001). It's sharing editorial content with a popular local Spanish-language music radio station, as well as sharing news and promotional efforts with local Univision and Telemundo affiliated television stations. The *Sentinel* started publishing a free weekly bilingual edition called *El Sentinel*, too, so they're really getting their name out there in the Hispanic community. Given the multicultural nature of Metropolis, this seems like something we might consider when we're thinking about new content and promotional ideas.

Coy said,

We can start by reviewing the results of the Impact Project study conducted by Northwestern University's Readership Institute for the American Society of Newspaper Editors and the Newspaper Association of America (Fitzgerald, 2001; *www.readership.org*). They suggest implementing eight changes to reverse the long-term decline of newspaper readership. For example, they found running in-paper promotions of their stories improved the paper's market image and increased reader satisfaction. The Institute said developing high-quality customer service, making the paper easier to navigate and read, emphasizing everyday people in articles, using the feature style for hard news stories, using image ads to promote the paper, using advertising to improve readership throughout the paper, and changing the military-style corporate culture found at most papers would help. (Fitzgerald, 2001; *www.readership.org*)

Coy continued,

Frankly, I haven't done any of this because it seems opposed to good journalism as I've always practiced it. I think most radio and TV news is "gossipy" and full of fluff. I'm not wild about having to work with reporters and editors at the radio and TV stations, even those owned by the same company. I've always prided myself in scooping everybody else in town. I really wonder whether these ideas will work or whether it's all just the latest buzzword we've got to try to make our owners happy.

Jackson replied,

Coy, I'm sympathetic. But if we don't have any readers who read our scoops, it doesn't matter how many scoops we get. You know newspaper readership is stronger among older age groups and weaker among the youngest adult groups. Only 18 percent of 18-to-22-year-olds read a newspaper daily in 1996, down from 47 percent in 1972. Our older readers are dying off faster than our younger ones are being created (Morton, 2002, p. 64). And kids born into newspaper-reading families tend to read them; those born in non-reading families don't. We've got to figure out how to attract non-readers and young readers while maintaining the journalistic standards we believe in. The bottom line is change is coming and we've got to find a way to adapt.

Jackson continued,

MegaMedia wants us to improve our Web site and make it economically viable. There have been a few complaints about racist and sexist comments in our chat room so we've got to figure out how to take care of that. We need to build interest in and traffic to our Web site, especially among young adults. Should we drop the chat room? Should we impose some kind of controls on it? How should we change our Web site? What else can we do to improve revenue and interest in the site? We need to find out how to better use our Web site to build readership and revenues.

Coy returned to his office for a meeting with Aliah Shebib, a naturalized American Citizen from Lebanon, who had arrived early today and was waiting for him when he arrived at work. Aliah said, "I've been covering 'Sock Jobs' part-time for seven months now." (Sock Jobs were what employees derisively called the society articles and columns they wrote for the paper's Society section. Covering such social events, fundraisers, charity golf tournaments, and so on was historically unpopular with the editorial staff. Sock Jobs were typically assigned to the newest general assignment reporter with the shortest tenure at the paper.) Coy said, "Yes, and you've been doing an excellent job." Aliah responded, "Thank you. And I appreciate the opportunity you've given me. But I'm ready to tackle new challenges. Now that my six-month probationary period is over I'd like to be reassigned to a different beat."

"Are you unhappy with your job?" Coy asked. "I'm unhappy covering society stories. Like most journalists, I'd rather cover hard news stories or do investigative reporting full-time. I understand the paper may not have the resources to support a full-time investigative reporter. But if I were given a serious news beat I could turn in my daily stories and work on major investigative pieces on the side. I'd be willing to do that."

Coy replied, "What beat would you like?" Aliah responded,

We have a number of minority communities in the city that really aren't covered in depth by the paper. Why hasn't the paper ever really made a serious effort to cover social, economic, and racial issues regarding the major Hispanic and Asian communities here? We've got a significant number of immigrants from Mexico as well as Central and South America. Our Vietnamese and Korean communities are among the largest in the U.S. We've also got a fairly large Muslim population. And like most big cities we have a large African-American population. Yet we've never done any significant coverage or investigative reports of these communities. Lately it seems we cover incidents of harassment or do 'look how these folks have achieved the American Dream' stories. Why haven't we done any in-depth coverage from minority viewpoints about minority issues? More important, why aren't we covering such issues in the context of the community as a whole?

Coy was surprised by Aliah's comments and said, "I thought we did a good job of covering minority stories. Why just last week Greg Johnson did the story on the successful Korean grocer." "That was a good, heart-warming story," said Aliah. "But some Koreans privately told me they thought it was patronizing. They said, 'Why doesn't the paper ever cover discrimination or check into the allegations of tougher inspections by the Health Department of minority restaurants?'" Coy replied, "You mean there are allegations that the Health Department is discriminating against minority restaurants?" "Yep," said Aliah, "and I've heard they're asking for bribes." "Where'd you hear that?" "It was in the Korean language weekly. A reporter there told me about it," Aliah said. "Well, that's something we ought to be covering, too," Coy said.

Coy thought a moment and then told Aliah,

Jackson and I were just discussing how to rebuild readership. I'm going to talk to the staff about it soon. Please start formulating your ideas and come up with as many specific suggestions as you can. I'm going to be asking everyone to think about potential new content and types of stories or sections to develop. Then we'll probably conduct research to discover what readers want and figure out what to do. We also need to consider how to build interest in our Internet site.

"OK," said Aliah, "I'll come up with some ideas. Oh, Greg said he wants to talk to you too." "Send him in," Coy said.

Greg Johnson, the *Herald's* respected business columnist and reporter, who was African-American, came in and sat down. "What's up?" Coy said. "Well, I've gotten an offer from the Los Angeles Times. Are you going to counter?"

Coy sat dumbfounded for a moment and then said, "Of course I'm going to make a counter offer! Didn't you know I would?" "Honestly Coy, no, I'm not sure how you feel about my work or me. You appear to have a few favorite reporters you talk to all the time. You rarely talk to me so I don't know what you think. I've wondered whether you're just uncomfortable in general with people of color."

"No, that's not it at all," said Coy. "You just never seemed interested in talking so I thought I was respecting your wishes and leaving you alone to do your work."

"It's not that I don't want to talk," replied Greg, "and I mean no disrespect; it's just that I don't want to talk about old newsroom war stories all the time. I wasn't here then. The *Herald* didn't employ any reporters of color at that time. And that's all you, Dave, and Edwin seem to want to talk about: what things used to be like." Dave Creighton and Edwin James, who were White, had been reporters at the *Herald* for more than 30 years. Coy had worked there for more than 35 years.

"Well, I'm sorry, Greg. I didn't know you felt that way. I'm really surprised you didn't think I'd go to bat with Jackson and MegaMedia to keep you here." Coy continued, "You've gotten good performance reviews the two years you've been here. Because of that I thought you know how much I respect what you do."

Greg replied,

Well, your performance evaluations are very different than the ones I had before I came here. I was given very specific comments, detailed suggestions for improvement, and goals to achieve. Mostly what I recall from your evaluations are vague comments like, "You're doing a pretty good job. Work on your writing style. Expand your business contacts." That really doesn't give me much direction. And from the way I hear Dave and Edwin talk, it sounds like I haven't gotten the raises they did. The performance evaluation system and compensation practices would have to change if I stayed.

"I can't tell you about their evaluations, that's confidential. But what I can tell you is that I've always recommended you for higher than average raises. I'm surprised you'd think otherwise. Why didn't you talk to me about this before?"

Greg replied,

Coy, I wasn't sure you'd be receptive. I feel like you and I work in two different newsrooms. Aliah and I can talk about a lot of things that I haven't felt comfortable talking about with you. That's another reason I went on the interview at the Times. I want more challenges and a more comfortable work environment. I really love it here in Metropolis. But if I'm going to stay the environment will have to change.

Coy said,

I'm glad you're being honest with me, Greg. I do value you and I want to keep you. I didn't realize all of this and I'm glad you've pointed it out to me. I'm certainly willing to update the performance evaluation system. I think it's pretty archaic myself. I'd like to work with you to improve the newsroom environment. If a reporter and columnist of your caliber can't be comfortable here, then I want to change that. I hope you'll give me the chance.

Greg said, "Thanks. I really appreciate your attitude, Coy. But realize that I'm serious. It's going to take more than a better compensation package to keep me here. I think changes are needed in the newsroom culture and performance evaluation process."

Dave and Edwin walked in Coy's office and shut the door right after Greg left. "Is it true he's gotten an offer from the L.A. *Times*?" asked Dave. Coy nodded and Edwin said, "Good riddance. He's never been a team player anyway."

Coy said, "What are you talking about? He's the best business columnist and reporter we've ever had at this paper?" "Big deal," said Dave. "He's not much fun at parties. He never wants to talk about the old days. And he works so hard he makes the rest of us look bad."

Coy replied, "I hope we're lucky enough to keep Greg. And I hope you two will think about what you just said to me. Greg's work ethic got him that good offer. And not wanting to talk about things that happened long before he got here doesn't make him a bad guy. It just means he wasn't here then." His two old friends looked surprised and walked out.

Coy shut the door to his office. He thought about everything that happened today. For the first time, he really thought about how his relationship with Dave and Edwin might appear to the other newsroom employees. Dave and Edwin always rushed into his office after something big happened to get the scoop. He thought about how and why Greg became so alienated, and how Aliah made him realize how out of touch he was with the local ethnic communities. He wondered if Aliah and other reporters felt alienated. Perhaps the Jewish female sports reporter, Sarah Rosenstone, felt as Greg did because she rarely talked to him either.

"How ironic," Coy thought to himself, "that Greg thinks I've given Dave and Edwin higher raises and performance evaluations than him. If Greg and the others knew how small Dave and Edwin's raises were over the past 5 years and how much I've had to deal with these guys just to get them to work half as much as Greg, Aliah and Sarah!" He sat a bit longer in silence, absorbing the day's events. Then he got up and said, "Well, this old dog is going to have to learn some new tricks." He got up to talk to Greg again about the counteroffer.

ASSIGNMENT

Select a major daily newspaper in the city where your university is located or in a nearby major metropolitan area. Pretend it is the *Metropolis Morning Herald*. Conduct a market analysis, develop new content and/or section(s) for the paper and Internet, evaluate legal problems associated with the Web site, consider how to cross-promote the paper and Internet site using the other local MegaMedia-owned outlets, change the organizational culture, and develop a new performance evaluation system for the Herald.

Such major changes require extensive research and planning as well as cultural changes to implement. By carefully planning and considering many factors before these changes are implemented, the ultimate changes should be easier to manage when the process starts. Also formulate your plans to reach Mega Media's overall goals: (a) to be the multimedia news leader in Metropolis; (b) to use new technologies to foster excellence in news and cross-promotion among its local outlets, developing partnerships to share news content and promotional opportunities to reach a broader audience in Metropolis; (c) to attract the major ethnic communities, nonreaders, and the younger audience to the newspaper for more in-depth coverage of important local stories using cross-promotion; and (d) to use new approaches and technologies to create operational efficiencies and increase revenue.

Before you formulate plans, begin by conducting a market analysis for the *Herald* (and pretend it is the major paper you have selected in a nearby city). Many sources are noted here, but ask your professor about these and other sources to use. Find out the number and types of existing local media outlets by reviewing publications such as the *Gale Directory, Broadcasting & Cablecasting Yearbook, Editor & Publisher Market Guide*, and others (these sources may include data about your city too). Ask your reference librarian for help to find these or other publications listing major media outlets in your city. If nothing else exists, look in the Yellow Pages. Check out the Web sites of the outlets in your major city to see how they identify and promote themselves.

Also obtain as much information as you can about the demographics, psychographics, and other characteristics of the city's residents. If available in your library, obtain the SRDS Lifestyle Market Analyst and copy the demographic and lifestyle pages for your city. Analyze the major demographic and lifestyle characteristics of residents. (Think about whether content could be developed to attract major readership segments based on the lifestyle categories with large numbers of residents and high indexes.) If Mediamark or Simmons are available in your library, check to see whether a report on your city is included.

When you are ready to conduct a computer search, you and your class might search together if your class is taught in a computer lab. The class as a whole could develop a comprehensive list of terms and objectives to use in a search. Your professor could assign different search terms or objectives to each student or team. Then the class could share all the useful information and data they find with each other to make the search process quicker and more efficient. Each person or team could be responsible for developing a list of useful articles, cites, and/or Web addresses to share with the class.

Here are some search strategies to try. Enter the name of your city and relevant search terms (such as demographic, lifestyle, income, etc.) to conduct searches in electronic databases like ABI Inform/ProQuest and Lexis-Nexis. Go to the News library in Lexis-Nexis, click on the U.S. Newspapers link, select the state where your city is located, and conduct a search there. Then select the region where your city is located and conduct another search. Also enter the names of other major media outlets in your city to obtain good background information on competitors in your market. Check *Mediaweek* magazine because it occasionally publishes articles on various TV markets around the country (e.g., see Hudson, 2002).

There are a variety of online resources with economic and other data. Go to FedStats (*www.fedstats.gov*), click on the MapStats link, and select your state and county to obtain information on your city. Look for economic data at the U.S. Department of Labor's Bureau of Labor Statistics site (*http://stats.bls.gov/*), click on Regions, States, and Areas at a Glance, and review the state data. Scroll to the bottom of the page to access reports on major cities in the state.

Visit the U.S. Department of Commerce Bureau of Economic Analysis (*www.bea.doc.gov*), click on the state and local data link, and examine data such as the regional economic profiles and personal income. Check out the overview of the economy link at the bottom of the home page to obtain a current snapshot of the U.S. economy.

If you still need more information, go to the U.S. Census Bureau (*www.census.gov*), click on the Search link, and type in the name of your city. Review and print any relevant tables or information of interest. However, realize that searching the Census Web site can be time-consuming and difficult. Ask your professor to identify what you should be looking for and search terms to use.

Review the Introduction to Census 2000 Data Products (*www.census.gov/dmd/www/products.html*) for an overview of available data, and then review relevant Census 2000 data (*www.census.gov/main/www/cen2000.html*). Find the Data Highlights link and select the state where your city is located. Review and print any data reports of interest. Try the U.S. Census Bureau's State and County Quick Facts (*http://quickfacts.census.gov*) for additional information. Click on the state where your city is located and examine the major data regarding your state as compared with the United States as a whole. Then select the major county where the city is located and view the data. Do not forget to click the link for more data sets on your county. There you will find links for demographics, ethnic composition, income, and other socioeconomic data. Next review the same data for all other counties in your city of interest, printing or downloading all you find helpful. Check out the demographic profiles (*www.census.gov/Press-Release/www/2002/demoprofiles.html*). Finally, you might examine the American Community Survey data (*www.census.gov/acs/www/index.html*) if you still need more information.

Once you have completed your research into your city, consider conducting a search using online databases again. The research process helps you identify new search terms to enter. Now that you know what you are lacking, you can conduct a more focused database search. You will also be confident that you have explored all your information search options fully.

There is a wealth of information available online to use in developing new content and changing organizational culture (as well as the information in various chapters of this book). Visit the Readership Institute (*www.readership.org*) and review its Imperatives to Grow Readership (a downloadable report is available there). These imperatives include developing excellent service, improving high-potential content areas, focusing on a particular type of local news, making the newspaper easier to read and navigate, improving advertising content, promoting content more effectively within the newspaper, building a positive brand relevant to readers, and developing an adaptive, constructive, reader-centered culture.

Also review the High Potential Content Areas page and data tables for ideas on the types of content to change or add (*www.readership.org/content/editorial/hp_content.htm*, especially the content area by age group table to compare scores for readers in different age groups). Be sure to read Branding: From Consumer Insight to Implementation; it provides specific suggestions for appealing to younger readers (e.g., using updates, talking points, enrichment, and guides; at *www.readership.org/brand/relevance.htm*). Also read High Potential Brand Areas (*www.readership.org/brand/hp_brand.htm*) to analyze brand perceptions by gender, age, and ethnic origin. Print and save these tables as you may refer to them often during the project.

Review relevant Web sites, including those discussed in the online resources section of chapter 6, to develop a perspective on the diversity and cultural issues raised in the case. Visit the Cherokee Nation Web site (*http://www.cherokee.org*) and review the information there on the Cherokee culture, history, language, literature, Cherokee Phoenix, and clans (e.g., see *www.cherokee.org/Culture/CulturePage.asp?ID=53* for information about the Aniwaya clan). From chapter 6, review links such as the U.S. Equal Opportunity Commission's federal equal employment laws (*www.eeoc.gov/qs-employers.html*) and the SPJ's diversity link (*www.spj.org/diversity.asp*), as well as the sites of the NABJ (*www.nabj.org*) and NAJA (*www.naja.org*), for example.

Your professor might ask a local newspaper publisher, editor, or manager to visit your class to discuss managing concerns like developing synergy among media outlets, personnel and culture issues, budgeting, research, and developing new project proposals. Ask the manager to bring a copy of the newspaper's organizational structure. If the company owns other media outlets in the same city, try to obtain organizational charts of those outlets as well. Use them as the organizational structural models of the *Metropolis Morning Herald* and its sister outlets.

Use the information and data obtained from all sources and the text to answer the following questions:

1. Identify and describe the major diversity issues that exist at the paper. For example, identify the major cultures that exist and explain why they developed. How have differences among managers and employees in gender and race, as well as ethnic and/or religious background, contributed to the development of these cultures? Provide detail and examples. Review chapters 2 and 6 before answering.

2. What can you do as a manager to avoid fostering the development of separate cultures in an organization? Review chapters 1, 2, 3, 4, and 6 before answering. Also review your answer to question 1 before completing this answer. Then consider whether and how your own gender, race, ethnic background, and/or religious or atheistic beliefs may have affected your answer to question 1. In other words, do your own experiences and background affect your perceptions? If yes, how? Finally, after reading the relevant chapters and completing your self-assessment, answer this question by describing what can you do when you are a manager (such as Coy) to avoid fostering the development of separate cultures in an organization.

3. Identify and describe Coy's leadership style. What is positive about the way he leads? What is negative about the way he leads? What did Coy do that led to the problems he is facing now? Review chapters 1, 2, 3, and 4 before answering.

4. What steps should Coy take to solve the cultural and other personnel problems in the newsroom? Why? Is any organizational restructuring needed? Why? Review chapters 1, 2, 3, and 4 before answering.

5. Design a new performance evaluation system for the paper. Consider all the problems Coy is facing. Be sure to address the issues Coy is dealing with fairly and equitably. Review chapter 6 and the American Arbitration Association's (*www.adr.ogr*) Web site before answering this question. Also review sources like the U.S. Equal Opportunity Commission's (*www.eeoc. gov*) quick start link (*www.eeoc.gov/qs-employers.html*); its link for laws, regulations, and policy guidance (*www.eeoc.gov/policy/index.html*); and the SPJ's diversity link (*www.spj.org/diversity.asp*) before completing your answer.

6. Conduct a market analysis of Metropolis (e.g., the major city you selected). Review chapters 7, 8, and 9 before answering. Use the information in those chapters as a guide for what to include in your market analysis.

7. Develop a content proposal for the paper and Internet. Identify the types of sections, features, stories, columns, and/or personalities to include. If possible, provide a preliminary budget. Review chapters 5, 6, 7, 8, 9, and 10 before answering. Also review the Readership Institute's (*www. readership.org*) Imperatives to Grow Readership.

8. Develop legal guidelines for the Web site to deal with any obscene or objectionable material. Also develop guidelines for protecting the Internet site against libel, slander, or privacy actions. Include a complaint procedure for employees to use when complaints occur about content on the Internet site. Review chapters 5 and 6 before answering this question. Check out the Internet Advertising Bureau's (IAB) privacy link that includes guidelines and a resource center (*www.iab.net/privacy/index. html*). If available, also review Delta and Matsuura (2002). (Delta and Matsuura [2002] included appendixes with advice on handling a variety of Internet legal concerns for managers, such as Guidelines for Handling Personal Data [p. App. 1-1], Electronic Records Management Checklist [p. App. 2-1], Network Use and Security Guidelines [p. App. 3-1], Web Site Notice/Disclaimer Checklist [p. App. 4-1], Checklist for Link Licenses [p. App. 5-1], World Wide Web Site Development Agreement [p. App. 6-1], Model Electronic Data Interchange Trading Partner Agreement and Commentary [p. App. 7-1], E-Commerce Business Practice Guidelines [p. App. 8-1], On-Line Content Management Checklist [p. App. 9-1], Guidelines for Managing On-Line Conflicts [p. App. 10-1], Avoiding Problems Caused by Obscene and Indecent Materials [p. App. 12-1], and Minimizing Potential Liability from Internet Operations [p. App. 14-1].)

9. Develop a research proposal to find out whether the new newspaper and Internet content will be popular with the desired readers before and after it is introduced. Evaluate reader reactions to the content before it is introduced to the general public, as well as the success of the proposed new content after its introduction. In other words, develop a research plan for evaluating the new content before it is made available to the general public in the newspaper and Internet. Also develop a research proposal to gauge reaction to the new content after it appears. Be sure to develop a research plan that helps the paper adjust the content, if needed, after it is introduced. Review chapters 5 and 9 before answering this question.

10. Once the new content is selected, what is the best way to cross-promote it among the newspaper, TV station, radio stations, and Internet? What

should MegaMedia's brand identity and the position of the newspaper be and why? Explain your answer in as much detail as possible. Review chapters 8 and 9 before answering. For more information about Internet advertising, review the IAB's site (*www.iab.net*), including the different types of interactive advertising units (*www.iab.net/iab_banner_standards/ bannersource.html*). The tables in chapter 9 include a variety of other links to use for information on different types of advertising and promotion.

11. What would be the best decision-making process to develop the proposed new content once it is identified through the market analysis and research? Should Coy make this decision alone? Should this be a group decision? Who should be involved? Why? Explain your answer in detail. Review chapters 1, 2, 3, 4, and 5 before answering.

12. What would be the best decision-making process for Coy to use when making assignments on who is to cover what new content? In other words, should Coy change his decision-making style? Why? How? Explain your answer. Review chapters 1, 2, 3, 4, and 5 before answering.

13. Once the new content for the paper and Internet is selected, should the newsroom or other departments be reorganized, or new departments added, to handle the new assignments? Should any new newsroom managerial positions be developed? If yes, who should be promoted? Why? Suggest organizational changes to make implementation of the content and promotional plans easier. Review chapters 4 and 5 before answering.

14. Develop a plan to implement the introduction of the new content. Develop steps, timetable, alternatives, and so on to show how and when the new section will be introduced. If possible, develop a preliminary budget. Identify steps in succession to show what must be done to ensure that the section is introduced as planned. Review chapters 7 and 10 before answering.

Extended Case 2
The Case of the Newsroom Restructuring

Charlene Gray, president of Northeast World Network (NWN), leaned back in her chair and stared grimly at the two men on the other side of the table. Bill Ligon, vice president of News, and Terry Russell, vice president of Operations, stared back. There was no good news anywhere in the piles of the paper scattered across the table between the three of them.

"This is going to be ugly," Gray said. "It's going to mean layoffs. Lots of layoffs." Both men slowly nodded agreement.

NWN was a 24/7 regional cable news network serving the northeast United States. It had started as a family-owned independent station. In the early 1990s, the owners had switched the station to an all-news format that became known for featuring a few longer, more thoughtful stories every hour. NWN's style was more like that of the BBC than the fast, flashy approach typically used by U.S. TV news, but the station had found an audience and, as its ratings and reputation grew, cable system operators took notice. Eventually, it was reinvented as a regional cable news network that focused on stories of interest to audiences in the Maine–Washington, DC corridor.

Two years ago, the family that owned NWN sold it to a major publicly held media corporation, Outlook Media. Outlook was on an acquisition spree, and its top management was under pressure from Wall Street to improve earnings. Last week, Outlook's Chief Financial Officer had visited NWN and told Gray she had to drastically increase NWN's operating profit margin next year. Gray, Ligon, and Russell had spent the past week trying to devise a way to do that. The answer was clear: cut jobs, including 120 positions from the newsroom.

"We have several problems," Gray said.

We've got to cut enough jobs to hit the numbers that Outlook has given us. But we won't be able to continue to produce news the way we've been doing it with a much smaller staff. So we'll also have to restructure our news product so that it requires fewer people to produce. Finally, we have to manage this organization through these changes in such a way that our entire staff doesn't quit.

"That's a real concern," Russell responded.

At my last job, we restructured our operations, trying to redesign jobs in the newsroom so that everyone was multi-tasking across jobs and media. For example, we wanted our TV producers to be able to produce broadcast stories and then re-edit them for the newspaper and Web. At the same time we had to buy new production systems to support the restructuring so everyone had to learn to use new equipment. We thought we would be more efficient, but it was a disaster. Morale disintegrated. The staff became openly hostile to management, and people quit in droves. By the time it was over, we had lost most of our best people, and it had become a very unpleasant place to work.

Gray and Ligon both nodded. "I've had similar experiences," Gray said. "The most important reason people seek careers in journalism is the desire for a changeable, non-routine job*. But it's one thing to want variety in your work, and another thing to accept changes in your job. Journalists are human. They don't adapt well."

"But there are still some things you can do to try to manage the process," Ligon noted. "It doesn't mean that it will be easy, but it might make it easier. I went to a seminar on managing organizational change last year. We looked at a lot of research that suggests some approaches that may help."

"For example?" Gray asked.

Well, first, research on change management in newsrooms shows journalists will most resent those changes they think hurt their ability to meet high professional journalistic standards for quality (Bergen & Weaver, 1988; Stamm & Underwood,

---

*See acknowledgments p. 300.

1993; Pollard, 1995). So, as we restructure our news product, we can expect to meet the most resistance—and generate the most morale problems—with changes the staff thinks are going to lower the quality of what we're doing.

Gray nodded. "What else?"

Several things. Providing continuous information and communication about the proposed changes, the processes to be used to make them, and the expected outcomes improves employees' openness to change and their job satisfaction, and reduces their likelihood to quit (Nadler, 1987; Miller & Monge, 1985; Wanberg & Banas, 2000). So does giving them the chance to have input into the process (Cummings & Worley, 1993). Particularly important is to try to help staff see the connection between the changes we're making and the organization's long-term needs and goals. (Beckhard & Harris, 1987)

"Of course," Ligon added wryly,

we shouldn't expect them to feel inspired by the goal of boosting the company's operating profit margins. So when we restructure, we need to think beyond financial outcomes and see this as an opportunity to develop new ways to improve the quality of our news and public service. If we can do that and focus our discussions of how the changes will help us meet those goals, we'll have better success managing this process.

"Anything else we should be considering?" Russell asked.

"Yes. Older staff members are more likely to resist change, but they're also less likely than younger employees to actually quit (Daniels & Hollifield, 2002). Of course, that means you can wind up with people who would like to leave but can't because of personal reasons," Ligon said.

Studies also show that the most resisted changes are, in rank order, those seen as hurting the quality of the news product, layoffs, changes in production technologies and systems, and changes in production processes. Research also suggests that no matter what you do, people are unhappy with change, most consider quitting in response to it, and they blame their managers for what's happening more than they blame the company—even though the company ordered the changes. We also can expect there to be staff turnover afterwards, even among those not released. The good news is that the attitudes of the people who stay *will* improve over time, but despite that, they still will perceive the change process as having been negative and believe they were happier before any of it happened. (Daniels & Hollifield, 2002)

Gray sighed.

In other words, we can expect a lot of unhappiness and resistance no matter what we do. But despite that, we're going to do our best to handle this well. In my previous job, we went through layoffs. It was done strictly on the basis of seniority, which is justifiable at one level but creates a lot of problems in other ways. The process used to handle the layoffs was brutal. Management called people in one-by-one to give them notice. Everyone in the newsroom saw who was being summoned. People walked out of those meetings sobbing in front of everyone and were escorted directly to the front door with no idea what they would do next or how they would find another job. That is *not* going to happen here. This may be an ugly process, but we can find a humanitarian way to handle it!

ASSIGNMENT

You are consultants brought in by Gray and NWN to help develop a plan for restructuring their news operations. You have three tasks:

1. Develop a vision for a new approach to producing a high-quality 24/7 news program that requires 120 fewer staff members than NWN currently uses. Be prepared to justify your proposed redesign and explain to staff members how it will reflect—or even improve on—their standards for journalistic quality and public service.

2. Develop a specific and detailed plan for communicating the changes to the staff. Use what Ligon reported about successful change management. When will you begin informing staff? What will your specific messages be? How will they be communicated? Who will communicate them? If you bring staff members into the decision process, whom will you bring in, when, and why? What decisions will you allow them to share in making? Who will you leave out of the decision process and why? What processes will you create for staff input? How will you deal with proposals from the staff that you do not think will work or that you do not like? How will you deal with staff members who become openly hostile and try to organize resistance? When in the change-management process will you put your plan into operation? After you have developed at least part of a concrete plan for the changes? Or before you even start? When will your plan end? Right after the layoffs? When the newscast redesign is finished? At some period following the point at which you are no longer implementing changes? Again, your communication and change management plan must be *very* detailed and specific.

3. Develop a termination plan for the layoffs. How can you minimize the potential legal ramifications that may result? How will those laid off be informed? Who handles that process and how will it be done? When will they be told in relationship to the beginning/end of the restructuring and the actual date when their jobs will end? What are the pros and cons of terminating people immediately or having their final day fall sometime after they have been notified? How will you handle the problems that result from the option you choose for notification/termination process? What will the severance package be? What other support or assistance, if any, will you offer those you are letting go? How will you inform the people who will *not* be laid off about the layoffs and about who is being terminated? Given the resentment that layoffs generate among those who keep their jobs, what is your proposal

TABLE C.1
NWN's Current Newscast Design per Hour
of Programming on Average

Type of Story	Length (min)	No. per Week	FTE Staff Requirements[1]
In-depth investigative or analytical	5	35	70
News package stories	1:30	195	130
Reader, voiceover w/video	30 sec	400	50
General newsroom operations and support			90[2]
Total staff			340

[1] FTE means the number of full-time equivalent staff members required to produce that type of news story in the quantity used each week.

[2] Includes management team, anchors, directors, studio camera operators, technicians, and assignment editors. Of the 90 positions, 50 must remain for the network to be on the air. The remainder is production assistants, writers, clerical staff, and other support personnel. Yet at least some of these positions must be retained to maintain operations.

for managing the remaining staff through the separation and grief process? Your proposal must be detailed, realistic, and legally acceptable.

ACKNOWLEDGMENTS

The author gratefully acknowledges the assistance of George Daniels, Dr. Lee B. Becker, and Mr. Robert Furnad with the development of this case.

*Unpublished data from the 1998 and 1999 Annual Survey of Journalism & Mass Communication Graduates, conducted by Dr. Lee Becker and the James M. Cox, Jr. Center for International Mass Communication Training and Research at the University of Georgia.

References

Aaker, D.A. (1995). *Developing business strategies* (4th ed.). New York: Wiley.

Accola, J. (2002, January 24). Scripps report shows News cut losses. *Rocky Mountain News*, Business, p. 5B.

Adams, J.S. (1963). Toward an understanding of inequity. *Journal of Abnormal and Social Psychology, 67*, 422–436.

Adams, R.C., & Fish, M.J. (1987). TV news direcors' perceptions of station management style. *Journalism Quarterly, 64*, 154–162, 276.

Adams, W.J., & Eastman, S.T. (2002). Prime-time network entertainment programming. In S.T. Eastman & D.A. Feguson (Eds.), *Broadcast/cable/web/programming* (pp. 111–150). Belmont, CA: Wadsworth.

Akhavan-Majid, R., & Boudreau, T. (1995). Chain ownership, organization size, and editorial role perceptions. *Journalism and Mass Communication Quarterly, 72*, 863–873.

Albarran, A.B. (1996). *Media economics: Understanding markets, industries and concepts*. Ames, IA: Iowa State University Press.

Albarran, A.B. (1998). The coalescence of power: The transformation of the communication industries. In R.G. Picard (Ed.), *Evolving media markets: Effects of economic and policy changes* (pp. 8–24). Turku, Finland: The Economic Research Foundation for Mass Communication.

Aldag, R.J., & Brief, A.P. (1978). *Task design and employee motivation*. Glenview, IL: Scott, Foresman & Co.

Alderfer, C.P. (1972). *Existence, relatedness, and growth*. New York: Free Press.

Allen, M.W., Seibert, J.H., Haas, J.W., & Zimmermann, S. (1988). Broadcasting departmental impact on employee perceptions and conflict. *Journalism Quarterly, 65*, 668–677.

AMA board approves new marketing definition (1985, March 1). *Marketing News*.

Amari, J. (2000). Toto, we're not in Kansas anymore. In ASNE Interactive Media Committee (Eds.), *The new journalists: A report from ASNE's Interactive Media Committee* (p. 2). Reston, VA: American Society of Newspaper Editors Foundation.

Another glass ceiling study: Women in communications field losing ground. (2002, Winter). *Media Report to Women, 30*(1), 6.

Argyris, C. (1962). *Interpersonal competence and organizational effectiveness*. Homewood, IL: Dorsey.

Argyris, C. (1974). *Behind the front page*. San Francisco: Jossey-Bass.

Armour, S. (1997, December 6). Team efforts, technology add new reasons to meet. *USA TODAY*, pp. 1A–2A.

Armour, S. (2002, March 24). Companies are hiring, but with new strategy. *USA TODAY*, p. D-1.

Armour, S. (2002, March 12). More moms make kids their career of choice. *USA TODAY*, p. B-1.

Ashkenas, R., Ulrich, D., Jick, T., & Kerr, S. (2002). *The boundaryless organization: Breaking the chains of organizational structure*. San Francisco: Jossey-Bass.

ASNE reports huge talent drain; Larger percentages of women depart. (2002, Spring). *Media Report to Women, 30*(2), 1–2.

Barge, J.K. (1994). *Leadership: Communication skills for organizations and groups*. New York: St. Martin's Press.

Barker, J.R. (1999). *The discipline of teamwork*. Thousand Oaks, CA: Sage.

Barkin, S.M. (2001, September). Satellite extravaganza. *American Journalism Review, 23*(7), 48–51.

Barlow, J. (2001, December, 9). Education crucial to coming job crisis. *Houston Chronicle*, p. 1D.

Barnard, C.I. (1938). *The executive functions*. Cambridge, MA: Harvard University Press.

Barron, J., & Dienes, C. (2000). *First Amendment law in a nutshell* (2nd ed.). St. Paul, MN: West Group.

Bartlett, C.A., & Ghoshal, S. (1989). *Managing across borders: The transnational solution*. Boston, MA: Harvard University Press.

Bartlett, C.A., & Ghoshal, S. (1990). *Transnational management*. Homewood, IL: Irwin.

Bass, B.M. (1983). *Organizational decision making*. Homewood, IL: Irwin.

Baxter, R. (1983a, August 29). Avoiding liability in firing employees. *The National Law Journal*, pp. 20–21.

Baxter, R. (1983b, September 12). Managing the risks in firing employees. *The National Law Journal*, pp. 20–21.

Becker, L., & Kosicki, G.M. (1997). Annual survey of enrollment and degrees awarded. *Journalism and Mass Communication Educator, 52*(3), 63–74.

Becker, L.B., Huh, J., & Vlad, T. (2001, November). 2000 annual survey of journalism and mass communication graduates. *AEJMC News, 35*(1), 1, 6–7, 11.

Beckhard, R., & Harris, R. (1987). *Organizational transitions: Managing complex change*. Reading, MA: Addison-Wesley.

Bergen, L.A., & Weaver, D. (1988). Job satisfaction of daily newspaper journalists and organization size. *Newspaper Research Journal, 9*(2), 1–13.

Blackler, F., & Brown, C. (1985). Evaluation and the impact of information technologies on people in organizations. *Human Relations, 38*(3), 213–231.

Blanchard, K., Carew, D., & Parisi-Carew, E. (1990). *One minute manager builds high-performing teams*. New York: William Morrow & Co.

BLS releases 2000–2010 employment projections. (2001, December 3). *Technical Information: USDL 01-443* (*http://www.bls.gov/emp*).

Bramlett-Solomon, S. (1992). Predictors of job satisfaction among black journalists. *Journalism Quarterly, 69*, 703–712.

Bramlett-Solomon, S. (1993). Job appeal and job satisfaction among Hispanic and black journalists. *Mass Comm Review, 20*(3–4), 202–212.

Braus, P. (1992). What workers want. *American Demographics, 14*(8), 30–35.

Brown, D. (2002, March). Back to Earth. *American Journalism Review, 24*, 42–47.

Brown, K.F. (1990, July/August). The new newsroom: Challenges of hiring and keeping minorities will force newspapers to learn to adapt. *ASNE Bulletin*, pp. 9–10.

Brown, M.E. (1999, November 11). Surveys confirm tight job market. *American Journalism Review*, pp. 3–5.

Brown, S.L., & Eisenhardt, K.M. (1998). *Competing on the edge: Strategy as structured chaos*. Boston, MA: Harvard Business School Press.

Buchanan, D.A. (1985). Using the new technology. In T. Forester (Ed.), *The information technology revolution* (pp. 454–465). Cambridge, MA: MIT Press.

Burack, E., & Sorensen, P.F., Jr. (1976). Management preparation for computer automation: Emergent patterns and problems. *Academy of Management Journal, 19*(2), 318–323.

Burnett, R. (1992). The implication of ownership changes on concentration and diversity in the phonogram industry. *Communication Research, 19*(6), 749–769.

Butler, J.M., Broussard, E.J., & Adams, P. (1987). Stress and the public relations practitioner. *Southwestern Mass Communication Journal, 3*, 60–79.

Buzzell, R.D., & Cook, V. (1969). *Product life cycles*. Cambridge, MA: Marketing Science Institute.

Cameron, G.T., Hollander, B.A., Nowak, G.J., & Shamp, S.A. (1997). Assessing the potential of a full-featured electronic newspaper for the young adult market. In C. Warner (Ed.), *Media management review* (pp. 15–28). Mahwah, NJ: Lawrence Erlbaum Associates.

Carter, T., Dee, J., & Zuckman, H. (2000). *Mass communication law in a nutshell*. St. Paul, MN: West Group.

Carveth, R. (1992). The reconstruction of the global media marketplace. *Communication Research, 19*(6), pp. 705–724.

Chang, L.A., & Sylvie, G. (1999, August). *Job satisfaction, dissatisfaction of Texas newspaper reporters*. Paper presented at the meeting of the Association for Education in Journalism and Mass Communication, New Orleans, LA.

Child, J. (1972). Organization structure, environment and performance: The role of strategic choice. *Sociology, 6*(1), 318–323.

Childs, K. (1997). Problems persist despite CDA ruling. *Editor & Publisher, 130*(27), 3, 35.

Chyi, H.I., & Sylvie, G. (1998). Competing with whom? Where? And how? A structural analysis of the electronic newspaper market. *Journal of Media Economics, 11*(2), 1–18.

Chyi, H.I., & Sylvie, G. (2000). Online newspapers in the U.S.—perceptions of markets, products, revenues and competition. *The International Journal of Media Management, 2*(2), 69–77.

Collins, B., & Guetzkow, H. (1964). *Social psychology of group processes for decision making*. New York: Wiley.

Collins, J. (2001a, November 26). Beware the self-promoting CEO. *The Wall Street Journal*, p. 1.

Collins, J. (2001b). *Good to great*. New York: Harper-Collins.

Compaine, B., & Gomery, D. (2000). *Who owns the media?* (3rd ed.). Mahwah, NJ: Lawrence Erlbaum Associates.

Cook, B.B., Banks, S.R., & Turner, R.J. (1993). The effects of work environment on burnout in the newsroom. *Newspaper Research Journal, 14*(3–4), 123–136.

Coulson, D.C. (1994). Impact of ownership on newspaper quality. *Journalism Quarterly, 71*, 403–410.

Covington, W.G., Jr. (1997). *Systems theory applied to television station management in the competitive marketplace*, Lanham, MD: University Press of America.

Croteau, D., & Hoynes, W. (2001). *The business of media: Corporate media and the public interest*. Thousand Oaks, CA: Pine Forge.

Crupi, A. (2002, May 6). Ratings get personal. *Cable World, 14*, 80–84.

Cummings, T.G., & Worley, C. (1993). *Organization development and change*. New York: West Publishing.

Cunningham, B. (2001, September/October). The art of managing morale. *Columbia Journalism Review*, pp. 34–36.

Cyert, R.M., & March, J.G. (1963). *A behavioral theory of the firm*. Englewood Cliffs, NJ: Prentice Hall.

Daniels, G., & Hollifield, C.A. (2002). Times of Turmoil: Short- and long-term effects of organizational change on newsroom employees. *Journalism and Mass Communication Quarterly, 79*, 661–680.

Davis, R. (1957). *The fundamentals of top management*. New York: Harper & Row.

Day, G.S., & Schoemaker, P.J.H. (2000). *Wharton on managing emerging technologies*. New York: Wiley.

Dedinsky, M.L. (2000). An editor's primer: Lessons learned at the Chicago Tribune. In D.A. Zeeck (Ed.), *Extending the brand* (pp. 43–46). Reston, VA: American Society of Newspaper Editors.

Delta, G., & Matsuura, J. (2002). *Law of the Internet* (2nd ed.). New York: Aspen Law & Business.

Demers, D. (1996). Corporate newspaper structure, editorial page vigor, and social change. *Journalism and Mass Communication Quarterly, 73*, 857–877.

Demers, D. (1998). Revisiting corporate newspaper structure and profit making. *The Journal of Media Economics, 11*(2), 19–45.

Denison, D.R. (1990). *Corporate culture and organizational effectiveness*. New York: Wiley.

Deutsch, M. (1949, February). A theory of cooperation and competition. *Human Relations, 2*, 129–152.

Dreazen, Y. (2002, June 18). FCC sets simultaneous review of its media-ownership rules-acquisition-hungry firms face uncertain landscape for at least another year. *Wall Street Journal*, p. A2.

Driver, M.J., Brousseau, K.R., & Hunsaker, P.L. (1993). *The dynamic decision maker*. San Francisco: Jossey-Bass.

Drucker, P.F. (1983). The effective decision. In E. Collins (Ed.), *Executive success: Making it in management* (pp. 464–475). New York: Wiley.

Dyer, W.G. (1995). *Team building: Current issues and new alternatives*. New York: Addison-Wesley.

Earley, P.C., & Erez, M. (1997). *The transplanted executive: Why you need to understand how workers in other countries see the world differently*. New York: Oxford University Press.

Elliott, P., & Chavez, D. (1969, November). A sociological framework for the study of television production. *Sociological Review, 17*, 355–375.

Emling, S. (2002, July 7). DVDs ejecting VCRs from the scene. *The Austin-American Statesman*, pp. J1, J6.

Endres, F. (1988). Stress in the newsroom at Ohio dailies. *Newspaper Research Journal, 10*(1), 1–14.

Endres, F. (1992). Stress in professional classes: Causes, manifestations, coping. *Journalism Educator, 47*(1), 16–30.

Endres, F., Schierhorn, A.B., & Schierhorn, C. (1999, August). *Newsroom teams: A baseline study of prevalence, organization and effectiveness.* Paper presented at the meeting of the Association for Education in Journalism and Mass Communication, New Orleans, LA.

Ephron, E., & Gray, S. (2001, January/February). Why we can't afford to measure viewers. *Journal of Advertising Research, 41*(1), 86–90.

Falcone, P. (1997, February). The fundamentals of progressive discipline; employee discipline. *HR Magazine, 42*(2), 90.

FBI Advisory–If you receive a suspicious letter or package, What should you do? (2001). Federal Bureau of Investigation press release available at http://www.fbi.gov/pressrel/pressrel01/mail3.pdf.

Fedler, F., Buhr, T., & Taylor, D. (1988). Journalists who leave the news media seem happier, find better jobs. *Newspaper Research Journal, 9*(2), 15–23.

Fentin, S. (2002). Documenting performance problems — no surprises, please! *Massachusetts Employment Law Letter, 13*(3), 1.

Fink, S.L. (1993). Managing individual behavior: Bringing out the best in people. In A.R. Cohen (Ed.), *The portable MBA in management* (pp. 71–112). New York: Wiley.

Fitzgerald, M. (2001, April 9). Eight is enough: Ways to boost circulation. *Editor & Publisher, 134*, 25.

Fleishman, E.A. (1956). A leader behavior description for industry. In R.M. Stogdik & A.E. Combs (Eds.), *Leader behavior: Its description and measurement* (pp. 104–119). Columbus: Ohio State University Bureau of Business Research.

Fowler, G., & Shipman, J. (1982). Pennsylvania editors' perceptions of communication in the newsroom. *Journalism Quarterly, 61*, 822–826.

Frayer, C. (2002, February). Employee privacy and Internet monitoring: Balancing workers' rights and dignity with legitimate management interests. *The Business Lawyer, 57*, 857–874.

Fullerton, H. (1988). Technology collides with relative constancy: The pattern of adoption for a new medium. *Journal of Media Economics, 1*(3), 75–84.

Fulmer, W. (2000). *Shaping the adaptive organization: Landscapes, learning and leadership in volatile times.* New York: American Management Association.

Fuquay, J. (2002, May 12). TV Station, Fort Worth, Texas, newspaper announce alliance. *Knight Ridder Tribune Business News*, p. 1.

Gade, P., Perry, E.L., & Coyle, J. (1997, August). *Predicting the future: How St. Louis Post-Dispatch journalists perceive a new editor will affect their jobs.* Paper presented at the meeting of the Association for Education in Journalism and Mass Communication, Chicago.

Gardner, H., Csikszentmihalyi, M., & Damon, W. (2001). *Good work: When excellence and ethics meet.* New York: Basic Books.

Gaziano, C., & Coulson, D.C. (1988). Effect of newsroom management styles on journalists: A case study. *Journalism Quarterly, 65*, 869–880.

Gershon, R.A. (1997). *The transnational media corporation: Global messages and free market competition.* Mahwah, NJ: Lawrence Erlbaum Associates.

Gershon, R.A. (2001). *Telecommunications management: Industry structures and planning strategies*, Mahwah, NJ: Lawrence Erlbaum Associates.

Gersick, C.J.G. (1994, February). Pacing strategic change: The case of a new venture. *Academy of Management Journal, 37*(1), 9–45.

Giles, R.H. (1983). *Editors and stress.* New York: Associated Press Managing Editors Association.

Gillmor, D., Barron, J., & Simon, T. (1998). *Mass communication law: Cases and comment* (6th ed.). Belmont, CA: Wadsworth.

Giuliani, R.W. (2002, May 14). Keynote address at "The Celebration of Success Dinner." University of Colorado at Denver Business School, Denver, CO.

Glairon, S. (2002, July 9). Serious play: Companies use games to train employees and spur creative problem solving. *Boulder Daily Camera*, pp. 8–9.

Goldstein, N. (Ed.). (2002). *The Associated Press Stylebook and briefing on media law.* Cambridge, MA: Perseus. apstylebook@ap.org.

Gomez-Mejia, L.R., Balkin, D.B., & Cardy, R.L. (2001). *Managing human resources* (3rd ed.). Upper Saddle River, NJ: Prentice Hall.

Goodman, H. (2002, July). Electronic tear sheets hot items at Nexpo. *Newspaper & Technology.* <http://www.newsandtech.com/issues/2002/07-02/07-02_etear.htm>

Granger, C.W.J. (1980). *Forecasting in business and economics.* New York: Academic.

Green, A. (2002, June 17). The amazing game. *Advertising Age, 73,* 30.

Greene, C.N. (1972, October). The satisfaction-performance controversy. *Business Horizons*, pp. 32–40.

Griffin, R.W., & Moorhead, G. (1986). *Organizational behavior.* Boston: Houghton-Mifflin.

Gubman, J., & Greer, J. (1997, August). *An analysis of online sites produced by U.S. newspapers: Are the critics right?* Paper presented at the meeting of the Association for Journalism and Mass Communication, Chicago.

Hale, S. (2001, March). Freedom of information—Technology brings new issues to FOI. *The American Editor* (March). http://www.asne.org/kiosk/editor/01.march/hale1.htm.

Hall, L. (2001, August 27). Dear diary: Goodbye and good riddance. *Cable World, 13,* 18–20.

Halonen, D. (2002a, June 24). FCC taking slow path on deregulation; Ownership-rules decision delayed a year. *Electronic Media*, p. 1A.

Halonen, D. (2002b, April 15). FCC won't hurry on ownership. *Electronic Media, 21,* 4.

Hanson, K. (2002, July). Give me the story in 90 seconds, you ask. OK, I'll try . . . *Save Internet Radio.* http://saveinternetradio.org/90seconds.asp.

Harrison, E.F. (1987). *The managerial decision-making process* (3rd ed.). Boston: Houghton-Mifflin.

Heller, F.A., & Wilpert, B. (1981). *Competence and power in managerial decision-making.* Chichester, England: Wiley.

Hersey, P., & Blanchard, K. (1972). *Management of organizational behaviour utilizing human resources* (2nd ed.). Englewood Cliffs, NJ: Prentice Hall.

Herzberg, F., Mausner, B., & Snyderman, B. (1968). *The motivation to work.* New York: Wiley.

Hickey, N. (2001, September/October). Low—and getting lower. *Columbia Journalism Review*, pp. 37–39.

Hickey, N. (1992, May/June). Media monopoly—Where will we land? *Columbia Journalism Review.* pp. 50–54.

Hinkle, Hensley, Shanor, & Martin, L.L.P. (2002). Question corner: Performance evaluation can contribute positively. *New Mexico Employment Law Letter, 8*(5), 1–3.

Hofstede, G. (1980). *Culture's consequences: International differences in work-related values.* Beverly Hills, CA: Sage.

Hollifield, C.A. (1993, August). *The globalization of Eastern Europe's print media: German investment during the post-revolution era.* Paper presented to the Association for Education in Journalism and Mass Communication, Kansas City, MO.

Holtz-Bacha, C. (1996, May). *Media concentration in Germany: On the way to new regulations.* Paper presented to the International Communication Association, Chicago, IL.

House, J.R., & Dessler, G. (1974). The path-goal theory of leadership: Some post hoc and apriori tests. In J.G. Hunt & L.L. Larson (Eds.), *Contingency approaches to leadership* (pp. 60–75). Carbondale, IL: Southern Illinois University.

How to align performance management with corporate goals. (News you can use). (2002). *Business and Management Practices—T [plus] D, 56*(3), 19.

How to remake a sub-par performance management process. (2002, February). *Design Firm Management & Administration Report*, p. 6.

Huber, G.P. (1980). *Managerial decision making.* Glenview, IL: Scott, Foresman.

Hudson, E. (2002, June 3). Chicago. *Mediaweek, 12*, 12–17.

IFJ survey on women journalists: Fighting complacency, fighting on. (2001, Fall). *Media Report to Women, 29*(4), 1–4.

Ivancevich, J.M., Lorenzi, P., Skinner, S.J., & Crosby, P.B. (1994). *Management: Quality and competitiveness.* Burr Ridge, IL: Irwin.

Jacobs, R.D., & Klein, R.A. (2002). Cable marketing and promotion. In S.T. Eastman, D.A. Ferguson, & R.A. Klein (Eds.), *Promotion and marketing for broadcasting, cable, and the Web* (4th ed.). Boston: Focal Press.

Janis, I.L. (1982). *Groupthink.* (2nd ed.). Boston: Houghton Mifflin.

Johnstone, J.W.C. (1976). Organizational constraints on newswork. *Journalism Quarterly, 53*, 5–13.

Jones, G.R. (2001). *Organizational theory: Text and cases* (3rd ed.). Upper Saddle River, NJ: Prentice Hall.

Joseph, T. (1983). Television reporters' and managers' preferences on decision making. *Journalism Quarterly, 60*, 476–479.

Jurczak, P.R. (1996, August). *Newsroom cultures, newspaper acquisitions and the community: A case study of Pittsburgh newspapers.* Paper presented at the meeting of the Association for Education in Journalism and Mass Communication, Anaheim, CA.

Kanter, R.M. (2001, February). A more perfect union. *Inc.*, pp. 93–98.

Kaplan, C. (2002, May 27). A libel suit may establish e-jurisdiction. *The New York Times*, p. C1.

Katz, D., & Kahn R.L. (1978). *The social psychology of organizations.* New York: Wiley.

Keeton, W. (Gen. Ed.). (1984). Privacy. In *Prosser & Keeton on torts* (5th ed.). St. Paul, MN: West.

Kempner, M. (2002, July 31). Is end of free TV in sight? Execs ponder price of zapping ads. *Atlanta Journal Constitution*, p. 1A. [Online]. Available: Lexis Nexis database.

Kiesler, C.A., & Kiesler, S.B. (1969). *Conformity.* Reading, MA: Addison-Wesley.

Killebrew, K.C. (2001, August). *Managing in a converged environment: Threading camels through newly minted needles.* Paper presented at the meeting of the Association for Education in Journalism and Mass Communication, Washington, DC.

Klein, E. (2001, June). Using information technology to eliminate layers of bureaucracy. *National Public Accountant, 46*(4), 46–48.

Kodrich, K.P., & Beam, R.A. (1997, August). *Job satisfaction among journalists at daily newspapers: Does size of organization make a difference?* Paper presented at the meeting of Association for Education in Journalism and Mass Communication, Chicago.

Kolodny, H., & Stjernberg, T. (1993). Self-managing teams: The new organization of work. In A.R. Cohen (Ed.), *The portable MBA in management.* (pp. 29–314). New York: Wiley.

Kreitner, R. (1986). *Management* (3rd ed.). Boston: Houghton-Mifflin.

Labor Force. (2001–2002, Winter). *Occupational Outlook Quarterly: U.S. Bureau of Labor Statistics*, pp. 36–41.

Lacy, S., & Simon, T. (1992). *The economics and regulation of United States newspapers.* Norwood, NJ: Ablex.

Leavitt, H. (1965). Applied organizational change in industry. In J. March (Ed.), *Handbook of organizations* (pp. 1144–1170). Chicago: Rand McNally.

Lewis, M. (2000, September 10). The end of TV as we know it? *The Austin American-Statesman*, pp. J1, J5.

Likert, R. (1961). *New patterns of management.* New York: McGraw-Hill.

Lin, C.A., & Jeffres, L.W. (2001). Comparing distinctions and similarities across websites of newspapers, radio stations and television stations. *Journalism and Mass Communication Quarterly, 78*(3), 555–573.

Lindstrom, P.B. (1997). The Internet: Nielsen's longitudinal research on behavioral chanes in use of this counterintuitive medium. *Journal of Media Economics, 10*(2), 35–40.

Locke, E.A. (1968). Toward a theory of task motivation and incentives. *Organizational Behavior and Human Performance, 3*, 157–189.

Maslow, A.H. (1954). *Motivation and personality.* New York: Harper & Row.

Maucker, E. (2001, November/December). Newspapers adding to their disaster plans. *The American Editor*, 18–21.

Mauro, T. (1997). Internet feels court's embrace. *Quill, 85*(7), 30–32.

Mayo, E. (1945). *The social problems of an industrial civilization.* Boston: Graduate School of Business Administration, Harvard University.

McClelland, D. (1961). *The achieving society.* Princeton, NJ: Van Nostrand.

McDevitt, M., Gassaway, B.M., & Perez, F.G. (2002). The making and unmaking of civic journalists: Influences of professional socialization. *Journalism and Mass Communication Quarterly, 79*(1), 87–100.

McEwan, E.K. (1997). *Leading your team to excellence.* Thousand Oaks, CA: Corwin Press, Inc.

McGill, L. (2002, April). Surveys on retention are in agreement. *The American Editor*, http://www.asne.org/index.cfm?id=3646.

McGill, L.T. (2000). *Newsroom diversity: Meeting the challenge.* Arlington, VA: The Freedom Forum.

McGregor, D. (1960). *The human side of enterprise.* New York: McGraw-Hill.

McKean, R.N. (1975). Cost-benefit analysis. In E. Mansfield (Ed.), *Managerial economics and operational research* (3rd ed., pp. 549–561). New York: Norton.

McKee, M. (2002, April 17). "Chicken butt" can't be taken literally. *The Recorder*, News, p. 1.

McManis, C. (2000). *Intellectual property and unfair competition in a nutshell* (4th ed.). St. Paul, MN: West Group.

McQuarrie, F. (1992). Dancing on the minefield: Developing a management style in media organizations. In S. Lacy, A.B. Sohn, & R.H. Giles (Eds.), *Readings in media management* (pp. 229–239). Columbia, SC: Media Management & Economics Division of the Association for Education in Journalism and Mass Communication.

McQuarrie, F. (1999). Professional mystique and journalists' dissatisfaction. *Newspaper Research Journal, 20*(3), 20–28.

Miller, A., & Davis, M. (2000). *Intellectual property-patents, trademarks, and copyright in a nutshell* (3rd ed.). St. Paul, MN: West Group.

Miller, P., & Miller, R. (1995). The invisible woman: Female sports journalists in the workplace. *Journalism & Mass Communication Quarterly, 72*, 883–889.

Miller, K.I., & Monge, P.R. (1985). Social information and employee anxiety about organizational change, *Human Communication Research, 11*, 365–386.

Moore, G. (2002, Summer). We must win the battle—now. *Poynter Report*, p. 8.

Morgan, A.N. (2001, May/June). Committed to diversity. *The American Editor*, pp. 29–32.

Morton, J. (2002, January/February). Why circulation keeps dropping. *American Journalism Review, 24*, p. 64.

Moses, L. (2000, August 28). A smooth handoff at Scripps. *Editor & Publisher*, pp. 17–19.

Mueller, J.E. (1997). Delivery system disaster: Circulation problems of the *St. Louis Sun*. In C. Warner (Ed.), *Media management review* (pp. 115–125). Mahwah, NJ: Lawrence Erlbaum Associates.

Munk, N. (2002, July). Power failure. *Vanity Fair*, pp. 128–131, 167–170.

Nadler, D.A. (1987). The effective management of organizational change. In J. Lorsch, (Ed.), *Handbook of organizational behavior.* (pp. 358–369) Englewood. Cliffs, NJ: Prentice Hall.

Nanus, B. (1992). *Visionary leadership.* San Francisco: Jossey-Bass.

Napoli, P. (1997). The media trade press as technology forecaster: A case study of the VCR's impact on broadcast. *Journalism and Mass Communication Quarterly, 74*(2), 417–430.

National Association of Broadcasters. (2001). *Television financial report.* Washington, DC: National Association of Broadcasters.

Newkirk, P.T. (2000a, September/October). Guess who's leaving the newsrooms: Too many journalists of color don't stick around. Why? *Columbia Journalism Review, 39*(3), 36–39.

Newkirk, P.T. (2000b). *Within the veil: Black journalists, white media.* New York: New York University Press.

Newman, S. (2002, April 5). Remarks made at 3rd Symposium on Online Journalism, The University of Texas at Austin.

Newspaper Association of America. (1999). *Daily newspaper readership trends.* Available online @ www.naa.org/marketscope/databank/tdnpr.htm

Noon, M. (1994). From apathy to alacrity: Managers and new technology in provincial newspapers. *Journal of Management Studies, 31*(1), 19–32.

Occupational Employment. (2001–2002, Winter). *Occupational Outlook Quarterly*, pp. 8–23.

O'Guinn, T., Allen, C., & Semenik, R. (2003). *Advertising and integrated brand promotion* (3rd ed.). Mason, OH: South-Western, Thomson.

Orlando Sentinel reaches into Hispanic community. (2001, November). *Quill, 89*, p. 39.

Ouchi, W. (1981). *Theory Z*. New York: Avon Books.

Pearce, J.A., & Robinson, R.B. (1997). *Strategic management: Formulation, implementation and control* (6th ed.). Boston: Irwin McGraw-Hill.

Pease, T. (1992). Race, gender and job satisfaction in newspaper newsrooms. In S. Lacy, A.B. Sohn, & R.H. Giles (Eds.), *Readings in media management* (pp. 97–122). Columbia, SC: Media Management & Economics Division of the Association for Education in Journalism and Mass Communication.

Petersen, B.K. (1992). The managerial benefits of understanding organizational culture. In S. Lacy, A.B. Sohn, & R.H. Giles (Eds.), *Readings in media management* (pp. 123–152). Columbia, SC: Media Management & Economics Division of the Association for Education in Journalism and Mass Communication.

Phillips, C.L. (1991). Evaluating and valuing newsroom diversity. *Newspaper Research Journal, 12*(2), 28–37.

Phillips, D. (1976). *A systematic study of the leadership process at the corporate level of two television group owners*. Unpublished doctoral dissertation, Ohio University, Athens.

Picard, R.G. (1998). Delusions of grandeur: The real problems of concentration in media. In R.G. Picard (Ed.), *Evolving media markets: Effects of economic and policy changes* (pp. 25–43). Turku, Finland: The Economic Research Foundation for Mass Communication.

Polansky, S.H., & Hughes, D.W. (1986). Managerial innovation in newspaper organizations. *Newspaper Research Journal, 8*, 1–12.

Policy Statement on Deception. (1983, October 14). Letter from then Federal Trade Commission Chairman James C. Miller III to Congressman John D. Dingell. Reprinted as an appendix to Cliffdale, 103 FTC 110 at 174 (1984).

Pollard, G. (1995). Job satisfaction among news workers: The influence of professionalism, perceptions of organizational structure, and social attributes. *Journalism and Mass Communication Quarterly, 72*, 682–697.

Porter, M. (1980). *Competitive strategy: Techniques for analyzing industries and competitors*. New York: Free Press.

Powers, A. (1990). The changing market structure of local television news. *Journal of Media Economics, 3*(1), 37–55.

Powers, A. (1991). The effect of leadership behavior on job satisfaction and goal agreement and attainment in local TV news. *Journalism Quarterly, 68*(4), 772–780.

Powers, A., & Lacy, S. (1992). A model of job satisfaction in local television news. In S. Lacy, A. Sohn, & R. Giles, (Eds.), *Readings in media management* (pp. 5–20) Columbia, SC: Association for Education in Journalism and Mass Communication.

Preston, I. (1994). *The tangled Web they weave: Truth, falsity and advertisers*. Madison, WI: University of Wisconsin Press.

Preston, I. (1996). *The great American blow-up: Puffery in advertising and selling* (rev. ed.). Madison, WI: University of Wisconsin Press.

Priest, C. (1994). *The character of information: Characteristics and properties of information related to issues concerning intellectual property*. Center for Information, Technology, and Society. [Online]. Available: http://www.eff.org/Groups/CITS/ Reports/ cits_nii_framework_ota.report

Progress stalled for newspaper women; greater numbers but not greater advancement. (2002, Winter). *Media Report to Women, 30*(1), 1–3.

Puritz, J. (1996, August). *Making headlines on the Internet: Online newspapers and the challenge of cyberspace.* Paper presented at the meeting of the Association for Journalism and Mass Communication, Anaheim, CA.

Rabasca, L. (2001, June). The next newsrooms: Benefits, costs & convergence. *Presstime 23*(7), 44–48.

Rauch, H. (1991, January). Editors beware! Improperly handled complaints mean trouble. *Folio, 108*, 110–112.

Reiter, D., Blumenfeld, E., & Boulding, M. (Eds.). (2001). *Internet law for the business lawyer.* Chicago, IL: American Bar Association.

Richards, J. (1990). *Deceptive advertising: Behavioral study of a legal concept.* Hillsdale, NJ: Lawrence Erlbaum Associates.

Rogers, E. (1983). *Diffusion of innovation* (3rd ed.). New York: Free Press.

Rogers, E. (1986). *Communication technology: The new media in society.* New York: Free Press.

Rosener, J. (1990). Ways women lead. *Harvard Business Review, 68*, 119–125.

Rudder, G. (1997, October). Newsprint '98. *Presstime*, pp. 33–39.

Russial, J.T. (1997). Topic-team performance: A content study. *Newspaper Research Journal, 18*(1–2), 126–144.

Schein, E.H. (1985). *Organizational culture and leadership: A dynamic view.* San Francisco: Jossey-Bass.

Schriesheim, J., & Schriesheim, C. (1980). *Test of the path-goal theory of leadership and some suggested directions for further research*: Personnel Psychology, 33(2), 349–371.

Severin, W.J., & Tankard, J.W., Jr. (1992). *Communication theories: Origins, methods, and uses in mass media* (3rd ed.). New York: Longman.

Shaver, M. (1995). *Making the sale: How to sell media with marketing.* Chicago, IL: Copy Workshop.

Sheppard, D.L. (1989). Organizations, power and sexuality: The image and self-image of women managers. In J. Hern, D. Sheppard, P. Tancred-Sheriff, & G. Burell (Eds.), *The sexuality of organization* (pp. 139–157). London: Sage.

Sherif, M. (1962). *Intergroup relations and leadership.* New York: Wiley.

Shih, S. (2002). Growing global: A corporate vision master class. New York: Wiley & Sons.

Simon, H. (1957). *Models of man.* New York: Wiley.

Simon, H. (1960). *New science of management decisions.* New York: Harper & Row.

Sissors, J., & Baron, R. (2002). *Advertising media planning* (6th ed.). New York: McGraw-Hill.

Skinner, B.F. (1971). *Beyond freedom and dignity.* New York: Alfred A. Knopf.

Skoler, Abbott, & Presser, L.L.P. (2002, January). Guidance for employee performance evaluations. *Massachusetts Employment Law Letter, 12*, 1–3.

Smith, G.D., Arnold, D.R., & Bizzell, B.G. (1985). *Strategy and business policy.* Boston: Houghton-Mifflin.

Sondhaus, E., & Gallagher, M.B. (2001). Teamworking. In E. Wilson (Ed.), *Organizational behavior reassessed: The impact of gender* (pp. 129–148). Thousand Oaks, CA: Sage.

Stamm, K., & Underwood, D. (1993). The relationship of job satisfaction to newsroom policy changes. *Journalism Quarterly, 79*, 528–541.

Stevens, R.E., Sherwood, P.K., & Dunn, P. (1993). *Market analysis: Assessing your business opportunities.* New York: Haworth.

Stewart, T.A. (1991, December 10). Gay in corporate America. *Fortune, 42*(50), p. 43.

Stigler, G.J. (1952). *The theory of price* (rev. ed.). New York: Macmillan.

Stoneman, P. (1983). *The economic analysis of technological change.* New York: Oxford University Press.

Strassmann, P. (1976). Stages of growth. *Datamation, 22*(10), 46–50.

Straub, J.T. (1984). *Managing: An introduction.* Boston: Kent.

Stroh, L.K., Northcraft, G.B., & Neale, M.A. (2002). *Organizational behavior: A management challenge* (3rd ed.). Mahwah, NJ: Lawrence Erlbaum Associates.

Strupp, J. (2000, August 21). Three-point play: Print, Web, and TV operations now live under the same roof in Tampa. Big Brother may not be watching, but everyone else is. *Editor & Publisher*, pp. 18–23.

Sukosd, M. (1992, October). *No title.* Paper presented at the Battelle-Mershon conference on Technology and Democracy, Columbus, OH.

Sundar, S.S., Narayan, S., Obregon, R., & Uppal, C. (1997, August). *Does Web advertising work? Memory for print vs. online media.* Paper presented at the meeting of the Association for Journalism and Mass Communication, Chicago.

Sylvie, G. (1995). Editors and pagination: A case study in management. *Journal of Mediated Communication, 10*(1), 1–20.

Sylvie, G. (1996). Departmental influences on interdepartmental cooperation in daily newspapers. *Journalism and Mass Communication Quarterly, 73*, 230–241.

Sylvie, G., & Danielson, W. (1989). *Editors and hardware: Three case studies in technology and newspaper management.* Austin, TX: The University of Texas at Austin.

Sylvie, G., & Witherspoon, P.D. (2002). *Time, change, and the American newspaper.* Mahwah, NJ: Lawrence Erlbaum Associates.

Tannenbaum, R., & Schmidt, W.H. (1973, May/June). How to choose a leadership pattern. *Harvard Business Review*, pp. 162–180.

Taylor, R.N. (1984). *Behavioral decision making.* Glenview, IL: Scott, Foresman.

Thomas, D.C. (2002). *Essentials of international management: A cross-cultural perspective.* Thousand Oaks: Sage.

Thompson, M. (2002). Age is no excuse for failing to meet high standards of performance. *New York Employment Law Letter, 9*(3), 1.

Toner, M. (1997). 1997: Another billion-dollar year. *Presstime*, pp. 76–77.

Turow, J. (1992). The organizational underpinnings of contemporary media conglomerates. *Communication Research, 19*(6), 682–704.

Two Tools to Boost a Sub-Par Performance Management Process. (2002, January). *Pay for Performance Report*, pp. 1–4.

Two Ways You Can Improve the Impact of Performance Management Programs. (2002, April). *Managing Training & Development*, pp. 1–2

U.S. Census Bureau. (2000). *Statistical abstract of the United States* (120th ed.). Washington, DC: U.S. Government Printing Office.

U.S. Census Bureau. (2001). *Statistical abstracts of the United States.* [Online]. Available @: http://www.census.gov/prod/2002pubs/01statab/labor.pdf.

U.S. Department of Commerce National Telecommunications and Information Administration. (1993). *The globalization of the mass media*. NTIA Special Publication 93-290. Washington, DC: U.S. Goverment Printing Office.

U.S. House of Representatives Committee on Government Operations. (1980). *International information flow: Forging a new framework*. Washington, DC: U.S. Government Printing Office.

U.S. House of Representatives Committee on Government Operations. (1981a). *International Communications Reorganization Act of 1981*. Washington, DC: U.S. Government Printing Office.

U.S. House of Representatives Subcommittee on Telecommunications, Consumer Protection, and Finance of the Committee on Energy and Commerce. (1981b). *Telecommunications and information products and services in international trade* (Serial No. 97-59). Washington, DC: U.S. Government Printing Office.

Van Maanen, J., & Barley, S.R. (1984). Occupational communities: Culture and control in organizations. In B.M. Staw & L.L. Cummings (Eds.), *Research in organizational behavior* (pp. 287–365). Greenwich, CT: JAI Press.

Vroom, V.H. (1964). *Work and motivation*. New York: Wiley.

Vroom, V.H., & Yetton, P.W. (1973). *Leadership and decision making*. Pittsburg: University of Pittsburg Press.

Wanberg, C.R., & Banas, J.T. (2000). Predictors and outcomes of openness to changes in a reorganizing workplace. *Journal of Applied Psychology, 85*, 132–142.

Wang, K. (2002, June 24–July 1). People meter standoff. *Electronic Media, 21*(25), 3, 29.

Warner, C. (1997). Compensating broadcast salespeople: Some recommendations. In C. Warner (Ed.), *Media management review* (pp. 157–176). Mahwah, NJ: Lawrence Erlbaum Associates.

Weaver, D.H., & Wilhoit, G.C. (1996). *The American journalist in the 1990s: U.S. news people at the end of an era*. Mahwah, NJ: Lawrence Erlbaum Associates.

Weaver, J. (2000). Orlando: Values are central to convergence strategy. In D.A. Zeeck (Ed.), *Extending the brand* (pp. 22–25). Reston, VA: American Society of Newspaper Editors.

Weber, M. (1947). *The theory of economic and social organization* (A.M. Henderson & T. Parsons, Trans.). New York: Free Press. (Original work published 1921.)

Whiting, C.S. (1995, October). Operational techniques and creative thinking. *Advanced Management*, pp. 24–30.

Wilhoit, G.C., & Weaver, D. (1994, August). *U.S. journalists at work, 1971–1992*. Paper presented at the meeting of the Association for Education in Journalism and Mass Communication, Atlanta, GA.

Williams, F., & Monge, P. (2001). *Reasoning with statistics: How to read quantitative research* (5th ed.). Fort Worth, TX: Harcourt.

Wimmer, R., & Dominick, J. (2003). *Mass media research* (7th ed.). Belmont, CA: Wadsworth.

Witcover, J. (1971, September/October). Two weeks that shook the press. *Columbia Journalism Review*, pp. 7–15.

Wolferman, E. (2001, June 18). Its "Perfect storm." *Editor & Publisher*, online http://www.editorandpublisher.com

Writers and Editors. (2001–2002). *Occupation Opportunities Quarterly: U.S. Bureau of Statistics*, pp. 145–148.

Yovovich, B.G. (2000, May 18). Web trend watch. Editor and Publisher. http://www.jup.com

Zachary, M. (2000, August). Performance evaluations trigger many lawsuits. *Supervision, 61*(8), pp. 23–26.

Zavoina, S., & Reichert, T. (2000). "Media convergence/management change: The evolving workflow for visual journalists." *The Journal of Media Economics 13*(2), 143–151.

Zipp, F. (2002, January–February). Case studies from a difficult year for FOI. *The American Editor.* <http://www.asne.org/index.cfm?id=3601>.

AUTHOR INDEX

SUBJECT INDEX